LEE

AND

HIS GENERALS

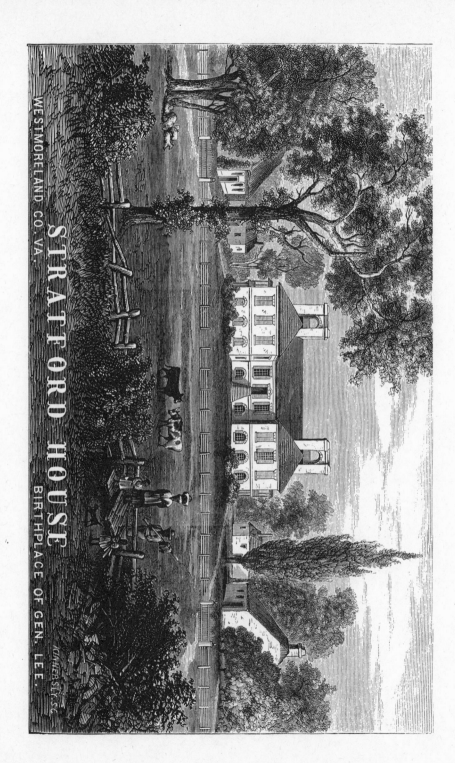

STRATFORD HOUSE

WESTMORELAND CO. VA.

BIRTHPLACE OF GEN. LEE.

KINNERSLEY SC.

LEE

AND

HIS GENERALS

CAPTAIN WM. P. SNOW

THE FAIRFAX PRESS
NEW YORK

Library of Congress Cataloging in Publication Data

Snow, William Parker, 1817-1895
    Lee and his generals.

    First issued anonymously : Southern generals. New York : Richardson, 1865.
    Reprint. Originally published : New York : Richardson, 1867.
    1. Confederate States of America. Army—Biography.
2. United States—History—Civil War, 1861–1865—Biography.
3. Generals—Southern States—Biography.   4. Lee,
Robert E. (Robert Edward), 1807–1870.   I. Title.
E467.S67   1982   973.7'42'0922 [B]   82-2343
ISBN : 0-517-381095   AACR2

h g f e d c b a

FOREWORD

THE compelling reasons for reissuing contemporary accounts of the Civil War such as this are the sense of immediacy, their first-hand impressions, and the power of their passionate, if biased, accounts in the language of the time.

This fascinating collection of wartime biographies of Lee and his foremost generals, relating their exploits in the conduct of their campaigns, was written immediately after the end of the Civil War, and was published in 1867. The events were fresh in the mind of Captain William P. Snow, and like other reports of the period, was heavily favored on the author's side. The earliest versions of the account of the war, such as *Southern History of the Civil War,* by E. A. Pollard, editor of *The Richmond Examiner,* published soon after the conclusion of hostilities, had not hesitated to call the Federal troops "the Union devils." By contrast, Captain Snow's account is more fair in its portrayal of both sides.

At the command level, there existed a gallantry and mutual respect between North and South that was not always present in the ranks nor in the treatment of prisoners of war. Among the officers of field rank—Confederate and Union, including Jefferson Davis—were many classmates who had earned their commissions at West Point. Several of them served together in the war against Mexico in the 1840s. And of course, Robert E. Lee had served as Commandant at West Point.

These colorful biographies of the Southern commanders and their conduct of the war should not only fascinate the great number of Civil War buffs but also those of us who, though born in the North, have always felt our sympathies were with the romantic South, certainly so in novels and in the movies. The Southern generals, for the most part, were products of the

aristocracy of the South. The manner in which they conducted themselves in battle and the fortitude with which their families endured the privations of war appealed to the sentiments of later generations.

It is with a great sense of discovery and excitement we bring Captain Snow's wartime biographies to light for modern readers.

January 1982   J. H. Reiner

PREFACE.

THE four fateful years of war which terminated in the surrender of the Southern armies to the overwhelming numbers of the Northern hosts, embrace within their scope one of those grand tragical episodes of history which arrest the attention and employ the investigation of succeeding ages. In the long history of the world, few contests have excelled this in magnitude; few have involved principles so important, marshalled armies so numerous, employed machinery so gigantic, or exhibited designs so vast; and none have displayed courage more conspicuous, devotion more lofty, or skill and genius more transcendent. The men who organized, inspired, and directed the great forces of this struggle, have won a renown as imperishable as history itself. While great distinction may properly be conceded to the commanders on the Federal side of the contest, an exalted reputation preeminently belongs, we think, to the Southern leaders. The Northern generals, with almost exhaustless resources, with daily increasing armies, and immense preponderance of strength, achieved the final triumph of their arms; but the Southern commanders, with greatly inferior forces, in the face of adverse circumstances, with armies suffering for want of food and clothing, and insufficiently armed, with no reserves to recruit the daily diminishing ranks, maintained during the last year of the war, a defence so obstinate and skilful, as to tax the utmost energies and capacity of the Union forces, with all their superiority; while often by some movement of brilliant audacity, victory was snatched from the very jaws of adversity.

The splendid campaigns conducted by Lee and his Generals have, indeed, filled the civilized world with wonder and admiration; and the skill, the genius, the devoted courage, exhibited by those generals when struggling in the face of accumulating misfortunes, against the overwhelming masses pressing and gathering around them, have won for them a fame even more exalted than that achieved by the splendid triumphs of the earlier periods of the war. It is only now, however, when the confusion and detraction incident to the contest have ceased, that we can begin fully to appreciate the magnitude of the struggle, measure its proportions, study its aspects, and by comprehending the nature and extent of the forces employed by the contestants, accurately judge of the genius exhibited in directing them. As a means towards forming this judgment, the volume here offered to the public has been prepared. It contains, briefly, a comprehensive view of all the military operations undertaken by the Confederacy; analyzes the military talents, and measures the capabilities of each commander; follows each expedition on its course—describes its fortunes, and traces its effects. But as the work is Biographical as well as Historical, it attempts to portray the characteristics of the great Confederate leaders, and to exhibit the personal traits of men who for so long a time were the centre of the world's observation.

It was impossible, within the limits of a single volume, to introduce all the Southern officers who have borne the rank of General; and even a narrative of the career of those justly conspicuous, would reduce the work to a mere encyclopedia. The author has, therefore, been compelled to make his selections from among the more prominent Generals, giving extended notice of the few towards whom, as the leading champions of Southern Independence, the attention of all Europe and America has been turned, since first the sounds were heard, telling of conflict and war in these long-peaceful States.

CONTENTS.

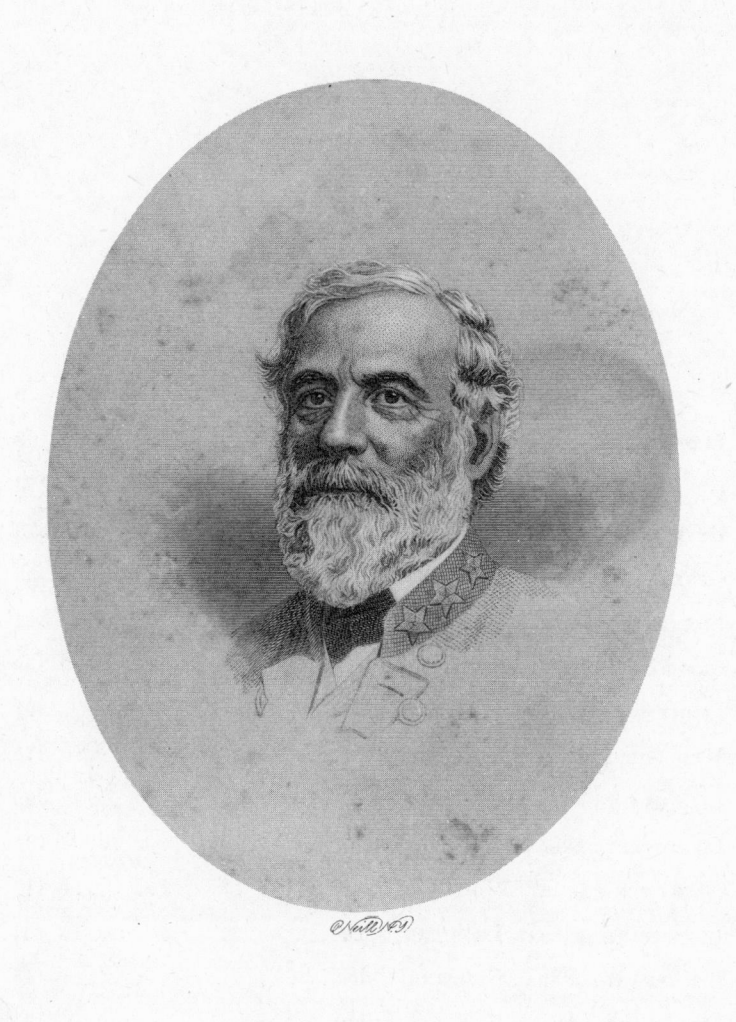

GEN. R. E. LEE.

LEE AND HIS GENERALS.

GENERAL ROBERT EDWARD LEE.

CHAPTER I.

Important Position held by General Lee.—A Sketch of his Life more needed in Detail.—His Ancestors.—Bishop Meade's Work on Old Virginia Families.—Thomas Lee.—Richard Henry and Francis Lightfoot Lee.—General Harry Lee.—Thanks of Congress to General Henry Lee.—His Children.—Robert Edward Lee.

THE subject of this memoir bears so important a part in the great political and national strife now unfortunately waging in our land, and his own personal position in the social and military world has been of so high a standing, that it seems necessary to enter more fully into the particulars of his life than may be deemed requisite as regards others. In common with several more well-known, and well-tried soldiers of rank, he has thought fit to take sides with his native South against the North in those sad disputes which have led to so much fearful blood and slaughter; and his past reputation in the army and on the battlefield, has placed him at the head of all the forces arrayed in hostile attitude against the flag to which he had formerly owned allegiance. Thus he is, and ever will be known, as the most prominent and important personage connected with all the military movements in the South, while boldly and persistently confronting the North. To his military skill and genius, to his calm and clear-thinking mind, his high moral and social status, and the family influence of his name, are undoubtedly due much of the strength of the South, and whatever success may have been achieved. There may be, and indeed there are some others in the Confederate ranks, whose spirit—whose mind and body—also maintain and keep infusing new life within the sometimes flickering elements of opposition in the South, but the name of *Lee* is in itself of additional weight to what they could bring forward. Of a Vir-

ginian family, whose members for more than two hundred
years had been settled in the State, and some of whom had
handed down to posterity names indissolubly connected with
all that was bright, and glorious, and god-like in the cause of
national freedom, besides being inseparably coupled with all
to be esteemed in the mind and intellectual qualities of man,
the present military Commander-in-chief of the Southern
forces is one on whom all eyes turn, with more than ordinary
interest, and whose influence is, perhaps, even greater than
that of the President of the Confederate States himself. To
give, therefore, any thing like a fair and impartial account of
his life to the present time, is no slight nor easy task. We
have to forget the hostile position he has assumed towards the
national power; and, keeping clear of all bias or feeling, save
that of a desire to picture the truth wheresoever it be found,
bear in mind that we are putting before the world the history
of a man, himself distinguished from his youth by his own
deeds, but distinguished equally as much by his close relationship to two of the signers of Independence—Richard Henry,
and Francis Lightfoot Lee,—to the Ludwells, Corbins, and to
that friend and eulogist of Washington, his own father, General
Harry Lee. Thus, in this memoir, we must take up the *man*
as well as the military chief in arms against the Government
of the United States, and we must deal with the individual in
his actions, and, as far as we can understand them, his motives,
as well as the public events that are connected with his name.
Nor must we forget that, in judging of the actions of our fellow-men—especially of those holding a prominent position in
the public eye—we ought always to take into consideration
the circumstances by which they are surrounded, and which
have often led them onward, almost irresistibly. Consequently, the various links which bind any man to a course of
conduct, frequently, to all appearance, inexplicable, and sometimes reprehensible, should be carefully examined, when placing him before the future in the position wherein he has become most prominent. It is not the passing hour that is to
canvass what he does; but it is the sons and daughters of
another day than this sad and painful one, who will have to
look at him and speak of him with a calmer and more impartial mind than can possibly now exist. To lead to this, to do

what present justice can be done to the individual, as well as
to the great military chief, is the object of the following memoir; and, to begin this aright, we will briefly introduce some
account of his family and their ancestors.

In the reign of Charles I., of England, there lived in the
county of Shropshire a good old family of the name of Lee.
Induced, probably, by the flaming reports connected with the
still very young colony of Virginia, then not more than a few
years discovered, a member of this family, Richard Lee, went
over there in an official appointment under the Governor.
He was "a man of good stature, comely visage, enterprising
genius, a sound head, vigorous spirit, and generous nature.
When he got to Virginia, which at that time was not much
cultivated, he was so pleased with the country that he made
large settlements there with the servants he carried over."*
Afterwards he made several voyages back to England, and on
one occasion, possibly considering his return not certain, " he
gave all the lands he had taken up and settled at his expense,
to those servants he had fixed on them, some of whose descendants are now possessed of considerable estates there."

Finally, however, he again visited the colony, bringing with
him more followers, for whom a certain portion of land was
granted him under the title of "Head Rights." He now settled definitely in that part of Virginia called the "Northern
Neck," and situated between the Rappahannock and Potomac rivers. Here, for a long time, he remained, acting as
secretary to Sir Wm. Berkeley, the Governor, during that portion of English history which beheld the master genius of a
powerful mind, in the person of Cromwell, triumphing over
the injustice and tyranny of the unhappy Charles, and finally,
when death took away the great Protector, saw the reinstatement of monarchy in the form of a dissolute and extravagant,
thoughtless, young man. Lee, however, was faithful to his
trust, and the loyal sentiments of his early days. With the
Governor, he contrived to keep the colony firm in its allegiance, and made it so respected by opponents that a treaty
was ratified in England, under Cromwell's hand, ranking it as
an independent State; and on the Restoration, having on its

---

* *Meade*; 137, Life of R. H. Lee, p. 5.

arms the motto, *En dat Virginia quintam*, changed since the Union of England and Scotland, to *En dat Virginia quartam*

Thus, even at the very commencement of the history of Virginia, we see the name of Lee identified with some of its most important affairs, and, in a measure, forming part and parcel of the land.

Richard Lee had two sons, *John* and *Richard*. The first was educated at Oxford, and was so clever and learned, that he could have been promoted to high dignities in the Church, had not his father determined that all his children should settle in Virginia. Accordingly, John returned there, and died before the old man.

Richard Lee, the father, died and was buried in the land of his love and adoption, leaving behind him a numerous progeny, and thus, afterwards, endearing the soil to every member of the family name.

Richard Lee, the son, was even more learned, if possible, than his brother John. He "spent almost his whole life in study, and usually wrote his notes in Greek, Hebrew, or Latin —many of which are now in Virginia. He was of the Council, and also in other offices of honor and profit." His wife was a Miss Corbin, of England, and by her he had five sons and one daughter. His death occurred in Virginia, about the year 1690.*

Of the children of this Richard Lee, the daughter married a Mr. William Fitzhugh, of Eagle's Nest, King George county, Virginia,—son of the first William Fitzhugh ; and from this union, a son—William Fitzhugh, of Chatham—was born. Of the sons of the second Richard Lee, his eldest born, also a Richard, went to England as a Virginia merchant, in partnership with his maternal uncle, Thomas Corbin. After a time he married a rich heiress, Miss Silk, and by her had one son, George, and two daughters, who, on their father's death, went to Virginia and married and intermarried, respectively, into the families of Womley, Fairfax, Corbin, and Turberville. The next son, Philip, went into Maryland, where his descendants are numerously and honorably found to the present day. The third son died a bachelor. The fourth was a Thomas, who married

* *Meade,* p. 138.

a Miss Hannah Ludwell, of whose family a word must be said.

The Ludwells, according to Bishop Meade,* were an old and honorable family, allied by marriage to the famous Lord Francis Cottington, mentioned in Clarendon's History of the Rebellion. Two brothers, John and Philip, held high office here in the time of Charles II., the first in the Virginia Council, the second as Governor of Carolina, until, joining his brother, he married the widow of Sir William Berkeley, by whom he had a daughter (afterwards united to Colonel Parke, Governor of the Leeward Islands in the West Indies), and one son, *Philip*. The Ludwells had now acquired a considerable estate in Virginia, and this son, Philip, married a Miss Harrison, who bore him two daughters and a boy. One of the daughters married a Colonel Grymes of Virginia: the other, Thomas Lee. As for the son, he ultimately married into the Grymes family, and went to England for his health, where he died without male issue, thereby leaving the name extinct. Three daughters were, however, born to him, and these were considered heiresses of some wealth.

We now return to Thomas Lee, who, by his marriage, had allied to his family name that of the Ludwells and the Grymes.

Thomas Lee was a man of great parts and industry. He speedily learned the languages, without any assistance but his own genius, and became a tolerable adept in Greek and Latin; but, being a younger brother, with many children and a small paternal estate, he felt the necessity of perseverance to acquire that fortune which would properly establish them in life. This he attained to some considerable extent, and, moreover, was appointed to the Council, of which he became president,—holding the position for many years, until his death.† He was one of the first of the leading men of the colony who turned their attention to our western wilds, and he employed an engineer of note to explore them, especially about the Ohio river. But he had the keen foresight to tell of the future disseverance of the American colonies from England, and even while President of the Council, said to a friend that such must

---

* *Meade,* p. 138. † Memoirs R. H. Lee, p 6.

inevitably be the case, and that "the seat of government would be located near the Little Falls of the Potomac river," where he afterwards took up large tracts of land, which until lately were in possession of his descendants. His principal homestead, however, was at Stratford, where he had built a mansion, still standing in 1860, and considered "one of the most remarkable buildings in this country."* It appears that his original dwelling had been burned by a serious fire, and, so great was the esteem in which he was held, that Government and merchants alike, and it is said even Queen Caroline, contributed towards the erection of another suitable mansion for him. Mr. Lossing, in his valuable "Field Book of the Revolution," says: "There is no structure in our country to compare with it. The walls of the first story are two and a half feet thick, and of the second story two feet, composed of brick imported from England. It originally contained about 100 rooms. Besides the main building, there are four offices, one at each corner, containing fifteen rooms. The stables are capable of accommodating 100 horses. Its cost was about $80,000."

Thomas Lee died in the year 1750, leaving six sons and two daughters, all well provided for in point of fortune. Of these children but a hasty notice can here be given, though they belong to a day when men and women were the sires and mothers of a people thenceforth a great nation in themselves. But we have no need to say much. Their names dwell in the history of their country's independence, and to that we refer for those details our space and our purpose here forbid us to give.

Philip Ludwell Lee, the eldest born, succeeded his father, Thomas, at Stratford. He married a Miss Steptoe, and had two daughters, Matilda, who married her second cousin, the famous General Henry Lee of the Revolution (father of the subject of our present memoir), and Flora, who married her first cousin, Mr. Ludwell Lee, son of Richard Henry.

The second son of Mr. Thomas Lee was Thomas Ludwell Lee, and he married a Miss Aylett.

The third son was the Richard Henry just mentioned, who

---

* *Lossing*, ii., 217.

was born on the 21st January, 1732, and died on the 19th June, 1794. Educated, as was then customary, in England, it would have been supposed that his sentiments were any thing but favorable to Republican ideas; but when, after various appointments, and after frequently uttering strong opinions as to the necessity for a severance from the mother country, he became a member of the first Continental Congress, his was the first voice to move a resolution on the 7th June, 1776, "That these united colonies are, and of right ought to be, free and independent States; that they are absolved from all allegiance to the British Crown, and that all political connection between them and the State of Great Britain is, and ought to be, totally dissolved."

When this resolution was made public a son of his was at school in England, and one day a gentleman, standing by, asked his tutor, "What boy is this?" The professor replied, "He is the son of Richard Henry Lee, of America." The gentleman put his hand upon the boy's head, and said, "We shall yet see your father's head upon Tower Hill." The boy, however, promptly answered, "You may have it when you can get it." That boy was the late Ludwell Lee, Esq , of Virginia.*

Richard Henry Lee was married, first to Miss Aylett, by whom he had four children, Thomas, Ludwell, Mary, and Hannah; and secondly, to a Miss Pinkard, who bore him three daughters, Harriet, Sally, and Anne. These children married into the families of Alexander, Washington, Turbeville, Maffit, and their cousins, the Lee's.

The fourth son of Thomas Lee was Francis Lightfoot Lee, born October 14th, 1734; died, April, 1797. Like his brother, he was one of the signers of Independence, and his name also lives to posterity as a true patriot and good man. He married a Miss Rebecca Tayloe, daughter of Colonel John Tayloe, of Richmond county.

The fifth son was William, who settled in London, and became Sheriff and Alderman there, though effectively serving the American cause until war was declared, but ever after wards remaining true to it in private.

---

* *Lossing's* Americans, p. 187.

The sixth son was Arthur Lee, who, "as a scholar, a writer, a philosopher, a politician and diplomatist, was unsurpassed by none, and equalled by few of his contemporaries. The services rendered by him to his country as her minister, at foreign courts, were most valuable."*

In the preceding brief extract of family history we have omitted to the last, mention of one branch, viz., Henry Lee, brother of Thomas, and fifth son of the second Richard Lee. This Henry Lee married a Miss Bland, and had several children, amongst whom was also a Henry (the third son), who was united to a Miss Grymes. From this marriage came five sons and three daughters. The eldest was called Henry, born January 29th, 1756, whose military career during the Revolution, and whose patriotism, as well as his personal friendship for Washington, are too well known to need dwelling upon here. The following synopsis of his history, however, as given by Mr. Lossing, may be interesting.

Henry Lee was first educated by a private tutor, under his father's roof, and then sent to Princeton College, where, under the guidance of Dr. Witherspoon, he completed his studies, and graduated in 1774. Two years afterwards, Patrick Henry nominated him to the command of a cavalry company, raised in his native State, for Continental service, under the general command of Colonel Bland. In 1777, Lee's corps was placed under Washington's immediate control, and soon acquired a high character for discipline and bravery. Lee was speedily promoted, and, with his legion, performed many daring exploits. In July, 1779, he captured a British fort at Paulus Hook, for which Congress gave him thanks and a gold medal. In November, 1780, Lee was promoted to Lieutenant-colonel, and early in 1781 joined the army under Greene in the Carolinas. Here he performed efficient service for several months, the services of his legion being of vast importance, and himself ever in the front of success, as well as of danger.

About the beginning of the year 1782 Lee returned to Virginia from the battle of Eutaw Springs, and married Matilda, daughter of Philip Ludwell Lee, of Stratford. He resided there with his father-in-law, and, in 1786, was elected to a seat

---

* *Meade,* p. 140.

in Congress. In 1791 he was made Governor of Virginia, and in 1794 was appointed by Washington to command the troops sent to quell what was called the Whiskey Insurrection, in Western Pennsylvania. In 1799 he was a member of the Federal Congress, and was chosen by that body to pronounce a funeral oration on the death of Washington, in the House of Representatives. At the time, Lee was temporarily absent, and the oration was delivered by his friend, Judge Marshall. But in it were the well-remembered words, referring to Washington, " He was first in war, first in peace, and first in the hearts of his countrymen." In 1801 he retired to private life, but was subject to great annoyance from embarrassed circumstances.

His first wife having died, he again married, and this time to Anne, daughter of Charles Carter, of Shirley, by whom he had, in 1806, Robert Edward Lee, the subject of the present memoir, who was born at the family seat of Stratford, in the same chamber where Richard Henry and Francis Lightfoot Lee first saw the light.

In 1809 General Harry Lee wrote his Memoirs of the War in the Southern Department, and in 1814 he was severely wounded in an attempt to quell a disturbance at Baltimore. From this he never recovered. In 1817 he went to the West Indies for his health, but found no sensible relief. On his return, the following spring, he stopped to visit Mrs. Shaw, a daughter of General Greene, on the coast of Georgia, and there he expired on the 25th of March, 1818, at the age of 62 years.

The character of General Henry Lee, and indeed that of other members of his family name, not excepting the two signers of Independence, has been blackened by the venom of calumny; but time, through a close analysis of contemporaneous facts, ever establishes something of truth, and thus clears the fame of really great men. Such is the case with regard to the Lee family, and the impartial testimony of candid men gives to them a high meed of praise for their unswerving patriotism and fidelity to their native land. This is necessary to be understood; and, also, that in any comments upon the name of Lee, General Charles Lee, of the Revolutionary army, be not brought in with those of whom we here speak. He was, wholly and absolutely, another person, and

of another family, therefore his actions—good and bad—must not be confounded with those of the Lees of Virginia. Of them, Bishop Meade says : " I have been intimately acquainted with some most excellent specimens of true piety among them—too many to be specified and dwelt upon. If tradition and history, and published documents, are to be relied on, the patriotic, laborious, self-sacrificing, and eloquent Richard Henry Lee of the Revolution must have deeply sympathized with Washington and Peyton, Randolph and Pendleton, and Nicholas and Henry, in their religious character and senti-ments. . . . When the question about paying debts in depreciated currency came on, Mr. Lee evinced his high and honorable sense of morality in the earnest and eloquent op-position made to it. He declared that nothing so deeply distressed him as a proposition which he regarded as a viola-tion of honesty and good faith among men, and said that it would have been better to have remained the honest slaves of Britain than dishonest freemen !"

" Of the descendants of so great and good a man," continues the bishop, " I cannot refrain from adding, that many of them are characterized by exemplary piety, and that he has left a numerous posterity of children, grand-children and great-grand-children, who walk in the fear of the Lord, while they still belong to, and love the Church of their ancestors."

But, confining ourselves to the immediate parentage of the present General Lee, we find also abundant testimony in favor of excellence and worth inherent amongst them. The gold medal presented by Congress with a vote of thanks to " Legion Harry, " had, on one side, a bust of the hero with the words HENRICO LEE LEGIONIS EQUIT : PRÆFECTO COMITIA AMERI-CANA, and on the reverse, as translated, " Notwithstanding rivers and intrenchments, he with a small band conquered the foe, by warlike skill and prowess, and firmly bound by his hu-manity those who had been conquered by his arms. In memory of the conflict at Paulus Hook, 19th of August, 1779. "

Again, we read elsewhere, that General Greene in writing of him, said: " He had been under obligations to Lee which he

* *Lossing,* ii., 623.

could never cancel, " and, as to his military services, he added in a letter to Lee, " I believe that few officers either in Europe or America are held in so high a position of admiration as you are. Everybody knows I have the highest opinion of you as an officer, and you know I love you as a friend. No man in the progress of the campaign had equal merit with yourself."*

The "love and thanks, " expressed in a letter to Lee, from Washington, in 1789, exhibit the affection which his qualities had inspired in the bosom of his chief, and in Virginia he is still known by the name of " Legion Harry. " His remains reposed near those of his warm friend, General Greene. " His relentless creditors could rob him of his personal liberty, but could not chain his noble mind, nor rob him of a well-earned fame to the glorious title of an HONEST MAN."

General Lee, by his first wife, had a son, Henry, and a daughter, Lucy. The son (the late Major Henry Lee) wrote and published a work called "The Campaign of 1781," etc., vindicating his father from certain attacks made upon him. By his second wife, he had the following children : Charles Carter Lee, *Robert Edward Lee*,† Smith Lee, Ann, and Mildred.

---

* *Judson's* Sages and Heroes of Amer. Rev.

† THE PEDIGREE OF THE LEE FAMILY.—The Virginia Chronicle publishes the pedigree of the family of General Lee. It is from an old manuscript which has been shown to the editor. The Chronicle says :

"This venerable manuscript, which bears the date 1750, was received by Mr. Mead (who is a gentleman of intelligence and character) from his mother, Mrs. Mead (widow of the Rev. Zachariah Mead, formerly of Richmond). Mrs. Mead received it from her father, who received it from his father, General Hull. It consists of several large sheets, and is written partly in Latin and partly in English. Accompanying the pedigree are some mutilated deeds, which, although much injured, exhibit the descending rights and titles to several lands. These deeds are in Latin, and written on the old stamped paper of England, and, to the antiquarian, are a rare object of curiosity and interest.

"The genealogy of the Lees of Virginia, from 1666,—just where this pedigree breaks off,—is well known, and may be found in Bishop Meade's well-known work on the Old Churches and Families of Virginia.

"The manuscript commences abruptly with the name of Hugo de Lega, or de Le, without date. The first name with date is that of Johes de Lee, Miles, to whom Hugo de Hinton gave the land, as by the old chart. Opposite this name is the date 1333. The father of Johes de Lee was Thomas de la Lee. The simple name of Lee occurs first as Ricardus Lee of Langly, about the year 1500. The first name of Robert is Robertus de la Lee, son of Johes de la Lee he married Margarita, daughter and heir of Thomas Astly of Nordly, about

In October, 1860, a petition was signed by the cavalry and infantry companies, and other military officers encamped near Richmond, to be presented to the next Legislature, "for the removal to Virginia of the remains of General Harry Lee, from his burial-place in Georgia, upon the lands once owned by his companion in arms, General Greene." The locality of the encampment has since been called Camp Lee, " after the illustrious hero, Harry Lee."

1400. The first name written in English is Thomas Lee of Cotton, in King's Nordley, in the Parish of Alvely, who was the son of Johannes Lee.

"There are several coats of arms on the manuscript. That of Ricardus Lee, of the direct line, is as follows: A shield with a crescent of a squirrel sejant, eating a nut or flower; a lion rampant gardant in sinister chief; a star in precise middle chief; dexter chief, a blood-red field with embattled bars of blue and yellow. The dexter base, a black cross on white field, with a lion's head, crowned, in one corner. The middle precise base is a chevron of white, on a red field, a white bar, the fesse point on a green field. The sinister base the same as the dexter chief.

"The Lancelet arms are a shield with crescent squirrel—dexter chief, red field, with blue and yellow embattled bars. Sinister chief, a star on blue field. Dexter base same as sinister chief, and sinister base same as dexter chief. There are no middle divisions on this shield. The prevailing white indicates royalty; the star, grandeur; the lion, courage; the red, war; the cross, religion, and, with the crowned lion, denotes the Church of England.

"The pedigree was extracted from the London Tower, and is certified by Charles Townley, York, and John Pomfret, Rouge Croix, August 1st, 1750.

   *   *   *   *   *

"Henry Lee, the son of the first wife, was a major in the war of 1812, and wrote the Strictures on the Writings of Jefferson, also a Life of Napoleon Bonaparte. Sidney Smith Lee was a commodore in the old United States Navy, and is now Chief of the Bureau of Orders and Detail, Navy Department, in Richmond. He commanded at Drury's Bluff for a long time. Robert Edmund Lee is at Petersburg—the General Lee of this day.

"He married Miss Custis of Arlington, in Alexandria County, the daughter and heiress of George Washington Parke Custis, the adopted son of General Washington, who married Mrs. Custis, his mother.

"General Lee has three sons—Brigadier-general G. W. Custis Lee, aid-de-camp to the President (he passed No. 1 at West Point); Major General W. H. F. Lee, commanding a division of cavalry in the army of Northern Virginia, and Robert Edmund Lee, who entered the army at the instance of his father as a private in the Rockbridge artillery. He is now on the staff of General Fitzhugh Lee. Besides these children, General Lee had four daughters,—Mary, Anne, Agnes, and Mildred,—all of them unmarried, and one of whom (Anne) has died during the war. General W. H. F. Lee married a Miss Wickman, who died a year or two since.

"General Fitzhugh Lee, of the cavalry, is the son of Commodore Lee."

CHAPTER II.

Ancestry not to be lightly esteemed.—The parents of great men entitled to praise for the early promptings of youth.—They are not to be forgotten in the fame of the son.—Youth of Robert E. Lee.—Enters West Point as a Cadet.—Graduates, and is appointed a Lieutenant of Engineers.—Marries into the Custis family.—Made Captain, and appointed member of Board of Visitors to Military Academy.—Attached to Army of Mexico.—General Scott's high opinion of him.—Extracts from Scott's Autobiography.—Captain Lee's services in Mexico.—His companions in arms.—Wounded at Chapultepec.—Promoted for gallant and meritorious conduct.—Appointed Superintendent at West Point.—Made Lieutenant-colonel of Cavalry—Employed in the Border wars against the Indians.—Returns to Washington.—Sent by Government to quell the John Brown Raid.—Successfully accomplishes this, and returns to Washington.

IF, in writing an account of a son's career, we would be wholly just, and can at all give space to do so, let us not forget the sire that gave him good example, and, above all, the mother that is too oft neglected when speaking of the early promptings of youth. It is to that father, and to that soft maternal care—so truly and justly prized by all good men, howsoever great they may be—that virtuous deeds and noble acts take root, afterwards spreading abroad in rich and glorious-looking fruit. So, too, with the ancestry of a man, if that ancestry has been of public note. Few there are of mind and education, in this world, who would willingly disgrace their sires,—nay, who would not rather do increased honor to them by their own worthy acts. And so it has been with the family of the Virginia Lees. Truth, honor, unselfish patriotism, love to God and love to man, seem to have been mainly the characteristic traits belonging to them.

The youth of Robert Lee was passed amid exciting times. For more than twenty years prior to his birth, America had been at peace as an independent nation; but about this time, symptoms of a new struggle with England were manifested, in addition to hostile attempts by the Indians on the western frontier. This latter, however, was soon quelled, but the

former resulted in a declaration of war with Great Britain on
the 18th of June, 1812. What followed is well known to
every youth in the present day. A British fleet, under
Admiral Cockburn, entered the Chesapeake, and laid waste
such towns and districts upon the coast as were found assailable. Some of the ships ascended the Potomac, and, on the
29th of August, 1814, reached Alexandria, while the military
forces of England, under General Ross, were at work on the
Patuxent, the Patapsco, and finally against Washington, and
Fort McHenry, Baltimore. In the South, Pensacola was in
possession of the British until driven from there by General
Jackson, who, a few months afterwards, completely routed
them again at the celebrated battle of New Orleans. Peace,
however, was now declared, the treaty having been signed on
the 24th December, 1814; and, a few months afterwards,
Algiers was made to sue for peace, after a severe chastisement
at the hands of Commodore Decatur, for having seized American vessels, and enslaving their crews. In 1817 Monroe
succeeded Madison as President; and in the same year, the
Seminole war broke out at the South, General Jackson being
sent to quell the Indians then overrunning the country.

It was at this time the father of Robert Lee went to the
West Indies, and died on his return; the youth being then
twelve years old.

In 1820, Florida was ceded by Spain to the United States;
and in 1824, the visit of Lafayette to America, producing a
general burst of enthusiasm throughout the land, could not
fail to have been strongly impressed upon young Lee's mind.

He was now eighteen years of age, and in the following year,
1825, entered West Point as a cadet from his native State.
There he remained the usual four years, perfecting his studies,
and preparing for that military career in which he afterwards
became so conspicuous.

During the whole of this period Lee never once received a
reprimand, nor had any mark of demerit against him; and
when, at the expiration of his term, he graduated at the head
of his class, he was immediately selected for service in the
corps of topographical engineers, receiving his appointment as
brevet second-lieutenant in July, 1829.

From this time, until the year 1835, he was principally

employed on the coast defences, but, at that period, we find him appointed assistant astronomer, for the demarcation of the boundary line between the States of Ohio and Michigan.

In 1832, Lieutenant Lee married a daughter of Mr. Custis and thus, through her, became proprietor of Arlington House and the White House on the banks of the Pamunkey, afterwards so noted in the Peninsular campaign.

On the 21st September, 1836, he was promoted to a first-lieutenancy; and in July, 1838, was made captain. During 1844 he was appointed a member of the Board of Visitors to the Military Academy, and was, afterwards, from September 8th, 1845, a member of the Board of Engineers. In 1846, Captain Lee was attached to the central army of Mexico as Chief-engineer, under General Wool, and he retained that post throughout the whole campaign, under General Scott. When this latter general landed in Mexico, Captain Lee was one of the first selected to be of his personal staff and council, and the high opinion Scott entertained of him is well known. A few extracts, however, from the general's own autobiography, lately published, may be serviceable. He says, of his first council at Vera Cruz:

"In my little cabinet, however, consisting of Colonel Totten, Chief-engineer; Lieutenant-colonel Hitchcock, Acting Inspector-general; *Captain R. E. Lee*, Engineer; and (yet) First-lieutenant Henry L. Scott, Acting Adjutant-general, I entered fully into the question of storming parties and regular siege approaches. A death-bed discussion could hardly have been more solemn. Thus powerfully impressed, I opened my subject, substantially as follows:

"We, of course, gentlemen, must take the city and castle before the return of the *vomito*—if not by head-work, the slow scientific process, by storming—and then escape by pushing the conquest into the healthy interior. I am strongly inclined to attempt the former, unless you can convince me that the other is preferable. Since our thorough reconnoissances, I think the suggestion practicable, with a very moderate loss on our part. The second method would, no doubt, be equally suc cessful, but at the cost of an immense slaughter on both sides, including non-combatants—Mexican men, women, and children—because the assault must be made in the dark, and the

assailants dare not lose time in taking and guarding prisoners without incurring the certainty of becoming captives themselves, until all the strongholds of the place are occupied."*

Vera Cruz and the Castle of San Juan de Ulloa surrendered, and Scott marched forward to Mexico on the 12th of April. The enemy made a stand at Cerro Gordo, and here, again, the commander-in-chief thus speaks of Lee. He says:

"Hearing that Twiggs, supported by Patterson, found himself confronted at Plan del Rio, some fifty miles in the interior, by a strong body of the enemy, and that both divisions were desirous of my presence, I left Vera Cruz on the 12th of April, with a small escort of cavalry, under Captain Philip Kearney (who fell in 1862, a distinguished major-general), and hastened to the front. Major-general Patterson, though quite sick, had assumed the command on joining Twiggs, in order to prohibit any aggressive movement before my arrival, according to the universal wish of the troops. No commander was ever received with heartier cheers,—the certain presage of the victories that followed.

"The two advanced divisions lay in the valley of the Plan del Rio, and the body of the enemy about three miles off, on the heights of Cerro Gordo. Reconnoissances were pushed in search of some practicable route, other than the winding, zigzag road among the spurs of mountains, with heavy batteries at every town. The reconnoissances were conducted with vigor under *Captain Lee*, at the head of a body of pioneers; and, at the end of the third day, a passable way for light batteries was accomplished—without alarming the enemy—giving the possibility of turning the extreme left of his line of defence, and capturing his whole army, except the reserve, that lay a mile or two higher up the road. Santa Anna said that he had not believed a goat could have approached him in that direction. Hence the surprise and the results were the greater."†

In alluding to this reconnoissance made by Lee, the brave old general, in his official report, thus again speaks:

"The reconnoissance begun by Lieutenant Beauregard was continued by Captain Lee, Engineers, and a road made along

---

* *Scott*, ii., 423–4.   † *Ibid.*, ii., 431.

difficult slopes, and over chasms, out of the enemy's view though reached by his fire when discovered—until arriving at the Mexican lines, further reconnoissances became impossible without an action. The desired point of the debouchure, the Jalapa road, was not, therefore, reached, though believed to be within easy distance; and to gain that point it now became necessary to carry the heights of Cerro Gordo. . . . . . Twiggs' division, reinforced by Shields' brigade of volunteers, was thrown into position on the 17th, and was, of necessity, drawn into action in taking up ground for its bivouac, and the opposing heights for a heavy battery. It will be seen that many of our officers and men were killed or wounded in this sharp combat—handsomely commenced by a company of the Seventh Infantry, under brevet First-lieutenant Gardner, who was highly praised by all his commanders for signal services. Colonel Harney, coming up with his rifle regiment and First Artillery, also parts of his brigade, brushed away the enemy, and occupied the heights, on which, in the night, was placed a battery of one 24-pounder and two 24-pound howitzers, under the superintendence of *Captain Lee*, Engineers, and Lieutenant Hagner, Ordnance. These guns opened next morning, and were served with effect by Captain Steptoe, and Lieutenant Brown, Third Artillery; Lieutenant Hagner, Ordnance; and Lieutenant Seymour, First Artillery."*

The details of the victory at Cerro Gordo are well known, and, moreover, need not be mentioned here. We have only to refer to the part Captain Lee performed therein; and again we quote General Scott. After expressing his "indebtedness for able assistance" to several gallant officers, particularly named, General Scott then says : "I am compelled to make special mention of Captain R. E. Lee, Engineer. This officer greatly distinguished himself at the siege of Vera Cruz; was again indefatigable during these operations in reconnoissances, as daring as laborious, and of the utmost value. Nor was he less conspicuous in planning batteries, and in conducting columns to their stations, under the heavy fire of the enemy."

The troops now marched onward to Jalapa and Puebla,

Scott, p. 450.

where we find that, among other well-known names mentioned as among the chief officers comprising the army, the following were in close companionship:

Engineer Corps.—Major J. L. Smith, Chief; *Captain R. E. Lee*, Lieutenant P. G. T. Beauregard, G. W. Smith, George B. McClellan, J. G. Foster.

Quartermaster's Department.—Captain J. McKinstry.

Harney's Corps.—Major Sumner, Major McReynolds, Captain Kearney, and also Captain Magruder of the field battery.

These heroic brothers in arms—then conjointly fighting against a national foe, have now all become prominently known as battling in fierce strife against each other in this sad war, and some of them have given their lives for the cause in which they served.

The battles of Contreras, Cherubusco, and Chapultepec followed, in all of which Captain Lee again highly distinguished himself. Indeed, so greatly was his meritorious conduct esteemed by Scott, that, even at the present time, in his own autobiography, he is continually praising him. A few passages only, and to mark the opinion entertained of Lee by so eminent a military authority, and so high a personage as General Scott, we again quote. He says:

"The same day (August 18th, 1847) a reconnoissance was commenced to the left of San Augustin, first over difficult grounds, and further on over the same field of volcanic matter which extends to the mountain, some five miles from San Antonio, towards Magdalena. This reconnoissance was continued to-day by *Captain Lee*, assisted by Lieutenants Beauregard and Tower, all of the engineers, who were joined in the afternoon by Major Smith, of the same corps. Other divisions coming up, Pillow was advanced to make a practicable road for heavy artillery, and Twiggs thrown further in front to cover the operations; for, by the partial reconnoissance of yesterday, Captain Lee discovered a large corps of observation in that direction, with a detachment of which, his supports of cavalry and foot, under Captain Kearney and Lieutenant-colonel Graham, respectively, had a successful skirmish. . . . . . These corps, over the extreme difficulties of the ground—partly covered with a low forest—before described, reached Contreras, and found Cadwallader's brigade in po-

sition, observing the formidable movement from the capital and much needing the timely reinforcement.

" It was already dark, and the cold rain began to fall in torrents upon our unsheltered troops, for the hamlet, though a strong defensive position, could only hold the wounded men, and, unfortunately, the new regiments had little or nothing to eat in their haversacks. Wet, hungry, and without the possibility of sleep, all our gallant corps, I learn, are full of confidence, and only waiting for the last hour of darkness to gain the positions whence to storm and carry the enemy's works.

" Of the seven officers dispatched since about sundown from my position, opposite the enemy's centre, and on this side of the volcanic field, to communicate instructions to the hamlet, not one has succeeded in getting through these difficulties, increased by darkness. They have all returned. But the gallant and indefatigable Captain Lee, of the Engineers, who has been constantly with the operating forces, is (11 o'clock P. M.) just in from Shields, Smith, Cadwallader, etc., to report as above, and to ask that a powerful diversion be made against the centre of the intrenched camp towards morning.

" Brigadier-general Twiggs, cut off, as above, from the part of his division, beyond the impracticable ground, and Captain Lee, are gone, under my orders, to collect the forces remaining on this side, with which to make that diversion, at about 5 o'clock in the morning.

This " diversion," however, became a real attack, " under the command of Colonel Ransom, of the Ninth, having with him that regiment, and some companies of three others, guided by Captain Lee. . . . . . At 3 A. M. the great movement had commenced on the rear of the enemy's camp. The march was rendered tedious by the darkness, rain, and mud ; but, about sunrise, Riley had reached an elevation behind the enemy, whence he precipitated his columns, stormed the intrenchments, planted his several colors upon them, and carried the work, all in seventeen minutes. Cadwallader had also brought up two of his regiments, and, at the appointed time, Colonel Ransom, with his temporary brigade, conducted by Captain Lee, not only made the movement in front to divert and to distract the enemy, but, after crossing the deep

ravine, advanced and poured into the work, and upon the fugitives, many volleys from his destructive musketry."*

The victory of Contreras being complete, General Scott, after giving necessary orders on the field, in the midst of prisoners and trophies, and sending instructions to Harney's brigade of cavalry (left at San Augustin) to join him, personally followed Pillow's command.

Arriving at Coyoacan, two miles, by a cross-road, from the river of San Antonio, General Scott first detached Captain Lee with Captain Kearney's troop, First Dragoons, supported by the Rifle regiment, under Major Loring, to reconnoitre that strong point, and next dispatched Major-general Pillow, with Cadwallader's brigade, to make the attack upon it, in concert with Major General Worth on the opposite side. At the same time, by another road, to the left, Lieutenant Stevens, of the Engineers, supported by Lieutenant G. W. Smith's company of sappers and miners of the same corps, was sent to reconnoitre the strongly fortified church or convent of San Pablo, in the hamlet of Cherubusco,—one mile off. Twiggs, with one of his brigades, Smith's, less the Rifles,—and Captain Taylor's field battery, were ordered to follow, and to attack the convent. Major Smith, senior Engineer, was dispatched to concert with Twiggs the mode and means of attack, and Twiggs' other brigade, Rifles, were soon ordered up to support him. Next, but all in ten minutes, Pierce was sent, though just able to keep his saddle with his brigade (Pillow's division), conducted by *Captain Lee*, by a third road a little further to our left, to attack the enemy's right and rear, in order to favor the movement upon the convent, and to cut off a retreat towards the capital. Finally, Shields, with the New York and South Carolina Volunteers (Quitman's division), was ordered to follow Pierce closely, and to take command of our left wing. All these movements were made with the utmost alacrity by our gallant troops and commanders.

General Scott now found himself at Coyoacan, from which so many roads conveniently branched; and without escort or reserve, he had to advance, for safety, close upon Twiggs' rear. The battle then raged from right to left of the whole line.

Captain Lee now returned and informed General Scott that Shields, in the rear of Cherubusco, was hard pressed and in danger of being outflanked, if not owerwhelmed, by superior numbers; thereupon Major Sumner, Second Dragoons, the Rifles, and Captain Sibley's troop, Second Dragoons, were immediately sent to support our left, guided by Captain Lee.

"The victory of the 8th (September), at the Molinos del Rey, was followed by daring reconnoissances on the part of our distinguished Engineers—Captain Lee, Lieutenant Beauregard, etc. Their operations were directed principally to the south—towards the gates of the Piedad," and on the heights of Chapultepec. Here Captain Lee was wounded, and, though still eager to advance, was compelled to retire from loss of blood. But he had well and nobly contributed towards the glories of the day ; and when the colors of the United States were hoisted on the national palace of Mexico, he could justly feel entitled to share in the praises so generously and nobly bestowed by Scott on his heroic followers. " In the glorious conquest," says that distinguished officer, " *all* had contributed —early and powerfully—the killed, the wounded, and the fit for duty, as much as those who fought at the gates of Belena and San Cosme."

In his official report, General Scott again highly compliments Captain Lee " as distinguished for felicitous execution as for science and daring." And, furthermore, he says, " Captain Lee, so constantly distinguished, also bore important orders from me (September 13th), until he fainted from a wound and the loss of two nights' sleep at the batteries."*

A writer in "Harper's Weekly"† has very justly remarked that " no one who reads the voluminous Reports of Scott's Campaign in Mexico can fail to observe the frequency with which special honorable mention is made of three young officers of Engineers,—Captain R. E. Lee, First-lieutenant Beauregard, and brevet Second lieutenant G. B. McClellan. Lee seems to have been the special favorite of the veteran General, and there is hardly a single dispatch in which his name is not honorably mentioned. . . . . . . The careful reader of the whole series of dispatches respecting the campaign in Mexico

---

* *Scott*, pp. 507, 533.   † Nov. 1, 1862.

will come to the conclusion that the three men who, after the veteran General, displayed the highest military talents, were the three young officers of Engineers, Lee, Beauregard, and McClellan. . . . . . . Lee and McClellan are now (November, 1862) virtually at the head of the two armies of the North and South, and by the almost unanimous consent of both sides they are the most capable men to fill these posts."

In the above remarks there may be some modification required, even as the Editor himself, at a later period, has expressed ; for there were, most undoubtedly, many other eminent men of great skill and bravery, in the Mexican War, who received due praise, and still prove in the present war their full right to the credit of it. But our province is simply to show what Lee has done, and how every one, from his highest superior officer, to those of equal rank with himself, united in awarding to him that eminence in his military profession, which, as Commander-in-chief of the Confederate forces, he has since invariably displayed.

During the war in Mexico he was promoted for gallant and meritorious conduct,—the first time at the battle of Cerro Gordo, as brevet major,—the next at Contreras and Cherubusco, an additional brevet, which made him a lieutenant-colonel ; and, for the wounds he received at Chapultepec, with his bravery there, he was nominated for still higher rank.

The campaign over, Lee returned home, and again filled the duties of a member of the Board of Engineers. In the early part of 1852 he appears to have been ordered with his regiment to New Mexico. The following letter, said to have been found by a soldier at Arlington House, lately appeared in the "New York News" and some southern and western papers, and as it serves to illustrate the personal character of the writer we give it entire.

"ARLINGTON HOUSE, April 5, 1852.

"MY DEAR SON: I am just in the act of leaving home for New Mexico. My fine old regiment has been ordered to that distant region, and I must hasten on to see that they are properly cared for. I have but little to add in reply to your letters of March 26, 27, and 28. Your letters breathe a true spirit of frankness; they have given myself and your mother great

pleasure. You must study to be frank with the world: frankness is the child of honesty and courage. Say just what you mean to do on every occasion, and take it for granted you mean to do right. If a friend asks a favor, you should grant it, if it is reasonable; if not, tell him plainly why you cannot: you will wrong him and wrong yourself by equivocation of any kind. Never do a wrong thing to make a friend or keep one; the man who requires you to do so, is dearly purchased at a sacrifice. Deal kindly, but firmly, with all your classmates, you will find it the policy which wears best. Above all, do not appear to others what you are not. If you have any fault to find with any one, tell him, not others, of what you complain; there is no more dangerous experiment than that of undertaking to be one thing before a man's face and another behind his back. We should live, act, and say, nothing to the injury of any one. It is not only best as a matter of principle, but it is the path to peace and honor.

"In regard to duty, let me, in conclusion of this hasty letter, inform you that nearly a hundred years ago there was a day of remarkable gloom and darkness—still known as "the dark day"—a day when the light of the sun was slowly extinguished, as if by an eclipse. The legislature of Connecticut was in session, and as its members saw the unexpected and unaccountable darkness coming on, they shared in the general awe and terror. It was supposed by many that the last day—the day of judgment—had come. Some one, in the consternation of the hour, moved an adjournment. Then there arose an old Puritan legislator, Devenport, of Stamford, and said, that if the last day had come, he desired to be found at his place doing his duty, and, therefore, moved that candles be brought in, so that the house could proceed with its duty. There was quietness in that man's mind, the quietness of heavenly wisdom and inflexible willingness to obey present duty. Duty, then, is the sublimest word in our language. Do your duty in all things, like the old Puritan. You cannot do more, you should never wish to do less. Never let me and your mother wear one gray hair for any lack of duty on your part.

"Your affectionate father,

"R. E. Lee.

"To G. W. Custis Lee."

On the 1st of September, 1852, Colonel Lee was appointed to succeed Captain Brewerton as Superintendent of the Military Academy at West Point. Here, under his administration, and on the 28th of August, 1854, the course of study was, by direction of the Secretary of War, extended so as to embrace a term of five years.

On the first of April, 1855, Colonel Lee, having been promoted to the Cavalry arm of the service, and thereby incapacitated by law from exercising superintendence at the Military Academy, was succeeded by Major J. G. Barnard.

The regiment to which Lee was now appointed was the Second U. S. Cavalry, a new regiment organized under the act of March 3, 1855, its colonel being Albert Sydney Johnson, afterwards a Confederate General. This regiment was much employed in the Indian wars on the prairies of Texas, which created so much excitement at the time; and here again Lieutenant-colonel Lee highly distinguished himself. But, for how long he was so employed, we are unable to say. This is certain, however, that in 1859 he was on his estates at Arlington, or perhaps at Washington on duty, because he then appeared in connection with the John Brown raid at Harper's Ferry, to which we must now refer.

The news of the insurrection of this enthusiast and his followers, and their seizure of Government property, had no sooner reached Washington than President Buchanan consulted with the Secretary of War as to the best measures to be adopted. To this consultation Colonel Lee (then Lieutenant-colonel of the Second Cavalry, U. S. Army) was summoned, and, after arranging plans to prevent additional outbreak, he was dispatched to command the regular troops concentrating at Harper's Ferry. Accompanied by his Aid, Lieutenant J. E. B. Stuart—lately a General in the Confederate Army—he set out on a special train on the evening of October 17th, and sent a telegraphic dispatch to the United States Marines, in advance of him, directing them what to do. Other troops—the militia from Virginia and Maryland—had promptly reached the scene, and when Colonel Lee arrived during the night, were awaiting his orders to act. He immediately placed his command within the armory grounds, so as to completely surround the fire engine house where the insur-

rectionists had taken refuge. This building was, no doubt, the
most defensible one in the armory, having dead brick walls
on three sides, and, on the fourth, large doors with window-
sashes above, some eight feet from the ground. In it, Brown
and his party had confined Colonel Washington, Mr. Danger-
field, and some other citizens whom they had surprised and
taken prisoners the night before; and therefore to use the cannon upon it now, would be to endanger the lives of friends as
well as foes.   Accordingly, at daylight, Colonel Lee took
measures to try and capture the insurgents, if possible, without bloodshed.   While doing so, one of them came out of the
door, and, presenting a flag of truce, proposed terms of capitulation.   These, however, could not be accepted; but, still desirous of avoiding more bloodshed, Colonel Lee at seven A. M. sent
his Aid, Lieutenant Stuart, to summon them quietly to surrender,
promising to hold them in security from the threatened ven-
geance of the citizens, until the President's pleasure was known.
Brown refused all terms but those he himself had proposed,
viz. : " That they should be permitted to march out with their
men and arms, taking their prisoners with them; that
they should proceed unpursued to the second toll-gate, when
they would free their prisoners, the soldiers then being permitted to pursue them, and they would fight, if they could not
escape."

Finding the insurgents thus madly bent on their own destruction, Lieutenant Stuart, by direction of Colonel Lee, earnestly remonstrated with them, but, after staying there a while
in a dangerous proximity, and evincing that coolness and
courage ever since so conspicuously displayed in him, he came
away.   At this moment, perceiving all his humane efforts to be
thrown away, Colonel Lee gave orders for an attack. A strong
party of marines under Lieutenant Green had been previously
posted so near the building that, at a concerted signal, they
advanced by two lines quickly on each side the door.   When
near enough, two powerful men sprang between the lines, and,
with heavy sledge-hammers, attempted to batter down the
doors, but failed. They then took hold of a ladder some forty
feet long, and, advancing with a run, brought it with tremendous effect upon the door. At the second blow it gave away,
and immediately the marines, headed by Major Russell and

Lieutenant Green, rushed to the breach as a volley from within came right upon them.   One of the marines instantly fell, and another was severely wounded; but it was necessary, if possible, to avoid firing upon the friends within; and accordingly great care was taken.   Fortunately, this was successful.   The marines marked their men, and, as the captured citizens, by advice of Colonel Washington, held up their arms, not one of them was hurt.   In a moment, more of the soldiers rushed in and secured the rioters, after two of them were killed, and two more wounded.   The next instant all was over: the liberated citizens were hailed with shouts of congratulation by the excited crowd of spectators without, and the captured rioters met with execrations.   Indeed, only for the precautions wisely taken by Colonel Lee, it is more than probable they would have been shot down on the spot.

Colonel Lee at once telegraphed to Washington for further instructions, which were promptly returned to him, stating that Mr. Ould, District Attorney for the District of Columbia, would immediately arrive to take charge of the legal proceedings, and bring the rioters to trial.

Thus ended the John Brown affair, so far as the military and Colonel Lee were concerned.   The prisoners were handed over to Mr. Ould, and Colonel Lee returned to his cavalry command.

CHAPTER III.

Commencement of Civil War.—Lee at Texas.—Returns home and Resigns his Commission.—Difficulty of his Position.—His Letters on the Subject.—Parting between him and General Scott.—His family Mansion.—Arlington House.—General McDowell's noble feeling in reference to it.—Description of the Estate.—Washington Relics.—Lee appointed to the Command in Virginia.—Organizes troops around Richmond.—Succeeds General Garnett in Western Virginia.—Battle of Cheat Mountain.—Retreat of Lee.—Appointed to take charge of Coast Defences.—Summoned to Richmond and made Commanding General of the Forces.—Commencement of Siege of Richmond.—General Johnston.—Defensive Operations.—The White House.—Mrs. General Lee Captured.—Battle of Seven Pines.—Johnston Wounded, and Lee appointed to Command the Army.

WE now come to the commencement of that period in the life of Lee which has made his name so conspicuous throughout the world. In the beginning of 1861, he was with his regiment at San Antonio, Texas, and it was there that news reached him of his native State contemplating a withdrawal from the Federal Union.

At this time it appears evident that a great struggle was going on within his breast as to the course he should pursue in relation to the strife then commencing. His natural attachment to the State in which he was born, and where all his family had resided during so many past years, drew him to her fortunes, whatever they might be. On the other hand, all his public career, his fame and rank, were identified with that flag he had so well and so bravely fought under. Then, too, there were his gallant associates in arms,—his friend and admirer General Scott, who, when applied to by the President to recommend some one of the army officers qualified to fill the place made vacant by the death of General Jessup, named him first on the list of four.* Added to all this was the inevitable reflection that, once in arms against the Government of the

---

* *Miss. Rep.*, June 24, 1861.

United States, his high and lofty position as a noble gentleman and an officer of exalted rank, with an unblemished reputation, would be thenceforth coupled, in history and state
documents, with the terms "Rebel and Traitor." Still more,
there was the terrible results certain to accrue from joining in
the war, and the inward sorrow he must feel on beholding the
devastation and misery following the first blood spilled on his
native soil. His house, his fortunes,* his family, had all to be
considered, and, turn whichever way he might, it would seem
that no escape from being involved in the national calamity
presented itself—one side or the other was alike injurious to
him. Early in the year, the Governor of Virginia had been
authorized by the State Legislature to raise and organize a
military force of from ten to twenty thousand men, under an
officer of experience, with the title of Major-general; but still
Lee remained true to his allegiance, perhaps hoping that Virginia would not, after all, secede. That hope, alas! was futile.
Events followed one another rapidly from the time of his appointment in the regular army as colonel, to the hour when,
Fort Sumter having surrendered, on the 14th of April, open
war between the North and South commenced. He could no
longer hesitate. Other high and experienced officers, born in
the South, were resigning, and his native State called upon
him to do likewise, and come to her aid. In vain his friend
and former chief, General Scott, begged of him not to relinquish his position in the regular army. "For God's sake,
don't resign, Lee," the veteran General is reported to have
said; but the response was, "I am compelled to. I cannot
consult my own feelings in this matter," and he threw up his
commission, his resignation being received on the 20th of
April.†

---

* It was publicly stated in the "Baltimore American," May 23, 1861, that
"Lee's baggage and papers were seized at New York *en route* from Texas to
Virginia."

† Lee's final letter to Scott was as follows:

ARLINGTON, VA., April 20th, 1861.

GENERAL: Since my interview with you on the 18th instant, I have felt
that I ought not longer to retain my commission in the army. I, therefore,
tender my resignation, which I request you will recommend for acceptance.
It would have been presented at once, but for the struggle it has cost me to

GENERAL ROBERT EDWARD LEE.

It has been stated that the parting between Scott and Lee was very painful;—and naturally so.* Two warm friends who had often been in intimate relationship during a war where all fought together, even closeted in serious council when military measures of importance—as at Vera Cruz—were to be adopted, could not now sever and take opposite sides in an intestine

---

separate myself from a service to which I have devoted all the best years of my life and all the ability I possessed.

During the whole of that time—more than a quarter of a century—I have experienced nothing but kindness from my superiors, and the most cordial friendship from my comrades. To no one, General, have I been as much indebted as to yourself for uniform kindness and consideration, and it has always been my ardent desire to merit your approbation. I shall carry to the grave the most grateful recollections of your kind consideration, and your name and fame will always be dear to me.

Save in defence of my native State, I never desire again to draw my sword. Be pleased to accept my most earnest wishes for the continuance of your happiness and prosperity, and believe me, most truly yours,

R. E. LEE.

LIEUTENANT-GENERAL WINFIELD SCOTT,
Commanding United States Army.

A copy of the preceding letter was inclosed in the following letter to a sister of the General, Mrs. A. M.:

ARLINGTON, VA., April 20th, 1861.

MY DEAR SISTER: I am grieved at my inability to see you . . . . . I have been waiting "for a more convenient season," which has brought to many before me deep and lasting regret. Now we are in a state of war which will yield to nothing. The whole South is in a state of revolution, into which Virginia, after a long struggle, has been drawn, and *though I recognize no necessity for this state of things*, and would have forborne and pleaded to the end for redress of grievances, real or supposed, yet in my own person I had to meet the question, *whether I should take part against my native State*. With all my devotion to the Union, and the feeling of loyalty and duty of an American citizen, I have not been able to make up my mind to raise my hand against my relatives, my children, my home. I have, therefore, resigned my commission in the army, and save in defence of my native State, with the sincere hope that my poor services may never be needed, I hope I may never be called on to draw my sword.

I know you will blame me, but you must think as kindly of me as you can, and believe that I have endeavored to do what I thought right. To show you the feeling and struggle it has cost me, I send a copy of my letter to General Scott, which accompanied my letter of resignation. I have no time for more.

. . . . May God guard and protect you and yours, and shower upon you every blessing, is the prayer of your devoted brother,

R. E. LEE.

* *Newspaper*, June 22, 1861, M. R.

strife without much pain. Then, too, the knowledge which
as experienced officers each must have had, in common with
other soldiers of rank and skill, of the terrible effects of such
a strife, would compel them to most sad and gloomy thoughts.
They had seen and well knew the calamities and the horrors
of war, and could too clearly see the fearful misery sure to
attend a civil war above all other wars. Politicians, Lawyers,
Civilians, Theorists, " Humanitarians," knew it not, save in the
fancy of their brain. Thus the two military friends *knew* what
was to follow, and could be well excused—nay, even admired for their good feeling—if, as is said, tears came into
their eyes when they were about to part, perhaps forever, and
take up opposite sides in deadly strife.

What Lee's struggle of mind must have been at the time,
may be gathered from the following passage in a letter sent
by Mrs. Lee in the Christmas of 1861 to a Union friend. She
says, " My husband has wept tears of blood over this terrible
war, but he must, as a man of honor and a Virginian, share
the destiny of his State, which has solemnly pronounced for
independence." *

Of the great estimation Lee was held in by the highest military authorities in the United States, an idea may be formed
from General Scott's remark, that "it were better for every
officer in the army, including himself, to die, than Robert
Lee."†

At this time, Lee's family resided at the famous Custis
Mansion, called Arlington House, on the heights, and the
following particulars relating to it may not be uninteresting.
A writer in the " New York Daily News," July 9th, 1861,
says:

" General McDowell would not occupy the evacuated ' Lee-
House,' preferring the tented field and a soldier's fare to the
luxury of enjoying the General's abandoned quarters. This
act, of itself, has greatly endeared him to the soldiers, who are
ready to follow him anywhere. His tent is a few paces distant
from the south wing of the house. In front of the door stands
a small plain table—without paint, varnish, covering, or any
such thing. A few books and writing materials upon it, with

---

* *Sun*, Oct. 1, 1862.   † *Mobile Adv.*, May 3, 1861.

a single chair alongside, tell plainly that the General, and he alone, sits at that table.

" Southeastward some sixty rods, and at gentle descent, the visitor beholds two monumental pillars of white marble, standing at the head of two graves. The largest of the monuments reads thus : "George Washington Parke Custis, died 1853 ;" the other, " Mary L. Custis, died 1857." Those departed ones, —once united in life, and not separated in death—were of family kin with the immortal Washington ; and what a sad, sad comment does the present read of the past !

" All around here, Arlington Heights presents a lovely picture of rural beauty. The 'General-Lee House' (as some term it) stands on a grassy lot surrounded with a grove of stately trees and underwood, except in front, where is a verdant sloping ground for a few rods, when it descends into a valley, spreading away in beautiful and broad expanse to the lovely Potomac. This part of this splendid estate is apparently a highly cultivated meadow, the grass waving in the gentle breeze, like the undulating bosom of Old Atlantic. To the south, north, and west, the grounds are beautifully diversified into hill and valley, and richly stored with oak, willow, and maple, though the oak is the principal wood.

" The view from this height is a charming picture. Washington, Georgetown, and the intermediate Potomac, all before you in the foreground—while the white tents of troops quartered in the suburbs over the river, at almost every point, with mountain high, and valley deep, in the background."

In connection with the above, the following has an especial interest.

When Mrs. Lee was obliged to leave Arlington House on its being occupied by General Sandford and the New York troops, it is related in the " Evening Post"—and with no delicacy of language—that " she undertook to carry with her all the Washington relics which had been so jealously preserved by her patriotic father, Mr. George Washington Parke Custis. Repeatedly she wrote to General McDowell, with whom she had been acquainted as her husband's associate on the staff of General Wool during the Mexican War, that she had left nothing at Arlington in any way connected with the public or domestic life of the father of his country.

"For a long time after the flight of the Lees, General McDowell, though quartered on the grounds, refused to enter Arlington House. A scrupulous respecter of private rights, he would not occupy, nor allow to be occupied by his officers or men, any portion of the mansion, which, in his opinion, belonged to General Lee quite as much as though he still made his home within its massive walls. When the Confiscation Act was passed by Congress, and a telegraphic operator had taken possession of one of the best rooms, he was still reluctant to enter the old building on account of the Washington memories clustering around it, and it was at last by force of circumstances rather than by his own free will, that he made it his headquarters.

"For a long time access to the upper rooms was forbidden, and even the cellar was not opened to the curious visitor. The historical paintings of Mr. Custis, which, from their want of merit, clearly demonstrate that however true a patriot that worthy descendant of the Washington family may have been, he was by no means an artist, and which Mrs. Lee had shown good taste in leaving behind, were most carefully guarded. Never did tenant use a house more gingerly. Relics of inestimable value might have slumbered in its upper chambers, or had quiet preservation in its basement-rooms forever and aye, for none but General McDowell entered the venerable premises.

"But there lately came to Washington a curiosity-hunter— an antiquarian, vigorous and insatiable—an enthusiast in Washington relics—Caleb Lyon by name—he of Lyonsdale, who, disdaining the letters of Mrs. Lee, sought permission to unveil the deepest recesses of the establishment. He searched the house from foundation to roof-tree. Fortunate search! for in an inner cellar he found a priceless prize, in a variety of household articles identified as belonging to Washington; but which one less familiar with the history of Mount Vernon and Arlington would have passed by as of no especial interest or value.

"Among these articles are a number of pieces of the Martha Washington China. The centre of each piece has the monogram 'M. W.,' from which four golden rays diverge, each point reaching to a blue oval, in which, in distinct rings, con-

nected by golden links, are written the names of the original States and Kentucky; while around the rim, the Egyptian symbol of eternal union—a green serpent with its tail in its mouth—and a crimson ribbon bearing the legend, " *Decus et tutamen abillo*," exquisitely painted, completes the decoration, which for richness and appropriateness has never been excelled at Sevres.

"This set of porcelain was presented by General Lafayette and his brother officers, including Rochambeau and Count De Grasse, as a fitting testimonial to the lady whose house had been their home while fighting the battles of the Revolution, and also with the sanction and subscription of the Mayor of the municipality of Paris. The set originally contained four hundred pieces. A plate, a saucer, or a cup, were occasionally presented by Mrs. Washington or Mr. Custis as the choicest *souvenir* they could give of the household relics of Mount Vernon. Specimens are in possession of the widow of Major-general Brown, the family of the late Alderman Peters, Major Mopham, Caleb Lyon, and others ; and it was from a familiarity with the one given to the latter gentleman some years ago by Mr. Custis, that he was able to promptly identify the remainder of the set remaining at Arlington.

"Two of the rich porcelain vases presented to Washington by Mr. Vaugh, and sketched by Lossing in his 'Mount Vernon and its Associations'—those ornamented by lions and tigers—were also brought to light by Mr. Lyon. The one decorated with leopards has not been discovered, and is probably lost. The ground-work of these vases is of the finest and rarest blue, but they are somewhat broken.

"It will be remembered that the officers of the Revolutionary army belonging to the Society of the Cincinnati, sent to China an order for a thousand pieces, including breakfast, dinner, and tea sets, of the finest India ware, for presentation to Washington. The ornamentation is blue and gilt, with the coat of arms of the society, held by Fame, with a blue ribbon from which is suspended the eagle of the order, with a green wreath about its neck, and on its breast a shield representing the inauguration of the order. Altogether, fifty pieces of this set yet remain at Arlington, more or less perfect. The tea-table used by Washington, and one bookcase, also remain. General

McDowell rendered Mr. Lyon every facility for brushing up these interesting relics, and expects an order from the War Department to place them in the Patent Office or Smithsonian institute. They would be perfectly safe at Arlington, while the General remains here, but to guard against the carelessness of those who may come after him, when the long-promised advance begins, and to gratify the public, it is doubtless wise to so dispose of the precious articles."

Immediately upon Lee's resignation in the regular army, he was appointed, by Governor Letcher, Major-general in command of all the military forces in Virginia. This appointment was confirmed, and made known to him, on the 23d day of April, by the Convention then assembled, through the President, John Lanney, Esq. The following particulers of his reception are given in the Richmond papers of the day :

"The Convention having assembled, the Honorable A. H. Stephens, Vice-president of the Confederate States, entered the Hall, accompanied by Governor Letcher, and was introduced to the President by Mr. Johnston, of Lee county, a member of the committee appointed to invite and conduct that gentleman to the Hall.

"Mr. Johnston next introduced Judge Allen, a member of the Advisory Council of the Governor; and following him were Colonel Smith and Captain M. F. Maury, both introduced as the other members of the Advisory Council.

"Every delegate was on his feet during this ceremony. The Governor and Mr. Stephens were assigned seats on the right of the President, and the three members of the Advisory Council on the left.

"At this time Major-general Lee entered, leaning on the arm of Mr. Johnson, of Richmond, the Chairman of the Committee appointed to conduct the distinguished military chief to the hall. As they reached the centre of the main aisle, Mr. Johnson said, 'Mr. President, I have the honor to present to you, and to the convention, Major-general Lee.'

"The President then said, 'Major-general Lee, in the name of the people of our native State, here represented, I bid you a cordial and heartfelt welcome to this hall, in which we may yet almost hear the echo of the voices of the statesmen, the

soldiers and sages of by-gone days, who have borne your name, and whose blood now flows in your veins.

"We met in the month of February last, charged with the solemn duty of protecting the rights, the honor, and the interests of the people of this Commonwealth. We differed for a time as to the best means of accomplishing that object; but there never was, at any moment, a shade of difference among us as to the great object itself; and now Virginia having taken her position, as far as the power of this Convention extends, we stand animated by one impulse, governed by one desire and one determination, and that is, that she shall be defended; and that no spot of her soil shall be polluted by the foot of an invader.

"When the necessity became apparent of having a leader for our forces, all hearts and all eyes, by the impulse of an instinct which is a surer guide than reason itself, turned to the old county of Westmoreland. We knew how prolific she had been in other days of heroes and statesmen. We knew she had given birth to the Father of his Country, to Richard Henry Lee, to Monroe, and last, though not least, to your own gallant father, and we knew well by your deeds that her productive power was not yet exhausted.

"Sir, we watched with the most profound and intense interest the triumphal march of the army led by General Scott, to which you were attached, from Vera Cruz to the capital of Mexico. We read of the sanguinary conflicts and the blood-stained fields, in all of which victory perched upon our own banners. We knew of the unfading lustre that was shed upon the American arms by that campaign, and we know, also, what your modesty has always disclaimed, that no small share of the glory of those achievements was due to your valor and your military genius.

"Sir, one of the proudest recollections of my life will be the honor that I yesterday had of submitting to this body confirmation of the nomination made by the governor of this State, of you as Commander-in-chief of the military and naval forces of this commonwealth. I rose to put the question, and when I asked if this body would advise and consent to that appointment, there rushed from the hearts to the tongues of all the members, an affirmative response, told with an emphasis that

could leave no doubt, or the feeling whence it emanated. I
put the negative of the question, for form's sake, but there was
an unbroken silence.

"Sir, we have by this unanimous vote, expressed our convictions that you are at this day among the living citizens of
Virginia, 'first in war.' We pray to God most fervently,
that you may so conduct the operations committed to your
charge that it will soon be said of you, that you are 'first in
peace,' and when that time comes, you will have earned the
still prouder distinction of being "first in the hearts of your
countrymen.' I will close with one more remark.

"When the Father of his Country made his last will and
testament, he gave his swords to his favorite nephews with an
injunction that they should never be drawn from their scab-
bards except in self-defence, or in defence of the rights and
liberties of their country, and, that if drawn for the latter purpose, they should fall with them in their hands, rather than
relinquish them.

"Yesterday your mother, Virginia, placed her sword in your
hand, upon the implied condition that we know you will keep
it to the letter and in spirit, that you will draw it only in defence, and that you will fall with it in your hand rather than
the object for which it was placed there shall fail."

Major-general Lee.—"Mr. President and gentlemen of the
Convention : Profoundly impressed with the solemnity of the
occasion, for which I must say I was not prepared, I accept
the position assigned me by your partiality. I would have
much preferred, had your choice fallen upon an abler man.
Trusting in Almighty God, an approving conscience, and the
aid of my fellow-citizens, I devote myself to the service of my
native State, in whose behalf alone, will I ever again draw my
sword."

The chair was then vacated, and some time was spent in the
introduction of delegates to Major-general Lee, and the tender
to him of congratulations by the members.

The appointment of General Lee seemed to give universal
satisfaction in Virginia. One of the leading papers said, in
reference to some disquietude about an attack on Richmond :
"Our people must rest quiet upon the fact that the military
preparations, for our defence, are under the direction of shrewd,

skilful, indefatigable, experienced, and patriotic officers. Our
commanding general, Robert E. Lee, has long been the pride
of the service, and he is supported by subordinates of acknowledged capacity and large experience."

One of Lee's first acts was to fortify Arlington Heights.
Heavy batteries were erected, and some five thousand Virginia
troops were concentrated there.* But the principal efforts of
General Lee were devoted to the organizing and equipping of
the military forces arriving from the South. Every train
brought in troops, and it required all the skill and experience
of a practical mind to establish discipline and order. The
military council at the State-house, Richmond, consisting of
Governor Letcher, Lieutenant-governor Montague, Lieutenant
M. F. Maury, of the Navy, General Lee, and others, was incessantly occupied in effecting for speedy service, the raw material
promptly brought forward. Virginia speedily became a great
camp. The valleys and the hills swarmed with soldiers eager
for the fray. Forty-eight thousand men, May 3d, were under
arms, and distributed as follows: † at Richmond 10,000, at
Harper's Ferry 10,000, Alexandria 3,000, Staunton 2,000, Petersburgh 5,000, Lynchburg 5,000, Fredericksburg 3,000, Norfolk 10,000 ; and it was stated that " the thorough and complete organization of the Quartermaster and Commissary Departments, which General Lee had perfected, would enable the
immediate concentration of troops upon the borders of the
State, wherever the movements of the enemy might demand
the presence of the troops. At any moment General Lee
could leave Richmond at the head of a large force; and it is,
indeed, surprising what he accomplished in so short a space of
time. " With the army to organize and drill, the materials of
war to create out of almost nothing, the troops to arm, clothe
and feed, after they had been collected, and all the duties of a
minister of war to discharge, in addition to those more immediate of general-in-chief,"‡ it would seem to be almost impossible for one man to effect what he did. Yet it was done, and
so efficiently, that the Northern papers, in speaking of military
movements, said, " Should the United States troops succeed in
entering the State of Virginia, they will be compelled to en-

---

* *Mob. Adv.*, Ap. 25-28, 1861.   † *Mob. Adv.* May 18, 1861.   ‡ Sthrn. Biog.

counter, at various points on the route, large bodies of troops, strongly posted in positions capable of being maintained for many days against an invading army. By the way of Alexandria, a general of superior ability will be required, as he will probably be compelled to encounter, at some point on the route to Richmond, General Lee, himself, or Magruder."

On the 6th of May, Virginia was admitted to the Southern Confederacy, and consequently, her forces formed part of the entire Southern army, under control of the Secretary of War, then at Montgomery, Alabama. But on the 10th of May General Lee was temporarily retained in the post he was so well occupying, until the entire military organization of the South was complete. On the 29th of May President Davis arrived at Richmond ; but it was not until the 20th of July that the Southern Congress assembled there, in the hall of the House of Delegates. It was then that Lee's rank was fixed as Brigadier-general, following, according to previous seniority in the United States' Army, Generals Cooper and A. S. Johnson. Beauregard, after the battle of Bull Run, was made a full general ; but there seems to have been something like doubt, and perhaps jealousy, amongst the authorities in council at Richmond, as to Lee. However, he waited his time, and while others were sent forward, and were actively engaged at the advanced posts, he cheerfully gave his valuable services to the cause at Richmond, and employed his engineering skill to great advantage in its defence.

After the retreat of General Garnett from Rich Mountain, and the death of that officer, General Lee was appointed to succeed him, and, with as little delay as possible, repaired to the scene of operations.* He took with him reinforcements, making his whole force, in conjunction with the remnant of General Garnett's army, about sixteen thousand men. On the 10th of August he reached the neighborhood of Cheat Mountain, and found it strongly fortified. The position was known to be an exceedingly strong one, and not easily turned. Nevertheless, General Lee was confident that he would be able, by strategic movements, to dislodge the enemy from his strong-

---

* *Pollard*, First Year of the War, p. 168.

hold, capture his forces, and then march his victorious army into the heart of Northwestern Virginia. Rosecrans was then the ranking officer of the Union troops in that department, but General Reynolds was in command of the forces at Cheat Mountain, and in its vicinity, his force being estimated at from ten to twelve thousand men.

General Lee felt his way cautiously along the road leading from Huntersville to Huntonsville, and, reaching Valley Mountain, he halted for some time, arranging his plans for attacking the enemy, who were about eight miles below him, at Crouch's, in Tygart Valley river, five or six thousand strong. His plans were arranged so as to divide his forces for the purpose of surrounding the enemy. After great labor and endurance of severe hardship on the mountain spurs, where the weather was very cold, he succeeded in getting below the enemy, on Tygart Valley river, placing other portions of his forces on the spurs of the mountains immediately east and west of the enemy, and marched another portion of his troops down the Valley river, close to the enemy. The forces were thus arranged in position for making attack upon the enemy at Crouch's, and remained there for some hours. It was, doubtless, in the plan of General Lee, for his forces to remain in position until the consummation of another part of his plan, viz., that some fifteen hundred of General H. R. Jackson's forces, stationed at Greenbrier river, should march around another position of the enemy, at the celebrated Cheat Mountain Pass, where he was five or six thousand strong. Jackson's forces did march around this position, under command of Colonel Rust, of Arkansas, through extraordinary difficulties and perils, and under circumstances of terrible exhaustion. The troops had to ascend the almost perpendicular mountain side, but finally succeeded in obtaining a position in front of, and to the west of the enemy. The attack of this force upon the enemy at Cheat Mountain, was understood to be, in the plan of General Lee, a signal for the attack by his forces upon the enemy at Crouch's. Colonel Rust, however, discovered the enemy on the mountain to be safely protected by block-houses, and other defences, and concluding that an attack could not be made with any hope of success, ordered a retreat. The signal was not given according to the plan of General Lee, and no at

tack was made by his forces, which retreated, without firing a
gun, back to Valley Mountain.

This plan of General Lee's, a finished drawing of which
was sent to the War Department, was said to have been one
of the best laid that ever illustrated the rules of strategy,
or ever went awry on account of practical failure in its execution.

Having failed in his plans for dislodging the enemy from
Cheat Mountain, and thus relieving Northwestern Virginia,
General Lee determined to proceed to the Kanawha region,
with a view of relieving Generals Floyd and Wise, and possibly
driving the enemy to the extreme western borders of Virginia.
Accordingly, in the latter part of September he ordered the
principal portions of his command to take up a line of march
in that direction.

It has already been stated, that General Floyd had fallen
back with his forces, to Meadow Bluff, while General Wise
stopped east of the summit of Big Sewell. In this position
General Lee found them on his arrival. He took up his headquarters with General Floyd, and, after examining his position,
proceeded to Sewell, where General Wise still remained in
front of the enemy. He decided to fortify Wise's position.
General Floyd's command, except a garrison at Meadow Bluff,
returned to Big Sewell. He had been largely reinforced since
he had left the Gauley river. The position of Big Sewell was
made exceedingly strong by a breastwork, extending four
miles.

The whole Confederate force here, nnder command of General Lee, was nearly twenty thousand; and for twelve or fifteen
days it remained in position facing the enemy, each party awaiting an attack from the other. At the end of that time, one
morning, it was discovered by General Lee, that Rosecrans had
disappeared in the night, and reached his old position on the
Gauley, thirty-two miles distant. Lee was unable to follow,
on account of the leanness of his artillery-horses, and the
swollen streams and mud impeding his way, with such poor
cavalry.*

On the 3d of October, General Reynolds with a force of

---

* *Pollard,* First Year of the War, p. 172.

about five thousand strong, taking the opportunity of Lee's absence in the Kanawha, suddenly came down upon the Confederate troops at Cheat Mountain, but was repulsed.

With reference to the inability of General Lee to pursue Rosecrans the following letter from Richmond, under date of October 22d, gives some explanation. It says: " A gentleman of this city, occupying a high position in the Government, has just reached Richmond from General Lee's headquarters. The enemy, under Rosecrans, was in full retreat toward the Ohio; but pursuit was impossible. The roads were in the most awful condition. Dead horses and mules that had perished in their tracks, broken wagons, and abandoned stores, lined the road to Lewisburg. There was no such thing as getting a team or wagon through uninjured. The road beyond Big Sewell was, if any thing, worse than on this side of it."

Meanwhile, as the approaching rigors of winter in the mountains gave warning of the speedy termination of further active operations in that region, General Lee was recalled, and soon afterwards appointed to take charge of the coast defences of South Carolina and Georgia.

The services of General Lee, in this department, were admitted to have been very valuable, though not of that active nature which afterwards made his name so famous and so revered. His duties consisted principally in superintending the fortifications along the coast, and exercising his engineering skill in making them more secure. On the 30th of December, in company with his staff, he visited the military district of Brigadier-general Evans, and made important observations in that quarter. Several additional troops were forwarded from Richmond to them, and every effort made to resist the attempts of the enemy to invade the land. In the latter part of February, 1862, it was much desired by many members in the Southern Congress, that General Lee should be appointed Secretary of War, but this was overruled, though, afterwards, he was virtually acting as such. Meanwhile, he had got the army in South Carolina into a very high state of efficiency. His district was placed in an admirable state of defence, and, in commenting upon him, the Southern papers remarked, that " the time would yet come when his superior abilities would be vindicated, both to his own renown, and the glory of his

country." At Charleston, where he was in command, on the
28th of February, every confidence was placed in his power
to defend the city against any force of the enemy, if the people
themselves only helped him aright. But in a few days afterwards, he was summoned by President Davis to Richmond,
and after various delays and difficulties between parties acting
from jealous motives, he was appointed to the newly formed
office of commanding general of the forces.

It was at this time the valuable services of General Lee
began to be rightly understood. Richmond and Virginia
were both in a state of great agitation in the public mind,
owing to the advance of the Northern army towards the capital. While the foe was at a distance, the people flattered
themselves that success would yet attend the movements of
their leaders; but, the moment that foe—a power, be it remembered, that, only fourteen months previous, had been
acknowledged as the sovereign authority in the land—approached the portals of their doors, tremor seized them. Disasters, also, in the West, had tended to depress their minds,
and doubts began to arise as to the wisdom and policy of the
course then pursued. McClellan, with a large army, had
already commenced a march along the Peninsula from Yorktown, which, with Williamsburg, the Southern forces had
been compelled to abandon, while McDowell, in the southern
part of the State, was prepared to join him. Would Richmond be the next city to be yielded? Would the Confederate
Executive desert them by retreating further inland, and leave
them to their fate? Was President Davis, after all, the man
to meet such an emergency as this? Were the generals, then
at the head of a fine and powerful army assembling around
Richmond, and, a part of it, holding in check the Union forces
in the North, sufficiently capable of standing against the
military chiefs—McClellan, in particular—opposed to them?
These were serious questions, and questions, too, that were
openly discussed, even in their Senate. True, Richmond had
been placed in a good position of defence; and J. E. Johnston,
who commanded the army, was a man of acknowledged ability
and skill. Still there was perplexity and doubt, as there ever
will be where men have taken a bold step in opposition to a
long-established constituted authority, and, at length, find

that authority at their doors, menacingly calling them to ac
count for what they have done.

What the state of the capital was at this important moment,
when, had not circumstances with which we have nothing
now to do prevented him, McClellan could soon have had
Richmond in his power, may be gathered from the following
brief statement of facts: On the 14th of May, the General
Assembly of Virginia, passed a resolution expressing a *desire*
that the capital *should* be defended to the last extremity, " *if*
such defence be in accordance with the views of the President."
That such was doubtful, was to be inferred from seeing many
large boxes on the side-walks, in front of the various official
departments, labelled "Lynchburg," as if ready for departure
thither. Iron safes, and valuable property were consequently
moved away by timid persons; and, not a few began to con-
vert every thing into cash at ruinous rates of discount, sometimes paying four hundred dollars in paper for one hundred
dollars in cash, while others changed goods into tobacco, which
they stowed away in cellars. Fortunately, some relief to the
agitated mind of the people was given, when, in response to
the above resolution, and, on a personal interview with the
President, Governor Letcher was assured that "it would be
the effort of Mr. Davis' life to defend the soil of Virginia, and
to cover her capital;" and, moreover, "he had never entertained the thought of withdrawing the army. If, in the course
of events, the capital should fall,—the necessity of which he
did not see or anticipate,—that would be no reason for withdrawing the army from Virginia. The war could still be successfully maintained on Virginia soil for twenty years."

Thus reassured, a popular outburst of feeling followed.
The people swore to defend their capital with the last drop of
their blood. The Governor, in warm language, echoed this
sentiment, and called upon all persons to unite in rallying to
the rescue. The Mayor, Joseph Mayo—a descendant of the
founder of the city—said it should never be surrendered by
him, for he would sooner die; and if any persons wished Richmond to be abandoned, they must elect another mayor in his
place. The press advocated, rather the total destruction of the
city than its surrender.* "To lose it was to lose Virginia;

* *Cook's* Siege of Richmond, p. 106.

and to lose Virginia was to lose the key of the Southern Con federacy. Better fall in her streets ; for such would be bliss, in comparison with that of basely yielding. The loss of Richmond would sound in Europe like the loss of Paris or London, and the moral effect would scarcely be less."

Thus, then, the determination to fight to the last, was made manifest, and the fears of the people were somewhat allayed. But still there was cause for great anxiety. The Union forces by this time (the end of May) had vigorously pushed forward advances to the neighborhood of the capital, and the right of their line was only four miles distant from it—their left about seven miles. This made it imperative on the part of the Government, to adopt every measure for preventing a nearer approach, and to secure the safety of Richmond ; and now, in this trying time, and in the midst of all this agitation and excitement, the calm mind, smiling, though ever thoughtful countenance, and kindly tones of General Lee, came forward to give strength and courage to the feeble and the drooping. His great engineering skill had already done much towards surrounding the capital with defences. The earthworks designed by him around it were of considerable magnitude, and were constructed in different shape, to suit the conformation of the ground. They swept all the roads, crowned every hillock, and mounds of red earth could be seen, in striking contrast with the rich, green aspect of the landscape. Redoubts, rifle-pits, casemate-batteries, horn works, and enfilading batteries, were visible in great number, in and out of the woods, in all directions. Some were mounted with heavy siege pieces, of various calibre, but the majority were intended for field-guns. Heavy ordnance was scarce, and home-made cannon often proved worthless and brittle, in many instances killing those who put them to the proof. Strong works had also been hastily erected and mounted at Drury's Bluff ; and the immense raft on the river was considered impregnable. Several large rifle pieces were manned by the crew of the late Merrimac, while the banks and woods swarmed with sharpshooters, and a number of rifled field-batteries were ready, with supports, to the rear.

Meanwhile General Lee himself was not unmindful of the serious aspect of affairs. Should Richmond be laid siege to, the wives and families of those engaged in conflict would be

better away, and General Lee seems to have previously sent his wife to the family seat called the White House. This celebrated mansion was, to a certain degree, looked upon as sacred by both the North and the South, on account of its connection with Washington, through his wife, who, while living there, as the widow of Mr. Custis, had been visited by the "Father of his Country" before marrying her. It came into the possession of General Lee when he married, and had we space, several interesting incidents belonging to the place could here be given. One only, as immediately referring to the subject of our memoir, may, however, be recorded.

The White House, known as such at this time, was not the original, but one built upon the site of that where Mrs. Custis had lived. It was in the form of a centre building and wings, its entire front being about forty feet, and its depth twenty, plainly built, two stories high, with a peaked roof, and porches. Inside there were main halls, and a staircase occupying the centre, with a room on each floor in each wing.* Two attics were under the roof, and the whole structure was of frame. Such a building could have been erected in the North for about fifteen hundred dollars.† The grounds around the house were simply a grass field, in which grew several trees. The house was about fifty yards back of the Pamunkey River, and some twenty-five miles northeast of Richmond. The negro huts and garden were on the bank of the stream below. When General Stoneman's troops (the advance of McClellan's army *en route* to Richmond, from Williamsburg) occupied White House on the evening of May 10th, the guard placed to protect the mansion found a paper pinned to the wall of the main corridor, on which was written, in a lady's hand, the following words:

"Northern soldiers who profess to reverence Washington, forbear to desecrate the home of his first married life, the property of his wife, now owned by her descendants.
              "A GRAND-DAUGHTER OF MRS. WASHINGTON."

This was signed by Mrs. Robert E. Lee, and below it, upon the wall, one of the guards wrote an answer:—

---

* *Cook*, p. 169.   † See McClellan's official correspondence.

"A northern officer has protected your property in sight of the enemy, and at the request of your overseer."

About a fortnight afterwards, the advance forces having moved nearer Richmond, found, in a house, distant seven miles from the capital, the family of General Lee, consisting of his wife, her daughter-in-law, the wife of Colonel Lee, of the Kent Cavalry, and two nieces. Probably they had moved there from the White House, when finding it was to be occupied by the Northern forces. But they were now again surrounded, and placed under guard of Union soldiers. A party had been sent to search the house, with a view of securing some valuable papers, supposed to be secreted there. Finding nothing, they were about to depart, when Mrs. Lee handed a note to the officer in charge. This note was directed to the commanding officer of the division, with the request that it should be handed to him in person. It was delivered as required, and was found to be as follows:

"To THE GENERAL IN COMMAND,—Sir, I have patiently and humbly submitted to the search of my house, by men under your command, who are satisfied that there is nothing here that they want. All the plate and other valuables have long since been removed to Richmond, and are now beyond the reach of any northern marauders who may wish for their possession.

"WIFE OF ROBERT LEE, GENERAL C. S. A."

The Union forces had now been in position around Richmond about a month, and after various skirmishes Hanover Court-house had been captured by them on the 28th of May. This, with other successes to the North, made the Confederates again very dissatisfied, and the Richmond papers were once more clamorous. The Enquirer said:

"We are now looking to General Johnston with great interest, and not without some solicitude. . . . . The time has come when retreat is no longer strategy, but disaster. It must, therefore, give place to battle. The temper of the army is opposed to retreat. The men are weary of toilsome marches, and almost clamor to be led against the enemy. . . . The campaign has ripened for the battle, and a battle is at hand."

It was even so as desired. Almost before the printer's ink was dry, the sound of a general engagement was heard. On

the 31st of May, General Johnston attacked the Union forces under General Casey, and drove them back; but his success was checked afterwards by fresh troops from McClellan, coming to the rescue. Johnston himself received a severe wound in the groin, and was conveyed from the field, at that time with little hopes of recovery. Longstreet then for the moment took command; but, on renewing the battle next day, the North maintained their ground, and made any advantage to the South exceedingly doubtful.

During the engagement, which has been termed the Battle of Seven Pines, there was a violent rain and thunder storm, and the Chickahominy river was greatly flooded, some of the bridges having been washed away. The city of Richmond, during the night, was also placed in total darkness, owing to the gas-works becoming flooded. All this, however, did not prevent renewed eagerness for a continuance of the fight, and now, at last, the President yielded to the common desire, by appointing General Lee, on the 3d of June, to the command-in-chief of the army. On assuming his position, he issued an address to the army, which was read at the head of the regiments. Its sentiments created the liveliest enthusiasm. The address informed them, in a very few words, that the army had made its last retreat, and that henceforth every man's watchword must be "Victory or Death!" The response was cheers from all the regiments.

CHAPTER IV.

Lee's Plan of Operations.—General Stuart's Cavalry Raid around McC.ellan's army.—General Jackson's arrival from the Shenandoah Valley.—Battle of Mechanicsville.—Lee's Headquarters at Hogan's House.—Personal Description of Lee and his Generals.—Battle of Gaines' Mills.—General Cobb's gallant Charge.—Meagher and the Irish Brigade.—Their Heroic Defence.—Battles of the Chickahominy, White Oak Swamp, and Malvern Hill.—Tribute to McClellan.—Richmond Relieved.—Departure of the Federal Army.—Pope's Operations.—Battle of Cedar Mountain.— Second Battle of Bull Run.—Lee's Report.—Invasion of Maryland.—Capture of Harper's Ferry.—Battles of South Mountain and Antietam.—Retreat of the Confederates. —Stuart's Raid into Maryland.—Movements of the Federals.—McClellan Relieved by Burnside.—Rapid March of the Confederates to the Rappahannock.—Battle o' Fredericksburg.—Retreat of Burnside.

It was now that an entirely new policy in the Confederate military affairs was adopted. General Lee had, for some time past, been virtually Secretary of War, though General Randolph bore that title, and he now was able to carry out the whole of his plans in reference to army movements. At a glance, he perceived that the siege of Richmond could not be raised without beating the enemy out of their formidable works in which they had intrenched themselves, and he immediately set about devising means to accomplish it. To attack their intrenchments merely in front, he saw was not only a hopeless undertaking, but was the thing above all others that they would naturally desire. He saw that a strong force must be brought from without, to operate upon the flank and rear of the enemy, and to turn his formidable works, in co-operation with an attack in front from the direction of the city. He therefore determined to bring Jackson down upon the left flank of the Union forces. To do this, great caution was necessary so as not to excite the enemy's suspicion. To that end, powerful reinforcements were sent to him with a great appearance of mystery, and it began to be whispered (that such might reach McClellan's ears), that he was to invade Maryland by way of Harper's Ferry, and strike a blow directly at Washington.

Meanwhile, General Lee strengthened anew the fortifications around Richmond, in order that he might be able to spare as many men as possible from his right and centre, to operate

upon his left. He was now seen on horseback more frequently, and scarcely a day passed without his being met ambling along the roads, and in all kinds of out-of-the-way places. Though naturally quiet, thoughtful, and polite, the responsibility resting on him rendered his deportment even more so than usual, and to strangers, his manner was so calm and placid, his dress so humble, and his gait so slow and unofficial, that he could not have been recognized as one whose genius and resources commanded the unbounded confidence and hopes of the entire Confederacy. Brigadiers, with couriers and orderlies at their heels, dashing to and fro, would have presented a much more impressive idea of importance and dignity, than the meek, gray-headed gentleman passing along without the distinctive color or uniform, or blazing stars on his shoulder-straps.

With reference to General Lee's important services at this period, when it is very evident that immediately following upon the battle of Seven Pines, Richmond could have been captured, even if, as the people said, all its inhabitants shed their blood in its defence, a writer observes:

"The shell which wounded General Johnston was the saddest shot for Federal success that had been fired during the war. It changed the entire Southern tactics. It removed the first commander of the Confederate army, and 'replaced him by a most eminent leader, General Robert E. Lee,' who brought to the field 'skilful generalship, excellent plans, and good discipline.' Before the battle of Fair Oaks, the Southern troops were sickly, half fed and clothed, and had not a full heart for the work. On the 1st of June, General Lee commenced his efforts to reorganize the army. He removed their camps from the swamps, and placed them in healthy situations. He procured supplies of wholesome provisions, particularly fresh beef and bread. He redressed many wrongs the men had suffered, attentively listening to their just complaints, and he soon found his efforts crowned with success. Mutiny and dissatisfaction almost universally disappeared. There were no more cries for food, no more outcries against oppression. The troops improved in appearance, cadaverous looks became rare among prisoners. The discipline became better: they went to battle with shouts, and without being urged, and, when in it, fought like tigers. A more marked change for the

better never was made in any body of men than that wrought in his army by General Lee."

The preparations in progress made it evident to all, that operations would soon recommence on a scale surpassing any thing hitherto attempted. Frequent reconnoissances were made towards the interior, to ascertain the enemy's strength and position on their left wing. McClellan never opposed these movements, being probably ignorant of them, as they were made principally at night-time, or in unpropitious weather. The Confederate Generals would sally forth on a march of ten miles, and return, almost without the knowledge of the main body of the army.

But the most important and extraordinary reconnoissance among these, was that dashing raid of J. E. B. Stuart, through and around McClellan's army, as far as the Pamunkey river, and back. Accompanied by Colonel Fitz Hugh Lee, the son of General Lee, and another Colonel Lee, his nephew. This bold cavalry officer succeeded in accomplishing his purpose, and returned with valuable information.

By these movements Lee had satisfied himself of McClellan's true position; and, in a general order, he felt bound to express " his admiration of the courage and skill so conspicuously exhibited throughout by Brigadier-general Stuart and the officers and men under his command." In addition to the officers, General Lee deemed it but just, to specially name some of the privates who had been mentioned by their several commanders as particularly deserving commendation.

At length, on the 25th of June, Jackson, in pursuance of his orders, reached Ashland, and Lee prepared for the grand attack he had contemplated upon the enemy.

On Thursday, June 26th, Jackson began his march from Ashland, at 3 A. M., and passed down the country on the left bank of the Chickahominy. He then quickly came upon the advanced guard of the Union forces, driving them in, and continuing his march towards Mechanicsville. His force was in three columns, himself on the left, General Branch in the centre, and General A. P. Hill on the right, next the river. About 5 P. M., Hill assaulted Mechanicsville, where the enemy was strongly posted, and in two and a half hours carried their batteries. But the victory was not complete, for, at Ellison's

Mills, about a mile from Mechanicsville, and on the right of his line, the Union forces were in great strength, defended by sixteen pieces of cannon. Feeling the importance of settling this affair as soon as possible, General Lee now gave orders to storm this battery. Several attempts were made to carry it; but these proving, for the time, abortive, the troops desisted at ten o'clock, and during the night the enemy, having burned his platforms, withdrew a portion of his force.

That night, however, was not to give rest to either party of the combatants. Ambulances, carriages, and litters were busy in collecting and conveying the wounded to Richmond; prisoners were collected, spoil secured, and various divisions put in proper order and position for the next day's operations. The tramp of men was incessant; artillery and ammunition-wagons toiled along; stragglers were brought in; captured cannon and stores sent to the rear; and from Brook Church turnpike to Mechanicsville, a distance of several miles, lights were flitting in fields and woods, searching for the wounded, or burying the dead. Amidst all this scene of excitement General Lee had to be calm, and fully prepared in his mind to direct every movement. Positions had to be taken, and orders given to the several corps and division commanders as they came in. At midnight Featherstone and Pryor were sent up to Beaver Dam Creek, and Gregg towards Ellison's Mills. Featherstone reached his post about 4 A. M., and found the enemy on the alert. The twilight had just begun to appear, and in that dim shadowing of the coming day, his men boldly advanced to the conflict. Pryor's division ably seconded him; and both rushed forward, with the wild yells peculiar to Louisiana soldiers. Wilcox now came on the scene, with reinforcements of Alabamians, and then the sight was awfully grand. Men were standing on the parapets of batteries, fighting in every conceivable attitude, and as the sun brilliantly rose over the tree-tops, illumining the scene, the semicircular line of fight, with its streams of fire, bursting of caissons, shouts, yells, and charging on the right and left—the centre occupied by a strong redoubt, crowds of combatants rushing in and out, with a sea of heads swaying to and fro round the banners floating on the wall—all was soul-stirring, sublime, and horrible! Finally, the Southern troops gained the point, and Wilcox

again advanced, while Featherstone and Pryor rested awhile
on the spot.

Meantime General Gregg had been as successful at Ellison's
Mills, which was taken at the point of the bayonet, and thus
both of the enemy's advance posts—strong impediments in the
way of the Confederate movements—were removed.

It was now past 8 A. M., and Lee felt the vast importance of
not losing an hour of time. He had received information, to
be relied upon, that McDowell, who was to have supported
McClellan, was still inactive, but how long he might remain
so was very uncertain. McClellan himself, however, was not
to be despised. Lee knew him well : they had been companions in arms ; and the strategy of both was familiar to each
other. Moreover, his army was a splendid one, and a brave,
determined body of men, well posted behind various strong
intrenchments. Accordingly, a general advance must immediately take place ; and thus, by nine o'clock, the several divisions of the Confederate forces were approaching the enemy, towards Gaines' Mills, the commander-in-chief accompanying them ; and, on arriving, at once formed them in line
of battle.

General Lee's headquarters were now at Hogan's House, a
place about six miles and a half to the northeast of Richmond.
It was a square mansion of frame, two stories high ; and at
about two hundred yards from it, in front, on a lane leading
out to the road, was an enormous oak, of faultless beauty.
Almost a perfect sphere, it was covered with foliage without
break or imperfection. It was the cynosure of all eyes, and
many of the Union officers had expressed themselves not only
in terms of admiration, but with a desire that it could have
been conveyed to the North. This house, at first, was used
by the Federal generals as headquarters, but, on the retreat of
the Union Army, General Lee, accompanied by Longstreet,
fixed his post there. In an adjoining orchard, a fine field-work
had been abandoned by the northern soldiers, and several
other important structures nearer the river. The building was
badly shattered by shot and shell from the Confederates during
the previous fights, and was very shaky. In the upper rooms
were large stains of blood, near where a shell had entered ;
and the outhouses bore every appearance of having been used

for hospitals, while numerous mounds of earth spoke of sepulture.

As soon as the Confederate chief took possession, the whole yard and orchard was occupied by general officers, aids, couriers, and prisoners. Says an eye-witness, Lee sat in the south portico, absorbed in thought. Dressed in a dark blue uniform, buttoned to the throat, his fine, calm, open countenance and gray hair would have tempted an artist to sketch him in this thoughtful attitude. Longstreet sat in an old garden-chair, at the foot of the steps, under shady trees, busily engaged in disposing of a bunch of sandwiches. With his feet thrown against a tree, he presented a true type of the hardy campaigner; his once gray uniform had changed to brown, and many a button was missing; his riding-boots were dusty and worn; but his pistols and sabre had a bright polish, by his side, while his charger stood near, anxiously looking at him, as if expecting a morsel of bread and meat.

Maxcy Gregg was sitting on his horse in the shade, conversing with a few about the affair at Ellison's Mills. Wilcox, Pryor and Featherstone were also present, talking freely and gaily, as if about to start on some pleasant picnic. Some other generals likewise surrounded the commander-in-chief, and a few civilians, principally landowners in the neighborhood, who had come to see the havoc made during the past engagements.

Presently General Gregg was called, and leaning his head through a window, conversed with General Lee. The substance of the communication he received was brief, and immediately afterwards he rode away to take post in a quarter assigned him. Wilcox, Featherstone, and Pryor then received orders, and rode off at a gallop. The next moment a courier rode up, and delivered some papers to General Lee, he calmly perusing them. The General then mounted, and, with Longstreet and their staffs, proceeded to New Coal Harbor, three miles distant, where it was now understood Jackson's right wing had already arrived.

The position of the Union army was such as showed great forethought, talent, and coolness on the part of General McClellan. With one portion of his troops he had crossed to the south side of the Chickahominy, and there confronted Magru-

der, who was in command of the Confederate right, while, with the larger portion of his force, he had taken up a position more to the rear and nearer the railroad, where he was resolved to accept battle. The different divisions of his army took their positions with admirable precision, and awaited the onset with firmness.

On the side of the Confederates, their forces were thus arranged: D. P. Hill, Anderson, and Whiting formed the centre, moving towards Coal Harbor; while Jackson, Ambrose Hill, and Longstreet formed the left, and marched down along the bank of the river. Magruder, as we have said, commanding the right wing, was, on account of the swampy nature of the ground he occupied, ordered to hold himself merely on the defensive. General Wise had command of the defences at Fort Darling, on the James river.

The advance was begun on Gaines' Mill about one o'clock, P. M., by Longstreet moving forward, with skirmishers thrown out, and driving in the enemy's outposts as he proceeded. The divisions of Anderson, A. P. Hill, and Pickett co-operated with him, while Jackson had already commenced work on the extreme left. The attack now began in fearful earnest. "With thundering hurrahs the gallant masses rushed forward upon the musketry of the foe, as though it were a joy to them. Whole ranks went down under the terrible hail, but nothing could restrain their courage. The struggle was man to man, eye to eye, bayonet to bayonet." The Union brigade of Meagher, composed chiefly of Irishmen, offered heroic resistance. The Confederates began to give way, and at length all orders and encouragements were vain—they were falling back in the greatest disorder. At that critical moment, infuriate, foaming at the mouth, bareheaded, sabre in hand, appeared on the field General Cobb at the head of his legion, and with him the Nineteenth North Carolina and Fourteenth Virginia regiments. The attack was at once renewed, but in vain. The Irish held their position with a determination and ferocity that called forth the admiration of the very officers opposed to them, and, notwithstanding that they had to stand their ground without other support, from four until eight, P. M., they firmly resisted every attack. It was only when the news came that Jackson was upon them in the rear, that the gallant defenders of Gaines'

Mill—the Irish Brigade—retired before the enemy, and then marched on with streaming banners and rolling drums, carrying with them their baggage and wounded.

Gaines' Mill had been won, but at a fearful slaughter, and when night at last put an end to the horrible carnage, it was as if the Deity had mercifully spread a pall over man's ferocious doings in his madness, to hide them from his eye when more calm and sane. Quiet gradually returned, except where the noise of the preceding night was repeated in the task of attending to the wounded and the dying. To use the words of a Prussian field-officer of the Confederate army: "The scene of ruin was horrible. Whole ranks of the enemy lay prone where they had stood at the beginning of the battle. The number of wounded was fearful too, and the groans and imploring cries for help that rose on all sides had, in the obscurity of the night, a ghastly effect that froze the blood in one's veins." Upon many battlefields had this officer been, in Italy and Hungary, yet "never had his vision beheld such a spectacle of human destruction." He adds: "It was a most heartrending task to get the wounded into Richmond. Many expired just as succor arrived, and many more received no aid at all in the darkness of the night. Finally, by midnight, the first train of the most seriously wounded, about two hundred, in sixty wagons, was taken to the city."

We need not dwell upon the feelings and the anxieties that must have filled the breast of General Lee and his several commanding officers. There are moments when the nature of man rises above all art and education, and we very much err if such be not the case with the greater number of those who are placed in command, even perhaps more so than with those who have merely to obey. But no exterior emotion must display itself on the features of him who has to direct great and important movements. Better he appear cold, passive, and heartless, than alarmed, doubtful, or weak. Thought, sensation, inward agony, no matter how great, must all be restrained, that the one object alone shall be accomplished. Thus was it with General Lee. Still calm, still unruffled, in the midst of all the excitement, he has been described as just the man suited for the moment. There was, neither for him nor his officers, rest to be obtained until the work was done.

The gates of the city—the threshold of their homes—had been menaced by a determined foe, and that foe must be driven back, no matter what the cost to all who had volunteered to defend the capital. The blood that had been freely offered to save that city and its inhabitants, was now flowing in streams around the walls, while heaps of slain lay on the ground never to rise again. Yet, more blood must run; more human bodies must be destroyed, and more terrible scenes enacted ere it could be hoped the enemy had gone. So it was, and four long days more saw the terrible drama of blood repeated, until, finally, the invading force was driven far beyond the walls, and Richmond was free!

The incidents connected with these battles around Richmond would fill a large volume full of heroic deeds and interesting detail. But we can only touch upon the leading points. On Saturday, June 28th, the enemy was pressed heavily on the Chickahominy, and General Jackson had succeeded in cutting off McClellan's communication with the base of his supplies at the White House. At ten P. M., the last of the Federal army had left Woodbury bridge, on the Chickahominy, and were in full retreat towards Savage Station, where, until one o'clock that night, General McClellan had his headquarters. But at that hour he ordered his tents to be struck, and, with his staff and escort, proceeded towards White Oak Swamp. On Sunday, the 29th, about two P. M., the Confederate forces again came upon the Union troops near Peach Orchard and Savage stations. The battle lasted until eleven at night; and resulted in the Federals again retreating, but with great loss to both sides. The same day General Stuart captured the White House, and large supplies intended for McClellan's army.

On Monday morning, June 30th, Jackson crossed the Chickahominy in pursuit of the Federals, along the Williamsburg road, while Longstreet, A. P. Hill, and Magruder, followed them along the Charles City road. Jackson came upon the right of the enemy, after he had burned the bridge over the White Oak creek. A long artillery fight ensued, and the Federals again fell back. On their left, the battle raged with great fury, and for some time, towards evening, the Confederates were compelled to retire, but, by great exertions, they

were again brought forward, and thus succeeded in holding their position while McClellan continued the retreat of his army to the James river.

In this engagement of Monday, General Lee was on the immediate field of action, personally encouraging and pushing forward his men, whenever showing symptoms of discouragement. To his commanders of divisions, as was his wont, he left all movements, after having once given them his plans, but when his presence was needed, he was ever at hand.

It is also stated that General McClellan was personally on the battle-ground, but there is much dispute in the Northern accounts on the subject.

The following morning, Tuesday, July 1st, saw the pursuit renewed by the Confederate army, and about three P. M. the Federals were again encountered at Malvern Hill. A desperate battle ensued, the enemy's gunboats in the river aiding in the scene of carnage, by throwing in shell. Night came, and the battle slackened, finally ceasing at dark. The carnage had been frightful, and the Confederate loss very heavy, with no successful result, except the empty one of occupying a field which had been held by the enemy only until his retreat was safely accomplished. Still, the foe had been driven away, and General Lee, by a series of skilful combinations in war tactics, had forced McClellan from his strong intrenchments, round Richmond, to a place thirty miles below, thus relieving all fears for the safety of the Southern capital. The siege had been raised; an army of 150,000 men had been pushed from their strongholds and fortifications, and put to flight; and the great moral effect of this on the minds of the people could not be otherwise than immense. Still, such is the extraordinary perversity of poor human nature, that, because such a large amount of success had been achieved, there was grumbling that it had not been greater. Lee and his brave officers and men had done so well in repelling the enemy, that it was speedily a cause of repining that they had not done even more, by completely capturing the foe. Yet, a little thoughtful consideration would have shown otherwise. General Lee, it has been well said, was, like every general-in-chief, but a workman on a large scale, using many different instruments in his work; and it may happen, especially in new operations with a por-

tion of untried material, that all do not fit and accord exactly as planned. There was an equal amount of mental and physical opposing force on both sides, and it is therefore to the credit of Lee and his brave army—impelled by that strong feeling which prompts men to greatest deeds in defence of their homes—that they succeeded so well against such a brave and splendid force as that which McClellan had under his command. Nor let us forget that chief himself. Few even of his military opponents but award to him the highest praise for the skill, spirit, and masterly generalship he displayed in this retreat through the difficult and pestilential swamps of the Chickahominy; and impartial persons competent to judge—men of high military rank and experience here and abroad—speak of it in the highest terms. What may have been the secret causes that impeded General McClellan's plans in every thing he undertook,—as he and his friends assert,—it is not our province to inquire into. It is enough that we venture this humble tribute to the merits of a gallant chief, a brave man, and a patient, forbearing gentleman, and at the same time bear cheerful testimony to the high courage and daring of his noble army.

The effect in Richmond produced by the relief from this immediate presence of an enemy before its doors, may be surmised. Joy and congratulation were everywhere felt, though not much outwardly displayed. There was still too much cause for anxiety, to be overboastful. But there was a calm and sober thankfulness not to be doubted. In the churches, prayers were offered up in gratitude for deliverance from peril, and in humble supplications, that, if possible, further effusion of blood might be averted. Elsewhere it was evident, however, that more work had yet to be done. The War Office department was particularly busy, and General Lee was constantly seen actively employed on some new important duty. Where and when the next blow would be struck, was, however, a secret, except to himself and those necessarily in his councils.

About this time, or rather on the 21st of July, General Lee had occasion to communicate with General McClellan, then at Harrison's Landing, on the subject of citizens (non-combatants) of the State of Virginia being compelled by the United States to take the oath of allegiance, or be imprisoned, when falling

into the hands of the Union forces.   He complained, that some had been so imprisoned at Fortress Monroe, and, by order of the Confederate Government, he was directed to say, that if such was persisted in, retaliatory measures would be adopted. President Davis, and the Adjutant-general at Richmond, also wrote in a similar strain ; and, finally, not receiving a reply— for General McClellan had referred the communications to Washington—Lee addressed General Halleck on the subject. After some time replies came, but couched in any thing but satisfactory terms; and finally, General Lee received a letter from General Halleck, as follows :

" Your two communications, of August 9th, 1862, and of the 2d instant, with inclosures, are received.   As these papers are couched in language exceedingly insulting to the Government of the United States, I most respectfully decline to receive them.   They are returned herewith."

Whether or no General Lee's language was " insulting," those who care to read the correspondence can judge. Shortly afterwards, in a letter to General McClellan, General Halleck, on the part of the Government, disavowed authorizing any such measures as complained of.

Much of the cause of this correspondence arose from certain orders issued in July by General Pope (who had assumed command of the Federal forces in Northern Virginia), to arrest all disloyal male citizens within the Union lines, or within reach of his several divisions; and, on refusing to take the oath of allegiance, they were to be banished from their homes, and, if found to have returned, would be subject to the extreme rigor of military law.   Moreover, " if any person, having taken the oath of allegiance as above specified, be found to have violated it, he shall be shot, and his property seized and applied to public use."   In addition to this, there was another order, to hold under arrest prominent citizens as hostages for any of the Union soldiers shot by roving bands of the South.

Now, we need hardly say, that this caused a great amount of bitterness on the part of Southerners towards Pope and his army, and it was with something more than ordinary joy the news was finally received that General Lee was on the way to attack him.   This, however, did not occur until after it was seen that McClellan was not in a position to molest Richmond

again ; and yet it was necessary to do it before the three hun
dred thousand recruits called for by the Washington Government should be brought into the field. Consequently, while
Lee still remained watching over the capital, Jackson was dispatched to hold Pope in check.

As this was, evidently, to be an important campaign, it was
intrusted solely to General Lee, who directed and controlled
every movement ; and, when the Union forces finally evacuated
the Peninsula, hastened, himself, in the middle of August, to
the scene of action.

Meanwhile Jackson had crossed the Rapidan, at Barnett's
ford, in heavy force, after marching for two days, and attacked
that portion of Pope's army stationed near Cedar Mountain,
under General Banks. The fight began at about 6 P. M., and
lasted nearly two hours. The contest was very severe ; but
General Banks bravely held his position until darkness ended
the engagement, with great loss on both sides. On the next
day, according to well-conceived plans, Jackson rapidly and
secretly withdrew from the Rapidan, intending, by a flank
movement on Pope's right, to menace his rear, while General
Lee came up in front. This was accomplished by the 17th of
August, when Lee assembled before Pope a force sufficient to
contest his further advance, and balk his threatened passage of
the Rapidan.

It was, probably, the design of General Lee, with the bulk
of the Confederate army, to take the front, left, and right, and
engage General Pope at or near the Rapidan, while Jackson
and Ewell were to cross the Shenandoah river and mountains,
cut off his supplies by way of the railroad, and menace his
rear ; but Pope's retreat to the Rappahannock partly frustrated
the design, and compelled Lee to keep the enemy's attention
drawn to his front. Jackson, however, succeeded in getting
behind Pope, and surprised his troops at Bristow and Manassas
stations. On the 27th, 28th, and 29th fighting occurred between Pope and the forces under Jackson and Longstreet ;
but, hearing that more soldiers were coming to reinforce Pope,
General Lee at once determined to give him battle. Accordingly, on the 30th of August, he attacked him on the old battlefield of Bull Run.

The account of this battle may be best given, for our present

purpose, nearly in the words of General Lee himself, and from what has already been published.

It appears that on Friday night (August 29th) the Confederate forces were resting upon their arms, and ready for the engagement next day. The following morning the pickets of the two armies were within a few hundred yards of each other, and the line of battle of each party was as follows.*

The Confederates were placed in the form of an obtuse crescent, at least five miles long, with Jackson's division stretching from Sudley, on Bull Run, along the partly excavated track of the Manassas Independent line of railroad, for a portion of the way, and thence towards a point on the Warrenton turnpike, about a mile and a half west of Groveton. His extreme right came within about six hundred yards of the turnpike.

Longstreet's command, which formed the Confederate right wing, extended from Jackson's, beyond the line of the Manassas Gap railroad. Thus the centre of Lee's army was not far from the same position that the right wing of McDowell's army was in at the first battle of Bull Run, July, 1861. Indeed, the whole ground covered by the fight of this day, was identical with the scene of McDowell's and Beauregard's hard-fought field thirteen months before.

In the centre of Lee's army, between Jackson and Longstreet, eight batteries were placed on an important elevation, under command of Colonel S. D. Lee, of South Carolina. This spot was one of the best that could have been selected, as it had the advantage of overlooking all the locality around. Pope's army had formed in line of battle similar to that of Lee's, with its advanced centre at Groveton, and its wings declining obliquely to the right and left. Heintzelman had the extreme right (his old ground), and McDowell the left, while the corps of Fitz John Porter, and Siegel, with Reno's division of Burnside's detached forces, were in the centre.

Early in the morning, the battle began with artillery, but little damage was done until the afternoon, when the engagement became very severe. Jackson's infantry raked the enemy most fearfully, causing him to break and run several times,

---

* *Pollard*, Second Year of the War.

yet as repeatedly rallying again under the appeals of their
officers. Finally, however, they were compelled to retreat,
apparently designing to fall back in the direction of Manassas.
But General Lee, with Jackson and Longstreet, had been carefully watching their every movement, and frustrated any such
attempt, had it been really intended. For a short time, a pause
now ensued, when suddenly the roar of artillery again shook
the ground, and the gallant Federals were seen advancing
with heroic determination upon Lee's centre. They were met
by a murderous discharge from Colonel Lee's well-posted artillery, which almost annihilated them, as the shot and shell
raked and tore them to pieces. It was impossible to withstand
this terrible discharge, and the advancing columns fell back,
only to be succeeded, however, by another gallant brigade of
Federals charging as before. Again the iron storm crashed
through their ranks, and again they broke and ran. A third
force, heavier than before, now advanced with mad rapidity,
and, in the midst of the awful fire of the Confederate batteries,
threw themselves upon Jackson, engaging him most desperately. Reserves followed, and the fight became furious. Presently the Union troops were compelled to give way, amidst a
scene of horrible slaughter. Swift in pursuit, Jackson's men
rushed forward, and at the same time Longstreet dashed with
impetuous force upon the Federal left flank. The whole Confederate army was now in motion, and the battle raged in all
its power. Jackson on the Union right, and Longstreet on
their left, was forcing their extended flanks inward, while
General Lee with his centre, and artillery, now moved on from
hill to hill in advance, was ploughing a way in huge gaps
through their heart. The effect was terrible. "The Confederates came on," says a Northern journalist, "like demons
emerging from the earth." Up the old, and, to some of the
regiments, the well-known Warrenton turnpike; down the
steeps of the plateau around the famous Henry House; across
the fields and over the hills on the left, as you come from Sudley to the Dogan farm; pell-mell, mad with excitement, rage,
and that fearful desire for blood which all feel at such times,
over heaps of dead and dying, rushed the wild Southern soldiers upon their foe, still combating foot by foot the ground
whereon they had to retreat. But, this time, it was not as

before, when a sudden panic drove the Northern soldier madly forward, in terrible confusion, anxious to escape. It was a well-contested movement backwards; and as the sun went down, once again upon that gory battlefield, as it had done on the evening of July 21st, of the preceding year, the defeated forces of the North could boast of having fought bravely to the last, and only retreated when to longer stand would have been complete annihilation. Forced across Bull Run, with their dead covering every acre from Groveton to the Stone Bridge, and the enemy in overwhelming numbers pursuing, nothing remained for them but to try and check the foe's advance. This was done by destroying the bridge, and making the fords, as General Lee himself says, doubtful to pass. Pursuit, therefore, ended, and the remnant of Pope's heroic army marched at once to Centreville, where it encamped in strong position.

Thus ended the second battle of Bull Run, and General Lee had again achieved a victory, for which he and his brave army soon afterwards received the grateful thanks of President Davis and the Confederacy.

In the battle, Generals Lee, Jackson, Longstreet, Hood, Kemper, Evans, Jones, Jenkins, Stuart, and other generals, were everywhere conspicuous, sharing in all the dangers of their men, and personally directing and encouraging the onward movements. The colonels and subordinate officers are also highly spoken of, and the conduct of the too often forgotten private was justly remembered by Lee, as was ever customary with him.

Night had now put an end to the scene, and the troops bivouacked on the battlefield. But, next morning, Sunday 31st, it was necessary to put the army in motion again towards the Little river and Chantilly, for the purpose of trying to turn Pope's right, or drive him further back. Accordingly, Jackson's corps was pressed forward, and Stuart pursued with his cavalry, fighting the Union rearguard at Cub Run bridge, which they burned after them. Stuart then struck into the turnpike towards Chantilly, and found the Federal army, on Sunday evening, retreating towards Fairfax Court-house.

Meanwhile, General Pope, on the day after the battle, had found it necessary to send a flag of truce to General Lee with

reference to his wounded left on the field uncared for, except so far as attention was humanely given them by the Confederates. The reply of General Lee gave consent to ambulances coming within his lines, and promising every assistance, but did not agree to any suspension of military operations.*

---

* The following is General Lee's Report of this battle, and the correspondence we have referred to:

HEADQUARTERS, ARMY NORTHWESTERN VIRGINIA,
CHANTILLY, Sept. 3, 1862.

HIS EXCELLENCY, JEFFERSON DAVIS, PRESIDENT CONFEDERATE STATES OF AMERICA:

MR. PRESIDENT: My letter of the 30th ult. will have informed your Excellency of the progress of this army to that date. General Longstreet's division, having arrived the day previous, was formed in order of battle on the right of General Jackson, who had been engaged with the enemy since morning, resisting an attack commenced on the 28th. The enemy, on the latter day, was vigorously repulsed, leaving his numerous dead and wounded on the field. His attack on the morning of the 29th was feeble, but became warmer in the afternoon, when he was again repulsed by both wings of the army. His loss on this day, as stated in his published report, herewith inclosed, amounted to 8,000 killed and wounded.

The enemy, being reinforced, renewed the attack on the afternoon of the 30th, when a general advance of both wings of the army was ordered, and after a fierce combat, which raged until after nine o'clock, he was completely defeated and driven beyond Bull Run. The darkness of the night, his destruction of the stone bridge after crossing, and the uncertainty of the fords, stopped the pursuit.

The next morning, the enemy was discovered in the strong position at Centreville, and the army was put in motion towards the Little River turnpike, to turn his right. Upon reaching Ox Hill, on the 1st of September, he was again discovered in our front, on the heights of Germantown, and about 5 P. M. made a spirited attack upon the front and right of our columns, with a view of apparently covering the withdrawal of his trains on the Centreville road, and masking his retreat. Our position was maintained with but slight loss on both sides. Major-general Kearney was left by the enemy dead on the field. During the night the enemy fell back to Fairfax Court-house, and abandoned his position at Centreville. Yesterday about noon, he evacuated Fairfax Court-house, taking the roads, as reported to me, to Alexandria and Washington.

I have, as yet, been unable to get official reports of our loss or captured in these various engagements. Many gallant officers have been killed or wounded. Of the general officers, Ewell, Trimble, Taliaferro, Fields, Jenkins, and Mahone, have been reported wounded: Colonels Means, Marshall, Baylor, Neff, and Gadberry, killed. About 7,000 prisoners have already been paroled, about the same number of small-arms collected from the field, and thirty pieces of cannon captured, besides a number of wagons, ambulances, etc. A large number of arms still remain on the ground. For want of transportation, valuable stores had to be destroyed as captured, while the enemy, at their various depots, are reported to have burned many millions of property in their retreat.

The results of General Lee's strategy were indicative of the resources of military genius. Day after day the enemy were beaten, until his disasters culminated on the plains of Manassas. Day after day the officers and men manifested a daring and skill rarely, if ever, surpassed. The summer campaign in Virginia had been conducted by the same army that had relieved the siege of Richmond in the seven days' battles. The trials and marches of these troops are most extraordinary. Transportation was inadequate; the streams which they had to cross were swollen to unusual height; and yet, forcing themselves onward, they ultimately succeeded in their crowning triumphs of the Second Battle of Bull Run; or, as termed in the South, "Manassas."

General Lee now followed up his success by an attack on the enemy massed in the neighborhood of Chantilly, at Ox Mill,

---

Nothing could surpass the gallantry and endurance of the troops, who have cheerfully borne every danger and hardship, both on the battlefield and march

I have the honor to be, very respectfully, your obedient servant,

R. E. LEE, General.

[Chantilly is north of Centreville and northwest of Fairfax Court-house, about six or eight miles from each. The "letter of the 30th," referred to in the above, was not received. The Little River turnpike leads from Middleburg to Alexandria, and intersects the Centreville turnpike about a mile this side of Fairfax Court-house. Germantown is on the Little River turnpike, about half a mile west of its intersection with the Centreville turnpike.]

The following correspondence will illustrate the thoroughness of the enemy's defeat in the battle of the 30th. It bears date, as will be seen, of the next day.

CENTREVILLE, August 31, 1862.

SIR—Many of the wounded of this army have been left on the field, for whom I desire to send ambulances. Will you please inform me whether you consent to a truce until they are cared for? I am, sir, your obedient servant,

JOHN POPE,

Major-general United States Army, Commanding.

COMMANDING OFFICER Confederate forces, near Groveton.

HEADQUARTERS, ARMY OF NORTHERN VIRGINIA, August 31, 1862.

Major-general JOHN POPE, U. S. A., Commanding, etc.:

SIR—Consideration for your wounded induces me to consent to your sending ambulances to convey them within your lines. I cannot consent to a truce nor a suspension of military operations of this army. If you desire to send for your wounded, should your ambulances report to Dr. Guilet, medical director of this army, he will give directions for their transportation. The wounded will be paroled, and it is understood that no delay will take place in their removal.

Very respectfully, your obedient servant,

R. E. LEE, General.

just above Germantown. Here, in the afternoon, an engagement took place, which was exceedingly obstinate, though not lasting. It was here that the gallant and lamented Kearney fell—the admired and esteemed of all, who had come expressly from Europe to join the Union cause, the cause of his native land; and his body lay undiscovered until the next day, when the Confederates carried it to his comrades under a flag of truce. That evening the battle was interrupted by a severe thunder-storm, and darkness coming on, the engagement ceased. On the next day it was found that the Union forces had fallen back within the defences of Washington, and the Confederates thereupon once more took possession of Fairfax Court-house. Immediately afterwards, demonstrations were made near the Chain Bridge, and the fords of the Potomac above Washington, as if Lee intended to assault the fortifications. But this was merely a feint to mislead the foe,—Jackson, ordering maps of the locality, and inquiring all about the roads around the capital, quietly and suddenly went forward in another direction, in pursuance of previous plans and the wishes of his whole army.

General Lee's determination now was to invade Maryland, and see if that State might not be aroused to join the South.* On the 4th of September, 1862, leaving to his right Arlington Heights, to which Pope with his army had retreated, he crossed the Potomac in the neighborhood of Leesburg, and marched to Frederickton, throwing the whole State of Pennsylvania into great alarm. The people of Maryland, however, did not join him as anticipated, and he resolved, therefore, to mark his invasion by an attack on Harper's Ferry. General Miles, of the United States army, held the post with 11,500 men, and Lee sent against him General Jackson with his corps, while Longstreet with his troops covered the movement, and D. H. Hill was stationed at Boonesboro to check the advance of McClellan, who had been reappointed to the command of the Union army. Lee himself kept with Longstreet, and continued, by various feints, to lead the North into continual doubt and anxiety as to his real object.

On the 14th of September, General D. H. Hill was posted

* *Pollard,* "Second Year of the War," p. 124.

in and around a gap in the South Mountain, close to Boones
boro. This pass is known as Boonesboro Gap, being over the
broad back of the mountain, a continuation of the National
turnpike. The road is winding, narrow, rocky, and rugged,
with either a deep ravine on one hand, and the steep sides of
the mountain on the other, or like a huge channel cut through
the solid rock. Near the crest are two or three houses, which
to some extent overlook the adjacent valley, but elsewhere
the face of the mountain is unbroken by a solitary vestige of
the handiwork of man.

It was here that McClellan with his new forces encountered
Hill. The battle commenced soon after daylight by a vigorous cannonade, under cover of which, two or three hours later,
first the skirmishers and then the main body became engaged.
A regular line of battle on the Confederate side, either as
regards numbers or order, was impossible, and the theatre of
the fight was therefore limited. The fortune of the day, which
was desperate enough in the face of overwhelming numbers,
was stubbornly contested by the Confederates. The brigade
of General Garland, of Virginia, the first engaged, lost its brave
commander. While endeavoring to rally his men, he fell,
pierced in the breast by a musket-ball, and died upon the field.

While the Confederate lines were giving way under pressure
of McClellan's troops, the welcome sounds of reinforcements
were borne on the air. The corps of General Longstreet was
at Hagerstown, fourteen miles distant, and at daylight commenced its march towards the scene of action, General Lee
accompanying it. Hurrying forward with all speed, stopping
neither to rest nor eat, the advance arrived at the Pass about
4 M., and were at once sent into the mountain. Brigade
after brigade, as rapidly as it came up, followed, until, by five
o'clock, nearly the entire command was in position, and a
portion of it already engaged. The accession of fresh numbers
at once arrested the backward movement of Hill, who, having
gallantly fought all the day, was now overpowered on his right
wing. But the reinforcements had arrived in time, and when
night came on, the two armies were in much the same position
as at the commencement of the battle, with no advantage to
either, except that which the Confederates wished, of holding
McClellan in check.

While this action was in progress, the capture of Harper's Ferry was effected by the army corps of General Jackson. During the night of the 14th he had planted his guns, and early next morning opened, in all directions, on the Federal forces, drawn up in line of battle on Bolivar Heights. Soon after seven o'clock, however, a white flag was raised, and Harper's Ferry, with its fine army, its splendid park of artillery, and a large number of small-arms, surrendered.

Meanwhile General Lee fell back to Sharpsburg, to concentrate his forces, and give battle to the still advancing foe. Sharpsburg is about ten miles north of Harper's Ferry, and eight miles west of Boonesboro. The town lies in a deep valley. The country around it is broken. Ascending a hill, just on the outer edge of the town, and looking towards the Blue Ridge, the eye ranges over the greater portion of the eventful field. To the right and left is a succession of hills which were occupied by the Confederates. In front is the beautiful valley of the Antietam, divided longitudinally by the river, which empties into the Potomac on the right, forming a background to the picture. Two miles distant are the steep, umbrageous sides of the Blue Ridge.

The morning of the 17th of September found General Lee strongly posted when the battle commenced. The Union forces, commanded by McClellan in person, were in line of battle, between four and five miles long, with their left stretching across the Sharpsburg road. General Burnside was on this extreme left, and General Hooker on the right.

During the afternoon of the 16th, McClellan had opened a light artillery fire on the Confederates; but not until daybreak of the 17th did the battle, in all its fury, commence. Then began one of those severe contests which showed the indomitable bravery and determination of each side. In the morning, some of the divisions belonging to the Confederate army had not come up from Harper's Ferry; but, later in the day they arrived, and then the conflict raged throughout the entire line. A portion of the Southern army on the left was driven back; and though the troops under McClellan were, in a great measure, composed of raw levies, they behaved so well, that even Lee's veterans, for a time, became staggered. At length, however, the new recruits of the Northern army were compelled

to fall back, and allow the longer-tried soldiers to maintain the ground, and this they did most bravely. Furiously the battle raged, and " backwards and forwards, swaying like a ship in a storm," were the various columns of the contending parties seen in motion. Nobly did the soldiers of the South, also, perform their duty, and even their enemies could not help praising them. " It is a wonder," wrote a Federal officer, " how men such as the rebel troops are, can fight as they do. That those ragged wretches, sick, hungry, and in all ways miserable, should prove such heroes in fight, is past explanation. Men never fought better."

In the afternoon, the Union forces pushed forward on Lee's right, where General Jones' division was posted. There General Toombs' brigade was guarding a bridge, spanning Antietam creek, and, as the enemy advanced, they fought until nearly cut to pieces, and obliged to retreat. The movement was followed up by Burnside crossing the bridge in force, and with an irresistible impulse that nothing could resist. But night now approached, and, after a hard-fought day, the two parties rested in the positions they had respectively secured, without, however, either gaining material advantage over the other. Burnside held the bridge, but in other parts of the field the Confederates maintained their own.

This battle was one of the most bloody and terrible that had yet been fought. " Many of the dead had to be left unburied for a time on the battlefield. Some of them laid with their faces to the ground, whither they had turned in the agony of death ; others were heaped in piles of three and four together, with their arms interlocked, and their faces turned upwards towards the sky. Scores of them were laid out in rows, as though the death-shot had penetrated their breast as they were advancing to the attack. Covered with mud and dust, with their faces and clothes smeared with blood and gore, there they rotted in the sun."

The close of this battle left neither army in a condition to renew the conflict. The next morning, General Lee found that McClellan had moved his army from the front, and, knowing the superiority of Northern troops in numbers, and expecting a rapid movement to cut him off, he crossed the Potomac without delay, taking position near Shepherdstown.

It has been asserted in the North, and denied by the South, that McClellan had here gained a victory over Lee. But, the truth of history must admit that both sides were victorious, and yet both also suffered a defeat. They were victorious— the North in effectively arresting the enemy from advancing further—the South in preventing their foe from entrapping them ; and they were equally defeated, when neither could further accomplish his designs, and when both had to leave the battlefield on the next day without attempting more. To General Lee and his army, in the enemy's own country, it was a victory, because he could and did move backward at will, and without molestation. To General McClellan and his brave soldiers it was also a victory, for it effectively stopped the Southern advance and compelled them to retire.

McClellan had now retreated to Harper's Ferry, which was again in possession of the North ; but, on the 1st of October, his cavalry under General Pleasanton drove back the Confederate pickets in front of Shepherdstown. The Ninth Virginia Cavalry, on picket duty, bravely disputed the ground, step by step to the main body. General Lee, in his official report, says : " By the time his artillery reached him, Colonel W. F. H. Lee, who was in command of the brigade, was obliged to place it on the west bank of the Occoquan, on the flank of the enemy as he approached Martinsburg. General Hampton's brigade had retired through Martinsburg, when General Stuart arrived and made dispositions to attack. Lee's brigade was advanced immediately, and Hampton's ordered forward. The enemy retired at the approach of Lee along the Sheperdstown road, and was driven across the Potomac by the cavalry, with severe loss, darkness alone preventing it from being a signal victory. His rear was overtaken and put to flight, our cavalry charging in gallant style under a severe fire of artillery, driving squadron after squadron, killing a number, wounding more, and capturing several. He was driven through Shepherdstown, and crossed the river after dark, in no case standing a hand-to-hand conflict, but relying upon his rtillery and carbineers at long range for protection."

General Lee's headquarters were now established near Winchester, and there, by the skilful disposition of his forces, he rendered it impracticable for McClellan to invade the Shenan-

doah valley, but forced him to adopt the route on the east side of the Blue Ridge into Virginia, which was still looked upon, by the North, as the great field where battles should be fought.

Shrewd, careful, and far-seeing, however, Lee was not to be deceived into fancied security by any display of the enemy's movements. Under that calm exterior of his, there was a fire of enthusiasm and an energy of mind—well and ably seconded by the brave and faithful chiefs, officers, and soldiers around him—that was capable of the most masterly generalship and prompt execution of plans. Hardly had the Marylanders recovered from their dismay at finding Lee's army in their midst, and their after thankfulness at his departure, than they were astonished by another daring incursion amongst them. This was accomplished by that bold cavalry officer General Stuart, and was started by Lee on the 8th of October, according to the following directions.

Stuart was to take from 1,200 to 1,500 well-mounted men, cross the Potomac above Williamsport, and proceed to the rear of Chambersburg, where he was to destroy the railroad bridge, and commit any other damage possible, on the enemy, or his means of transportation. Every information of the position, force, and probable intention of the enemy was to be gained; and, to avoid news being forwarded by citizens to the Union forces, they were, upon suspicion, to be arrested. Officials under the Federal Government were to be seized and held as hostages; but, in all cases, every respect and consideration was to be shown them. Horses, and any other necessary articles, were to be captured; and then every expedition used to rejoin the army.

Full reliance was justly placed on General Stuart to carry out these instructions as he might consider best; and Colonel Imboden was directed to draw the enemy's attention away from such parts of the Potomac where the Confederates might cross.

These instructions were faithfully carried out by General Stuart, and his command,—Brigadier-general Hampton, Colonels W. F. H. Lee, and Jones, forming a part of it,—and on the 12th the entire expedition returned safely, without the loss of a single man, and with only a few slight wounds received

in skirmishes. They had passed through several important places, and entered Chambersburg, where possession of the town was immediately given to them, and where, as well as in other places, every care was taken, according to orders, that the peaceful inhabitants should not be ill-treated. Several official persons and prominent citizens were captured as hostages for Southern non-combatants imprisoned by the North, and a large amount of provisions and a great number of horses were also secured. Altogether the expedition was most successful, and General Lee, in his official report, very highly complimented Stuart and his command for its execution.

Towards the end of October, fresh movements, on the part of the Union forces, began to take place. Several minor engagements had occurred, and, finally, the disposition of the respective troops was as follows: "The Northern army occupied all the region east of the Blue Ridge mountains, with the right resting on Harper's Ferry, and the left near Paris, on the road from Aldie to Winchester. The centre was at Snickersville, with Snicker's Gap in its possession. The Confederate line was on the south side of the Blue Ridge, with the Shenandoah river immediately in its front, extending from Front Royal down to Charleston, with the great body of their troops massed between Berryville and Winchester. On the 4th of November, Ashby's Gap was occupied, without opposition, by the Federal troops. The approaches to Manassas Gap were also held by the Federals, and, on the 6th, General McClellan had his headquarters at Rectortown, near Front Royal." Thus, to all appearance, the Confederate forces were thoroughly hemmed in, and General Lee confined, hopelessly, near Winchester. Great, therefore, was the surprise of the Union army when it was found that Lee had intuitively judged their plans, and forestalled them by detaching the greater part of his troops, and accompanying them to the south bank of the Rappahannock, leaving Jackson to guard the Shenandoah until circumstances would indicate whether he should unite with him.

The available force of General McClellan was about 120,000 men, and its condition and spirit was unequalled by that of any force before organized: that of General Lee consisted of about 60,000 able men, at Culpepper and Gordonsville, and 30,000 in the Shenandoah valley, and we have already seen

what was their state, away from all their immediate resources, and enfeebled, but not dispirited, by a long campaign. Thus, then, it is evident that it was again a very critical juncture for the South, and one that required the most consummate ability, on the part of Lee, to guard against. The two former close companions in arms—the general-in-chief of the Northern army, and the commander-in-chief of the Southern forces—were, as they had been only three months previously, when Richmond was in danger, face to face with each other, ready to renew a contest for " victory or death." Yet, just at that moment, by the supreme Federal authority, McClellan was removed, and a new, a brave, but hitherto untried, military chief in the field, General Burnside, was placed in command. What followed is familiar to every one who knows aught of the history of the heroic army of the Potomac and its beloved commander. McClellan bade his troops farewell amidst scenes of deep feeling, and wild, impassioned tokens of affection, on the part of his officers and men, such as rarely witnessed since Napoleon's adieu at Fontainebleau. Latterly it has been made to appear that this love and esteem of his soldiers had decreased, but impartial history cannot fail to do justice, by recording the truth as here narrated.

With McClellan's departure, Lee found that a new change of programme, on the part of the enemy, was to commence. On the 12th of November a consultation took place between General Burnside and General Halleck, at Warrenton, and by the morning of the 18th the Northern forces had all left, *en route* for Fredericksburg, which, at that time, was held by the South. Lee immediately followed, and with that promptitude and sagacious skill which characterized his every movement, had his army concentrated on the heights, in the rear of Fredericksburg, at the same time Burnside had massed his forces at Falmouth, on the oppposite side of the Rappahannock river. Here was another surprise for the North. A very short time previous, General Lee and his worn-out troops were cooped up at Winchester, in the Shenandoah valley ; now, he and his hardy veterans were in readiness for the fight at Fredericksburg, and had actually blocked the passage of the Rappahannock! So confident, it is said, was Burnside and his army of success attending his stratagem—a stratagem

whereby he had hoped to get on to Richmond by the neaici route from Fredericksburg, left, as he supposed, unguarded,—that the most sanguine expectations were raised of a speedy downfall of the Southern capital. The quick and energetic steps taken, however, by Lee, so dashed these hopes to the ground, especially on seeing the way to Richmond thus again barred by the same daring chief and his undaunted soldiers, who had before stayed the invaders at the very threshold of the coveted city, that gloom and distrust were again speedily manifested. Delays on the part of the Union forces followed, and these delays the more enabled General Lee to make his position impregnable, and to increase his reserve of resources within his own intrenchments, all unknown to the enemy. Finally, on the night of the 10th of December the battle was begun; and here we cannot do better than let General Lee speak for himself, as he does in the report sent by him to President Davis.

"HEADQUARTERS, ARMY OF NORTHERN VIRGINIA, Dec. 14, 1862.
"The Honorable Secretary OF War, Richmond, Va.

"SIR,—On the night of the 10th instant the enemy commenced to throw three bridges over the Rappahannock—two at Fredericksburg, and the third about a mile and a quarter below, near the mouth of the Deep Run. The plain on which Fredericksburg stands is so completely commanded by the hills of Stafford, in possession of the enemy, that no effectual opposition could be offered to the construction of the bridges on the passage of the river, without exposing our troops to the destructive fire of his numerous batteries. Positions were, therefore, selected to oppose his advance after crossing. The narrowness of the Rappahannock, its winding course, and deep bed, afforded opportunity for the construction of bridges at points beyond the reach of our artillery, and the banks had to be watched by skirmishers. The latter, sheltering themselves behind the houses, drove back the working parties of the enemy at the bridges opposite the city; but at the lowest point of crossing, where no shelter could be had, our sharpshooters themselves were driven off, and the completion of the bridge was effected about noon on the 11th.

"In the afternoon of that day the enemy's batteries opened

upon the city, and by dark had so demolished the houses on the river-bank, as to deprive our skirmishers of shelter; and, under cover of his guns, he effected a lodgment in the town. The troops which had so gallantly held their position in the city under the severe cannonade during the day, resisting the advance of the enemy at every step, were withdrawn during the night, as were also those who, with equal tenacity, had maintained their post at the lowest bridge.

" Under cover of darkness and a dense fog, on the 12th, a large force passed the river, and took position on the right bank, protected by their heavy guns on the left.

" On the morning of the 13th, his arrangements for attack being completed, about nine o'clock, the movement, veiled by a fog, he advanced boldly, in large force, against our right wing. General Jackson's corps occupied the right of our line, which rested on the railroad; General Longstreet's the left, extending along the heights to the Rappahannock, above Fredericksburg; General Stuart, with two brigades of cavalry, was posted in the extensive plain on our extreme right. As soon as the advance of the enemy was discovered through the fog, General Stuart, with his accustomed promptness, moved up a section of his horse-artillery, which opened with effect upon his flank, and drew upon the gallant Pelham a heavy fire, which he sustained unflinchingly for about two hours.

" In the mean time the enemy was fiercely encountered by General A. P. Hill's division, forming General Jackson's right, and after an obstinate combat repulsed. During this attack, which was protracted and hotly contested, two of General Hill's brigades were driven back upon our second line. General Early, with part of his division, being ordered to his support, drove the enemy back from the point of woods he had seized, and pursued him into the plain, until arrested by his artillery.

" The right of the enemy's column, extending beyond Hill's front, encountered the right of General Hood, of Longstreet's corps. The enemy took possession of a small copse in front of Hood, but were quickly dispossessed of it, and repulsed with loss.

" During the attack on our right the enemy was crossing troops over his bridges at Fredericksburg, and massing them in

front of Longstreet's line. Soon after his repulse on our right he commenced a series of attacks on our left, with a view of obtaining possession of the heights immediately overlooking the town. These repeated attacks were repulsed in gallant style by the Washington Artillery, under Colonel Walton and a portion of McLaw's division, which occupied these heights.

"The last assault was made after dark, when Colonel Alexander's battalion had relieved the Washington Artillery, whose ammunition had been exhausted, and ended the contest for the day.

"The enemy was supported in his attacks by the fire of strong batteries of artillery on the right bank of the river, as well as by the numerous heavy batteries on the Stafford Heights.

"Our loss during the operation, since the movements of the enemy began, amounts to about eighteen hundred, killed and wounded. Among the former, I regret to report the death of the patriotic soldier and statesman, Brigadier-general Thomas R. R. Cobb, who fell upon our left; and among the latter, that brave soldier and accomplished gentleman, Brigadier-general M. Gregg, who was very seriously, and, it is feared, mortally wounded, during the attack on our right.

"The enemy to-day has been apparently burying his dead. His troops are visible in their first position, in line of battle; but, with the exception of some desultory cannonading and firing between the skirmishers, he has not attempted to renew the attack.

"About five hundred and fifty prisoners were taken during the engagement, but the full extent of his loss is unknown.

"I have the honor to be, very respectfully, your obedient servant,   "R. E. LEE,
                                        "General in command."

On the day following the dispatch of this Report, Burnside determined to withdraw across the river, from Fredericksburg, and reoccupy his old position. This was most skilfully done, during the night and early morning of December 15th and 16th; and every man, with all the property, was safely brought away, the pontoon bridges removed at the same time, before General Lee and his army were aware of it. Thus ended an-

other terrific battle, wherein immense slaughter occurred, and no positive advantage was gained to either side. The ghastly field was such, that even those most inured to sickening scenes of blood shuddered. The loss of brave men on both sides was great, though far greater on the North than on the South ; and the destruction of peaceful homes and private property such as to make the most indifferent pause thoughtfully on beholding it. General Lee, with the well-known sensibilities of his kindly nature, felt this acutely, especially as these were the native scenes of his early youth, and every thing around him reminded of cherished family ties, and associations. But honor and duty forbade any display of his own personal feelings. Neither had he time to dwell upon painful memories of the past. His native soil had chosen him to defend her rights and privileges as an independent State, and the united South had elected him for its chief. Thus he had to keep himself actively employed, and not allow one moment to be taken away from carefully watching over, and, as far as possible, protecting the interests of the people confiding in him.

When the news concerning Lee's victory at Fredericksburg reached Richmond, the hopes of the South at first rose high that some important results would attend the success of their arms. But these hopes were speedily dashed to the ground, when it was found that the Northern army had been able to effect a successful retreat. People at a distance fancied that Lee could and should have wholly annihilated Burnside and his men, but they little knew the almost utter impossibility of such a task on either side. There was the same amount of indomitable courage, the same skill, more or less displayed— the same fertility of resources—the same perseverance, and the same remarkable personal bravery (with rare exceptions) amongst officers and privates alike, on the part of the North as well as the South, and with the latter as the former. Neither could justly claim a superiority in these respects. Both of the contending parties were akin in all the fearlessness of character and heroism of mind for which they of old, in the days of Carthage and of Rome, have been remembered. And it is only the difficulty of trying to compress, within a limited space, details belonging to prominent individuals, that forbids us dwelling with an admiring pen (though also, with a

saddened heart, to find such brave men fighting against each other) upon the many heroic deeds on record. We must let them pass now, and merely confine ourselves to general events. A master mind occasionally does arise amongst the many great and brave; and it is evident that, for the South, in its great emergencies, General Lee was that master mind; yet he could not do more than direct, and plan, and personally encourage his brave men. He could not annihilate foes who were equally brave and daring as himself, and, moreover, fought with the knowledge that theirs was a cause about which there could be no dispute as regarded its loyalty and national right. There-fore, when cavils, at any time, were raised by thoughtless men against their general, he only showed a more noble and su perior mind, by calmly pursuing his way, regardless of them.

The public approbation, however, of the Confederate au-thorities, of the Southern Congress, and of those competent to judge, as well as the people generally, was fully awarded to General Lee, and no terms of laudation and esteem seem to have been strong enough to express what was felt concerning him. Nor was he, himself, unmindful to bestow just praise upon those who had so ably and cheerfully seconded his efforts In a general order, issued on the 31st of December, 1862, he expressed himself very warmly on the endurance and good conduct of his troops.

CHAPTER V.

THE commencement of the year 1863 was signalized by no event of any military importance as connected with General Lee personally. A family affliction, the death of his daughter, Annie Carter Lee, at Jones' Spring, Warren county, North Carolina, may, however, be recorded; but the private history of the Confederate chief—that inner life of a great man which all love to hear about, and to read—cannot yet be written, until by himself, or another authorized, those particulars are given to the world. But a summary of cavalry exploits undertaken by his direction towards the close of the past year and the beginning of this, in which, as usual, his sons, nephew, and personal friends bore themselves bravely, may be aptly noticed here. In his general order, February 28th, Lee says:

"About the 1st of December, General Hampton, with a detachment of his brigade, crossed the upper Rappahannock, surprised two squadrons of Union cavalry, captured several commissioned officers, and about one hundred men, with their horses, arms, colors, and accoutrements, without loss on his part.

"On December 4th, General W. F. Lee's brigade crossed the Rappahannock below Port Royal, in skiffs, attacked the enemy's cavalry pickets, captured forty-nine officers and men, etc., and recrossed the river without loss.

"On the 11th and 16th of December, General Hampton made two successful raids to Dumfries and the Occoquan.

"On the 25th of December, General Stuart, with detachments of Hampton's, Fitzhugh Lee's, and W. F. Lee's brigades,
under command of those officers, made a successful attack
upon the enemy's rear at Dumfries, Alexandria, the Occoquan, and north of Fairfax Court-house, returning to Culpepper with more than two hundred prisoners and twenty-five
wagons."

On February 16th, 1863, Captains McNeil and Stamp, of
General Imboden's cavalry, with twenty-three men, attacked
a Union supply-train near Romney, routed the guard, and took
a number of prisoners.

The 25th of February, General W. F. Lee attacked and
damaged two of the enemy's gunboats at Tappahannock, driving them down the river. The same day, General Fitz Hugh
Lee, with four hundred of his brigade, crossed the Rappahannock, and reconnoitred the enemy's lines to within a few
miles of Falmouth, broke through his outposts, fell upon his
camps, killed and wounded many, took one hundred and fifty
prisoners, and safely returned with only a loss of fourteen
killed, wounded, and missing.

The next day, Brigadier-general W. E. Jones made an attack
upon two cavalry regiments of Milroy's command, in the Shenandoah valley, and routed them, taking two hundred prisoners, etc.

Major White, of General Jones' command, attacked the
enemy's cavalry near Poolesville with success.

Captain Randolph, of the Black Horse cavalry, had also
made several bold reconnoissances.

Lieutenant Mosby, with his detachment, had likewise done
much to harass the enemy.

Sergeant Michael, with seventeen men of Hampton's bri
gade, had, in like manner, performed a heroic act in routing
a large body of Federals; " and, in conclusion, adds General
Lee, " the commanding general takes special pleasure in ad-
verting to the promptness of the officers in striking a successful
blow whenever opportunity offered, and the endurance and
gallantry with which the men have always supported their
commanders."

We will now return to the main body of the army and its
movements.

After the battle of Fredericksburg, Burnside kept his position at Falmouth, until about the middle of January, when he began to move higher up the Rappahannock, with the object of trying to cross the fords, and make an attack upon the flank of General Lee. Various causes prevented this. At first the roads were dry and hard, but, by the time delays were ended and the army really prepared for the march, the weather suddenly became so bad that the roads were almost impassable, and finally the Union forces returned to their former quarters. Of course these movements could not be wholly concealed from the keen eyes of General Lee and his officers. Accordingly, at any moment, the Confederate army was fully prepared for a renewed engagement. Meanwhile, however, another change in the command of the Northern forces occurred. Burnside, at his own request, was relieved, and Hooker was appointed General-in-chief, on the 26th of January, 1863. From this date, for nearly three months more, both armies remained comparatively inactive. The winter season was too inclement for any operations to be carried on successfully. Raids on both sides occasionally relieved the monotony of camp-life, and in one of these, on the 12th of March, a portion of Lee's cavalry made a bold dash within the Federal lines as far as Fairfax Court-house. Brigadier-general Stoughton was taken from his bed and carried off, and a detachment from his brigade, with guards, horses, &c., captured. On the 17th of March a sharp conflict took place between a body of cavalry under the Union General Averill, and an equal number of Lee's dashing horsemen at Kelly's ford, wherein both sides suffered. At length, on the 13th of April, Major-general Stoneman, with detachments of cavalry, infantry, and artillery, proceeded to several places in the neighborhood of the Rappahannock and the Rapidan, as an advance to reconnoitre the ground. No opposition of any importance was met with, and, therefore, General Hooker finally determined to make the grand attack.

At this time, the end of April, General Lee's army was encamped along the Rappahannock, from above Fredericksburg on the left, to Port Royal on the right, and numbered about 70,000 men, while Hooker's army consisted of about 120,000 men, in the highest condition and spirits. To attack Lee,

therefore, and fight him with hopes of success, Hooker thought it a good plan to make a feint on the right of the Confederate army, about three miles below Fredericksburg, and at the same time carry on a vigorous flank movement on the left, and thus compel Lee to come out of his intrenchments. The execution of this plan was commenced on Monday, the 26th of April, by three corps of the Union army marching up the river, northwest, some twenty miles, to a place called Kelly's ford, where they arrived and crossed on the next evening and following morning. They then promptly turned round to the south, and before night, had reached the Rapidan which runs from the west and unites with the Rappahannock at about twelve miles from Fredericksburg. Due south of this junction, at about four miles, is a place called Chancellorsville, and thither the three Union corps, joined by Stoneman's cavalry, and afterwards by another corps—the Second—made their way. They all arrived without the slightest interruption, on Thursday night, April 29th, and General Hooker here made his headquarters.

Meanwhile, the other part of Hooker's plan of attack was being carried out at the same time. Three other corps were sent down the river to a place called Deep Run, there to cross and make show of attacking Lee in great force. This was done, still without molestation, and so certain did the Federal troops now appear of success that Hooker, on the next day, April 30th, issued the following order:—

"It is with heartfelt satisfaction that the commanding general announces to the army that the operations of the last three days have determined that our enemy must either ingloriously fly, or come out from behind his defences and give us battle on our own ground where certain destruction awaits him. The operations of the Fifth, Eleventh, and Twelfth corps have been a succession of splendid achievements."

That such elation did seem justifiable at the time, may be gathered from the fact that, apparently, Lee and his army were indeed completely entrapped. Longstreet, at that period, was not with Lee, having previously been detached with his corps, and sent to face the enemy then advancing upon Suffolk, in Southeast Virginia. But, on the other hand, Stonewall Jackson and his veterans had joined him, and was

now stationed on the right. Still, what means of retreat were
there, if it was necessary for the army to fall back? The only
road of communication with the rear, was by the railway from
Fredericksburg to Richmond, or the turnpike from the same
place to Gordonsville, passing through Chancellorsville, and
this was now in possession of the enemy. Moreover, the cav
alry force of General Stoneman had been sent to cut up the
communication by rail with Richmond, and thus completely
isolate Lee's army. Well, then, might the Federal commander congratulate himself and his forces at this having been
so speedily, and apparently so successfully accomplished.
But where, then, was the acute and clear-sighted Lee? Could
he be insensible to what was going on? Not he!—no, not
for one moment, had he allowed what was taking place to escape his closest observation; and beneath a calm and seemingly indifferent exterior—at least to those who knew him not
—not to his brave and trusting troops—he was silently planning the means for a more effectual overthrow of his enemy,
and even while the congratulatory order of Hooker was being
issued, Lee was in the act of bursting upon him with an effect
that soon completely altered the tone of joy to one of dismal
foreboding. He had allowed the crossing of the Rappahannock on his left, and likewise the crossing of the river on his
right, that he might thoroughly penetrate the enemy's design
before making any movement of his own that might possibly
weaken himself. It became evident to him that the strategy
of McDowell at the first battle of Bull Run, was now being
adopted by Hooker; and, therefore, on the night of Thursday,
April 29th, he ordered General Jackson to leave one division
to watch the enemy on the right—already lessened by the detachment of one of the three corps sent to join Hooker—and
march rapidly to the extreme left, where a portion of his forces, under Anderson and McLaws had already been forwarded
in advance to watch the Union army. Jackson, characteris-
tically, started on his march at midnight, and in the morning
joined the forces in advance. He then proceeded towards
Chancellorsville, and between that place and Fredericksburg,
encountered Sykes' division of General Meade's corps, thrown
forward by Hooker to reconnoitre. Some heavy firing ensued,
but the Union forces fell back according to previous orders,

and, as night approached, Jackson halted to get up the whole
of his command, and better prepare for the next day. That
evening General Lee arrived with such additional forces as he
deemed it prudent to withdraw from their intrenchments, and
immediately a consultation was held.

The position attained by Hooker was indeed a most formi
dable one. Chancellorsville is eleven miles from Fredericks
burg, and about four miles from the point of confluence of the
two rivers, and consisted of a large two-story brick house,
formerly kept as a tavern, and a few outhouses. It is situated
on the plank-road leading to Orange Court-house, and is easily
approached by roads from the several fords of the Rapidan
and Rappahannock. Between Chancellorsville and the Rapidan lies "The Wilderness," a district of country formerly
covered with a scrubby black-jack, oaks, and a thick, tangled
undergrowth, but now somewhat cleared up. The ground
around Chancellorsville was heavily timbered, and favorable
for defence. Seven miles from Chancellorsville, on the road
to Fredericksburg, and four miles from the latter place, is
Salem Church.

It was at Chancellorsville, Hooker had formed a double line
of battle, resembling the two sides of a square—his right rang-
ing along the plank-road nearly east and west, his left extending towards the river, nearly north and south—the apex, where
the two lines of battle joined each other, being near the Old
Chancellor house. In front of these lines the dense timber of
the region had been felled so as to form an almost impassable
series of abattis: in rear of this were elaborate ranges of earthworks for infantry; and behind, as upon either flank—wherever, indeed, a position could be obtained—the hills bristled
with artillery, completely protected from attack by felled
timber.

During the consultation between Generals Lee and Jackson,
it was seen that to storm Hooker in front would be vain, without a frightful loss of life. Consequently, a suggestion made
by the heroic Jackson, that he should attempt a flank movement to the left, was assented to. But even this was a task
almost impossible, as was thought, in the time necessary to be
effective. A road had to be actually *cut* through the forest
protecting Hooker's advanced right, and this was done under

the most extreme difficulties, and, necessarily, with much secrecy. General Fitz Hugh Lee's brigade of cavalry was disposed in such a manner as to guard the front and flanks of the column as it advanced, from observation on the part of the enemy, by driving off scouting parties and acting as pioneers.

Diverging to the left from the plank-road, the command, which now consisted of three divisions only, and the cavalry, moved to and passed the point known as "The Furnace," and thence proceeded towards the road leading to Gordonsville, crossing it near its junction with the road to Germania ford. It was along this road that the main body of Hooker's right was posted, and to get round this, it was necessary for Jackson to move still further to the left. Accordingly, the march was continued, the cavalry moving upon the flank, as well as the dense undergrowth of timber in the wilderness permitted. Thus, apparently screened from the enemy, the head of the column reached Germania ford, about half a mile east of the old Wilderness post-office. At this point, General Fitz Hugh Lee informed General Jackson that by ascending a neighboring hill, he could obtain a view of the position of the enemy, and perhaps be taken for a mere simple vidette. He did so, accompanied by one or two of his staff, and saw at a glance the enemy's position. Instantly, he turned to one of his aids, and said briefly, "Tell my column to cross that road," and then hastening back to the head of his command, gave orders to prepare for action.

It is not in our power, here, to give the details of this battle. All we can do is to hurriedly sketch such movements as were undertaken by the contending parties respectively, under Generals Lee and Hooker, while we occasionally introduce the names of the other actors in the engagement, that belong to this especial work.

The attempt of Jackson to effect a flank movement, by surprise on Hooker's right, was not so successful as he had supposed. The Union forces were commanded by shrewd and skilful generals, who closely watched every motion made by Lee and his men. Accordingly, the advance of Jackson had been perceived, and, to ascertain its true character, General Sickles was sent by Hooker with a reconnoissance in force

towards the quarter threatened. At the same time certain divisions were pushed to the front, and were speedily engaged with General Lee's command, under McLaws and Anderson.

It was about 5 P. M. on Saturday, May 2d, when the fight began, by Rodes' and A. P. Hill's divisions, under orders ot Jackson, rushing to the assault, and so fierce and sudden was the attack, that, in a short time, the Federal troops opposed to it (principally the Eleventh Corps) gave way. In a few moments more they threw down their arms, and fled towards headquarters in the wildest disorder, Jackson's men pressing the advantage with renewed vigor. Thus, on their right and rear, the Union forces found themselves furiously attacked and driven back by General Jackson's command, while in their front, Lee himself, with Anderson and McLaws, not only stood their ground, but succeeded in preventing any advantage being obtained by the entrapped foe. Hooker sent up reinforcements to his right, but it was evident that nothing could retrieve what had already been lost. Night came on, but a bright moon soon rose to shed its calm and holy light upon the terrible scene, and the fighting still continued, with the same success for the Confederate arms.

It was at this time, about nine o'clock, when Jackson—the esteemed and admired, alike of friend and foe—met his death, and that, most lamentably, at the hands of his own men. He had been, with his staff, reconnoitering, when, on returning, a regiment of his command, mistaking the general and his companions for a party of the foe, fired upon them, killing one or two on the spot, and so severely wounding their beloved commander that he died soon afterwards. No words can possibly convey the anguish and mourning that followed, not merely among his own soldiers, but everywhere. General Lee, on hearing that he was wounded, immediately addressed him a note, as follows:

"General: I have just received your note, informing me that you are wounded. I cannot express my regret at the occurrence. Could I have directed events, I should have chosen, for the good of the country, to have been disabled in your stead. I congratulate you upon the victory which is due to your skill and energy." And, when it was known that he was dead, a general order was issued by Lee, expressive of the

great grief felt, and eulogizing the departed hero in the highest terms.

General A. P. Hill now took command of the Confederate left, but soon afterwards was himself wounded, and obliged to relinquish it to General Rodes, who yielded it to General G. H. Stuart, on his arrival. The latter renewed the fight, and compelled the enemy's right wholly to give way.

Sunday morning the battle still raged, and with increased fury. In every direction the Union forces were made to retreat, and at one time it was thought by the Confederate army, that Hooker's was certain of entire capture, so completely did they seem hemmed in. But this was not so. General Lee soon perceived that the enemy were still in force, toward the river, and, moreover, heard that Sedgwick was advancing on his rear, from where he had crossed below Fredericksburg. This movement necessarily compelled Lee to turn and meet the new foe, who had succeeded in temporarily defeating the force, left at the lower crossing, under Early and Barksdale. Accordingly the divisions of Anderson and McLaws were sent back towards Fredericksburg, to check Sedgwick's advance. This was successfully done, not, however, without great loss to both parties, and, finally, night coming on, the conflict was for a short time closed.

The enemy, however, was not yet defeated. The same unconquerable spirit, and the same fierce bravery, which belonged to Lee's impetuous soldiers, was possessed also by Hooker's men, and every inch of ground was pertinaciously resisted. That the Union troops had made a mistake in strategy, or in maturing their plans, was sad, but it was no reason they should give way without a great struggle; and, therefore, during the night the Federals, on Hooker's extreme left, massed a heavy force against McLaws. Anderson moved rapidly to his support, and during the day, Monday the 4th, General Lee arrived, having secured the advantage he had gained in Hooker's front. About 4 P. M., the battle was renewed here with impetuous fury, and in a short time Lee's forces succeeded in driving back the enemy, and, finally, compelling them to cross the Rappahannock with great slaughter. There still now remained, however, the principal part of Hooker's army, on the south side of the river, at the United

States ford. No time, therefore, could be lost. One half of the enemy defeated and effectually forced back, there was yet the rest to conquer, and conquer them he must, at once, if possible. Accordingly, Anderson and McLaws were ordered back to Chancellorsville and the ford. But the weather now changed, a storm of wind and rain set in, continuing, without cessation, until Wednesday forenoon, and during this time Hooker recrossed the river, "leaving the dead on the battle-field unburied," and, owing to "the rapid rise of the river," unmolested from General Lee, who was thus unable to follow him. Even the wounded belonging to the Union army were left behind, under charge of the medical director, Dr. Luckley, and not until a week afterwards, May 12th, were they able, some 1,200 in number, to be returned to their own camp. They were, however, as kindly treated as possible, by General Lee, considering his already straitened means, and he even sent a flag of truce to General Hooker for supplies for them, stating that his own medicines and hospital stores were exhausted.

The two armies now re-established themselves in their old positions, remaining inactive for some little time; but the effect of the late week's battles was of even more importance than perhaps appeared. It proved the undoubted superiority of generalship on the part of Lee and his officers, while it also contributed greatly to strengthen the moral power and prestige of the South. Indeed, this was fairly and honorably admitted by several of the Northern journals when commenting on the battle, and, in speaking of the defeat the Union forces had received, it was said, "We had men enough, well enough equipped, and well enough posted to have devoured the ragged, imperfectly armed and equipped host of our enemies from off the face of the earth. Their artillery horses were poor, starved frames of beasts, tied on to their carriages and caissons with odds and ends of rope and strips of raw hide. . . . . . And yet they have beaten us fairly, beaten us all to pieces, beaten us so easily that we are objects of contempt even to their commonest private soldiers, with no shirts to hang out of the holes in their pantaloons, and cartridge-boxes tied round their waists with strands of rope."

On the 7th of May, General Lee issued an address to his army, congratulating his officers and men for "the heroic

conduct they had displayed under trying vicissitudes of heat and storm, in a tangled wilderness, and again on the hills of Fredericksburg," and inviting them to unite on the following Sunday "in ascribing to the Lord of Hosts the glory due his name." At the same time, a letter from President Davis was read, wherein he said to General Lee: "In the name of the people, I offer my cordial thanks to you and the troops under your command, for this addition to the unprecedented series of great victories which your army has achieved. The universal rejoicing produced by this happy result, will be mingled with a general regret for the good and the brave who are numbered among the killed and the wounded."

It might be supposed after this, that General Lee's mind would have been quietly resting awhile; but not so. Like his father, "Light Horse Harry," he was determined to follow up every advantage where, by so doing, an object of importance could be gained. That object, especially dear to himself and to every Virginian in his army, as well as necessary to the South, was to compel the Union forces to evacuate the State and fall back on their own Federal soil. Accordingly, various cavalry reconnoissances were made along the Rapidan, and, finally, Ewell, who had succeeded to Jackson's command, was rapidly marched across the Blue Ridge Mountains, by way of Front Royal, into the Shenandoah Valley, upon Winchester. There he quickly defeated General Milroy, and then promptly moved up to the Potomac, where he occupied all the fords.

Meanwhile certain movements in Lee's army, at Fredericksburg, led General Hooker to suppose that some of the Confederate forces had been withdrawn ; and, accordingly, on the 5th of June a strong reconnoissance was sent across the river on Lee's right. Some skirmishing ensued, but Lee's strategy was again displayed by masking his real strength, and by an appearance of greater means than he actually had, leading his enemy to suppose his entire army was still there.

At this time, the beginning of June, the Confederate Army had been completely reorganized, and filled up, and it was intended by Lee, in conjunction with the authorities at Richmond, once more to attempt a blow on the enemy, within their own States. For this purpose, on the 3d of June, a part of the

army left Fredericksburg for Culpepper Court-house, and, after
the Federal reconnoissance of the 5th, was joined, on the 8th,
by Longstreet and Ewell,—the cavalry under General Stuart
also being concentrated there. On the following day an at
tack was made by the Union cavalry, on this force of Stuart's.
A severe engagement ensued, and continued until late in the
afternoon, when the enemy was forced to retire, leaving nearly
four hundred prisoners behind.

Lee having evacuated Fredericksburg, now marched rapidly
forward in pursuance of his plans, while Hooker, withdrawing from the line of the Rappahannock, took up a strong position at Manassas and Centreville, so as to interpose his army
between the Confederate forces and Washington. But in the
mean time Lee had pushed on the rest of his forces, and merely
so played with the enemy as to mislead him entirely. Indeed,
so well was this done, that an impression began to prevail in
the North, that all fear of an invasion into Pennsylvania might
be cast aside, and the Governor of New Jersey went so far in
this feeling of confidence, that his troops were recalled. Lee,
however, was even then well on his way. Hooker had followed
him to the passes of the Blue ridge, but was so uncertain
whether he meant to give battle there or move up the valley,
that time was lost, and instead of bringing the point to an
issue at once in Virginia, the Federal commander had to hastily
cross the Potomac, and take position in Maryland. There he
was in hopes that Lee would give him battle, but again was
disappointed; for that able general had, after a skirmish between the cavalry of Stuart and Pleasanton, promptly followed
his advanced forces up the Shenandoah, and on the 24th of
June crossed the Potomac, in the vicinity of Shepherdstown.
The corps of General Ewell had preceded Lee two days before,
and on the 23d had occupied Chambersburg, where a most
praiseworthy order was issued against the sale or use of intoxicating liquors in his army without permission of a Major-
general. Lee himself, immediately after his arrival, issued
very stringent orders against "unnecessary or wanton injury
to private property," and enjoined upon his officers "to arrest,
and bring to punishment all who shall in any way offend."
Indeed his whole order on this subject is most praiseworthy,
and truly Christian in spirit.

On the 27th of June, the whole of Lee's army was at Chambersburg   Preparations had been made to advance on Harris burg, but the design was abandoned on the 29th, in consequence of information that the Federal army was moving northwards, and so menacing the communications of the Confederate army with the Potomac.   To check the Federal advance, therefore, Generals Longstreet, Hill, and Ewell were ordered to proceed to Gettysburg.   But, before we give any particulars of the battle that here followed, let us again, for a moment or two, speak of General Lee himself, not forgetting that since the sixth of June, and thus within twenty days, he had brought his entire army from Fredericksburg, by the way of the Shenandoah Valley, to Gettysburg, in Pennsylvania, without obstruction.   This, as has been justly said, will rank with some of the most remarkable marches on record, even though others have been performed by brave and enduring men, under Sherman, Rosecrans, Blunt, Grant, and other eminent leaders, not omitting the extraordinary and hazardous retreat with Hunter, across and along the mountains in Southwest Virginia.   But, when Lee set out upon this northern expedition, he was confronted by one of the largest and best-appointed armies the enemy ever had on the field.   Winchester, Martinsburg, Harper's Ferry, and Berryville were garrisoned by hostile forces, and the Union cavalry were in splendid condition.   Yet, General Lee marched along the Rappahannock, over the passes of the Blue Ridge mountains, up the Shenandoah Valley, and across the fords of the Potomac, into Pennsylvania, without his progress being arrested.

At this time, General Lee was in every respect a most popular man, and deservedly so.   Even his opponents, with some few partisan exceptions, gave him that honorable meed of praise which was his due.   Bearing in mind that he was a Virginian, and had forsaken a splendid home and rich estate in defence of what *he* considered to be the just cause, only one opinion as to the disinterestedness and integrity of his motives could be given, though the wisdom of his course may certainly be much questioned.   His personal character was also above reproach ; and, as we have shown, even in his military operations, every possible forbearance and kindly disposition was evinced by him towards a foe.   A foreign writer, in speak-

ing of him at this date, says : "General Lee is, almost with
out exception, the handsomest man of his age I ever saw. He
is fifty-six years old, tall, broadshouldered, very well made,
well set up—a thorough soldier in appearance—and his manners are most courteous, and full of dignity. He is a perfect
gentleman in every respect. I imagine no man has so few
enemies, or is so universally esteemed. Throughout the South
all agree in pronouncing him as near perfection as a man can
be. He has none of the small vices, such as smoking, drink-
ing, chewing, or swearing ; and his bitterest enemy never accused him of any of the greater ones. He generally wears a
well-worn, long, gray jacket, a high, black felt hat, and blue
trowsers, tucked into his Wellington boots. I never saw him
carry arms ; and the only marks of his military rank are the
three stars on his collar. He rides a handsome horse, which
is extremely well groomed. He himself is very neat in his
dress and person ; and in the most arduous marches he always
looks smart and clean."

The same writer adds, that he understood Lee never to have
slept in a house since commanding the Virginia army, and he
had invariably declined all offers of hospitality, fearing that the
person offering it might afterwards get into trouble on account
of having sheltered him. In fact, whatever may be the ideas
of persons interested on either side of the war as to its conduct
and that of its leaders, no one of honest impartiality can deny
to General Lee the credit of being a perfect Christian gentleman, a brave, skilful soldier, and a thoroughly unambitious,
unselfish man. And thus, under such a leader, united with
subordinate chiefs of similar virtues, and all devoted to the
cause in which they had embarked, did the Confederate army
march to the battlefield of Gettysburg.

On the 26th of June, General Lee encamped on the turn-
pike-road, three quarters of a mile from the town of Gettysburg, and so particular was he as regards any thing that might
seem to press harshly upon the inhabitants around, that he was
very chary of giving passes, even to officers of rank, to visit
Chambersburg, or elsewhere. No private houses were allowed to be entered on any pretence whatever, not even to
procure rations for the troops ; and the stringent order already
mentioned, was issued by him against all manner of retaliation

This order was tolerably well received by his troops, but, in such a large army, where so many bad characters are sure to be found, it was, as is always the case, impossible to prevent instances of plunder and pillage. This is true of both sides in the war, and should be fairly admitted when speaking of ruin and devastation, either by the North or the South; and no doubt it is equally true, as it assuredly is of Lee, that other generals, in common with him, not only used every effort to protect private property and non-combatants, but also severely punished delinquents when guilty of any breach of this command.

On the 1st of July, Hill's division, joined afterwards by Ewell's during the engagement, came up with the Federals, who were driven through Gettysburg with heavy loss. The Federals retreated to a high range of hills, and the attack was not pressed that afternoon, as the Confederates did not know the force of the enemy. General Lee, in his report, says: "It had not been intended to fight a general battle at such distance from our base, unless attacked by the enemy; but finding ourselves unexpectedly confronted by the Federal army, it became a matter of difficulty to withdraw through the mountains with our large trains. At the same time the country was unfavorable for collecting supplies, while in the presence of the enemy's main body, as he was enabled to restrain our foraging parties by occupying the passes of the mountains with regular and local troops. A battle thus became, in a measure, unavoidable. Encouraged by the successful issue of the first day, and in view of the valuable results which would ensue from the defeat of the army of General Meade,* it was thought advisable to renew the attack.

"On the following day, about two in the afternoon, the Federal position was again assaulted. Unfortunately, on the previous day, when the enemy were driven through Gettysburg, they had obtained possession of the high range of hills south and east of the town, and were so posted as to make its position almost impregnable.

"The town of Gettysburg is situated upon the northern slope of this ridge of hills or mountain range, and about one

---

* Hooker had been relieved at his own request, and Meade appointed.

and a half or two miles from its summit. The western slope
of this range was in cultivation, except small patches where
the mountain-side is so precipitous as to defy the efforts of the
farmer to bring it into subjection to the ploughshare. At the
foot of the mountain is a narrow valley, from a mile to two
miles wide, broken in small ridges running parallel with the
mountains. On the western side of the valley rises a long
high hill, mostly covered with heavy timber, but greatly inferior in altitude to the mountain range upon which the enemy
had taken position, only running nearly parallel with it. The
valley between this ridge and the mountain was in cultivation,
and the fields were yellow with golden harvest. About four
or five miles south of Gettysburg, the mountain rises abruptly
to an altitude of several hundred feet. Upon this the enemy
rested his left flank, his right being upon the crest of the range
near Gettysburg.

" The Confederate line of battle was formed along the western
slope of the second and inferior range described above, and in
the following order,—Ewell's corps on the left, beginning at
the town with Early's division, then Rodes' division ; on the
right of Rodes' was the left of Hill's corps, commencing
with Heth's, then Pender's, and Anderson's divisions. On
the right of Anderson was Longstreet's left—McLaw's being next to Anderson, and Hood on the extreme right of
the line, which was opposite the enemy's left on the highest
eminence."

It was not until the afternoon that the attack again commenced. General Lee gave the orders for Longstreet to begin,
and then, in quick succession, the other divisions to follow
him. This was done. Longstreet was gallantly met by General Sickles who, for two hours, stood firm against the assault,
and then fell back, but, the wavering line having been reinforced from Meade's centre, the Confederates were repulsed in
that quarter with great loss. The divisions of McLaws and
Anderson attacked the centre of Meade, and fought with terrific fury, but after again and again charging up the steep
sides of the hills on which the enemy were posted, they, also,
had to retire. On the Confederate left, Ewell had made an
attack upon the high ground before him, and General G. H.
Stewart achieved some success, but, here again, the enemy

came forward with reinforcements, and finally compelled him to retire. Thus, in this day's fight, the advantage was decidedly in favor of the North.

Meanwhile, and directly the firing began, General Lee had joined Hill just below a tree, and remained there nearly all the time looking through his field-glass, sometimes talking to Hill, and sometimes to Colonel Long, of his staff. But generally he sat quite alone, on the stump of a tree; and during the whole time the firing continued he sent only one message, and received only one report. It was evidently his system to arrange the plan thoroughly with the three corps commanders, and then leave to them the duty of modifying and carrying it out to the best of their abilities.

Soon after 7 P. M. the following report came to General Lee by signal from Longstreet, "We are doing well," and a little before dark the firing dropped off in every direction, and soon ceased altogether. Intelligence then came that Longstreet had carried every thing before him for some time, capturing several batteries and driving the enemy from his positions. But when Hill's Florida brigade and some other troops gave way, he was forced to abandon a small portion of the ground he had won, together with all the captured guns except three. His troops, however, bivouacked during the night on ground occupied by the enemy in the earlier part of the day.

By 6 o'clock next morning (July 3d) General Lee was again in the saddle, and, with Longstreet and his staff, commenced reconnoitering and making preparations for renewing the attack. As they rode along, and being rather a large party, they often drew upon themselves the attention of the hostile sharpshooters, and were two or three times favored with a shell. One of these shells set a brick building on fire which was situated between the lines. This building was filled with wounded, principally Union men, who thus must have perished miserably in the flames. As General Lee rode along, some of the dead were being buried, but great numbers were still lying about, also many mortally wounded, for whom nothing could be done. Amongst the latter were several of the Union troops dressed in the Zouave costume, and these opened their glazed eyes upon the Confederate general in a painful, imploring manner. Alas! with all his desire to abate their present suffering,

he could do nothing then. His mind, and all his faculties were engrossed by the important considerations involved in the next movement he should make.

During the morning of this eventful day—a day that was to decide the great battle—"one of the most terrific combats of modern times, in which more than two hundred cannon were belching forth their thunders at one time, and nearly 200,000 muskets were being discharged as rapidly as men, hurried with excitement and passion, could load them," the fighting was renewed on the Confederate left, and during this time General Lee ascended the College cupola in Gettysburg to reconnoitre. The issue was, perhaps, even then apparent to him; but no steps to alter previous plans were deemed necessary. At 11 A. M. there was a general cessation of firing, and for about two hours all was quiet. It was, however, merely that calm which is well known to precede the fierce hurricane in nature's storms. At a given signal, the shrill sound of a Whitworth gun broke the ominous silence, and then commenced a cannonading absolutely appalling, and certainly beyond the power of pen adequately to describe. One writer, who was in the Confederate army, says, "The air was hideous with most discordant noise. The very earth shook beneath our feet, and the hills and rocks seemed to reel like a drunken man. For one hour and a half this most terrific fire was continued, during which time the shrieking of shell, the crash of falling timbers, the fragments of rocks flying through the air, shattered from the cliffs by solid shot, the heavy mutterings from the valley between the opposing armies, the splash of bursting shrapnel, and the fierce neighing of wounded artillery horses, made a picture terribly grand and sublime."

But the day was not for the South. The most daring deeds, and the most earnest resolution could not gain the victory over the North at Gettysburg. Men fought on both sides with bravery, perhaps never surpassed, and the record of that three days' battle must ever arouse a thrill of admiration and astonishment.

In his report, General Lee says, " Our troops succeeded in entering the advanced works of the enemy, and getting possession of some of his batteries; but our artillery having nearly expended its ammunition, the attacking columns became ex-

posed to the heavy fire of the numerous batteries near the summit of the ridge, and after a most determined and gallant struggle were compelled to relinquish their advantage and fa'\l back to their original positions with severe loss."

Still the Confederate forces struggled on; and, during one period, when the Federal General Howard slackened the fire of his guns to allow them to cool, it was determined to make one more desperate attack, a storming party rushed forward without a moment's hesitation. The division of General Pickett, which had arrived since the previous day, led the advance supported on the right by Wilcox's brigade of Anderson's division, and on the left by Heth's division, commanded by General Pettigrew. These latter, however, being mostly raw soldiers, wavered; but Pickett's Virginians pressed forward under a terrible fire of grape, shell and canister from forty guns opened upon them. On they pressed, crossing the Emmitsburg road, and steadily approaching the masses of Federal infantry. Hundreds of them go down under the murderous fire, and still they falter not, but—up to the enemy's rifle pits they rush—over them they go, and then with a wild yell dash up to the very muzzle of the terrible guns belching forth flame and destruction upon them. Vain! vain! They are now unsupported. Pettigrew's line has been broken, and his men fly panic-stricken to the rear. The brave general, himself, is wounded, but still retained command, and strives to rally his men. But they heed him not, and he is left alone, while Pickett and his brave Virginians contend as best they can against the fearful odds opposed to them. Presently relief approaches. General Lee sends Wright's brigade to their support, and, finally, the remnant of them effects a retreat.

It was now that General Lee showed some of those admirable qualities, for which he was so noted and esteemed. Forgetful of himself, he rode about, quite alone, in front of the wood, rallying and encouraging the broken troops, the whole of his staff being engaged in a similar manner further to the rear. His cheerful and placid face displayed no signs of the slightest disappointment, care, or annoyance; and to the soldiers he met, some words of encouragement were addressed. To one he would say, "All this will come right in the end; we'll talk it over afterwards; but, in the mean time, all good

men must rally. We want all true men just now." To
another, he would speak in similar terms; and, to the slightly
wounded, words of exhortation were used for them to bind up
their hurts and take a musket again in the emergency. And
very few failed to answer his appeal, many even of the badly
wounded taking off their hats to cheer him. To a foreign
military officer of rank, who had come to witness the battle,
he said : "This has been a sad day for us, Colonel—a sad
day; but we can't expect always to gain victories," and, at
the same time, seeing this gentleman somewhat exposed,
advised him to get into a more sheltered position.

Notwithstanding the misfortune which had so suddenly be-
fallen him, General Lee seemed to observe everything, however
trivial. When a mounted officer began to ill treat his horse
for shying at the bursting of a shell, he called out, " Don't
whip him, Captain; dont whip him. I've got just such another
foolish horse myself, and whipping does no good."

There was a man lying flat on his face, in a small ditch,
groaning dismally; General Lee's attention was drawn to him,
and he at once appealed to the man's patriotism to arouse
himself, but finding such to be of no avail, he had him ignominiously set on his legs, by some neighboring gunners.

General Wilcox now came up to him, and, in very depressed
tones of annoyance and vexation, explained the state of his
brigade. But General Lee immediately shook hands with
him, and said, in a cheerful manner, " Never mind, General.
All this has been my fault. It is I that have lost this fight,
and you must help me out of it the best way you can." In
this manner did General Lee, wholly ignoring self and position,
encourage and reanimate his somewhat dispirited troops, and
magnanimously take upon his own shoulders the whole weight
of the repulse. "It was impossible," says the writer already
quoted, " to look at him, or to listen to him, without feeling
the strongest admiration, and I never saw any man fail him,
except the man in the ditch."

It is difficult to exaggerate the critical state of affairs as they
appeared about this time. General Lee and his officers were
fully impressed with a sense of the situation; yet there was
much less noise, fuss, or confusion of orders, than at any ordinary field day. The men, as they were rallied in the wood,

were brought up in detachments, and lay down quiet and coolly in the positions assigned them.

The result of this day's fight convinced General Lee tha the Federal position was impregnable, and his ammunition being nearly exhausted, offensive operations could not be resumed, even had it been desirable. On the following day, with rain falling in torrents, both armies were occupied in burying their dead ; and, at night, Lee retired with the whole of his troops and prisoners, except the wounded. The march, however, was so slow, owing to the storm, that not until after daylight of the 5th, had his rear column left Gettysburg ; yet no important effort was made to impede him. On Monday, the 6th, Lee arrived at Hagerstown, and on the following day the advance of Meade was at Funktown, six miles south of that place. Meanwhile, General Couch, in command of the department, had immediately sent forward General W. F. Smith, in command of the militia that had been called out from the several States, and directed a pursuit of the Confederate army. At Carlisle, General Smith was met by General W. H. F. Lee, who had there expected to find Ewell. Lee retired, and Smith now joined his raw troops to those of Meade ; but, by this time General Lee had reached the Potomac at Williamsport, ready to cross. Here a difficulty awaited him. "The Potomac," he says, "was so much swollen by the rains that had fallen almost incessantly since our entrance into Maryland, as to be unfordable. Our communications with the south side were thus interrupted, and it was difficult to procure either ammunition or subsistence ; the latter difficulty being enhanced by the high waters impeding the working of neighboring mills. The trains with the wounded and prisoners were compelled to await, at Williamsport, the subsiding of the river, and the construction of boats, as the pontoon bridge left at Falling Waters had been partially destroyed. The enemy had not yet made his appearunce, but as he was in a condition to obtain large reinforcements, and our situation, for the reasons above mentioned, was becoming daily more embarrassing, it was deemed advisable to recross the river. Part of the pontoon bridge was recovered, and new boats built, so that by the 13th, a good bridge was thrown over the river at Falling Waters."

Lee crossed over in face of the enemy (who had arrived on the 12th, and taken up position) " with no loss of material, except a few disabled wagons and two pieces of artillery, which the horses were unable to move through the deep mud. Before fresh horses could be sent for them, the rear of the column had passed."

Before finally retreating from Maryland, General Lee, on the 11th of July, issued an address to his army, acknowledging the gallantry and devotion of his troops, and concludes his modest report with a few words of kindly remembrance of the " brave officers and patriotic gentlemen who fell in the faithful discharge of their duty, leaving the army to mourn their loss and emulate their noble examples."

General Meade ordered a pursuit of Lee, and, at the Falling Waters, an encounter took place, which was the cause of some official correspondence on the part of both generals. The Federal commander stated that he had captured a brigade of infantry, besides the two pieces of artillery, etc., already mentioned ; and to this General Lee replied at some length in a denial. He says that " the enemy did not capture any organized body of men on that occasion, but only stragglers and such as were left asleep on the road, exhausted by the fatigue and exposure of one of the most inclement nights known at that season of the year. It rained without cessation, . . . and the last of the troops did not cross the river at the bridge till 1 A. M. of the 14th. While the column was thus detained on the road, a number of men, worn down with fatigue, laid down in barns and by the roadside, and though officers were sent back to arouse them as the troops moved on, the darkness and rain prevented them from finding all, and many were in this way left behind. . . . . . No arms, cannon, or prisoners were taken by the enemy in battle, but only such as were left behind, as I have described under the circumstances."

To this reply, General Meade, in an official letter to General Halleck, responds by reiterating his former statement, and inclosing the report of General Kilpatrick, who commanded the cavalry on the occasion. From this report, it would seem that General Lee had been misinformed as to the affair.

We have mentioned the preceding, because it not only belongs to matters connected with General Lee's personal

history, but because it shows, very strikingly, the condition and hardships of the soldiers (on both sides alike) during the war, although what is here narrated is but trifling, compared with what has been endured at other times.

The pursuit of Lee was resumed by a flank movement of the Federal army, crossing the Potomac at Berlin and moving down the Loudon Valley. The cavalry were pushed into several passes of the Blue Ridge mountains, but despite all efforts of the Union forces, General Lee succeeded in once more establishing his men on the Rapidan, while General Meade took position on the Rappahannock, and thus terminated the campaign.

CHAPTER VI.

Position of the two Armies.—General Meade's Order.—Grand Review of the Confederate Army.—Longstreet sent to reinforce Bragg.—Lee's sudden Flanking of Meade.—Minor Operations of the Army.—Imboden.—Fitzhugh Lee.—General Stuart.—Meade's Attack on Ewell.—Lee visits Richmond.—Question of Ranking Officer. —Bragg as Military Adviser.—Condition of the Confederate Army.—Religion in the Camp.—Amusements.—Thanks of Confederate Congress to Lee and his Army.—General Custer's Raid.—Position of Lee's Forces.—Reinforced by Longstreet.—Day of Fast.—Commencement of a New Campaign.—Grand Advance of the Northern Army.—General Ulysses Grant.—Battle of the Wilderness.—Heroic Achievements. —Spottsylvania.—Grant Crosses the Pamunkey.

THE pursuit of Lee by General Meade had been as follows: On the 18th of July the latter moved across the Potomac; on the 19th he was at Lovettsville; on the 20th and 21st at Union; on the 22d at Upperville; on the 23d at Markham station; on the 24th at Salem, and on the 25th at Warrenton, with the army occupying the same line which it did two months previous.

On the 30th of July, General Meade issued an order of a very stringent character, concerning "numerous depredations committed by citizens, or rebel soldiers in disguise harbored or concealed by citizens along the Orange and Alexandria railroad," within his lines, and threatened not only severe punishment to offenders, if caught, but held the "people within ten miles of the railroad responsible in their persons and property" for any injury done.

During General Lee's advance into Pennsylvania, some correspondence had taken place between him and President Davis on the subject of reinforcements, and the latter intimated that there was some doubt as to whether the capital might not be left too defenceless, owing to certain movements of the enemy again on the peninsula. From this, it appears that General Lee must have felt some difficulty about staying long across the Potomac, lest Richmond should be endangered while his army was at too great a distance to go quickly to its rescue.

True, there were other forces, and other commanders, but they were all much occupied elsewhere, and it was mainly upon the army of Virginia that the Confederate authorities at the capital had to depend.

That there was some cause for doubt may be seen from the fact that General Dix, then in command at Fort Monroe, had made a diversion towards Richmond, and also to threaten the communications of Lee, and while thus occupied, Tunstall's station was seized, and Brigadier-general W. F. Lee—one of the general's sons—was captured. The return, however, of the army from across the Potomac to its old quarters on the Rapidan, relieved the public mind, South, and again cleared the peninsula.

It was now necessary for a time that some rest should be obtained to recruit the army, and prepare for future work. Consequently a short period of relaxation followed, and furloughs were granted to the men. The system adopted by General Lee, with regard to these furloughs, was very good. His order on the subject stated that, for the purpose of allowing " as many of the brave soldiers to visit their families and friends as can be done consistently with the service, and at the same time give some reward for meritorious conduct, a system of furloughs is instituted in the army." First, two for every one hundred men present for duty, and afterwards at the rate of one in a hundred. Commanders were to forward urgent and meritorious cases for approval, and the time of leave varied, according to the State, from fifteen days in Virginia to thirty days in Louisiana.

On September 9th, General Lee held a grand review of his army, at which were present Generals Ewell, Longstreet, Hill, Stuart, Wilcox and others of note. The condition of the troops was excellent, and the only fault the strictest disciplinarian could find was the irrepressible manifestations of affection for the generals. The number of troops reviewed is not stated, but it must have been considerable, for in passing along the lines and returning, the various generals had to gallop over nine miles.

About this time affairs in the western departments led to a withdrawal of Longstreet's portion of the Virginian army, for the purpose of reinforcing Bragg. At first, it had been sup-

posed at Washington, that Lee was receiving more reinforcements; but on the 14th of September General Meade reported
that, in his opinion, and from all that he had learned, Lee had
been reduced in his forces by Longstreet's withdrawal, and by
some regiments from Ewell and Hill.   To meet this additional
force in the west, the North dispatched General Hooker, with
nearly two corps from Meade's army, to reinforce Rosecrans
in Tennessee.   Thus the two armies in Virginia still confronted
each other with about the same comparative numbers. A period
of total inaction, except occasional skirmishes, seemed to have
settled on both parties.   The Federals were in a good position,
and the North clamorous for another onward movement, but
none took place.   Neither did it appear that General Lee felt
inclined to take the initiative in a fresh struggle.   In fact, a
sort of lethargy had apparently fallen upon all, and in the
beginning of October so much quiet reigned, that people both
in the North and South began to wonder and to speak aloud
in murmuring tones.

Suddenly, however, unexpectedly, and in a marvellous, un-
intelligible way, it was reported that General Lee and his army
had flanked Meade, and was several miles in his rear, between
him and Washington.   Then came alarm and dismay. A
hasty retrograde movement of the Northern army; an ineffectual attempt to check the Confederate advance; a severe
engagement with the rear guard; affrighted sutlers, and panic-
stricken teamsters pouring in throngs along the roads to Washington; provisions and *matériel*, worth hundreds of thousands
of dollars, given to the flames, are the primary results of Lee's
new and masterly strategy.   Finally, the Northern army,
jaded with a week's incessant marching, disheartened by an
instinctive sense of the enemy's superior strategy, takes up a
position on the old ground again.   And thus it was, as we have
already stated, Lee had posted his army on the line of the
Rapidan, with his right wing at Fredericksburg, and his left
near the Orange Court-house, while the Northern forces occupied the banks of the Rappahannock.   On the 8th and 9th of
October Lee suddenly dispatched a portion of his troops
towards Madison Court-house, and by circuitous and concealed
roads, contrived to get up near Culpepper without notice of the
enemy.   Lee himself with the bulk of his army, except a show

ot force, under General Fitzhugh Lee, left in his old lines, swiftly followed, and on the 11th was at Culpepper, where he found Meade had retreated along the line of railroad running to Alexandria. Lee immediately pursued, having now been joined by the commands of Stuart and Fitzhugh Lee, who had repulsed Buford's attack on the remaining force of the Confederates at the Rapidan, and driven him back to his main army. On the 11th Lee arrived on the Rappahannock, at Warrenton Springs, after a skirmish with the Federal cavalry at Jefferston. The next day, after a short march to Warrenton, where the whole army was reunited, a halt was made to supply the troops with provisions. On Thursday, the 14th, Lee again pushed on in two columns, and by different roads, towards Bristoe station, where the rear guard of General Meade, under General Warren, was attacked by the advance of General Hill. A sharp fight ensued, ending in the repulse of Hill, with considerable loss, before Lee could send to his assistance. The advance thus checked, and Meade, having retreated to the old battlefields around Bull Run and Centreville, which he was strongly fortifying, it was deemed unwise by General Lee to continue the pursuit any further, especially as the intrenchments around Washington and Alexandria would render abortive any success that might attend efforts to turn Meade's new position. Accordingly, after destroying the railroad from Cub Run southwardly, Lee, on the 18th, returned to the line of the Rappahannock, leaving his cavalry in front of Meade. Next day this force was attacked, and compelled to retire, until General Fitzhugh Lee arriving, a severe action followed, and the Confederates advanced nearly to Haymarket and Gainesville. There Meade's infantry were met, and Fitzhugh Lee fell back unpursued.

While this flank movement and advance of Lee's was taking place, directions had been sent to General Imboden, of the Confederate forces, in the Shenandoah, to guard the passes of the mountains on Lee's left. This was done in a most admirable manner, and was then swiftly followed by the capture of Charlestown in West Virginia, by that gallant officer, on the 18th of October. The Union forces stationed there, consisting of the Ninth Maryland regiment, and three companies of cavalry, with their stores and transportation, were nearly all made

captive. But, on a strong Federal force appearing from Harper's Ferry, Imboden had to retreat. .

General Lee had placed his troops again in position, on both sides of the railway, upon the line of the Rappahannock, with Ewell on the right, Hill upon the left, and the cavalry protecting each flank. It was fully expected that Meade would advance upon the Confederate forces as soon as he could, and this was seen to be the case on November 6th, when, having repaired the broken railroad, he came in force upon Lee's army at Rappahannock station and Kelly's ford. An engagement followed, which was continued after dark, and resulted in the Confederates being defeated with great loss. General Lee then fell back to Culpepper, but finding that position untenable, he once more retired to his old lines on the Rapidan. There, on the 27th of November, Meade again advanced upon the Confederates at Germania ford. General Edward Johnson, of Ewell's corps, with his division, was in advance, and the two armies came into collision about a mile and a half from the river, and near the plank-road, noted in the battle of Chancellorsville. A desperate conflict ensued, which was maintained on both sides with great obstinacy, until night caused a cessation of the fight. The engagement was not again renewed; but Meade withdrew next day from the front, and reoccupied his post about Brandy station, on the Orange and Alexandria railroad. This virtually ended the campaign for that year. With the exception of some skirmishes, and a slight engagement on the road to Orange Court-house, nothing more was done by the two armies.. The Union forces went into winter quarters on the line of the Rappahannock about the 6th of December, and the Confederate army did the same on the Rapidan.

Soon afterwards General Lee made a visit of some length, to Richmond, which was, no doubt, necessary to give himself some change, and to see his family; but it was also for the purpose of assisting in certain war-councils, especially with regard to new appointments in the military departments. General Bragg had been relieved from his command in the West, and was intended for the post of "consulting or advising officer" to the Executive—in other words, virtually commander-in-chief of the Southern armies—while General Lee was to keep the

field in Virginia; but many difficulties were in the way of such an arrangement, though Bragg was not only the ranking general, his friends claimed for him far greater merits than the public generally acknowledged. General Lee, as he had invariably done, was ready to relinquish self to the service of his country; but, naturally, his old classmate, friend, and former companion, J. E. Johnston, had his warmest recommendations in the matter of new appointments. The difficulty arose thus: Generals Cooper, A. S. Johnson, Lee, Beauregard, and J. E. Johnston had been appointed under the provisional government, in 1861. When A. S. Johnson fell at Shiloh, in 1862, after the organization of the permanent government, Bragg was appointed to the vacancy, and this was at once confirmed by Congress. The appointments of Cooper, Lee, and the others, were also confirmed by the same Congress, but *subsequently* to that of Bragg, therefore he was considered, in reality, the senior general. The matter was however settled, at this time, by Bragg's appointment at Richmond, and Generals Lee and Johnston keeping their important positions in the field.

There were many other causes tending to much anxiety in the mind of General Lee. His brave army had been subject to great depletion, and was suffering from those accursed evils, which, even more than the battlefield itself, belong to war, and help to destroy lives to a greater extent than the cannon-ball and rifle-shot. Richmond was no more exempt from this than any other capital, where a market is made by hordes of base contractors, who seize the opportunity of a nation's hour of peril to gorge themselves with golden spoils. The honorable and just-dealing man, who fairly turns his goods to ordinary profit at such times, can make no headway in such a greedy crowd, and consequently has but faint conception of the frightful and inhuman wrongs heaped upon the heroic soldiers bleeding for their country's weal. Well may a famous general in the Napoleon wars have expressed a wish that the whole class of fraudulent contractors had but one neck, that he could have the pleasure of hanging them at once with a single rope; for, if ever men deserve to be strangled or guillotined those do who thus take advantage of their country's need, and recklessly plunder government and soldier alike, by the vile supplies they cunningly substitute for the good samples speciously

submitted to inspection. Again, these same men, and their innumerable hangers-on, are too comfortable at home to risk their precious lives on the camp-ground, in the maintenance of that cause they, on both sides, talk so much about as a good and righteous one. The consequence is, that when inaction among the ranks of the army occurs, and, especially when cold and hunger—arising from short rations and ill-made garments—are felt, desertions, repinings, apathy, and general discontent, are sure to be found. The subordinate officers, even those of higher grade, experience this, and the generals in command have, in such, far more to contend with than the greatest difficulties connected with strategic movements or a battlefield.

In the case of the Northern army of Virginia there was, about the winter of 1863–4, much of this for General Lee to contend with. The line officers, it was said, who had marched many weary miles with their men, and had cheerfully borne all ordinary privations and want, bitterly felt the contrast between themselves and the shirkers who staid at home, speculating upon the miseries of citizens and soldiers alike. The consequence was that desertions were not unfrequent, and the commander-in-chief had to use all his own personal popularity in procuring fresh men to fill the ranks. Every thing he could possibly do to promote the welfare and comfort of his troops, it was universally admitted he did, and his example, not only in this respect, but by being constantly with them for so long a time, sharing their privations and often shelterless bivouacs, was of immense benefit. "He was truly the soldiers' idol, not merely on account of his great genius, but—like the first Napoleon—he ever studied the wants of his private soldiers, and personally looked into their supplies." Yet, what could he, what can any human being do, especially one of mind, of talent and masterly ability in great things, adequately to oppose the mean and contemptible trickery of little souls backed by the gold they have so avariciously contrived to make? Absolutely nothing! And, when the calm future arrives in the yet unconceived history of the great and mighty people such as *must* exist on this continent, the eye will look with amazement on the prolongation of this sad struggle, and truth will then admit, it was chiefly occasioned by the greed and infamy of designing speculators, and base men throughout the land.

To meet these difficulties, General Lee had to exercise every available faculty of his mind. A tithe-tax was instituted, whereby the people in Virginia, around his troops, furnished supplies to the army, and in various ways did he so continue to lessen some of the evils spoken of, that several old regiments re-enlisted for the war, and new ones numerously came forward. He increased the length of furloughs, and it was truly gratifying to find the soldiers so promptly return at the expiration of their leave. Nor was another important subject in the welfare of the army forgotten. Say, or think what some will to the contrary, there *is* a sure safeguard for the moral, and even physical good of man, in unaffected, honest-hearted religion, particularly when he is thrown amongst his brethren without the usual restraints of home society. Therefore, the exercises of religion, even in its mere form alone, are of real practical good, and we find that it was much evinced in Lee's army. In accounts of what was then passing, it is said " the religious interest in the army is unchilled by the cold weather. Meetings are still held in every part of the army ; and, in many, if not all the brigades, meeting-houses have been constructed by the soldiers, for their own use, and faithful chaplains nightly preach to large and deeply attentive congregations."

But, beside the more serious duties incumbent on a wise general to regard and encourage among his men, the lighter occupations of life were not forgotten. No one who has ever been called to headship over others—if he be at all capable of right feeling himself—can fail to know the importance of maintaining a healthy spirit of mirth and cheerfulness around. Give the soldier, or the sailor, or the employed artisan, a fair proportion of life's joys, whenever it can be done, and let him see and experience the pleasant smile or the uproarious glee of others around him, and assuredly it will do him immense good, no matter what his privations or even his sufferings may be. Accordingly we find many wise commanders especially attending to this, and in Lee's army (as it was also to be seen amongst the Union forces) sports and pastimes were not omitted in the military economy established. A newspaper, called *The Rapid Ann*, was issued by some of the soldiers, with pen and pencil, and the following is a specimen of its good humor:

"TACTICS OF KISSING.—Recruit is placed in front of the piece First motion—Bend the right knee; straighten the left; bring the head on a level with the face of the piece; at the same time extend the arms, and clasp the cheeks of the piece firmly in both hands. Second motion—Bend the body slightly for ward; pucker the mouth, and apply the lips smartly to the muzzle mouldings. Third motion—Break off promptly on both legs, to escape the jarring or injury should the piece recoil."

It may seem trivial to bring forward such incidents as this, in writing a biographical sketch of a great man, but we conceive that nothing which tends to illustrate the character of such a one, and of those under his control, who as a glass throw back the reflection of his own face, should be omitted. Lee had been now, March, 1864, for more than twenty months in command of that army, and much of the reflex of himself was sure to be found in the general actions of his men, when free to display the bent of their own inclinations. Thus, their pleasures and amusements, their sense of religious duty, and their devotion to the cause they served, were all indicative of that kindly and wise spirit which ruled over them. Nor was his family less thoughtful and friendly disposed toward the soldier. Like the angels of goodness and mercy in the North, who are ever seeking to relieve the wants and sufferings of the Union soldiers, so were there in the South, vast numbers of ladies constantly at work for the benefit of their own troops, and amongst them was ever prominent, Mrs. General R. E. Lee. On one occasion, hearing that a detail of men from the Fifty-third North Carolina regiment were engaged, during severe weather, in rebuilding the plank-road near Orange Court-house, Virginia, she made and presented to them thirty-seven pairs of most useful gloves, a gift the more valuable on account of the difficulty and the cost, at that time, to a soldier in procuring them.

One more trait illustrative of General Lee's personal character as a man, and yet as a military chief, and we pass to other and sterner things. A soldier had deserted, and had gone back to his wife, who, however, in spite, as she said, of her love for him, and the suffering and hardship she endured in consequence of his absence, would not shield him when officers came in search. The army needed every man in her country's

hour of tribulation, and to protect him while other brave men perilled their lives, and other women had to be separated from their husbands, brothers, and sires, was against her sense of duty. Therefore, he was arrested, though she was aware the sentence for his crime would be death. But, having done her duty, her woman's nature strove all in her power to get him pardoned, and that heroic wife, that true woman, had the bliss of succeeding. General Lee, hearing of the case, granted his reprieve at the moment of execution, giving as his reason for doing so, that it was on account of the noble-minded, patriotic wife, and as an encouragement for other wives to be equally true to their country and their duty.

Let us now turn to the general occurrences connected with Lee, from the beginning of 1864.

On the 2d of January, in the Confederate Senate, at Richmond, Mr. Johnson, of Arkansas, submitted the following, with reference to General Lee and his army:

"*Whereas*, the campaigns of the brave and gallant armies covering the capital of the Confederate States, during the two successful years of 1862 and 1863, under the leadership and command of General Robert E. Lee, have been crowned with glorious results; and,

"*Whereas*, these and other illustrious services rendered by this able commander, since the commencement of the war of independence, have especially endeared him to the hearts of his countrymen, and have imposed on Congress the grateful duty of giving expression to their feelings; therefore, it is

"*Resolved*, by the Congress of the Confederate States of America, That the thanks of Congress are hereby tendered to General Robert E. Lee, and to the officers and soldiers of the Confederate armies under his command, for the great and signal victories they have won over the vast hosts of the enemy, and for the inestimable services they have rendered in defence of the liberty and independence of our country.

"*Resolved*, That the President be requested to communicate these resolutions to General Robert E. Lee, and to the officers and soldiers herein designated."

After some remarks by senators, highly complimentary to General Lee and the army, the resolutions were unanimously adopted, and were afterwards made known, by the commander

in-chief, in handsome terms, to his officers and men.   At about the same time he announced, in a special order, to the Mississippi soldiers under his command, the resolutions of thanks of their own State Legislature.

The month of January now passed without any military event of importance, except cavalry raids, and the capture of a Union wagon train by General Rosser, of Early's division, at Petersburg, in Northwest Virginia, on the 30th, and the further destruction, on February 2d, of bridges over the Patterson creek, and north branch of the Potomac, besides taking a number of prisoners.

In the month of February, on the 6th, the Federals crossed in large force at Morton's ford, but, after a sharp contest, were repulsed by General Edward Johnson's division, and driven back over the river.   They also attempted to cross at Barnett's ford, but were repulsed by General Scales' North Carolina brigade and Lomax's cavalry.

On February 28th, General Custer of the Union cavalry, made a raid on the left flank of Lee's army, and succeeded in getting as far as the vicinity of Charlottesville, where a camp of Stuart's horse artillery was stationed, near the Ravenna river.   The huts of this camp were arranged with mathematical precision and soldierlike regularity.   On one side were the horses, quietly standing at the time Custer's men approached ; on the other side, pieces of artillery were packed with all the appurtenances neatly arranged, and close to the caissons.

It was about noon on Monday when the Federal horse approached this camp, and immediately the Confederates sounded alarm.   But the surprise was so sudden, that it was found impossible to save the caissons in the prompt retreat which had to be made.   Captain Moorman, who commanded the post, ordered the men to retire, with what guns they could save, to a neighboring hill, whence they kept up a galling fire upon the Union cavalry, now engaged destroying the camp. This done, and the Southerners obtaining reinforcements, General Custer and his men retreated towards their own lines. On the way, General Stuart, having swiftly followed on receipt of the news, met Custer near Stannardsville, and a sharp encounter took place, the Union commander gallantly charging through, and ultimately reaching his own camp in safety.

This expedition of General Custer's was mainly for the purpose of drawing away the Confederate cavalry from the Central railroad to Richmond, so as to allow General Kilpatrick the better to accomplish an object then in view, of penetrating within or to the fortifications. This bold exploit was eminently successful, except in the cutting off of Lee's communications, and getting within the works around the capital.

But we must now hasten on to the more important events that were shortly to occur.

At this period, the beginning of March, the strength of the Confederate armies was estimated at 344,000.

Lee's force was, as we have said, stationed along the Rapidan, and Meade's on the banks of the Rappahannock. But now another important actor was to appear upon the scene. Ulysses S. Grant, who had made himself famous as the hero of Fort Donelson, Shiloh, and Vicksburg, had been appointed Lieutenant-general and Commander-in-chief of all the Union forces. Modest and unpretending, calm and thoughtful in his mind, he was considered well fitted to cope with Lee; and, immediately upon the assumption of his rank he prepared for active exertions in the field.

General Lee, now reinforced by Longstreet, was not idle in adopting all precautionary measures to meet him. He strongly intrenched his lines, dug rifle-pits at the fords of the Rapidan, and kept a good force on the Gordonsville road so as to hold the communication open to Richmond by that route, while by the way of Fredericksburg he destroyed the bridges and rails in order to prevent, or make more difficult, the enemy's advance in that direction. Thus, then, when the battle between the two parties was likely to commence, it was sure to be again a bloody one. What the plan of the new campaign would be no one but the few initiated knew. General Grant was exceedingly reticent, and Lee equally so. Indeed, on both sides, all communications respecting movements of the army were forbidden to be published. The visit of General Grant to Butler at Fortress Monroe, indicated some important strategic operation in connection with the campaign, but nothing appeared as to the actual object in view.

On the 7th of April General Lee issued a general order directing the morrow to be observed "as a day of fasting, hu-

miliation, and prayer." All military duties, unless absolutely
necessary, were to be suspended, and the chaplains were de
sired to hold divine service in their regiments and brigades
Officers and men were "requested" to attend. This passed
the final preparations were made for the deadly struggle that
it was evident, would soon commence. The Northern army
was strong, fresh, vigorous, and anxious for the fight. The
Southerners were firm, defiant, and maddened with the sense
of wrongs they felt had been inflicted upon them and their
homes. "For your stricken country's sake, and ours," said
the "wives, daughters, sisters, and friends" of these soldiers in
a published address to them, "be true to yourselves and our
glorious cause. Never turn your back on the flag, nor desert
the ranks of honor, or the post of danger. You are constantly
present to our minds. The women of the South bestow all
their respect and affection on the heroes who defend them."
With such an appeal to them, who can doubt that the soldier
—with rare exceptions—remained true and undaunted ?

General Lee now sent to the rear all superfluous baggage,
and unnecessary incumbrances. The sick and useless were
removed from the camp, and due transportation provided for
the movement of stores, and the conveyance of wounded in
the forthcoming battles. Ever since Kilpatrick's "fruitless
raid," the Confederates had kept a battery in position at Ely's
ford, and, when a party of foreign officers, visiting the Union
army, rode to the front one day to examine Lee's position,
they expressed an opinion that it was all but impregnable, so
strongly and admirably had he fortified it. As to the South
itself, and what was thought there, we need hardly say that very
hopeful ideas were prominent in the printed opinions. General Grant was admitted to be "a man of far more energy and
ability than any that had yet commanded the army of the
Potomac," but "his performances would bear no comparison
whatever to those of General Lee."

Thus stood the two armies, and thus awaited and hoped the
people of the North and South, towards the end of April,
when at length some symptoms of an active movement oc
curred. About the 23d of April, General Grant, whose headquarters were at Culpepper, ordered portions of two army
corps to make a feint on Lee's left, and draw back Longstreet's

supposed movement in that direction. The result, however was merely a reconnoissance on the part of the Union forces and the occupation of Warrenton by the Confederates. In th latter part of April the famous Court-house at Madison wa destroyed by an expedition sent from Washington. The Con federates occupying the locality were attacked,—retreated and fought in the town. The result was that the Union troops compelled a retreat of their opponents by firing the place, and reducing nearly every house to ashes. On the 29th of April Mosby surprised a Union picket post of men at Hunter's Mill in Fairfax county, and captured six men, and eighteen horses. The rest escaped. Afterwards he was pursued, and the Federals recaptured five horses, and took prisoner one of his lieu tenants.

May now opened, and the great and bloody drama of the war recommenced. On Tuesday night, May 3d, the Union army broke up its encampments and at dawn of next morning crossed the Rapidan at the old fords—Ely's and Germania—and in much the same line that Meade attempted in the previous November, and where Lee had caused Hooker to retreat a year before. The Second corps, commanded by General Hancock, in front, crossed at Ely's ford, the Fifth corps, under Warren, took the Germania ford, while the Sixth (Sedgwick's) followed immediately upon it. Two corps of Lee's army were at once moved to meet them,—Ewell's by the old turnpike, and Hill's by the plank-road. The advance of Ewell's corps—Johnson's division—arrived within three miles of Wilderness run that evening and encamped. Rodes lay in his rear; and Early was next at Locust Grove, all ready to strike at Grant's advance the next morning. At about 6 A. M. the enemy was discovered by the skirmishers thrown out, and Johnson immediately pressed forward to gain a hill where he proceeded to form his troops in line of battle. The Union forces now advanced as well as they could through the thick tangled forest already mentioned in describing the battle of Chancellorsville, with a heavy line of skirmishers in front, and followed by a solid column four lines deep. At the first onslaught, the Confederate skirmishers were driven in, and the Fifth corps of the Union army came thundering along, unchecked by a terrible fusilade from Johnson's line, until with deadly fire, and after

a brief struggle, General Jones' brigade of Virginians were forced back. Jones strove, in desperation, to rally his broken troops, but with no avail ; and, as the brave general was imploring his men to stop their flight, a ball struck him, and he fell from his saddle a bleeding corpse. Captain Early, of his staff, was at the same time also killed. Now came the decisive moment. Warren's men poured forward with stern determination, but just then General Stewart moved from his position in line of battle and with a wild cheer dashed upon the advancing Federals, driving them back by the impetus of his charge, and capturing their guns. At the same time Ewell ordered Daniels' and Gordon's brigades of Rodes' division to form on the right and charge. They did so, crushing through the enemy's first lines, and capturing many prisoners, besides some guns. The Federal front, now thrown into confusion, fell back and retreated some distance. Meanwhile, the Union troops were engaged in a heavy conflict on the left of this part of the field, with General Stafford at the head of his Louisianians, who succeeded in repulsing them, but with the loss of the general, who fell mortally wounded. Sedgwick had now come up, and fiercely attacked the Confederate left flank, but was repulsed by Pegram's and Hays' divisions. But again the brave Federals came on in dense masses, and the fight was renewed till after dark with great slaughter, Pegram, himself, falling severely wounded. The engagement for that day now ended, and both parties maintained their position on the field.

Meanwhile, Hill's corps had moved along the Fredericksburg plank-road, Heth and Wilcox in advance, while Anderson remained behind for a time to guard some fords. The two divisions bivouacked for the night of the 4th near Verdiersville. Next morning the march was pursued along the same road, and parallel with that which, at the same time, Ewell was taking, though some three miles apart, the intervening space being the "Wilderness" heretofore described. While thus marching an incident occurred that must be narrated as personally affecting General Lee.

Between the two parallel lines of march, and in a part of the wilderness, was an open field, where, during the forenoon, the commander-in-chief, with General Hill and some other officers, were seated on the ground in consultation. At this

moment, some of the enemy's scouts and skirmishers, arrived near the spot, and might with the greatest ease have shot General Lee, had they not, on finding their dangerous position, hastily retreated, ignorant of who it was that had lain so closely at the mercy of their rifles.

General Lee now opened a communication with Ewell, and Wilcox's division moved forward to effect the junction. The line of battle thus completed, now extended from the right of the plank-road through a succession of open fields and dense forest to the left of the turnpike. It presented a front of six miles, and occupied a very irregular plane along the broken slopes of the stream known as the Wilderness Run. There was, however, in the front, an almost impenetrable thicket which, as necessarily occupied by the Union troops, prevented their artillery being used except in the openings of the roads.

It was now about 2 P. M. (May 5th), and large columns of the enemy were seen coming up, along the roads from the Union rear. The attack then began in front of Hill, Heth's division for some time bearing the whole brunt of the fierce onslaught of the Federal troops. This being perceived by General Hill, he ordered Wilcox from Ewell's right to come to the support, which was done in double quick, at about 4 P. M. The conflict now was again most fearful, and continued with no important advantage to either side, but with considerable loss in killed and wounded, until night closed in and compelled the combatants to cease.

During that night, the two armies lay so close to each other as to be within hearing. Indeed, a small stream on the Confederate left constituted their mutual supply of water, and was so near both, that men from either side going out to fill their canteens from it, were very often captured by some from the other. It was in this manner Colonel Baldwin, of the First Massachusetts regiment, while slaking his thirst, was taken prisoner.

We must now, for a moment, turn back to Longstreet's corps, which, on the 3d, was posted some thirteen miles southwest of the original position on the Rapidan. Ordered by Lee to march forward, it moved from Gordonsville on the morning of the 4th, and on the night of the 5th it halted within twelve miles of the advanced field of battle just described. News,

however, now reached Longstreet, at midnight, of Hill's danger in front, and, accordingly, at 2 A. M. of the 6th, he aroused his sleeping men from their bivouac, and marched on to the field of battle. That morning, at daylight, General Lee was himself well in the advance, but on renewing the engagement, such was the impetuous valor of the Union troops that, despite the most determined bravery of Heth's and Wilcox's divisions, they were overpowered, and had to give way. On rushed the victorious Federals, pushing the Confederates before them to within a hundred and fifty yards of Lee, when, at that moment, McLaws' division of Longstreet's corps arrived, and for a time checked the enemy in his victorious career. Then came up Anderson's division, and presently Longstreet himself rushed forward with his staff to the front. Loud were the cheers that greeted him and General Lee as each rode on,—the former taking the more advanced post, and the latter personally directing and encouraging the men. Longstreet galloped forward, and as he pushed on, General Jenkins spurred to his side to grasp his hand, with the true pleasure of a soldier-friend,—for, be it remembered, Longstreet had but newly arrived from several months' campaign in Eastern Tennessee. But, alas! hardly had the mutual congratulations passed each other's lips, when a deadly volley from one of their own brigades—mistaking Longstreet, Jenkins, and the rest, for a party of the flying foe—poured into them, at short range. Jenkins fell instantly from his horse a lifeless corpse, while Longstreet received a ball that entered his throat and passed out through his right shoulder. It was supposed that he was dead, but it was not so, and he was speedily taken to the rear for medical care.

The battle now became general, and the field was well contested on both sides. At one time, however, the aspect of affairs was so alarming for the South that, fearing for the constancy of his troops under such fierce attacks, General Lee placed himself at the head of Gregg's brigade of Texans, and ordered them to follow him in a charge. But the wounded Longstreet, ere he was moved, raised his feeble voice to protest against it, and even the rough soldiers positively refused to move until their beloved general in-chief had gone to his proper position of safety.

Ewell, on the extreme left, was battling severely against the powerful onslaughts of the enemy, and by a successful movement completely repelled Burnside's attempt to outflank him, in the space between Lee's two wings left vacant by Wilcox's removal. Ewell then united with the right, and again and again were the most valiant charges made on both sides without the crown of victory alighting positively on either party. Success, in a detached form, undoubtedly attended the one side and the other. Both took prisoners, and captured guns, colors, and *matériel ;* but the general results were about equal, and when night again closed upon the scene, it was to blot out of sight, for a few hours, another terrible field of carnage, no more decisive than had been that of the day before. In this battle, General Lee so much exposed himself that President Davis wrote him a touching letter of remonstrance. The explosion of a shell under his own horse, the killing of the horse of his Adjutant-general, Lieutenant-colonel Taylor, and the wounding of another officer, Lieutenant-colonel Marshall, attached to his person, caused great and most affectionate anxiety in the army.

On Saturday, the seventh, both armies moved their position —Grant's to take an interior road towards Richmond by the Spottsylvania Court-house, and Lee's, back, apparently, towards Orange Court-house, but in reality it was to reach Spottsylvania before the enemy. Something like a neck and neck race took place, but the advance of Lee arrived first and took up a good position, the main army quickly following. Next morning, Sunday, May 8th, a part of Warren's Fifth corps of Federals, under General Robinson, tried to dislodge Longstreet's corps—now under Anderson's command—from their strong position, but were repulsed, and General Robinson wounded. Grant now placed his army in line of battle, Hancock being on the right, Warren in the centre, and Sedgwick on the left, the line reaching about seven miles. The day following, about 2 P. M., the engagement began, but consisted principally of skirmishing. It was, however, at that time General Sedgwick was killed.

Tuesday, May 10th, the struggle was renewed at an early hour, Warren's corps being the one most hotly engaged against the Confederates, though all were fighting heavily. About

half-past five two divisions of Hancock's second corps crossed the Po river and advanced against Lee's left, making a strong show of giving battle there. Lee, supposing the enemy was massing forces at that point, moved his troops during the night and next day to that quarter, but, in the morning of Thursday, the 12th, it was found that Hancock was again in the centre, and vigorously assaulting Johnson's division. The struggle, here, now became very fierce. Charge after charge was made by the Confederates to regain what ground they had lost, but they were met so determinedly that each time they fell back with broken and shattered ranks. The dead and wounded, according to the report of one eye witness, here lay piled over each other, " the latter often underneath the former." Generals Edward Johnson and G. H. Stuart were taken prisoners ; and, on the Union side, Generals Wadsworth and Hayes were killed, besides Sedgwick, as previously mentioned, and many more of lesser rank.

It was now evident that Grant's strategy was, by a series of flank movements on Lee's right, so to revolve around him, even as the fierce cyclones of a tropical clime gyrate in their rapid career, that a constant surprise might be created, and the Confederate army kept unsettled, until the Union forces had again reached the old battle-ground of McClellan's on the Peninsula. To aid in this, a cavalry expedition was dispatched by Grant, while Lee was on the Rapidan, down the Richmond railroad. This expedition was under command of General Sheridan, since so noted in the Shenandoah Valley. It first effected some damage at Beaver Dam, and thence moved rapidly to the South Anna and the Ashland station. But General J. E. B. Stuart promptly followed, and on May 11th overtook them at the latter place. A sharp fight commenced between Fitz Lee's advance and the enemy, which resulted in Sheridan's leaving the place and pushing on towards the " Yellow Tavern," six miles only from Richmond. Stuart quickly moved ahead to intercept them, while General Gordon was aiding him by attacking them in the rear. An engagement ensued, and it was here that the lamented Stuart lost his life.

After the engagement of the 12th, at Spottsylvania, little was done for a few days except skirmishing, but, on the

16th, Grant made a retrograde movement to the Ny river, where he received reinforcements, and prepared for another battle. Lee occupied the same position he had previously held, on the north side of the river Po. On the 18th Grant made an assault upon Ewell's line, with a view of turning Lee's left, but this failing, the Union troops returned to their camp, after a severe loss. At the same time Grant began another of his flank movements, by moving to Guinney's station, some ten miles east of Spottsylvania, on the railroad. The Union cavalry, under Torbert, went in advance to clear the way, and the right corps followed. Lee was thus necessarily obliged to evacuate his position on the Po, and by an admirable movement took up a new position between the North and South Anna rivers before Grant's army had arrived. On Friday, the 20th, the Federal cavalry had reached Milford station, and the next and following day, Hancock, Warren, Wright (late Sedgwick's corps), and Burnside, encamped there.

On Sunday, the 22d, the Union line of battle stretched in a curve from Milford to Guinney's, through Bowling Green, and on the next day Grant determined to attack the Confederate lines. Accordingly, Warren crossed the North Anna, principally at Jericho ford, the men wading waist-deep, while Hancock engaged at Taylor's bridge. These fords and bridges were just above Sexton's Junction. Warren's corps and the portion of Hancock's which had crossed, feeling their way towards the Little river and the Virginia Central railroad, were fiercely attacked, and were only extricated from a very perilous position by their determined bravery and the timely arrival of Burnside and Wright.

Next day, Tuesday, May 24th, the fighting continued at Taylor's bridge, and at a place called Oxford; and on Wednesday Grant found it necessary to make another flank movement, by recrossing the North Anna, and marching easterly towards the Pamunkey. To cover his plans, an attack was made on Thursday upon Lee's left, while a portion of Sheridan's cavalry tore up the Central Railroad track. As this was going on, the Union forces withdrew, merely keeping a strong body of skirmishers in front of the Confederates, in order to mislead them. But General Lee was fully master of the situation, and could

not be thus blinded. Comprehending Grant's tactics, he was as prompt in his movements, and as skilful in his strategy as the Union commander. Moreover, the scene of battle was now, once more, nearing the old ground where his first great victories had been won. Richmond, too, the home of trusting wives and families, was again to be menaced; and a wily, astute, and determined foe was bent on its destruction. Accordingly, no sooner did Grant's army, on the 28th, arrive at Hanovertown, on the Pamunkey, fifteen miles northeast of Richmond, than it was found the Confederates were in line of battle, from Atlee's station, on the railroad, ten or eleven miles north of Richmond, to Shady Grove, eight or nine miles north-northeast of the capital. To reconnoitre this position, on the same morning, Grant dispatched Torbert and Gregg's division of cavalry down towards Mechanicsville. But before arriving there, the Confederate cavalry, under Fitzhugh Lee and Hampton, were encountered at a place not far from Tolopatomoy creek. A severe engagement followed, ending in the Union cavalry remaining on the field, while Lee and Hampton fell back to the main lines, both sides suffering much loss.

On Sunday, the 29th, the whole of the Union forces were across the Pamunkey, marching towards Richmond, and reinforcements from Butler's army, on the James river, were arriving at White House, which once more formed the Federal base of supplies.

On Monday, May 30th, the Union cavalry pickets on the left were driven in, and a sharp fight ensued, with some slight loss. The same afternoon, Rodes' division of Ewell's corps hotly attacked Warren's corps, then moving along the Mechanicsville road, and Crawford's division was forced back. Warren's flank was also in danger, but reinforcements arrived, and though General Meade ordered an attack of the whole line, it was dark before any other of the Federals but Hancock could respond. He, with his accustomed gallantry, dashed on, and succeeded in obtaining good ground in the advanced Confederate lines, but with no other important advantage. On the next day, May 31st, the two armies were ready for a general engagement; and here, for a moment, let us review the whole situation as it was at that time, when the singular fortune of war had again made the Peninsula a deadly battle-ground.

One month had hardly elapsed since the present campaign had begun, and of those brave companions and friends already lost to Lee, and to the Confederacy, the following are some of the prominent names :—

Killed, Major-general J. E. B. Stuart; Brigadier-general Stafford; Brigadier-general Jennings; Brigadier-general J. M. Jones; Colonels Nances, Grice, Carter, Forney, Avery, Randolph, and Binney : *Wounded*, Lieutenant-general Longstreet; Major-general Heth; Major-general Pickett; Brigadier-general Walker; Brigadier-General Hays; Pegram; Benning; Colonels Gailland, Kenedy, Herbet, Ronlove, Jones, Sheffield, Whitehead, Board, Winston, Lane, Sanders, Falum, Miller, Davidson, Lamar, Crott, Hartsfield, Wilds, Hodge, and Willett; besides Major-general E. Johnson and G. H. Stuart captured.

When Lee stood in array against Grant at the Rapidan, his force was then estimated at less than 80,000; since then it had been considerably decreased by the many killed, and the wounded unfit for duty. But it had, also, been reinforced by Breckinridge with his troops, so that it now numbered about 110,000 men.

Grant's army, at this time, was estimated at 200,000, including all the reinforcements sent to him from Butler.

The position of these two armies was as follows:—Grant was between the Chickahominy and the Pamunkey, with his left thrown forward to Mechanicsville, his right withdrawn to White House, and his reserve massed in rear of his left, and Richmond somewhat behind his left flank.

Lee was posted from Atlett's station, on his left (with his advance parties towards Hanover Court-house), to Gaines' Mill, with outposts as far as Coal Harbor. This position of Lee's was nearly identical with that of Jackson's in 1862; and indeed, the whole Confederate line of battle was on ground occupied by both the armies at that time.

On Tuesday, the 31st of May, there was some skirmishing between the two parties, and a cavalry attack at Cold Harbor, by Sheridan, against Fitzhugh Lee; but it was not till next day, June 1st, the engagement fully began.

Lee, anticipating Grant's last gyratory movement, had determined to secure positions he knew, from the battles of two years before, to be good ones. Accordingly he sent forward

to the right, Kershaw's and Hoke's divisions of Anderson's corps, with orders to occupy the eminences around Gaines' Mill and Cold Harbor. As already stated, Grant's orders had also been to secure these places, and the cavalry engagement of Tuesday partly effected it. But on arrival of Hoke's division, shortly afterwards reinforced by McLaws', the Confederates obtained possession of the desired posts. At the same time Breckinridge and Mahone, of Hill's corps, were equally successful in gaining certain advanced positions.

In the afternoon an attack was made upon Heth's division, by the Federals, reinforced by Baldy Smith's Eighteenth corps; but after a severe and gallant fight, were unable to gain any advantage. Next morning it was found that Grant had made another gyratory movement, even as Lee suspected, and, therefore, he was closely followed. The Confederates were put in motion on a parallel line, while Early, commanding Ewell's corps (Ewell being sick), swung round, late in the afternoon, and took the enemy in flank, drove him from two lines of intrenchments, and inflicted great loss. Meanwhile Breckinridge, supported by Wilcox, proceeded, under orders from Lee, to attack the advanced Federals, now on the extreme right, at Turkey Hill, and there succeeded in driving them away. Thus another important position was obtained by Lee, for this hill commanded the approaches from the north and east to the military bridges which McClellan had formerly thrown over the Chickahominy. It was evident to Lee that Grant was aiming for those bridges, consequently he continued to move his army to the right, until he had thrown it across the intended path of the Federals. During the night, breastworks were hurriedly thrown up, and every preparation made for the attack. This commenced early on the morning of Friday, June 3d, when the Union army, now extending from Tolopatomony creek to and across the road from Cold Harbor to the Chickahominy, advanced, in full line of battle, upon the Confederate army.

The formation of the Union line of battle was as follows: From right to left, Burnside, Warren, Smith, Wright, and Hancock, the latter thus being opposed to Breckinridge, who was on Lee's extreme right, and Ewell's corps on the extreme left, opposite Burnside,—Hill's corps being in reserve. Taking

the Confederate right, Hancock, with his division commanders Gibbon, Barlow, and Birney, dashed gallantly forward, and, for the moment, carried the position held by Breckinridge, but speedily General Finnegan, with Milligan's Florida brigade and the Maryland battalion, rushed into the breach, and swept the brave Federals out, and compelled them to retire, though only to a short distance. On the right of Hancock, the sixth and eighteenth corps of Wright and Smith assaulted, with all their force, but with equally bad results; while Warren and Burnside vainly strove to gain some advantage over Lee's troops before them. Numerous were the assaults made by the Federals, but such was the determination of the Confederates not to be beaten, that no amount of bravery on the Union side could overcome them. The slaughter was again immense, but we may not dwell upon it. Enough that the battle of Cold Harbor was, after five hours' fighting, lost to Grant and won by Lee.

On the following two days, Grant renewed the attack upon Lee, but without success, and during the night of the 5th he withdrew his right wing about two miles, and placed it behind a swamp which protected both the flank and front of that portion of his army.

The battle of the 3d was fought upon the same ground as the battle of Gaines' Mill and Cold Harbor in 1862. It was at Cold Harbor that Jackson first struck McClellan's right and rear in his first grand flank movement, a fact well known to the Confederates, and from which they drew fresh inspiration. The position of the armies was reversed in some respects, the Federals occupying nearly the same ground the Confederates held in 1862. In the engagements of that year at Gaines' Mill and Cold Harbor, McClellan, though strongly intrenched, was driven from his position with heavy loss. Thus far Grant had found it impossible to dislodge the Confederates from the same ground. The latter availed themselves, upon some parts of the field, of the works from which they formerly drove McClellan.

Among the killed on the Confederate side were Brigadier-general Doles, of Georgia; Colonel L. M. Keitt, of South Carolina, formerly a distinguished member of the United States House of Representatives, and Colonel Edwin Willis, of

Georgia, a late graduate of West Point, and one of the most promising officers in the Confederate army. Among the wounded were Brigadier-general Law, of Alabama, Kirkland of Georgia, and Lane, of North Carolina, the two first slightly. Major-general Breckinridge had his horse killed under him in the night attack of the 4th.

On the evening of the 5th, General Grant sent a communication to General Lee, proposing that when the armies were not actually engaged, either party may, upon notification to the other, succor its wounded and bury its dead. General Lee replied that he preferred the custom common on such occasions—to wit, that the party desiring to remove its wounded and inter its dead should send in a flag of truce and ask permission to do so; adding, that the burial party should be accompanied by white flags. To this Grant rejoined, affecting to understand General Lee as accepting his proposition, and informing him that he would send forward a force between the hours of 12 and 3 P. M. of the 6th, to care for the wounded and killed, and that they would be instructed to carry flags of the kind designated by General Lee. The latter immediately informed him that he had misunderstood him, and that if he (Grant) should send out a party for the purpose indicated without first obtaining permission under flag of truce to do so, he would cause the party to be warned off by his pickets.

Accordingly, Grant made the usual request for permission to bury the dead, and Lee immediately granted it.

For several days after the battle of Cold Harbor there was comparative quiet, with the exception of a few unimportant skirmishes and picket firing. At length, on the 12th of June, Grant completed his preparations to abandon the late field of operations about the Chickahominy, cross the James' river, and occupy the south side towards Petersburg. To do this he had to make another movement round Lee's right, extending as far as Bottom's bridge, and march low down the Chickahominy as far as the next crossings at Long's and Jones' bridges. The movement was effected with consummate skill, and with hardly any impediment. On Monday evening, June 13th, the advance had reached Wilcox's landing on the James, near Charles' City Court-house, and the next day the whole Union army was safely transferred over to the opposite shore.

It may be a matter of surprise to some, that General Lee did not attack Grant in his movement to the James, but it must be borne in mind that Richmond and Petersburg had both to be guarded, not only against the army of the North, but also that of Butler, who had come up the river in force to co-operate with Grant. Consequently, it was the capital that had to be thought of, more especially as Hunter was advancing along the road to Lynchburg, with a view of throwing a third army, if possible, on the city. Lee, therefore, acted wisely in not forcing his troops into another conflict until they had been recuperated, and additional means of defence prepared. Some of his men he had to send away to assist in checking Hunter's advance, and it was about this time another brave Confederate general, J. W. Jones, was killed. Then, too, Sherman's operations in the Western part of Georgia had more in them than met the general eye. Hence there was much to guard against, and be prepared for. Petersburg was well able to withstand a siege, especially with the additional fortifications promptly erected around it and on the banks of the Appomattox, while at Fort Darling, Drury's Bluff, there was as good and strong a point of defence as need be wished for.

At the time Grant determined to cross the James, he had already sent the eighteenth corps, by way of the White House, back to Fortress Monroe, in transports. Thence it proceeded up the James, and, at 1 A. M. of June the 15th, disembarked at Bermuda Hundred. The different forces, thus united, now marched rapidly forward to invest Petersburg. It had been attacked once before, on the 9th, by an expedition from Butler's army, but, after making a gap in the Confederate lines, the Federals were repulsed. The first attack was made late in the afternoon of the 15th, by 15,000 men, under General Smith, Hancock then advancing along the road. The second, on the 16th, by the two corps combined, and the third on the 17th, with Burnside's forces in addition to those already engaged. The Union losses during these days were very heavy, especially so among the officers. On the 18th, a fourth attack was made, by four Union corps, and in several desperate assaults they were repulsed, with a slaughter even more terrible than the well-known carnage at Fredericksburg in 1862.

Meanwhile Butler, taking advantage of the Confederates in

his front having been withdrawn to Petersburg, sallied from behind his intrenchments and advanced towards the railroad, intending to tear it up, but Lee promptly prepared for him. The lines necessarily vacated by Beauregard, when he had to fall back and defend Petersburg, had already been taken possession of by the Federals; but directly Butler made his attempt, General Anderson was dispatched with his corps from Richmond to repulse him. This was done most effectively, Pickett's division being with difficulty restrained in their impetuous advance. The result was so satisfactory, and the exploit so gallantly accomplished, that General Lee issued the following congratulatory dispatch:

CLAY'S HOUSE, June 17—5½ P. M.

LIEUT.-GEN. R. H. ANDERSON, Commanding Longstreet's Corps:

GENERAL—I take great pleasure in presenting to you my congratulations upon the conduct of the men of your corps. I believe that they will carry any thing they are put against. We tried very hard to stop Pickett's men from capturing the breastworks of the enemy, but could not do it. I hope his loss has been small.

I am, with great respect, your obedient servant,

R. E. LEE, General.

That the statement made by General Butler, to the effect that he had destroyed the railroad, was a mistake, is evident from the fact that Lee was, all day, on the 18th, sending troops from Richmond to join Beauregard at Petersburg.

The same evening, Friday 17th, at 10 o'clock, an attack was made on Burnside's line of advanced rifle-pits by the Confederates, who drove the enemy back on his supports, and remained in possession until daylight, when they retired to their own works.

The strongest part of the Confederate intrenched line was in front of the Second Union corps (Hancock's), then under Birney's command; and on Saturday the 18th, the attempt already mentioned as the fourth attack was unsuccessfully made by the Fifth, Eighteenth, Second, and Tenth corps of Federal troops to capture this line.

This check to the Federals in regard to capturing Petersburg, by them, at one time, thought so easy of accomplish-

ment, was only what Lee felt convinced would occur. He had fully expected that city would be attacked, and as he well knew how impregnable it could be made, in addition to its original strength, none of Grant's movements affected him. On the contrary, they were quite in accordance with his own purposes. As for the siege itself, he knew it must be long, and this would give him ample time and opportunity to execute certain measures for the defence of Richmond on the south, which he might not otherwise have had.

On Wednesday, the 22d, an attempt was made by the Union forces to get possession of the Weldon railroad, but when they had reached the Jerusalem plank-road, the Confederates, consisting of A. P. Hill's corps and Anderson's, successfully encountered them, and drove them back with severe loss. General Wilson, however, on the Union side, succeeded in reaching the railroad at Ream's station, below where the combatants were engaged, and tore up some of the track, but which was repaired again by the Confederates soon afterwards. Wilson, joined by Kautz, then struck across to the Petersburg and Lynchburg railroad, destroying it in their progress. They then proceeded to the Southside railroad, and following that, came upon the Danville track,—on the way having a sharp engagement with a small Confederate force near Nottoway Court-house, night ending the fight. Continuing along the Danville railroad to the southwest, they arrived at the covered bridge over the Staunton river, about 3 P. M. of the 24th. There a body of Virginia and North Carolina militia met them, and after a brisk encounter Wilson and Kautz had to retire. This was the limit of their bold and adventurous raid. They returned as rapidly as they could, but at Ream's station were nearly all captured by a Confederate force under Hampton and Fitz Hugh Lee. Kautz's knowledge of the country only enabled him to escape. He, with his shattered band, reached the Union camp on the 30th of June, while Wilson, with his men in a pitiable and wretched condition, did not arrive till next day. It was a brave undertaking, but productive of only most disastrous results to themselves.*

---

* In General Lee's report, dated July 5th, he says the Federal loss was "one thousand prisoners, thirteen pieces of artillery, thirty wagons and am

General Lee was now in person at Petersburg, Beauregard still remaining in charge of the city; and on the 28th of June, five regiments from Lynchburg, where they were no longer required, reinforced him.

Meanwhile occasional demonstrations were made by the Federals against the Confederate lines, but with the same want of success as before; and, while this was going on in that quarter, with Grant fully occupied in the south of Virginia, General Lee was very quietly and skilfully sending another army of invasion into the Northern States. The occurrences pertaining to this great and audacious movement belong more to a history of the war than a biography of the able military chief who planned it.

Whether it was for the purpose of drawing Grant away from Petersburg and the vicinity of Richmond, or to throw terror and confusion into the very heart of those who sat in the executive and legislative chairs at Washington, the masterly skill and ability displayed by General Lee at this time, the future cannot fail to laud in the high terms it deserves.

Viewing the operations of Lee at this time, what do we find? Petersburg vainly assaulted and holding Grant at bay, the brave Union troops were almost themselves as if besieged, instead of being the besiegers; and feeling this to be the case—having full confidence in the result—Lee unhesitatingly withdraws a large portion of his forces for a new invasion of Maryland. Grant had to detach "Baldy" Smith's corps from his army, and hastily send it to Baltimore; while Lee left at Petersburg nearly "two divisions of Ewell's corps, one division of Longstreet's, and the whole of A. P. Hill's." This evidently shows an amount of confidence on Lee's part that could only be attained by the most masterly skill and experience in military affairs. Well might the veteran General Scott's words be remembered, when, as currently reported, he remarked to this effect, "it would be better to lose any one than Lee, so clear, far seeing, and almost omniscient was his judgment."

---

bulances, many small-arms, horses, ordinance stores, and several hundred negroes they had taken from the plantations on their route, besides many killed and wounded they had to leave on the field."

It was about this time, the middle of July, that a report be
came current that all the household effects of General Lee
would be sold at public auction. The sale was postponed,
however, in consequence of some doubt as to the real owner
ship of the property, it originally having belonged to his
father-in-law, Mr. Custis, by whom it was bequeathed to his
grandchildren; consequently the seizure of it might prove
illegal. Some months previous, Lee's family estate, the Arlington House, had been formally seized, confiscated, and sold by
order of and for the use of Government; and the White House
estate had long ago been taken from him for military purposes
when the Union troops arrived there, though, in the various
changes of war, it had come back and been lost several times.
Thus, few men and few families had abandoned so much, or
suffered so much loss and ruin by adherence to the Confederate
cause—a cause they believed to be a just one—than General
Lee and his devoted wife, with her brave sons and their
families. Right or wrong, the Lees of the South have undoubtedly proved themselves pure-minded and disinterested.

Towards the latter part of July, Grant had strengthened his
forces, by sending additional troops over to Deep Bottom, on
the north side of the James, where for some time he had stationed a large body of men; and, while little of importance was
going on actually before Petersburg, this force, amounting to
some 20,000 men and twenty-two pieces of cannon, attacked
the Confederate troops near Newmarket. The result, on either
side, was unimportant, but it was generally conceived that a
more determined effort would soon be made by Grant from
his three main positions, Deep Bottom, Bermuda Hundred,
and before Petersburg, and that operations on the north of the
James were merely a ruse to cover his real designs. On Friday, July 27th, the demonstrations on the Union side, at Deep
Bottom, were, however, so apparently important, that, in the
eyes of nearly all but Lee, it was looked upon as a new attempt
on Richmond. General Lee, however, was not deceived. He
knew it to be a ruse of some kind, and contented himself with
dispatching a force sufficient to check Grant's advance, while
he kept the remainder of his army behind the intrenchments,
calmly awaiting the Federal plans. That it is probable he had
heard all about them, or had a good idea of what they were,

may be inferred from several little matters coming from Federal sources, and appearing in the press. But the public generally, and especially the humane portion of the civilized world, could have formed no conception of the horrible truth as it was soon to be unfolded.

On the 25th of June a plan was suggested by Lieutenant-colonel Pleasants, of the Forty-eighth Pennsylvania, whereby a tunnel could be excavated right under the enemy's works. It was at once adopted by Grant, and on the 25th of July the work was completed. Its length was about five hundred feet, and at the end of the tunnel the mine was formed, running parallel with and directly under the fort that was to be destroyed. On the twenty-seventh, the enormous quantity of 12,000 lbs. of powder was placed in the mine, fuses were constructed and connected with the magazine, and every thing was in readiness for the grand explosion.

It was also arranged that immediately after the explosion, a grand charge should be made against the other parts of the enemy's lines, and the feint of operations on the north of the James was merely to try and weaken the enemy by deceiving Lee into sending away a portion of his troops. What ensued when the mine was sprung may be gathered from the following account in a Southern paper.

"The chasm caused by the enemy's explosion appears to be about forty feet in depth and some two hundred feet in circumference, and resembles more what one would imagine to have been the effects of a terrible earthquake than any thing else. Immense boulders of earth were piled up rudely one above the other, and great fragments of bomb-proofs, gun-carriages, timbers, etc., were lying promiscuously in every direction.

"The sides and bottom of the chasm were literally lined with Yankee dead, and the bodies were in every conceivable position. Some had evidently been killed with the butts of muskets, as their crushed skulls and badly smashed faces too plainly indicated, while the greater portion were shot, great pools of blood having flowed from their wounds and stained the ground.

"Between our breastworks and the enemy's, large numbers of dead and wounded were still lying, the latter begging piteously for water and praying to be cared for. The length of the

'sap' made by the enemy is supposed to have been about six hundred feet."

A Petersburg paper, describing the struggle for the repossession of the Confederate works captured by the enemy in the confusion consequent to the explosion, says:

"Arriving upon the ground, General Mahone found twelve of the enemy's flags waving upon the ramparts of that portion of our line carried by the explosion, and the whole vicinity swarming with white and black Yankee troops. Getting his men into position, General Mahone ordered his forces to retake a part of the works, and instructed Wright's brigade to come up in such a manner as would insure the recapture of the remaining portion. Under command of Colonel Weisiger, acting brigadier, Mahone's brigade formed into line, and were about to move up, when the enemy rallied out and made a charge. The Confederates reserved their fire until they could see the whites of the enemy's eyes, when they poured into them such a storm of bullets that the enemy recoiled and fell back in confusion. A charge was now ordered, and Weisiger's men dashed forward with a yell, driving the enemy up to and over the breastworks. On the works our men halted and delivered a plunging fire, which proved so destructive that the enemy never rallied again on this portion of the line, but left our men in undisturbed possession."

For some time after the mine explosion, but little was done by the Federals in front of Petersburg. Grant went to the north to direct some movements on the part of Sheridan in the Shenandoah Valley, and General Lee, accompanied by General Beauregard and a retinue of officers, visited the hospitals at Richmond, to see how their brave soldiers were faring. Speaking of it, a Richmond paper says: "It is pleasant to the eye, and gratifying to the heart, to behold these great champions of our national honor, turning aside for a season from the rigor of their martial duties, and lending the sympathies of their noble souls to the suffering and wounded, whom they have led to glory in the hour of battle. We love our generals the better when we witness them thus giving evidences of the tender affection they bear towards their men, knowing that they find narrow scope for the display of such virtues in the storm of combat upon the field of carnage."

In the middle of August, another attempt was made by Grant's army, on the north of the James, to defeat the Confederates, but again Lee's troops were successful. On the 18th and 19th, however, Grant's left, under Warren, after a defeat on the first day, succeeded on the next and following in holding the Weldon railroad, and enabling the Federal commander to form his plans with reference to the Danville road. "These plans," remarked a Richmond paper, "are now revealed, and all the energy and gallantry of the army under Lee and Beauregard will not be too much to beat back this bold movement to the south of Petersburg."

On the 25th, a severe engagement took place at Reams' station, between the Federals, Hancock's and Warren's corps, and the Confederates of A. P. Hill's corps, under Wilcox, Heth, and Mahone. The result was unfavorable to the Union troops, though they still held on to the railroad, where it was first gained, nearer Petersburg. The official report of General Lee stated that "seven stands of colors, 2,000 prisoners, and nine pieces of artillery remained in possession" of the Confederates. "One line of breastworks was carried by the cavalry under General Hampton, with great gallantry, who contributed largely to the success of the day."

General Hill's official report, at a later date, September 2d, says: "The correct results were, twelve stands of colors captured, and nine pieces of artillery, ten caissons, 2,150 prisoners, 3,100 stand of small-arms, and thirty-two horses." His own loss was, "in cavalry, artillery, and infantry, 720 men, killed, wounded, and missing."

This achievement at Reams' station, wherein many of the North Carolina soldiers were engaged, elicited from General Lee a highly complimentary letter to Governor Vance, concerning them. He says, under date August 29th, "I have been frequently called upon to mention the services of North Carolina soldiers in this army, but their gallantry and conduct were never more deserving of admiration than in the engagement at Reams' station, on the 25th instant." He then mentions the various brigades and divisions, and adds: "If the men who remain in North Carolina share the spirit of those they have sent to the field, as I doubt not they do, her defence may be securely intrusted to their hands."

A tribute like this, and many similar that General Lee gave to his soldiers, was particularly encouraging to the men, showing the kindly, just nature of him who wrote it, as well as convincing the troops that they had a commander whose eye was always upon them, ready to encourage and reward their good conduct.

It may be supposed that the stoppage of communication on the Weldon railroad, by Grant holding possession near Petersburg, would materially interfere with Lee's supplies, but this was not so. Other avenues to the fertile grain districts were open, and, meanwhile, his troops were employed, when not fighting the enemy, in building a branch line to connect the parts of the track not destroyed.

In the mean time, Lee's army "was being steadily and constantly filled to its original standard by men in the very prime and vigor of youthful manhood," and the daily routine showed a full determination on the part of the general and the Confederate authorities to remain firm at their post, while Grant was before the city. Nothing of importance, however, occurred in regard to the bombardment. A Confederate raid by General Hampton, on a large number of cattle, was so successful, and done with so much skill, that it proved of considerable annoyance and vexation to Grant's army, the poor soldiers thereby being subjected to much inconvenience. About the same time, Early's operations in the Shenandoah, where Sheridan was obtaining so much fame, called upon General Lee to reinforce him, which he did by sending troops along the Richmond and Gordonsville railroad, now in full working order under his control.

At length, on the 29th of September, General Grant recommenced active operations by another movement towards Richmond. His dispatch of that date, from Chapin's farm, stated that General Ord's corps had carried the Confederate line of intrenchments and fortifications below that place, and captured three hundred prisoners, with fifteen pieces of artillery. At the same time, General Birney moved from Deep Bottom and carried the Newmarket road. Simultaneous with these movements, General Meade, on the Union left, assaulted the Confederate right wing near Poplar Grove church. The latter retired to their earthworks, which were carried, and one gun

and sixty prisoners captured.   Advancing half a mile further, Meade was encountered by a strong force, and some desperate fighting ensued, without any additional success to the Federals. Indeed, the whole question of any real success at all was doubtful.   It is true that at one time reports were current in the North, of information, from reliable sources, having been given to the effect that Lee had evacuated Richmond, but these were soon afterwards changed to rumors of reverses again to the Union troops.   Lee, in an official report, stated that " Hill and Hampton had driven back the Federals on the right," while on the left they were effectually checked.   On the 7th of October, an engagement occurred on the Darbytown road, which the Confederates state to have been successful for them.   General Lee, in his official report, said that General Anderson attacked the enemy on the Charles City road and drove them from two lines of intrenchments, capturing prisoners and *materiel*, but with the loss of the brave General Gregg.

Various movements took place on both sides during the month of October, but at its close the position of Grant's army was as follows: North of the James the troops were disposed in a line from Fort Harrison, near Chapin's. Farm, across the Newmarket and Central roads, the Eighteenth corps holding the right, strongly protected by the fort, and the Tenth the left, flanked by the cavalry of Kautz.   Meade's army stretched from Petersburg across the Weldon railroad, to within four miles of the Southside road ; the Second corps on his right, the Ninth in the centre, and the Fifth on the left.

In the official report of General Lee, dated October 28th and 30th, he says : " The attack of General Heth upon the enemy, on the Boydton plank-road, was made by three brigades, under General Mahone in front, and General Hampton in the rear.   Mahone captured four hundred prisoners, three stands of colors, and six pieces of artillery.   The latter could not be brought off, the enemy having possession of the bridge.   In the attack subsequently made by the enemy, General Mahone broke three lines of battle ; and during the night the enemy retired from the Boydton plank-road, leaving his wounded, and more than two hundred and fifty dead on the field.

" About 9 P. M., a small force assaulted and took possession

of our works on the Baxter road, in front of Petersburg, but was soon driven out. On the Williamsburg road, yesterday, General Field captured upwards of four hundred prisoners, and seven stands of colors. The enemy left a number of dead in front of our works, and returned to his former position to-day."

In the latter part of October, General Longstreet was sufficiently recovered from his wound, received at the Wilderness battle, to be able to take up his command again, and General Anderson, who had held his post, now was appointed to that of Beauregard, which had been vacated by the latter going to the West.

General Lee, at this time, had occasion to open a correspondence with General Grant, on the subject of Butler's order concerning captured soldiers of the Confederate army being placed at labor in the Dutch Gap canal, then in process of construction; also, as regarded negro soldiers. The correspondence is too long to insert here; but it is alluded to, on account of some interesting remarks made by a correspondent of the *Savannah Republican,* on the chirography of the two parties. He says: "General Lee's handwriting is bold, and rather stiff; his letters being large, round, and very distinct. He bears heavily upon the pen—probably a goose-quill—and abbreviates many of his words, as if writing were a labor to him. The following is an exact transcript of the first sentence in his letter to General Grant:

"'General: I have read your letter of the 18th inst., accomp'g copies of letters from Judge Ould Comm'r of Exchange of Pris'rs on the part of the Conf'ate States & the Honb'le E. M. Stanton Sec'y of War & Lt. Col. Mulford Asst. Comm'r of Exc. of the U. States.'"

"He does not, as you perceive, punctuate closely; and nowhere in his letter does he write out the word 'and,' but invariably uses the abbreviation '&.' And yet he pauses long enough to dot all his 'i's,' and cross all his 't's.' All his letters are drawn nearly straight up and down the paper; in other words, they are like himself, round, full, bold, and upright, inclining neither to the right nor the left, and standing firmly on their base, as if they disdained all assistance. They are so clear and precise, so round, and weighty, and distinct,

that each letter reminds one of a solid cannon-ball, and each word of a cluster of grape-shot.

"General Grant's handwriting, on the contrary, though not so bold and distinct, nor the letters so large, and round, and erect, is, nevertheless, very legible, and very striking. It is full of energy and action, and his letters all incline to the right, and follow one after another, with a little space between them, as if they represented an equal number of his brigades on a rapid march round Lee's right. Among chirographers his hand would be called a running-hand. The words occupy much space from left to right, and still they are very clear and legible. He pays more attention to punctuation than General Lee, abbreviates less, and is equally careful of his 'i's' and 't's.' It may be the work of imagination, yet in reading his letter I cannot but picture the writer as a restless, nervous, energetic man, full of fire and action, always in motion, and always in a hurry."

The month of November chronicled but few changes in the position and advantages of the two armies. Movements, however, had been made, which seemed to augur a battle on an extensive scale; but if such was intended by Grant, it failed Any advances his army made were promptly met by Lee, and the result was, that the Federals fell back, and occupied their old camps again. We have not space to minutely relate, or even give an abstract of what was done; and, moreover, it belongs to the present hour, when each event comes daily before the eye of every one who chooses to read what the press so diligently and faithfully chronicles.

On the 1st of December fresh movements were made by a part of the Union forces. General Gregg's raid on the Petersburg and Weldon road was speedily followed by one under General Warren, who marched down the Jerusalem plankroad, and, crossing the Nottoway on pontoons, proceeded as far as the Meherrin River, where, finding the Confederate forces too strong, he turned about and safely reached his own camp. A cavalry reconnoissance had been thrown out between Grant's lines and this advance of Warren, with the view, doubtlessly, of ascertaining whether the Confederates had taken any steps for cutting it off. After forcing Lee's pickets across Hatcher's

Run, the Federal horse returned. In reference to these attempts General Lee makes the following report :

HEADQUARTERS ARMY NORTHERN VIRGINIA, Dec. 13.
HON. JAMES A. SEDDON, Secretary of War :

The expedition to Belfield, under General Warren, returned within the enemy's lines yesterday. The two divisions of the Ninth Corps which went to Warren's relief proceeded no further than Belcher's Mill. On meeting the returning column it turned back. On retiring from Belfield, the enemy moved easterly to the Jerusalem and Sussex Courthouse roads. Our troops, therefore, only encountered their rear-guard, and pursued no further than the Nottoway River. They have returned to camp, bringing in a few prisoners. Our loss is very slight. The superintendent of the railroad reports about six miles of the track torn up.

R. E. LEE.

Towards the close of the year, the Union calvary, under General Torbert, attacked the Confederates near Gordonsville, and another party of the Federal forces gained possession of Saltville. The following are General Lee's official announcements on the subject :

HEADQUARTERS ARMY OF NORTHERN VIRGINIA, Dec. 24, 1864.
HON. JAMES A. SEDDON :

General Fitz Lee reports that the force which attacked Lomax yesterday consisted of two divisions of the enemy's cavalry, under General Torbert.

General Lomax was posted across the Madison turnpike, two and a half miles from Gordonsville.

The enemy was handsomely repulsed, and retired about 3 P. M., leaving some of his dead on the field.

He travelled too rapidly last night to engage his rear, having passed Jack's shop, twelve miles from Gordonsville, one hour after dark.

Thirty-two prisoners captured at Liberty Mills on the 22d, being unable to keep up on their retreat, were liberated.

General Lomax's loss was slight.

R. E. LEE.

HEADQUARTERS ARMY OF NORTHERN VIRGINIA, Dec. 24, 1864.
HON. JAMES A. SEDDON, Secretary of War :

General Breckinridge reports that the enemy, after having
been roughly handled in the engagements of Saturday and
Sunday, near Marion, many having been killed and wounded,
gained possession of Saltville during the night of the 20th.

The garrison retreated up Rich Valley. His advance arrived
at daylight on the 21st, and the enemy retired that night and
the morning of the 22d towards Hector's Gap.

They are being pursued. Our troops are bearing the fatigue
and exposure with great cheerfulness.

The damage to the (salt) works can soon be repaired.

Many bridges and depots on the railroad have been burned.

                                        R. E. LEE.

Another subject, and that an important one, has yet to be
introduced before we close the year 1864 as regards General
Lee. In the month of November the legislative council of the
South seriously considered the question of arming the negroes
as Confederate soldiers, and the opinion of such a man as Lee
was naturally looked for with some eagerness. He soon gave
it, and the following remarks from the New York Herald, of
December 28th, embody what he says:

"In support of an argument for the arming of the slaves
of the 'Confederacy' in the cause of Southern independence, one of the Richmond journals recently asserted that
General Lee was in favor of the scheme, and that, such being
the case, the question ought to be considered as finally settled.
This statement, it now appears, was no random assertion ; for
a Richmond correspondent of the Liverpool Courier, in a letter to that journal of the 5th November, says he had been
spending a day with General Lee, who, in a conversation upon
the subject, said : 'I wish you to understand my views on this
subject. I am favorable to the use of our servants in the
army. I think we can make better soldiers of them than Lincoln can. He claims to have two hundred thousand of them
in his service. We can destroy the value of all such soldiers
to him by using ours against them. I do not see why I should
not have the use of such available material as well as he. I
would hold out to them the certainty of freedom and a home

when they shall have rendered efficient service. He has not given them a home, nor can he give them officers who can understand and manage them so well as we can.'"

At a later period, February 18th, 1865, in a letter to the Hon. E. Barksdale, he expressed himself in similar terms.

This, then, was General Lee's opinion, but events have since changed the whole circumstances as connected with the colored population of the South, and time has yet to show how far those events have or have not benefited the negro race.

The year 1865 commenced with many internal symptoms, on the part of the Southern Confederacy, that a severe and bitter struggle was yet to take place—not merely in regard to the military battle-field, but also with reference to the political and social state of things then existing. Dissension, doubt, and, to a certain extent, dismay, found a place nearly everywhere. At length, as with one mind, all men turned their eyes upon Lee. "His wisdom and firmness," it was hoped, would yet save their tottering cause at that "critical period," and accordingly, on the 17th of January, it was resolved by the General Assembly of Virginia, that his appointment to the entire control of the military forces in the South should be, confidentially, pressed upon Mr. Jefferson Davis. This was done by a letter to the President of the same date, and to which he replied without delay, cheerfully acknowledging the high regard felt for General Lee, and the great confidence placed in him. Mr. Davis, however, implied that Lee had once before, in 1862, been in the post now desired for him—viz., general-in-chief of all the armies of the Confederate States—but had been relieved at his own especial request when the duties became such as to prevent his more undivided attention to the army in the field within his own native State. Nevertheless, Mr. Davis assured the General Assembly, that, whenever it should "be found practicable by General Lee to assume command of all the armies of the Confederate States, without withdrawing him from direct command of the Army of Northern Virginia, he would deem it promotive of the public interests to place him in such command."

Accordingly, upon a resolution of the Confederate Congress, passed a few days afterwards to that effect, Mr. Davis signed the bill which created a general-in-chief, and on the 1st of

February, Lee was nominated by the President and confirmed by the Senate as commander-in-chief of the Confederate armies. The official order, promulgated February 6th, announcing this, is as follows:

General Robert E. Lee, having been duly appointed general-in-chief of the army of the Confederate States, will assume the duties thereof, and will be obeyed and respected accordingly.

General Order, No. 22, of 1864, is hereby revoked.

Lee now assumed entire command, and issued a general order to that effect, wherein he says:

"Deeply impressed with the difficulties and responsibility of the position, and humbly invoking the guidance of Almighty God, I rely for success upon the courage and fortitude of the army, sustained by the patriotism and firmness of the people, confident that their united efforts, under the blessing of Heaven, will secure peace and independence.

"The headquarters of the army, to which all special reports and communications will be addressed, will be for the present with the Army of Western Virginia. The stated and regular returns and reports of each army and department will be forwarded as heretofore to the office of the adjutant and inspector-general.

"R. E. LEE, General."

On the 11th of February, he published an address to the army and country, wherein he urges "constancy, fortitude, and courage in the hour of that adversity, suffering, and danger," then close upon them. In another order he speaks of "the discipline and efficiency of the army" as having been "greatly impaired;" and, on the 13th, he summoned his forces to prepare for the spring campaign.

But, though expressive of hope and confidence in his public addresses, it is evident that General Lee felt less sanguine in his private sentiments. He admitted that there was, among themselves even, a source of fear, and that was "the spreading of a causeless despondency among the people." This may have been a mild form of putting his inward convictions; but, probably, he had stronger ideas than these as to the back-

wardness and apathy of the masses in the South. Perhaps they were tired of the war, and were desirous of seeing it ended, hence the dilatoriness so often displayed in responding to fresh calls made upon them. At all events, Lee found it necessary to again renew these calls, and just prior to his new appointment we find him, on the 25th of January, appealing for arms, and, on the 28th, asking Georgia for general supplies for his army.

Meanwhile, the Federal forces were again in motion. On the 4th and 5th of February attempts were made by Gregg, Warren, and Humphreys, with their respective troops, against the Confederates stationed on the south of Petersburg, with what result, according to General Lee, the following shows:

HEADQUARTERS ARMY OF NORTHERN VIRGINIA, Feb. 6, 1865.

General S. COOPER, A. A. G.:

GENERAL—The enemy moved in strong force yesterday to Hatcher's Run. Part of his infantry, with Gregg's cavalry, crossed and proceeded on the Vaughn road—the infantry to Cat-tail Creek, the cavalry to Dinwiddie Courthouse, when its advance encountered a portion of our cavalry and retired. In the afternoon part of Hill's and Gordon's troops demonstrated against the enemy on the left of Hatcher's Run, near Armstrong's Mill. Finding him intrenched, they withdrew after dark.

During the night the force that had advanced beyond the creek returned to it, and were reported to be crossing. This morning Pegram's division moved to the right bank of the creek to reconnoitre, when it was vigorously attacked. The battle was obstinately contested for several hours, but General Pegram being killed, while bravely encouraging his men, and Colonel Hoffman wounded, some confusion occurred, and the division was pressed back to its original position. Evans's division, ordered by General Gordon to support Pegram's, charged the enemy and forced him back, but was, in turn, compelled to retire. Mahone's division arriving, the enemy was driven rapidly to his defences on Hatcher's Run. Our loss is reported to be small. That of the enemy not supposed great.

(Signed)   R. E. LEE.

There was, however, but little done, for some time, beyond desultory fighting similar to that just mentioned. Symptoms of a speedy termination of the struggle began to be more and more evident. Lee is reported to have said, in reply to questions of the Confederate Congress, that there were "not enough troops for the next campaign," and that their existence "could not last till midsummer." He added, moreover, as is stated, that "the cause of the South could not be saved, nor could any human power save it." Indeed, what was there for hope to dwell upon? Grant with his brilliant and powerful army of veterans—Sherman with his hardy and victorious campaigners—each had the Southern troops almost absolutely in their power; and this the Government at Richmond appeared to perfectly comprehend. The evacuation of the city, therefore, was seriously thought of, even so early as the month of February. The press began to discuss the route of Lee's retreat, ultimately concluding that Lynchburg would be the first place to fall back upon. Vainly did General Lee urge upon the Southern Congress some definite measure that would either give additional strength to the army, or bring about peace. To this latter, Lee was willing to use every means for its accomplishment. Certain unofficial communications had already taken place between the civil powers, but there were obstacles in the way of any thing like a treaty being made. The South was considered in "rebellion" against the national power, and, consequently, an unconditional submission was first required by the Federal authorities. But it was surmised that a military convention could be called for the purpose of bringing about an adjustment of affairs; and, owing to some misconceptions of General Grant's remarks on the subject of exchange of prisoners, General Lee was informed that an interview on the subject could take place. Accordingly, after communicating with Mr. Davis, he wrote to General Grant, under date March 2d, 1865, and stated his "sincere desire to leave nothing untried which might put an end to the calamities of war." He proposed a meeting at such time and place as General Grant should deem convenient.

To this letter, General Grant replied by explaining the misconception as to any meeting on such a subject, and stated that he had no power to accede to any such interview unless

on subjects of a purely military character.   No alternative remained, therefore, but submission, or war to the bitter end; and to carry out his duty, to the full extent of his means in this respect, Lee accepted the power at length yielded to him by the Senate, in the early part of March, of arming the negroes.

The 10th of March was appointed by Mr. Davis as a fast day, and, in issuing an order for its due observance, General Lee again shows his deep and earnest feeling. "Soldiers," says he, "let us bow with penitence and deep humility before Almighty God, who has sorely chastened us, beseeching Him to turn again and cause His face to shine upon us."

But now the time for a final struggle had come.   Grant had massed his forces with a view of making a vigorous movement on a plan of his own; and Lee anticipated this by a fierce assault on the Union right at Hare's Hill, on the Appomattox. Two columns of the Confederate army, under General Gordon, were sent at daylight of March 25th, to the attack.   On Hare's Hill was Fort Steadman, and this was quickly stormed and captured, its guns being turned upon other portions of the Union works.   But short-lived was this success, the last that the Confederate cause achieved.   Up rose other Federal forces near by, under Hartrauft, Potter, and Willcox, and with determined bravery forced back the Southern troops, capturing some two thousand that were cut off from the main body. Near about the same time, General Humphreys of the Second Corps, stationed on the extreme left of the Union army, hearing the firing on the right, at once pushed forward and captured the advanced Confederate lines south of Petersburg. This was the signal for a general move.   Grant advanced to the front, and sent Sheridan with his cavalry ahead to clear the way, which he did in a masterly manner by sweeping every thing before him.   The engagement at Five Forks, on April 1st, was a complete victory for the Federals; though every point on the headlong career of the elated Union troops was fiercely and gallantly contested by the Confederates. But in vain.   The last days of the Southern Confederacy had come.   Lee, in Petersburg, aided by his able and heroic generals and brave soldiers, did all that could be done by men fighting at the last gasp.   Petersburg fell on the morning of

Sunday, April 2d, and, almost at the same moment, Richmond was evacuated, and Lee with his discomfited troops on the way to Danville or Lynchburg, as might be.

That Richmond was to be abandoned, when Petersburg could no longer be held, seems to have been previously determined, for several important movements of individuals and effects had taken place, and President Davis himself, with some of his officials, left the capital, directly news arrived of the Union successes.

Meantime Grant, merely sending a force to occupy the captured cities, pushed on the whole of his army to intercept Lee. Sheridan with his cavalry dashed forward to Burkesville at the junction of the Lynchburg and Petersburg, and Danville and Richmond railroads, while the Fifth and Second corps encamped further on. Lee had crossed the Appomattox at Devil's Bend, and on Tuesday, April 4th, was in the vicinity of Amelia Courthouse.

Next day, Grant having reached Nottoway Courthouse, heard from Sheridan that Lee was intercepted, and accordingly pushed on to the support. Lee, finding himself thus cut off from Danville, made for Lynchburg by a westerly route through Farmsville and Deatonsville. Here, on the 6th, the Confederate rear was attacked by Sheridan with his cavalry and the Sixth Corps on the left, while the Second and Fifth corps supported on the right. A victory was again achieved by the Federals, and 13,000 prisoners, including Generals Ewell, Custis Lee, Anderson, and others of note, taken. Next day General Grant commenced the following correspondence, while Lee was pushing on towards Appomattox Court-house:

I.

GENERAL GRANT TO GENERAL LEE.

General R. E. LEE, Commander C. S. A.: April 7.

GENERAL—The result of the last week must convince you of the hopelessness of further resistance on the part of the Army of Northern Virginia in this struggle. I feel that it is so, and regard it as my duty to shift from myself the responsibility of any further effusion of blood, by asking of

you the surrender of that portion of the Confederate States army known as the Army of Northern Virginia.

Very respectfully, your obedient servant,

U. S. GRANT, Lieutenant-General,
Commanding Armies of the United States.

II.

GENERAL LEE TO GENERAL GRANT.

April 7.

GENERAL—I have received your note of this date. Though not entirely of the opinion you express of the hopelessness of further resistance on the part of the Army of Northern Virginia, I reciprocate your desire to avoid useless effusion of blood, and, therefore, before considering your proposition, ask the terms you will offer on condition of its surrender.

R. E. LEE, General.

To LIEUTENANT-GENERAL U. S. GRANT,
Commanding Armies of the United States.

III.

GENERAL GRANT TO GENERAL LEE.

April 8.

To General R. E. LEE, Commanding Confederate States Army:

GENERAL—Your note of last evening, in reply to mine of same date, asking the conditions on which I will accept the surrender of the Army of Northern Virginia, is just received.

In reply, I would say, that peace being my first desire, there is but one condition that I insist upon, viz.:

That the men surrendered shall be disqualified for taking up arms against the Government of the United States until properly exchanged.

I will meet you, or designate officers to meet any officers you may name for the same purpose, at any point agreeable to you, for the purpose of arranging definitely the terms upon which the surrender of the Army of Northern Virginia will be received.

Very respectfully, your obedient servant,

U. S. GRANT, Lieutenant-General,
Commanding Armies of the United States.

IV.
GENERAL LEE TO GENERAL GRANT.

April 8.

GENERAL—I received, at a late hour, your note of to-day in answer to mine of yesterday.

I did not intend to propose the surrender of the Army of Northern Virginia, but to ask the terms of your proposition. To be frank, I do not think the emergency has arisen to call for the surrender. But, as the restoration of peace should be the sole object of all, I desire to know whether your proposals would tend to that end.

I cannot, therefore, meet you with a view to surrender the Army of Northern Virginia, but so far as your proposition may affect the Confederate States forces under my command, and lead to the restoration of peace, I should be pleased to meet you at 10 A. M., to-morrow, on the old stage-road to Richmond, between the picket-lines of the two armies.

Very respectfully, your obedient servant,

R. E. LEE,
General Confederate States Armies.

To LIEUTENANT-GENERAL GRANT,
   Commanding Armies of the United States.

V.
GENERAL GRANT TO GENERAL LEE.

April 9.

General R. E. LEE, Commanding C. S. A.:

GENERAL—Your note of yesterday is received. As I have no authority to treat on the subject of peace, the meeting proposed for 10 A. M., to-day, could lead to no good. I will state, however, general, that I am equally anxious for peace with yourself; and the whole North entertain the same feeling. The terms upon which peace can be had are well understood. By the South laying down their arms they will hasten that most desirable event, save thousands of human lives, and hundreds of millions of property not yet destroyed.

Sincerely hoping that all our difficulties may be settled without the loss of another life, I subscribe myself,

Very respectfully, your obedient servant,

U. S. GRANT,
Lieutenant-General, U. S. A.

VI.
GENERAL LEE TO GENERAL GRANT.

April 9, 1865.

GENERAL—I received your note of this morning on the picket-line, whither I had come to meet you and ascertain definitely what terms were embraced in your proposition of yesterday with reference to the surrender of this army.

I now request an interview in accordance with the offer contained in your letter of yesterday for that purpose.

Very respectfully, your obedient servant,

R. E. LEE, General.

To LIEUTENANT-GENERAL GRANT,
Commanding United States Armies.

VII.
GENERAL GRANT TO GENERAL LEE.

April 9.

General R. E. LEE, Commanding Confederate States Armies:

Your note of this date is but this moment (11 : 50 A. M.) received.

In consequence of my having passed from the Richmond and Lynchburg road to the Farmville and Lynchburg road, I am at this writing about four miles west of Walter's Church, and will push forward to the front for the purpose of meeting you.

Notice sent to me on this road where you wish the interview to take place will meet me.

Very respectfully, your obedient servant,

U. S. GRANT, Lieutenant-General.

In accordance with this intimation, Lee designated a spot where he and Grant could discuss the terms of surrender. This was at Appomattox Courthouse—a small country village of some five hundred inhabitants. The building selected for the interview was a two-story brick house nearly square, rather old, but surrounded by a beautiful yard of shrubbery and flowers, with roses and violets in full bloom, and the trees decked in a coat of green. It belonged to Mr. Wilmer McLean, a well-to-do farmer. Here, about 2 P. M., General Lee arrived, accompanied by Colonel Marshal, his chief of staff, and was immediately shown into the parlor, a large room neatly furnished, where he took a seat at the table.

General Lee was dressed in the usual Confederate gray, and had donned a very handsome sword that had been presented to him by friends.   A few moments later General Grant arrived, accompanied by his aid-de-camp, Colonel Parker, formerly chief of the Six Nations—a man of a wonderfully acute mind, and a fast friend of the general's.   Grant was dressed in blue, and without his sword.   Lee immediately arose, and advancing towards each other they shook hands, and then introduced their respective chiefs of staff.   The business of the meeting then followed, and in a few moments was settled as follows:

THE TERMS OF SURRENDER.

APPOMATTOX COURT-HOUSE, April 9.

General R. E. LEE, Commanding C. S. A.:

In accordance with the substance of my letter to you of the 8th instant, I propose to receive the surrender of the Army of Northern Virginia, on the following terms, to wit:

Rolls of all the officers and men to be made in duplicate, one copy to be given to an officer designated by me, the other to be retained by such officers as you may designate.

The officers to give their individual paroles not to take arms against the United States until properly exchanged, and each company or regimental commander to sign a like parole for the men of their commands.

The arms, artillery, and public property to be packed and stacked, and turned over to the officers appointed by me to receive them.   This will not embrace the side-arms of the officers, nor their private horses or baggage.

This done, each officer and man will be allowed to return to their homes, not to be disturbed by United States authority so long as they observe their parole and the laws in force where they may reside.

Very respectfully,

U. S. GRANT, Lieutenant-General.

THE SURRENDER.

HEADQUARTERS ARMY OF NORTHERN VIRGINIA, April 9, 1865.

Lieutenant-General U. S. GRANT, Commanding U. S. A.:

GENERAL—I have received your letter of this date, containing the terms of surrender of the Army of Northern Virginia.

as proposed by you; as they are substantially the same as those expressed in your letter of the 8th instant, they are accepted. I will proceed to designate the proper officers to carry the stipulations into effect.

Very respectfully, your obedient servant,

R. E. LEE, General.

While the papers were being drawn up, the time was passed between these two eminent chiefs in recalling events that transpired long before the war, to which no further allusion was made on either side. When the articles of surrender were drawn up and signed, Lee remarked that many of his cavalrymen owned the horses upon which they rode, and he asked if the word "personal effects" included them. General Grant replied that he considered that they ought to be turned over to the United States, and with this General Lee coincided. "But," said General Grant, "I will instruct the officers who are appointed to carry out the capitulation to allow those who have their own horses to return to their homes; they will then do for spring ploughing." General Lee was struck by this liberal act, and with considerable feeling said, " Allow me to express my thanks for such consideration and generosity on your part. I think it cannot fail of having a good effect."

The following was the parole signed by General Lee and his staff-officers:

THE PAROLES OF GENERAL LEE AND HIS ARMY.

The following was the parole signed by General Lee and his staff-officers:

We, the undersigned, prisoners of war belonging to the Army of Northern Virginia, having been this day surrendered by General R. E. Lee, commanding said army, to Lieutenant-General Grant, commanding the armies of the United States, do hereby give our solemn parole of honor that we will not hereafter serve in the armies of the Confederate States, or in any military capacity whatever, against the United States of America, or render aid to the enemies of the latter, until

properly exchanged in such manner as shall be mutually ap•
proved by the relative authorities.

> R. E. LEE, General.
> W. H. TAYLOR, Lieutenant-Colonel and A. A. G.
> CHAS. S. VENABLE, Lieutenant-Colonel and A. A. G.
> CHAS. MARSHAL, Lieutenant-Colonel and A. A. G.
> H. E. PRATON, Lieutenant-Colonel and Inspector-General.
> GILES BROOKE, Major and A. A. Surgeon-General.
> H. S. YOUNG, A. A. General.

Done at Appomattox Courthouse, Va., }
   this ninth (9) day of April, 1865." }

The parole was countersigned as follows:

The above-named officers will not be disturbed by United
States authorities as long as they observe their parole and the
laws in force where they may reside.

> GEO. H. SHARPE,
> General, and Assistant Provost-Marshal.

The officers of the rebel army signed the following parole
for their men:

"I, the undersigned, commanding officer of ———, do, for
the within-named prisoners of war belonging to the Army of
Northern Virginia, who have been this day surrendered by
General Robert E. Lee, Confederate States Army, commanding said army, to Lieutenant-General Grant, commanding
armies of the United States, hereby give my solemn parole of
honor that the within-named shall not hereafter serve in the
armies of the Confederate States, or in military or any
capacity whatever against the United States of America, or
render aid to the enemies of the latter, until properly exchanged in such manner as shall be mutually approved by the
respective authorities."

The within named will not be disturbed by the United
States authorities so long as they observe their parole and the
laws in force where they may reside.

Done at Appomattox Courthouse, Virginia, }
   this 9th day of April, 1865.   }

Immediately on conclusion of the formal terms of surrender
General Grant telegraphed to Washington as follows:

HEADQUARTERS ARMIES OF THE UNITED STATES, }
April 9—4 : 30 P. M. }

Hon. EDWIN M. STANTON, Secretary of War:

General Lee surrendered the Army of Northern Virginia this afternoon, upon the terms proposed by myself. The accompanying additional correspondence will show the conditions fully.

(Signed)   U. S. GRANT, Lieutenant-General.

On the next day, General Lee issued the following farewell address to his army :

GENERAL ORDERS—NO. 10.

HEADQUARTERS ARMY OF NORTHERN VIRGINIA, April 10.

After four years of arduous service, marked by unsurpassed courage and fortitude, the Army of Northern Virginia has been compelled to yield to overwhelming numbers and resources. I need not tell the survivors of so many hard, fought battles, who have remained steadfast to the last, that I have consented to this result from no distrust of them, but holding that valor and devotion could have accomplished nothing that could compensate for the loss that would have attended the continuation of the contest, I have determined to avoid the useless sacrifice of those whose past valor has endeared them to their countrymen. By the terms of agreement, officers and men can return to their homes and remain there until exchanged. You will take with you the satisfaction that proceeds from the consequences of duty faithfully performed, and I earnestly pray that a merciful God will extend you His blessing and protection.

With an increasing admiration of your constancy and devotion to your country, and a grateful remembrance of your kind and generous consideration of myself, I bid you an affectionate farewell.

ROBERT E. LEE, General.

General Lee remained with his army for a few days to carry out the terms of capitulation, and then went to Richmond, where he arrived on the afternoon of April 15th. His reception there was of such a character that we cannot pass it over

without a few words in the language of those who were eye witnesses.

It was towards 3 P. M., when General Lee, with some half-dozen of his staff and a few cavalry, approached the city by the Lynchburg turnpike. When he arrived at the pontoon bridge, spanning the James River between Richmond and Manchester, an immense crowd had collected to receive him, and he was greeted with cheers upon cheers. Several Union officers and soldiers were also there, and these, with the true characteristic of all brave and noble-minded men, raised their caps to the fallen commander-in-chief of the Southern armies—he who, for the whole period of four years had been the leading and only general in the State of Virginia, and who had so long stood up against the daring and heroism of the North. As he now passed along the streets towards his residence, in Franklin-street, windows and doors flew open, and the softer sex spontaneously appeared waving their 'kerchiefs as a welcome. These tokens of respect and esteem evidently affected him, especially as he marked the sad tokens of the past in the aspect of men and things around. What were his thoughts we can only judge from a knowledge of the whole previous history connected with him and with the city itself. But, except an occasional bow, as he recognized an acquaintance, and an acknowledgment of the salutations made to him, he gave no sign or token of his mind. His hair white as snow, his face care-worn, and his air and manner jaded, he rode on with a quiet and thoughtful countenance. At every step the crowd increased. Strong men, alike with women, wept aloud, for the glory of Richmond—as its people once felt—had departed, and its great chief and popular idol now came, not as a victorious general, but as a conquered man.

The residence of General Lee, at Richmond, was a large three-story brick house, built without ornamental flourishes, with a hall at one side, a basement, and the general arrangement of rooms. As he dismounted here and ascended the steps, the crowd spontaneously gave him three cheers, and called upon him for a speech, while, for a moment, he stood upon the balcony and bade his staff good-by. But, no doubt too much affected, Lee merely raised his hat to the crowd, and bending his head in salutation, passed within his doors,

and was lost to sight as the high military chief who had won so much renown in the cause he had—rightly or wrongly—from a sense of duty to his native State, espoused.

It is due to Lee, says a Philadelphia correspondent, to state that " he entered the city with the least possible display, and that he took the shortest route to his house, trying to avoid all kind of public demonstration. But the people loved as well as admired the man, and his simple presence—fallen as conquered, but not disgraced—stirred them to the last sign of emotion. It was no words that he spoke, for he said not a word. It was no mute appeal that he made, for he avoided them ; but it was his presence and its signification that moved them." To this may we not add that man's truer and better nature is ever keenly susceptible of loftier and nobler emotions when beholding a spectacle of fallen greatness. There is in disaster and suffering, a something which tends to soften our sterner and more repellant character. Truly, as the writer from whom we obtain our information says, " The animate corpse of Napoleon, pacing the walks of Longwood, drew tears from many besides the worshippers of the empire. Lee riding, a prisoner of war, through the streets of the city he had so long defended, is the latest parallel of that sad scene. We must forgive this people."

Happily, as the public press stated at the time, General Lee found the noble-minded partner of his life, Mrs. Lee, in good health, though reports to the contrary had gone forth ; and in a few days afterwards he received the visits of his friends. But, there were other visits, however, of a character that soon became annoying. He became troubled by calls, from many whose sole object was curiosity or a desire to catch what he might say and make something—for good or for evil—out of it. We have several instances of this before us; but pass them over now. One anecdote illustrative of this may alone be mentioned.

A free negro had about three hundred dollars owing to him from the Southern Confederacy ; and, hearing that General Lee had arrived, he went to him and asked for his money. The general was seated in his back piazza with a portion of his family around him, when the following colloquy took place :

General. Well, Edward, how do you do? I am glad to see you!

Edward. I am right well, sah: had mighty hard time here, sah.

General. Yes, we have all had a hard time, Edward.

Edward. Ise been very poorly, and dey owes me three hundred dollars, and I come to get it.

General (somewhat surprised). Oh, Edward, I have nothing to do with that. Mr. Trenholm attended to that.

"Yes, sah," said the old messenger, and taking himself off, hat in hand, left General Lee, no doubt in a state of bewilderment at this new development of negro strategy and business tact.

From the date of Lee's arrival in Richmond as a prisoner of war, there is little to chronicle that of right belongs to the public to become acquainted with. The *general* has merged into the *private citizen*, honorably doing his duty in that new station of life to which Providence has called him. One or two events alone have to be recorded as attached to his past military career, and to the position he now holds in connection with the Literary Institute of Virginia. For the rest, the pen has no right to enter upon it more than he himself may choose to put down.

When the news of President Lincoln's assassination reached General Lee, he was powerfully affected. Like all properly constituted minds, and especially of such a stamp as Lee's, his was filled with horror at the atrocious deed, and, for some time, he remained wholly secluded. At length a new order of things called him forth to attend to his personal position. President Johnson's proclamation of amnesty led him to apply for a special pardon; but just at this time a Federal judge at Norfolk thought fit to frame an indictment for treason against him. Thereupon General Lee inclosed his application to General Grant, who, in the most complimentary and friendly terms, forwarded it to Washington. But, owing to some misconception, his name got mixed up with those mentioned in the indictment prepared against Wirz, and only for prompt action on the part of the Executive, it would have so stood. But the sense of the people in the North as well as the South was against it, and, finally, General Lee received his full acquittal.

In August he was offered the Presidency of Washington College, and as soon as he found himself at full liberty to do so, he accepted it. In his letter of acceptance he says:

"It is the duty of every citizen, in the present condition of the country, to do all in his power to aid in the restoration of peace and harmony, and in no way to oppose the policy of the State or General Government directed to that object;" and that "it is particularly incumbent on those charged with the instruction of the young to set an example of submission to authority."

The rector of the college, John W. Brockenbrough, then issued an announcement, dated September 1st, that General Lee had been appointed, and spoke of him in very high terms, indorsing the sentiments uttered in his letter, and concluding his remarks as follows:

"In dedicating his future life to the holy work of educating the youth of his country, General Lee presents a new and interesting phase of his grand and heroic character, a character than which no more perfect model exists among living men. 'Tis a solid fabric, and will well support the laurels that adorn it. Let the young men of the country, North as well as South, be wise and profit, not less by his precepts, than by his great example."

On the 2d of October the amnesty oath was taken by General Lee; and the same day, at Lexington, Va., he was formally installed with becoming ceremonies as president of Washington College.

* * * * *

We now close our sketch of General Lee with the following illustrations and remarks on his character.

A foreign gentleman who had been in the South during a great portion of the war, said:

"I assure you that Lee is more than ever a sight for gods and men. The same tranquil modesty, utter absence of vanity, egotism, or self-seeking, and determination to spend and be spent in discharge of his duty. It is certainly one of the most beautiful characters I ever read of—certainly the most beautiful that I ever encountered."

A characteristic incident concerning him is thus related:

"A gentleman who was in the train from Richmond to

Petersburg, a very cold morning, not long ago, tells us his at
tention was attracted by the efforts of a young soldier, with
his arm in a sling, to get his overcoat on. His teeth as well
as his sound hand were brought into use to effect the object;
but, in the midst of his efforts, an officer rose from his seat,
advanced to him, and very carefully and tenderly assisted him,
drawing the coat gently over the wounded arm and buttoning
it up comfortably, then, with a few kind and pleasant words,
returning to his seat.

"Now, the officer in question was not clad in gorgeous uni
form, with a brilliant wreath upon the collar and a multitude
of gilt lines upon the sleeves, resembling the famous labyrinth
of Crete, but he was clad in 'a simple suit of gray,' distinguished from the garb of a civilian only by the three stars
which every Confederate colonel in the service by the regulations is entitled to wear. And yet he was no other than our
chief, General Robert E. Lee, who is not braver and greater
than he is good and modest."

But apart from what his personal friends, his companions
in arms, or impartial strangers may say, we need only refer to
the honest opinions of those generous-minded men who were
his opponents. The estimation of Scott and others has been
recorded, and the dignified, manly act of General McDowell—
the act of a true soldier and a man—who had once been his
friend, in refraining from trespassing on Lee's private property,
till military necessity forced his compliance with official
orders, cannot be forgotten, nor the considerate and generous
demeanor of General Grant. True, there have been those
who, through the press, have allowed party feeling of late to
malign Lee and all his family—even the dead—forgetting the
numerous testimonies of their worth found in letters of Washington, Judge Marshall, and other eminent men; but, when
the fierce tide of passion and sad strife is ended, justice, we
are sure, will yet award a truthful panegyric to his name.

As aptly illustrating our remarks, the following able analysis
of his character, from the *American Phrenological Journal* of
September, 1864, deserves to be brought forward.

"The likeness of General Lee herewith presented is said to
be an excellent one. The position, however, is not the best
for phrenological and physiognomical purposes, a three-quarter

or a side view being better. The skilful reader of character will be able, however, to make out much even from this.

"First, it may be observed that General Lee is a large man and well built, each part being in perfect proportion and harmony with every other part and with the whole. The chest is capacious, the heart, the stomach, etc., are amply developed, and he is said to be the picture of perfect health and manly beauty.

"The temperaments are well balanced, the vital and motive, however, predominating, with not too much of the mental; and he is naturally cool and collected, rather than nervous, fiery, or fidgety. He thinks before he speaks, and looks before he leaps. His head is in harmony with his body, being large—even massive—and both long and broad. There is nothing pinched up, contracted, or little about him. He has been literally endowed with all the natural talents vouchsafed to man; and in addition to this, he has been thoroughly educated, intellectually, religiously, and socially. If he is not a philosopher or a statesmen, he is at least a first-class scholar, and would everywhere pass for a gentleman.

"His intellectual faculties, without an exception, are prominent. Causality and comparison are especially large, but language is less conspicuous.

"The moral sentiments, as a class, are scarcely full. Benevolence, conscientiousness, self-esteem, firmness, and approbativeness are among the largest organs. Combativeness, destructiveness, secretiveness, and cautiousness are full. The organs comprising the social group are also full or large, and he is affectionate, loving, and warm-hearted. As a citizen in civil life, he was without reproach; as a military man, he stands in the front rank. No one will dispute his ability in this department. Were he on the side of the Unionists, instead of the Confederates, the entire North would be proud of him, and claim equality for him with a Napoleon or a Wellington. We claim for him only what phrenology indicates, and what he has proved himself to be. Nature made him a man, circumstances made him a slaveholder and a soldier. He answers well the ends of his creation and position. We are charitable enough to attribute to him no wrong motive, for we remember that George Washington was no less a rebel than is

General Lee, though on the side of freedom instead of slavery
But we may affirm, judged from *our* standpoint, that both he
and all his associates have acted unwisely and from a mistaken
judgment. May he see the error of his ways, and correct
them."

In conclusion, we now offer the following remarks as coming
from a paper (the London *Daily News*) ever most warm in
favor of the Northern cause. It says:

" General Lee and the relics of his army have surrendered.
The most honored and the most trusted of the Confederate
leaders, the man who but a few weeks back was appointed
commander-in-chief of the whole armies of the Confederacy,
expressly that he might retrieve its fortunes and establish its
independence, has laid down his arms. In thus acting he has
been faithful to his character and his honor. He fought gallantly while by fighting he could hope to achieve any practical result, to hold the capital, to save the army, or to maintain
the existence of the State which had confided to him its
defence; but when the course of events and the fate of war
satisfied him that none of these objects could be served by
resistance, he spared the useless effusion of blood. The respect
which he has won from friend and foe will be heightened by
this conduct. His military reputation suffers nothing from
succumbing to superior numbers; his patriotism shines the
brighter for this evidence that not even the passionate chagrin
of defeat could induce him to set personal ambition or false
pride above the true interests of his country."

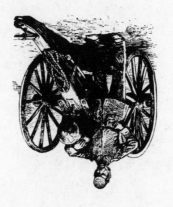

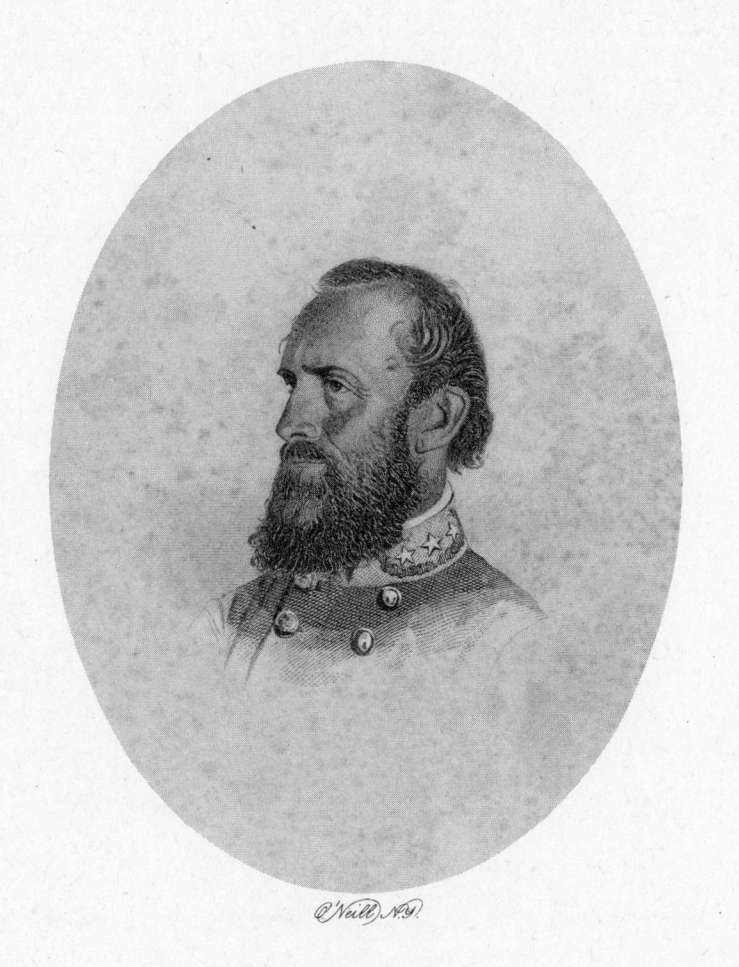

LT. GEN. T. J. JACKSON.

From a Photograph taken a few days before his death.

GENERAL THOMAS JONATHAN JACKSON.

CHAPTER I.

ONE day, in the year 1841, a lad, seventeen years old, might
have been seen wending his way, on foot, towards the great
city of Washington, the seat of government of the United
States. There was nothing particularly striking about this
lad, except, perchance, a stolidity of expression upon his countenance, and, rather than otherwise, a want of those marked
features of vivacity and intelligence, generally so characteristic of the youthful American. Indeed, he would have seemed
to be rather a dull and ungainly lad, than a bright one. But,
there was evidently a stubbornness of purpose about him, as
he plodded along on his way, that showed a dogged perti-
nacity in his will as to whatsoever he had set his mind upon.
Plain in appearance and indifferently dressed, it was clear that
his life had not been passed amidst city scenes, or in polished
society. There was nothing courtly or refined about him,
beyond the simple manners nature herself teaches. And
whatever he was, or whatever he might become, assuredly to
himself alone did and would belong all the credit due.

We have said this lad was on his way, a-foot, towards Washington; and now we must add, that, having an irresistible desire to enter upon a military career, he was bent upon trying

to see if he could not, possibly, get an appointment as a cadet
at West Point. But, what had he to help him in procuring
such an appointment? In those days it was not easily obtained, and, especially, it needed some influential or prominent
introduction. Had he got this, then, that solitary youth plodding along the highway? Had he wealthy friends, or relatives
of political note? Was he linked to any of the old established
families of the land? No, reader! Not one of these things,
or any thing else save perhaps some political friends to help
him along, had he: but he had energy, perseverance, a strong
heart, and, even young as he was, a firm belief that what he
wished for would be. In other words, he was a believer in
the doctrine of predestination, and hence his desires, he conceived, would be granted, because his desires were just exactly
what might occur, whether for good or for evil. A stern
fatalist, he was a passive, though ready worker in the hands
of destiny.

Still, it was necessary that some human means should be
found to aid his inclinations. Were these, then, to be found?
Let us see.

The lad himself was, as we have said, about seventeen years
old, and, at the time we introduce him, had just left a farm,
where, first as a laboring boy, then as something of assistant
manager, he had been working for all the past period of his
life. An orphan, dependent in his childhood upon a paterna.
uncle, with whom he had ever since remained honorably earn-
ing his bread, the early lessons received by him were those of
poverty, though at the same time of honest ennobling labor.
Yet, at his birth there might have been hopes far different.
His father had been a lawyer at Clarksburg, in West Virginia;
his grandfather, a surveyor of the county in which he resided,
and represented it in the Legislature. But when this lad
was only three years old his father died, and, through some
previous unfortunate circumstances, left this youngest child,
with an elder brother and two sisters, completely penniless.
His uncle took the orphan to his home, where, as we have
seen, he remained for the next fifteen years. During this
time the boy worked hard: in summer, always in the field—
in winter, devoting all spare hours to school, where he gained
the rudiments of a plain education. Conscientious in the dis-

charge of his duties,—grave and seriously disposed, he was noted for his industry, intelligence, and probity. Indeed, it is believed he was, when only sixteen, elected constable of the county, in consequence of his remarkable high qualities oi mind and conduct.

At length he determined to enter upon a new career. A military life seemed to be that which was, to his nature, most inviting; and with promises, from political friends, of kindly aid to pave the way in his first movement—John Tyler, of Virginia, at that time being president—this lad started on foot, to try if his object could be accomplished. Did he succeed, that sturdy farmer lad? We shall see.

*   *   *   *

There is, in Mexico, and close to the great city itself, a very strongly fortified place called *Chapultepec*. It is a natural and isolated mound of great elevation, and, at the time we are about to refer, contained the military college of the republic, with a large number of sub-lieutenants and other students. The works about this place were of great magnitude; and, in fact, it was the key on the west side to the city of Mexico, and to get possession of the latter, it was necessary to capture the former. Now, in the month of September, 1847, a gallant army of Americans, under the leadership of General Scott, was engaged in vigorously assaulting this place, prior to the great victory they soon obtained, both there and in the capital of the Montezumas itself. Among the bold assailants, there was one officer holding a lieutenant's commission in a field-battery. This officer was in charge of one section of artillery in the advance. He was cool, self-possessed, and seemingly in utter indifference to the storm of shot and shell which came pouring down from the besieged. There, with unflinching nerve, he stood his ground, only moving *forward*, when he moved at all. At length, an order to charge was given by the general in command. The lieutenant promptly prepared to obey, but his men, appalled by the terrible fire poured upon them, hesitated, and remained under cover. Seeing this, without a moment's hesitation, the young officer stepped into the exposed road, and said, " See, my men: there is no danger. Follow me!"

Chapultepec was taken; and among the many heroic inci

dents of that day, September 13th, this one of the bold lieu·
tenant has been recorded.

*   *   *   *

Fourteen years after the preceding occurrence, there is another battlefield we must cast our eye upon, but, this time, it
is at our own doors.   Friend to friend, brother with brother—
sons born of the same flag—contend for mastery, and fierce,
most deadly fierce, is the strife!   Already has the carnage been
dreadful!   Heaps of slain cover the ground, and the whiz of
shell and shot seems as if complete annihilation to every man
and beast upon that blood-stained field must ensue.   Yet,
cool, calm, stern, and self-collected, one man sits upon a
charger as though he were a mere spectator at a review!   On
a rising ground, which commands a full view of the battle, at
that time fearfully grand, his keen glittering eye takes in the
whole scene, as he remains there apparently insensible to all.
For a moment or two, let us take a closer glance at this
strange man, so seemingly immobile amidst such terrible
strife; let us approach him and examine his appearance.
See!   He is evidently a powerful man, and, when erect on
foot, must be some five feet ten inches high, rather thick-set,
with a full chest, broad stalwart shoulders, but somewhat
clumsy looking.   His face is slightly bronzed, but showing
the picture of health, and denoting a mixture of several qualities that might puzzle one to say which was most predominant.
Raising his hat, the broad forehead indicates clearness of intellect, courage, self-command, perseverance, and indomitable
will.   His eyes express a singular union of mildness, energy,
and concentration; his cheek and nose are both long and well
formed.   In his dress, simplicity is characteristic,—a common
suit of gray, faded cassimere, but just sufficiently braided to
show his rank is that of a general.   On his horse, he has a
most unmilitary appearance.   The stirrups are short—his
knees are cramped up, with his heels stuck out behind, and
his chin, now and again, falls drooping on his breast.   But his
eye, that piercing, eagle eye, when looking on the field, even
at the very time he so droops his head, tells of the man, and
at once proclaims him a true hero.   And now mark his every
motion.   See!   The troops on his own side are evidently overpowered!   Appalled at the fierceness of an heroic attack made

upon the hill on which they are stationed, they gradually fall back, and seem as if about to fly. Yet, still he sits, calm, immovable, and like a statue. His orders had been given; he waits for one decisive moment to effect another movement; and his presence thus to the brave soldiers who know him well, acts as a charm to stay their flight. Who then is he, that thus so strangely appears amidst such a wild and terrible scene? Listen, and observe.

An officer of rank, dashing furiously up, amid the fiercest of the fight, approaches him. "General," said he, "they are beating us back! We're obliged to give ground!" For a second or so, the general looks at the officer, but his stern, silent face betrays no answering emotion. The keen eye glitters for a moment; then a speaking animation spreads across his features: his lips open; and in curt, peculiar tones, he replies, "Aye, sir? Well, then, we must give them the bayonet!" The gallant officer—himself meeting his death immediately afterwards—gathers new inspiration from his words. He gallops back to the remnant of his command, and, pointing to the statue-like general, says to his men, "Look! there is JACKSON, standing like a *stone wall*. Come! Let us conquer or die! Follow me!"

Yes! that strange, apparently immobile general, was the now well-known heroic Thomas J. Jackson, thenceforth called by the term here applied to him, "Stonewall" Jackson,*— the same calm, sturdy, energetic being who, as a lad, walked his way, twenty years before, to Washington for the appointment he obtained as a cadet to West Point, and who, as the young lieutenant at Chapultepec, encouraged his men onward by personally showing them the road, heedless of the danger!

*   *   *   *   *

---

* The above is the currently received idea of Jackson's receiving the name of *Stonewall* affixed to his own. But it has been asserted, with some good evidence, that the soubriquet of "Stonewall" originally came *from his brigade,* which was so called because principally recruited in a stone-wall country—the valley counties of Jefferson, Frederick, Page, and Warren. The brigade bore this name before the battle of Bull Run, and thus lent its name to its stout leader—not derived it from him—and Jackson, even in his last hours, was particular in explaining to those around him, that the title belonged to his men and not to him.

We will now proceed to fill up the blanks in the above rapid sketches of the man, and then go more into detail with his after history.

The immediate ancestors of General "Stonewall" Jackson were settled in Western Virginia,—his grandfather being Edward Jackson, for a long time surveyor of Lewis county, and a member of the Legislature,—his father, Jonathan Jackson, a lawyer of some considerable reputation at Clarksburg. The mother of our hero was the daughter of a Mr. Thomas Neal, of Wood county, who bore to her husband four children, two sons and two daughters. The youngest of these children was Thomas, the subject of this sketch, who was born January 21st, 1824. When he was three years old, his father died in embarrassed circumstances, and, as we have already mentioned, the lad was left to the care of his paternal uncle, until, by his own perseverance, he contrived to get an appointment as cadet at West Point. It appears, from various statements, that the lad was at first strongly dissuaded, by his friends and relatives, from venturing on such a step ; but, he was not to be turned from his purpose. A member of Congress from his section of Virginia had a presentation to West Point, and young Jackson determined to ask for it. He obtained an introduction, and, with a slender wardrobe in his hand, journeyed, partly by stage and on foot, to Washington, and that, too, during the muddy season. His perseverance met a reward. Introduced to the secretary of war, that eminent official complimented him for his energy, and gave the appointment. But Jackson had other difficulties in himself to overcome. His education had been very poor, and he was thus inferior to all his classmates in every intellectual attainment. Still he persevered ; and those who remember him there, speak of him as an earnest worker, plodding onward in his tasks with unwearied assiduity. He was, however, looked upon as dull and slow, taking three times as long to learn any thing as did his companions. Nevertheless, what he did learn was learned well, and his tutors felt much pleased with him. He was of a retiring and taciturn disposition, but when brought out in conversation on subjects of interest, his face would light up with a pleasant smile, and his whole countenance beam with intelligence.

After the usual four years' residence, he graduated number seventeen in his class; and in July, 1846, was brevetted second-lieutenant, with orders to report for duty in Mexico, under General Taylor.   When General Scott took command, Jackson served under him during the several battles made so famous to the American arms by the skill of that great military chieftain.   His conduct, as we have already seen, was marked by daring and firmness, and his promotion, consequently, was rapid.   In August, 1847, he was made a first-lieutenant, in Magruder's battery; in August, 1848, he was brevetted captain, for gallant and meritorious conduct in the battles of Contreras and Cherubusco; and in March, 1849, brevetted major, for like good conduct at Chapultepec.   In 1852, finding his health such as would interfere with the conscientious discharge of his duties, and peace having been restored, he resigned his commission and returned to Virginia.   Just prior to this time, "there was a vacancy in one of the professorships at the Virginia Military Institute, and General Smith, the superintendent, was instructed by the Board of Visitors to seek, by private inquiries, some one suitable for the position.   Among those to whom he first applied was General D. H. Hill, then a professor in Washington College.   Hill warmly recommended T. J. Jackson, then serving with the army in Florida.   Hill had, at that time, no family connection with Jackson; but he knew him well, and with a penetration and sagacity that did him much credit, declared that he was not only a competent, faithful, reliable man, but had a great deal of 'outcome' in him.   Repairing subsequently to West Point, General Smith addressed his inquiries to the faculty there.   They recommended as eligible for the position, McClellan, Rosecrans, Foster, Peck, and G. W. Smith.   Upon General Smith's stating that Jackson had been recommended, they said of him that he was an indefatigable man, and would do well, but had come to the academy badly prepared.   Inquiries elsewhere developed the fact, that the persons recommended at West Point were considered better *book-men* than Jackson, but all bore testimony to his great personal worth and energy, and his sterling qualities.

"When the Board of Visitors met, General Smith reported the name of Jackson, together with a statement of the recommenda-

tions and encomiums already referred to. It happened that there was on the Board a member who appeared there on that occasion for the first time and the last. He at once advocated Jackson's appointment, though evidently taken by surprise at the suggestion of his name. He spoke in very high terms of Jackson, whose townsman he said he was, and told of the great pleasure which his appointment would give to the people of Northwest Virginia. This member, who thus eulogized Jackson, was J. S. Carlile. He was the only one of the Board who knew Jackson, and he warmly advocated him before that jury of strangers. Influenced by what they had thus heard, the Board, without the usual delays, at once ordered the appointment to be tendered to Jackson, and as his health was feeble, he resigned his commission and accepted it."

The post he now undertook to fill was Professor of Chemistry and Natural Science, and the mere fact of his having been chosen for such a position from among other eminent names put forward, is strong evidence of the extraordinary abilities he possessed, and the innate genius of his mind. The farmer lad, of so poor an education that ten years before he was hardly qualified to enter West Point, was now selected by experienced judges to sit in a professor's chair, and instruct youthful members of the Military Institute in two of the sciences requiring great mental acquirements to fully comprehend. But he was not found defective in the task he had undertaken. Zealous and persevering in the discharge of his duties, he soon became marked as one of the most competent that could have been found for the position. His peculiar character, however, did not make him a favorite with his pupils, and perhaps we may ourselves slightly err in saying that he was too much of a martinet, with too little of that valuable experience in life which enables a wise teacher to sow good and lasting seed, by winning his way into the hearts of more youthful blood than his own. Jackson will be ever deservedly admired for his high qualities as a Christian soldier, and a moral, upright man. But the natural bent of his mind was such as could not exactly see where to draw the line between actual excesses and those irregularities of youth which most men are liable to in their early days, though it appears, in his case, he had been exempt from. Certain it is, however, he

was not popular with the students; and, it is said that one instance occurred where his life was in danger from a youth he had expelled owing to misconduct. It seems that this youth, in the heat of passion, determined to have revenge, and way-laid the Professor on his return home from college. A friend apprized Jackson of the possible danger, as he was walking towards the place where the mad boy was concealed; but Jackson exclaimed aloud, "Let him shoot me, if he will!" and walked on. The intended murderer was near, and heard the remark. It took effect. Reflection instantly came, and he slunk away, saved from the commission of a great crime, and thus allowing Jackson to fulfil the destiny he ever seemed to think was allotted him.

That there was something more than ordinarily peculiar about Jackson's mind, must be inferred from the many circumstances currently reported of him. One statement goes to assert, that "he was afflicted with different forms of hypochondria, and had a mania for believing that every thing he ate went down and lodged in his left leg. At another time he would never eat except by the watch, at the precise moment; and he would take out his watch, lay it on the table, and eat at that moment. If the meal was behind-hand, he would not eat at all."

Many other singularities are reported of him, some few may be yet mentioned in their place; but, whatever may have been those peculiarities, it is certain that, even in other things, he was very different from most men. Perhaps his early struggles in life, and the hard lessons of poverty, may have somewhat soured his temper, and inclined him to asceticism, though to a really healthful mind the tendency is the reverse. The experiences of a painful past should make us more forbearing and indulgent to others in the present; but all men cannot be thus, especially when holding fast to the tenets of religion in one of the strictest sects of the Christian faith. And such was his case. A conscientious and devout member of the Presbyterian church, of which he was an elder, we can understand how it was that no allowance could be made, in his position, even had his inclination ever tended that way, for the errors and infirmities of those placed under his tuition. "Independent of his work in the professorship, he was indefatigable

in the duties of his creed. He taught in the Sunday-school, he visited the sick, and took a lively interest in the spiritual welfare of the negroes. Every Sunday he expounded the Scriptures to a class of negro children, and, though in all things else modest and retiring, his voice was heard, and his influence exerted to the utmost, in all questions that related to the moral and spiritual welfare of the colored race.

Soon after entering upon his professorship, he married Miss Junkin, a daughter of the Rev. Dr. George Junkin, principal of the Washington College. This lady died in the year 1855, and her children also lived only a short time. Jackson, then, on leave of absence, visited Europe, and upon his return resumed his duties both at the Institute and in the church. He was now married again, to Miss Morrison, daughter of the Rev. Dr. Morrison, late President of Davidson College, N. C., and sister of the wife of the present Confederate general, D. H. Hill, already mentioned as favoring his appointment at the Institute. From this period until the year 1861, Jackson continued in the quiet methodical duties of his position. He was not known, at any time, to mix in the political questions of the day, though he must have watched, with keen anxiety, the violent agitation which resulted in the disruption of the Union. Hidden from the great world without, it is probable that the name of " Stonewall" Jackson would never have been heard in history, certainly not with such fame as now, had not the gigantic strife of civil discord burst forth in his native land. But, like many of the stern enthusiasts of times before him, he suddenly appeared like a blazing meteor, and by the swiftness and striking energy of his movements, made for himself a niche in the temple of fame, which will stand to all posterity with those of Cromwell, Cameron, and others.

The history of the secession of Virginia is well known. Hesitating and doubtful for a time, that State at length passed an ordinance of disunion on the 17th of April, 1861, and immediately it was determined to drive the Federal forces away, if possible, beyond the border-lines. Harper's Ferry and the Arsenal there was then garrisoned by a detachment of United States dragoons, under Lieutenant Jones, who, on the 18th of April, evacuated the place, in consequence of a large force of Virginians coming to take possession of it. But, it was neces-

sary for Virginia to keep an " army of observation" there, and Governor Letcher immediately issued a commission to Jackson, appointing him a colonel in the State troops, with command in the Shenandoah Valley, the headquarters being at Harper's Ferry. It is, however, stated that previous to this, Jackson was commandant of the camp of instruction at the Fair Grounds, Richmond; but even if so, it is certain that his was the first regular military commission issued by his native State, and that on the 3d of May he took command at Harper's Ferry.

On the 23d of May, the military forces of Virginia having been more fully organized, General J. E. Johnston took command at Harper's Ferry, and assigned Jackson to the infantry then concentrating in the Valley. Stuart was appointed to command the cavalry, and Pendleton had charge of the artillery, and it was thus conceived that under such leaders the new Confederate troops would be successful against any Federal attacks, especially as Jackson had already placed the soldiers under excellent drill, and moulded them "into that impenetrable phalanx which stood stern and unbroken afterwards, amid scenes of the most frightful carnage." But, early in June, General Patterson advanced with a large Union force, and necessitated the evacuation of Harper's Ferry by Johnston. The Confederates retired to Winchester, but had scarcely arrived there when information was obtained that the Federals were still advancing, and therefore Jackson, with his brigade, was sent to the neighborhood of Martinsburg to aid Stuart's cavalry in destroying what they could of the Baltimore and Ohio railroad stock, and thus check the enemy's movements. Patterson, however, still came on, though not by the way of Harper's Ferry, which remained unoccupied, but intending to cross the Potomac near Williamsport, twenty-five miles higher up. There, on the 2d of July, Jackson, with his force of some 3,500 troops, all Virginians, prepared to resist the Union attempt. The ford across the Potomac at Williamsport is narrow, and the river so shallow at times, that a man may wade it without being wet above the waist. There, however, in the early morning of Tuesday, the 2d of July, the advanced Federal forces crossed, and, after some movements on both sides, Jackson fell back to Falling Waters, on the main road

to Martinsburg, a running fire being kept up. A detachment of Union troops was then sent forward to reconnoitre, and at 9 A. M. Jackson was encountered on the Porterfield farm, where he had formed his men in line of battle behind the house, and with a park of artillery (four guns) directly upon the turnpike along which the enemy was advancing. The battle now commenced, and for half an hour Jackson succeeded in maintaining his ground; but, the remainder of Patterson's army coming up, he was compelled slowly to fall back. This he did for a mile or two further, and then made a second stand, renewing the fight with great obstinacy. The odds, however, were too much against him, and finally he "retired, when about to be outflanked, scarcely losing a man, but bringing off forty-five prisoners." Jackson then rejoined the main army, under Johnston, at Winchester.

This engagement—it can hardly be called a battle—was the first that took place between the two armies, and from several circumstances related concerning it, wherein parties of both sides are said to have met each other without knowledge of either being foes, it would seem that regular organized warfare had hardly yet commenced. The commanding officers were schooled in military art, but the men were still raw and unused to a battlefield.

Shortly after this affair, Jackson was made a brigadier-general; and he then continued to march and countermarch in front of Patterson, thoroughly checking his onward movements, for a fortnight more. At the end of that time, July 18th, a dispatch reached General Johnston, at Winchester, that the great Northern army was advancing on Manassas, where the bulk of the Confederate forces under Beauregard were then concentrated, and that he was to go thither as speedily as possible. In two days from that date, Johnston had arrived with his army at Manassas, and General Jackson was posted, with his brigade, in the rear of Longstreet's forces, near Blackburn's ford, where an engagement with a portion of the Union troops had already taken place, viz., on the 18th of July.

Next morning, Sunday, July 21st, began that great battle, which, first in this memorable strife, was also remarkable for the great panic that occurred on the Union side, and the completeness of a hard-earned and nearly lost victory to the Confed-

erates.   But, in this hasty sketch of the life of one of the many
eminent commanders on both sides, engaged on that day, it is
impossible to do more than give a hurried outline of the entire
battle.   As is well known, the Union army was under General
McDowell, and the Confederates under Beauregard and Johnston,—the latter, though senior, allowing the former to conduct the engagement in accordance with his previous plans.
The several corps and division commanders on either side
were men of skill and ability, but the soldiers, though brave
even to rashness, were all, or nearly all, inexperienced, and
not yet fully disciplined.   The fight, therefore, was bloody
and severe.   A portion of the Union forces crossed Bull Run
stream, about 10 A. M., at a place called Sudley's ford, eight
miles higher up than where Jackson's brigade was posted, and
the remainder were stationed at the Stone bridge, also six
miles above Jackson's position.   Later in the day, however, a
part of this remaining Union force crossed the stream, and
engaged, hand to hand, in the conflict, while the rest still
defended the bridge.

The Confederate line of battle was from below Jackson's
position on the right, to the Stone bridge, and then diverging
along the Warrenton turnpike to near Groveton, on the left,
where the Union right had come forward, hoping to outflank
their foe.   Within this line was an irregular plateau, the
slopes of which reached down upon and slightly across the
turnpike road.   On the Confederate left of this plateau was a
farm-house, belonging to a widow lady named Henry, who,
during the engagement, being bedridden, was once or twice
carried out by her family, but ultimately met her death while
lying there during a part of the fiercest of the strife.   This
house was in a prominent position, and consequently became
the scene of several severe attacks for its capture and recapture on both sides.

On the morning of July 21st, Jackson was moved from his
position in the rear of Longstreet, more to the left, so as to
support either Bonham, in front of him, at the Bull Run
stream, below the Stone bridge, or Cocke, who was on the left.
Here he remained during the greater part of the morning, until,
finding that a portion of the troops already hotly engaged on
his left were exhausted and in disorder, he moved to reinforce

them. Marching along the back of the plateau, he suddenly
came out upon its eastern crest, a little below the Henry
House, and there with his artillery opened fire to great
effect. The Union forces, in spite of the most heroic charges,
and a tremendous fire aiding them from Griffin's and Rickett's
batteries, were completely held in check, until Johnston himself, with Beauregard, came up and reformed the shattered
columns, compelling the Federals for a time to retire. Jackson was now in the centre with four regiments and thirteen
pieces of artillery; and the most strenuous efforts were made
by him, and the other heroic commanders on his right and
left, to keep the advantage so far gained. But, the enemy
was again dashing on with irresistible power. Up the sides
of the plateau,—from the turnpike road, and from their right,—
forward they came with a determination and bravery that
justice must admit, and the truth of history cannot deny.
Heavily reinforced, they gained the summit, and all around
the Henry House, with other portions of the ground, was in
their possession. Then General Beauregard gave orders for
the entire right of his line, except the reserves, to advance.
With a wild yell, peculiar to the Southern troops, they did so,
Jackson's brigade piercing the enemy's centre, and recovering
what had been lost, though at a fearful sacrifice of life. But,
the triumph was shortlived. Again did the Federals rush
forward, and this time so overpoweringly, that the Confederates once more gave way. Now appeared Jackson, no more
as the calm, reserved college professor, but as a thorough im-
personation of the military chief. Everywhere in the thickest
of the fight, with the voice and the look of a warrior upon
him, he cheered and encouraged his men amid the deadliest
slaughter. He seemed to have a charmed life, so futile to
touch him were the efforts of the enemy's fire. But, hope was
nearly gone. The fortunes of the day were evidently waning
for the Confederate cause, and about 4 P. M., when a lull in
the battle occurred, he paused awhile, on his horse, to consider
anew what could be done. It was while thus reflecting, General Bee rode up, and, as we have already mentioned, spoke,
in the bitterness of his heart, of the lowering aspects of the
day. Then came that reply before recorded; and when again
the troops once more rallied to the bugle blast, Jack-

son was among them, foremost in the fray. Just then General Kirby Smith's reinforcement arrived, and the sight of their comrades so inspirited the Confederate soldiers, that nothing could withstand them. The Union forces broke in disorder. In vain their commanders tried to rally them. They fled, and ere darkness had commenced, the battlefield of Bull Run was in possession of the Southern army, and the victory was theirs.

Thus terminated the battle, in which Jackson obtained his *soubriquet* of "Stonewall." That there was any thing, up to this time, very extraordinary in his military talents above his brother commanders, may reasonably be questioned; but, a fortuitous circumstance gave him a name, and this, added to something of a Cromwellian charm about the man, has caused him to be spoken of, perhaps, in a higher degree than impartial justice to all would exactly warrant. However, he was one of the many deserving great admiration and respect.

The Union army having retreated towards Washington, Jackson remained with his brigade near Centreville. In September he was made a major-general, and, in the early part of October, assigned to the command of the Confederate forces in and around Winchester.

When the news of this appointment reached his old brigade, which was to remain with the main Virginian army, it caused general regret at the separation. On the 4th of October he took leave of his men, and, as they were drawn up before him, the silent but deep sorrow expressed in the countenance of every man was unmistakable. With the short abrupt tones peculiar to him, he addressed his soldiers in words of praise for the past and exhortation for the future, adding, that " he trusted whenever he should hear of the First brigade on the field of battle, it would be of still nobler deeds achieved, and higher reputation won." Then, pausing for an instant while his eye ran along the line, that outwardly cold, stern soldier was unable to master the emotion within him ; but, suddenly rising in his stirrups, and throwing the reins upon his horse's neck, he extended his arms, and exclaimed, with an emphasis that sent a thrill through every heart—

"In the army of the Shenandoah, you were the *First brigade !* In the army of the Potomac, you were the First brigade ! In the Second corps of the army, you are the First brigade !

You are the First brigade in the affections of your general; and I hope, by your future deeds and bearing, you will be handed down to posterity as the First brigade in this our second war of independence. Farewell !"

Three prolonged and deafening cheers then burst forth from his brave and hardy soldiers, which were renewed again and again. His face flushed for a moment as he listened to the sound, but he did not speak. Perhaps—for even stern generals are men—his heart was too full to say another word. But he looked the kindly thanks, and waving his hand, he galloped away.

When Jackson was ordered to the Shenandoah, he took with him several new regiments; and, attached to one of these was a gentleman, whose correspondence with another Confederate officer has been published by the latter. As portions of it aptly serve to illustrate the character and describe the movements of General Jackson at this time, we briefly transcribe them, with such trifling amendments as reference to other reports make necessary. The writer says:

" When we were ordered up the Valley with old Jackson, it was considered to be a source of congratulation to all for going into active service; but, believe me, I would willingly have gone back into winter-quarters again after a week's trial, for Jackson is the greatest marcher in the world. When we first moved up here, our orders were for a march to Charlestown; next day we moved back to Winchester; in a few days again back to Charlestown; and thence from one place to another, until at last I began to imagine we were commanded by some peripatetic philosophical madman, whose forte was pedestrianism. With little or no baggage, we are a roving, hungry, hardy lot of fellows, and are not patronized at all by parsons or doctors: the latter have a perfect sinecure amongst us. ' Stonewall ' may be a very fine old gentleman, and an honest, good-tempered, industrious man, but I should admire him much more in a state of rest than continually seeing him moving in front. And such a dry old stick, too ! As for uniform, he has none—his wardrobe isn't worth a dollar; and his horse is quite in keeping, being a poor lean animal of little spirit or activity. And don't he keep his aides moving about ! Thirty miles ride at night through the mud, is nothing of a job; and,

if they don't come up to time, I'd as soon face the devil, for Jackson takes no excuses when duty is on hand. He is solemn and thoughtful, speaks but little, and always in a calm decided tone; and, from what he says there is no appeal, for he seems to know every hole and corner of this valley as if he had made it, or, at least, as if it had been designed for his own use. He knows all the distances, all the roads, even the cow-paths through the woods, and goat-tracks along the hills. He sits horse very awkwardly, and has a fashion of holding his head very high, and chin up, as if searching for something skywards; yet, although you can never see his eyes for the cap-peak drawn over them, nothing escapes *his* observation. His movements are sudden and unaccountable: his staff don't pretend to keep up with him, and, consequently, he is frequently seen alone, poking about in all sorts of holes and corners, at all times of night and day. I have frequently seen him approach in the dead of night and enter into conversation with sentinels, and ride off through the darkness. . . . In my opinion, Jackson will assuredly make his mark in this war, for his untiring industry and eternal watchfulness *must* tell upon a numerous enemy unacquainted with the country, and incommoded by large baggage-trains. Jackson evidently intends to supply himself at Federal expense; and, as he is a true fire-eater, and an invincible believer in our 'manifest destiny,' Banks will find him a disagreeable opponent to confront in the mountain passes, or at the many fords."

Another writer, speaking of him at the same period, says:

"He is as calm in the midst of a hurricane of bullets as he was in the pew of his church at Lexington, when he was professor of the Institute. He appears to be a man of almost superhuman endurance. Neither heat nor cold makes the slightest impression upon him. He cares nothing for good quarters and dainty fare. Wrapped in his blanket, he throws himself down on the ground anywhere, and sleeps as soundly as though he were in a palace. He lives as the soldiers live, and endures all the fatigue and all the suffering that they endure. His vigilance is something marvellous. He never seems to sleep, and lets nothing pass without his personal scrutiny. He can neither be caught napping, nor whipped when wide awake. The rapidity of his marches is something

portentous. He is heard of by the enemy at one poirt, and before they can make up their minds to follow him, he is off at another. He keeps so constantly in motion that he never has a sick-list, and no need of hospitals."

The movements of Jackson at this period must now be briefly mentioned. At the time he was ordered to the Shenandoah, there was a strong force of the Federals at Romney and Bath, in Northwestern Virginia, while General Banks, with his army, was on the north of the Potomac, ready to cross into the Valley. Jackson, accordingly, determining to try and annoy the enemy, even if he could not beat them, conceived the idea of destroying the "dams" up the river, so that supplies could not be forwarded to the Union army at Washington by the canal. Accordingly, the attempt was made, and, amid the cold and snows of a severe winter in that region, his men were engaged, waist-deep, in the river, endeavoring to tear down Dam No. 5, near Williamsport. The attempt at first was unsuccessful, owing to the severity of the weather and a continual fire from the Federals on the river bank, but, ultimately, the task was accomplished in December, though with the loss of several men.

No sooner was this done, than Jackson, on the 1st of January, 1862, without allowing any one to know whither he was bound, started with his force of 2,200 men to surprise the Federals stationed at Bath, otherwise known as Berkley Springs. The day was fine, and the air soft and balmy, so that the men left their blankets and overcoats behind, expecting the wagons to follow and join them before those articles were needed. But, by some mischance, the wagons did not come up, and on the third day of the march, the weather changed again to all the severity of winter. Rain, snow, hail, sleet, beat upon the troops thus shelterless, and without their ordinary covering. The horrors of the march became fearful. "The country was exceedingly rough; unfrequented roads had to be taken; ice was on the ground, and neither man nor beast could maintain a footing. Men soon were bootless, hatless, and ragged; horses could scarcely stir, and, at night, the weary soldiers had to sleep out upon the snow as best they could. By and by, when the wagons came up, matters were in no ways mended, for, in toiling over the hills, horsemen, infantry, wagons and

all, would frequently slip over an embankment. One train of wagons and artillery took from daylight until 3 P. M. to pass a hilly point, heavy details of men steadying the wagons, and almost lifting the animals along."

This expedition appears to have been unnecessary and ill planned. . But the object of it was accomplished. Bath was occupied by Jackson, who "drove the Federals across the Potomac, on one of the coldest nights ever known in that region," and he immediately marched on towards Romney, which place was evacuated by the Union troops, under General Shields, before Jackson's arrival.

At this time, General Loring, with Jackson's old brigade, had joined him, and the former was now left at Romney, while the latter, with his "Stonewall" companions, rapidly returned to Winchester. Information, however, now came to him that Shields had united with Banks, and their whole army was on the march down the Valley. Accordingly, Jackson speedily collected his corps together from all points, and prepared to retire down the Shenandoah whenever necessary. On the 11th of March he evacuated Winchester, and slowly marched along the Valley, with all the spoils he had obtained, towards Staunton. But, on the 21st, after passing Strasburg, the enemy still following him thus far, he heard that General Shields was falling back, and a body of Union troops was moving by way of Snicker's Gap, to reinforce the Federals operating against General Johnston at Manassas. He therefore, at once returned and pushed forward with the greatest rapidity to Winchester. On the afternoon of the 23d, Jackson's army was again near that place, intending to bivouac for the night at Kernstown. But, finding the enemy likely to receive reinforcements, he at once determined upon attacking him. The battle began about 4 P. M. and continued until dark, ending in success to the Federals, and Jackson being compelled to fall back to Cedar creek.

In this engagement, it is understood that Jackson was completely outwitted by General Shields' feint of retreating back to the Potomac ; but the Confederates, however, "accomplished something of what they desired, in preventing a junction of Banks' command with other forces."

CHAPTER II.

Arrival of General Ewell.—Advance of General Milroy.—Jackson unit 3s w.th General Edward Johnson.—The Military Institute Cadets and General Smith.—Movements in the Valley.—Observance of the Fast-day.—Retreat of General Banks.—Divine Service in Camp.—Movements of Fremont and Shields.—Battles of Crosskey and Port Republic.—Jackson and the Bible Society.—McClellan's Army around Richmond.—Jackson's March to the Peninsula.—Battle of Cold Harbor.—Pursuit of the Federals.—Battle of Malvern Hill.—Jackson's Army in Camp recuperating.—On the March again.—Advance towards the Army of Pope.—Battle of Cedar Run.—Jackson Moves by the Federal Right Flank to Pope's Rear. — Attack on Manassas.—Affair at Bristoe Station.—Jackson falls back to the old Battlefield of Bull Run.—Battles of August 29th and 30th.—Rout of the Federals.—Pursuit.—Engagement at Ox Hill.—Movement into Maryland.—Arrival at Leesburg.—Crossing the Potomac.—Capture of Harper's Ferry.—Battle of Antietam.—Return to the Shenandoah valley.—Anecdote of Jackson.—Battle of Fredericksburg.

AFTER this battle, General Jackson retreated in the direction of Harrisonburg, pursued by Banks' army as far as that place. He then, on the 19th of April, crossed the south fork of the Shenandoah, and took position between that river and Swift Run Gap. General Ewell had also been directed to join the main body of Jackson's army, and arrived from Gordonsville on the 30th of April. Meanwhile it was ascertained that General Milroy, with another portion of the Union forces, was advancing from the west side of the Shenandoah mountains, with the intention of effecting a junction with Banks, and then both to attack Staunton. To defeat this, Jackson determined to join his own forces with the Confederate troops of General Edward Johnson, then near Buffalo Gap, west of Staunton, and, while Ewell was sent to keep Banks in check, Milroy should be attacked. This was done. At Staunton, Jackson found himself earnestly supported by Major-general Smith, his old friend, the superintendent of the Military Institute, and the cadets, who had all come forward to assist in defending that portion of the Valley; and on the 7th of May he directed Johnson to move in advance on Milroy's position. The latter retreated until he was reinforced by General Schenck, in the McDowell valley, where he stood his ground for an engagement. This took place on the 8th, and ended in the further

retreat of Milroy, pursued by Jackson to the vicinity of Frank-lin.   Here Jackson deemed it advisable to return to the Shen-andoah Valley again, with the intention of attacking Banks with all of the Confederate forces—his own, Johnson's, and Ewell's united—before those of the Union commander could be again concentrated.   On the 15th of May he had recrossed the mountains, and encamped for the night near the Lebanon White Sulphur Springs.   Here the troops were halted for a short time, to enable them to attend divine service, and observe the Fast recommended by President Davis.   On the 17th, the march was resumed towards Harrisonburg, and thence—hear-ing that Banks had fallen back to Strasburg, which he was strongly fortifying—he moved rapidly down the Valley to New-market, where a junction was again effected with Ewell. From this place Jackson crossed to Luray and Front Royal, hoping, by a surprise of the Union troops there, to get in the rear of Banks, or compel him to abandon his fortifications at Strasburg.   On Friday, May 23d, the Federals were attacked and defeated at Front Royal, and Jackson immediately pre-pared to advance upon General Banks.   But the next morning he was surprised to hear that the entire Union army was in rapid retreat up the Valley, towards Winchester.   The Con-federate cavalry had previously been posted near the Federals, and Ewell also sent on in advance, and now, together, these so completely harassed the Northern troops, that something like another Bull Run panic commenced.   The scene along the road is described as something never before witnessed.   " Every imaginable article known to campaigning was strewn about for miles : the fields were crowded with fugitives, while scores of ambulances were filled with foot-sore or wounded Federals. Now and again the rear of the enemy would rally, and try to check the impetuous advance of the victorious Confederates ; but it was only a vain effort.   The cavalry, under the gallant Turner Ashby, the infantry under Ewell, and the main body under Johnson, with Jackson himself and his old brigade amongst them, all swiftly followed on, capturing immense spoils and a vast number of prisoners.   "For many miles along the road towards Winchester and beyond, large and in-numerable fires told that the enemy were destroying their sup-plies, and already on their retreat towards the Potomac.   The

whole country seemed on fire, and on the night of the 24th the sight was awfully grand, for, whichever way the eye turned, fires illuminated the dark and distant landscape."

Early on the morning of the 25th of May, Jackson began to move on Winchester. Dense columns of smoke issuing from the town, made it evident that the enemy were busily engaged in burning stores : but Jackson, wishing to stop this, pushed forward, and, meeting with a feeble resistance, the Confederates rushed into the town, driving the foe through every street, and speedily causing the Federal troops again to hurriedly retreat. But swift upon their heels came the victorious Southern soldiers—Ashby, with his cavalry, hanging close to their rear. Soon it was discovered that Banks had shaped his course towards Williamsport, and ere he had crossed over to that town, the Confederate advance was well up with him. Now the scene became even more intensely exciting than ever. The dead and wounded along the road were so numerous, that it was more like the last of a battle-field than a retreat. "Hats, caps, muskets, boots, wagons, burning stores, sabres, pistols, etc., besides exhausted Union soldiers, lined every yard of the way, and could be found in the woods at either side. At last, Jackson's army, totally prostrated from fatigue, and helpless as children, reached the vicinity of Williamsport on the evening of the 26th of May, and found that all who remained of the enemy, had effected a passage across the river at different points, and were safe in Maryland."

On the following day " divine service was held in the camps of the Southern army, and thanks rendered to God for the success with which He had blessed their arms, and His continued favor implored,—a duty which General Jackson never failed to impress upon his troops." The men then rested ; but on the 28th, movements against the enemy were renewed. The Federals still had some of their divided army near Charlestown, but Generals Winder and Ewell were sent by Jackson to disperse them; and this accomplished, it was then necessary for Jackson to guard against a serious peril which menaced him behind. Shields was moving rapidly towards his right, and Fremont from near Romney, on his left, with a view of concentrating a heavy force in his rear, and cutting

off a retreat up the valley. To avoid this, Jackson, on the 30th of May, with all his troops, except Winder's and the cavalry, returned to Winchester. Before he reached there, however, news came that the Union cavalry had already appeared at Front Royal, and the Confederate force left in possession had abandoned it. Jackson, therefore, on the 31st, hurried forward, and moved towards Strasburg, encamping there that evening. Next morning, June 1st, Fremont's forces having arrived by the way of Wardensville, attacked Jackson's outposts in that direction. Ewell was now ordered to hold Fremont in check until the remainder of the Confederate forces under Winder arrived, which they did that evening,—a part of them, the Second Virginia, having marched thirty-six miles. The command being thus united again, the retreat continued towards Harrisonburg.

The incidents of this retreat now became numerous and most exciting. Fremont hung close upon Jackson's rear, but the gallant Ashby, by his skill and personal daring, materially checked the pursuit, and early on the morning of the 5th of June the Confederates reached Harrisonburg, and passing beyond the town, turned towards the east, in the direction of Port Republic. Next day an engagement took place between Ashby's cavalry, supported by General G. H. Stewart's brigade of infantry, and the Union cavalry, supported by the Pennsylvania "Bucktails." In this encounter, two important Union officers—Colonel Sir Percy Wyndham, and Lieutenant-colonel Kane—were captured by the Confederates, and their forces driven from the field; but this was dearly bought by the death of the heroic Ashby.

The main body of Jackson's command had now reached Port Republic, and were encamped on the high ground north of the village, about a mile from the South river, a tributary of the Shenandoah. Ewell's forces were four miles distant, near the road leading from Harrisonburg. Fremont had arrived with his forces in that vicinity, and Shields was fifteen miles below Port Republic. Jackson's position was about equidistant from both parties, and it was his object to prevent, if possible, a junction between them. Accordingly, when Shields had approached nearer, he was attacked by Jackson, at Port Republic, and driven back, while Ewell encountered

Fremont's advanced forces, and, after a sharp engagement at Cross Keys, on the 8th of June, defeated them.

The forces of General Shields having retreated, it was now easier to attack Fremont, when he again made his appearance; but that general deemed it more wise to concentrate his troops around Winchester, as a base of operations, and accordingly retreated thither, leaving Jackson to pursue his triumphant march unmolested.

On the 12th of June, Jackson recrossed South river, and encamped near Weyer's Cave; "and for the purpose," as he said, "of returning thanks to God for having crowned our army with success, and to implore his continual favor, divine service was held in the army on the 14th." The army remained in the same place until the 17th, when Jackson again took up the line of march, but, now, to join in the great movements then going on around Richmond.

It was about this time that General Jackson was made a Life Director of the Bible Society of the Confederate States; and the following is his letter of acknowledgment:

HEADQUARTERS VALLEY DISTRICT, VIRGINIA, July 21, 1862.
REV. E. A. BOOLES, General Agent
Bible Society of Confederate States of America:

DEAR SIR:—I gratefully acknowledge the honor conferred upon me by a portion of *God's people*, in constituting me a Life Director of the Bible Society of the Confederate States of America.

It is a cause in which I feel a deep interest, and my earnest prayer is, that God will make this infant Bible Society the means not only of giving His blessed Word to our own people, but of sending it freely to the remotest nations of the earth.

Inclosed is a check for one hundred and fifty dollars. Please acknowledge its reception, and believe me to be, very truly, your friend and brother in Christ,

T. J. JACKSON.

During the period of Jackson's labors in the Shenandoah, the Union army, under McClellan, had invested Richmond; but, on the 31st of May, at the battle of Seven Pines, General Johnston inflicted upon the Federals the first of those severe

checks that finally ended in their withdrawal before the Confederates under General Lee. We have already seen, in our sketch of General Lee's life, how this was accomplished, and i would be a needless repetition to go again into details. We shall, therefore, confine ourselves simply to the personal movements of Jackson.

On the 17th of June, General Jackson commenced his march from Weyer's Cave to the Peninsula, leaving a small force at Harrisonburg to watch the enemy. On the 25th he had arrived at Ashland, sixteen miles from Richmond, at the very time McClellan, probably hearing of his advance, "closed the siege, by changing his policy from offence to defence." The next day, Jackson, as directed by Lee, steadily advanced towards Cold Harbor, where he immediately took up a position to fall upon the enemy. On the 27th of June the great battle began. "Stuart, with his cavalry, was posted on the left of Jackson's troops, to charge and intercept the Federals if they attempted to retreat in the direction of the Pamunkey; and hardly had line of battle been formed, when heavy firing on the right indicated that General A. P. Hill, who had gone in that direction, was hard pressed. Jackson immediately ordered a general advance of his entire corps, which hastened forward, Whiting's division on the right of the line, and Jackson's, Ewell's, and D. H. Hill's, in the order named, from right to left. The welcome sound of Jackson's guns came to Lee and Longstreet as they were hastening forward from Gaines' Mill, and the entire Confederate force on the left bank of the Chickahominy, which had only waited the arrival of Jackson, advanced in one wild charge, and the battle began to rage with a fury until then unknown." The result is well known. The Union forces fought heroically, and occasionally gained some advantage; but, "just as night was descending, the general and decisive charge was made all along the line, and in obedience to Jackson's brief, stern order, 'Press them with the bayonet!' Hill's, Ewell's, Whiting's, and Jackson's divisions all charged. Hood's Texans, and the Stonewall brigade, in advance of all the rest, pressed forward, with cheers of defiance, over every obstacle; and before this terrible charge in front, and the storm of artillery on their right, the enemy wavered, broke, and were put to rout. Posted in advance of his batter-

ies, his figure clearly revealed by the fires which the enemy
had kindled to draw the artillery fire from their guns, Jackson heard the wild cheers of his men as they pursued the flying enemy in the direction of Grapevine bridge."

Next morning, Jackson sent Ewell forward to Dispatch station, on the York River railroad, General Stuart being in
advance with his cavalry. The cavalry attacked and routed
a party of the enemy, and Ewell tore up and destroyed the
railroad at that point.

Jackson remained on the battlefield directing movements,
as the Confederate forces pursued McClellan's army; and on
the night of the 29th, he crossed to the right bank of the
Chickahominy, hastily reconstructing the bridge destroyed by
the Federals. At Savage station, he gathered up about 1,000
stragglers from the Union army, and then proceeded to White
Oak Swamp, where he pressed heavily upon the enemy's rear,
to Frazier's farm. There he met Generals Lee and Longstreet, and was at once assigned to the front, infusing, by his
presence, new ardor into the pursuit. At Malvern Hill his
corps was confronted by the entire army of McClellan, and, in
that heavy engagement, lost some of its best men.

It was during these battles that Jackson and Lee met for
the first time in the war, and, having now seen each other at
work, there sprung up at once between them that profound
respect, confidence, and regard, which thenceforth knew no
diminution. Jackson's opinion of Lee was shown, when he
said, "He is a phenomenon—I would follow him blind-
folded;" and the appreciation of Lee for Jackson, after events
fully proved, when, on the occasion of Jackson's death, he expressed himself as having lost his right arm.

The day after the battle of Malvern Hill, Jackson was sent
forward towards Harrison's landing, and on the following day
there was a desultory skirmish between the opposing forces;
but the great and bloody drama of the Peninsula campaign,
on that occasion, was ended; and on the 8th of July, when the
Confederates were withdrawn, Jackson's corps returned to
Richmond, and went into camp on the Mechanicsville road.
Here, for a time, it might be naturally expected that he
and his hardy soldiers would have obtained some rest, after
the constant marching and countermarching, with the numer-

ous engagements they had gone through.   But it was not so.
Only a few days had elapsed when new movements had to be
made.   Pope was massing large bodies of Union troops on the
Rapidan, and threatening the Central railroad at Gordonsville,
consequently he must be promptly checked.   General Lee had
quickly perceived that the scene of action was rapidly changing from the James to the Rappahannock, and it was necessary to maintain the Confederate position at such an important
place as Gordonsville.   Accordingly, Jackson was directed to
proceed thither and guard that point against the threatened
assault upon it.

At the time this order was given, no one except the official
few had any idea where the destination would be; and, says
one writer, as for gleaning any information concerning it from
"the sharp-eyed, tart, sarcastic, crabbed-spoken Jackson," a
person might as reasonably "whistle jigs to a mile-stone."
When his corps received orders to move, some imagined merely a change of camps, or some such indifferent movement, yet
when Richmond was left far to the south, and the column proceeded rapidly in a northwestern direction, many thought it
was again to the Shenandoah Valley.   But facts soon became
known, when, on the 19th of July, Jackson with his own old
division and General Ewell's arrived at Gordonsville.   Here
Jackson received information that the Federal army in his
front was in great force, and, accordingly, upon his represen-
tation, General A. P. Hill's was sent to reinforce him.   It
was not long, now, before the advanced forces of cavalry, on
both sides, came into collision at Orange Court house, and the
Confederate horsemen had to retreat; but Jackson ascertaining
that only a portion of Pope's army was at Culpepper, he determined to advance and attack it before the remaining Union
forces could arrive.   Accordingly, on the 7th of August, he
moved with his entire force from Gordonsville in the direction
of the enemy.   On the 9th, Jackson reached a point about
eight miles from Culpepper, and found the Union troops, under
General Banks and General Sigel, posted in his front, near
Cedar Run, a short distance west and north of Slaughter mountain.   "A large body of Federal cavalry occupied a ridge on
the right of the road, and a Confederate battery, under Lieu
tenant Terry, at once opened upon it.   General Early then

advanced, keeping near the Culpepper road, while General Ewell diverged to the right along the slope of the mountain. Early, forming in line of battle, moved into the open field, and drove the enemy's cavalry before him to the crest of a hill. Along this hill the Federal batteries were posted, ready to open as soon as he appeared. In his front, the country was, for some distance, open and broken. A cornfield, and to the left of it a wheatfield, extended to the opposite hill, which was covered with timber." As soon as Early reached the eminence described, the Federal batteries opened upon him, large bodies of cavalry appearing in the wheatfield to the left. A rapid and well-directed fire was returned, and the engagement began.

By this time, General Winder, with Jackson's own division, had arrived, and he immediately disposed the several brigades under Garnett, Taliaferro, and his own under Colonel Ronald, in position behind various batteries. He was then proceeding to direct the movements of these batteries when he was struck by a shell, from which he expired in a few hours. The command of Jackson's division now devolved upon Brigadier-general W. B. Taliaferro, whose brigade, during the action, was commanded by Colonel A. G. Taliaferro.

Meanwhile, Ewell had reached the northwest termination of Slaughter mountain, and upon an elevated spot, about two hundred feet above the valley below, had planted Latimer's guns, which opened with marked effect upon the enemy's batteries. At 5 P. M. Banks had thrown forward his skirmishers through the cornfield, and advanced his infantry. Another body of infantry, at the same time, moved upon Early's right, and speedily the fight extended from the left to the centre, in a sharp and very warm contest. General Hill had sent one of his brigades to support Early, and while the fight was in progress here, the Federals fell with great vigor on the Confederate left, turning it, and pouring a destructive fire into the rear, compelling Taliaferro's brigade to fall back. At this critical moment, Branch's brigade, of Hill's division, and Winder's brigade, came up and succeeded in driving back the Federals with great slaughter. A general charge was now made by Jackson, and resulted in driving the enemy across the field into the opposite wood, strewing the narrow valley with their

dead. The victory for the Confederates was gained, and, as night fell, the full-orbed moon soared aloft, pouring its mellow light upon the field of carnage. Over the beautiful slopes of Culpepper, covered with the wounded and the dying, the battle-flag of the South floated proudly in the light of the calm August moon. But the contest was hard and desperate, and, at one time, the day seemed to be in favor of the Federals. I was then, however, that Jackson, carried away by the excite ment of the battle, threw aside his usual cool reserve, and rushed forward to the front, rallied, with his voice and mien, his confused troops, and ordering the decisive bayonet charge, retrieved the broken fortunes of the day.

Jackson being now anxious to reach Culpepper without delay, determined to advance through the night, but his front having encountered the enemy's batteries posted in the woods, it was deemed necessary to halt, and this was done. On the following morning, the 10th, he heard that the Federals had been reinforced, and, therefore, did not advance any further. General J. E. B. Stuart now arrived on a tour of inspection, and at Jackson's request took command of the cavalry to reconnoitre. On the 11th, a flag of truce was received from the Union commander, requesting permission to remove and bury the dead. This was granted until 5 P. M., when, hearing from Stuart that the enemy were too heavily reinforced to be wisely attacked, Jackson, during the night, fell back towards Gordonsville, with a view to strategic movements of his own.

On the 14th, as was customary with him, General Jackson rested his troops to "return thanks to God for the victory won," and also to await the main army, which was now rapidly marching, under General Lee, from Richmond to co-operate with him. General Lee soon arrived, united with Jackson near Culpepper, and immediately made various demonstrations at the fords of the Rapidan, lower down, to attract Pope's attention while Jackson attempted a flank movement on the left. On the 25th, with some 25,000 men, Jackson left the main army, and proceeded rapidly towards the head waters of the Rappahannock, crossed that river at Hinton's ford, dragging his artillery with difficulty up the narrow and rock-ribbed road beyond, and pushed forward with the utmost speed. It was something of a gigantic task.

Indeed, the undertaking was almost superhuman. Miles of weary marching—across open fields, by strange country roads and comfortable homesteads, past a little town called Orleans up the steeps, along and across the valleys skirting the Blue Ridge mountains; always on, on, and seldom resting even for an instant—footsore, hungry, and all but completely exhausted —did the daring band under Jackson (himself ever sharing the same fatigue and hardship) push forward to Thoroughfare Gap, that it might be reached before the enemy could be aware of their intention. At midnight the troops arrived at Salem, rested a few hours, and then, at dawn of day, on they marched again. At length they reached the Gap. It is, as is well known, a mountain gorge, and was then undefended by the Federals. Jackson, therefore, passed rapidly between the frowning ramparts with his little army, hungry, exhausted, but resolute as ever, and descended, like a hawk, upon Manassas.

General Stuart had pushed in advance with his cavalry, ascended the Bull Run mountain, by a winding and rocky road, to the right of the Gap, and descending the eastern acclivity, took his post again in front and on the flanks of the army, which, on the afternoon of Tuesday, the 26th, reached the neighborhood of Manassas.

Jackson was now completely in the enemy's rear, and speedily possessed himself of the railroad which supplied their army, while Lee was rapidly approaching in the Federal front. Manassas was quickly captured by Stuart, with his cavalry and some infantry, and the first symptoms of a general engagement now appeared. The old ground of the Bull Run battle was to be the scene of another great fight, and, on the morning of the 27th, reinforcements from Washington, under General Taylor, passed the Stone bridge, and advanced upon that portion of the Confederate troops at Manassas. An engagement followed, ending in the rout of the Federals, who were driven over Bull Run, by Blackburn's ford, with the loss of their commander, and hotly pursued by the Stuart horse-artillery, under Major Pelham. Later, on the same day, Ewell attacked Hooker at Bristoe station, but was compelled to retreat and fall back to the main army at Manassas. At the same time, General Fitzhugh Lee, with some cavalry, went

cn an expedition to Fairfax Court-house, to still further damage the Federal communications, and, if possible, cut off the retreat of Taylor's brigade. At nightfall, Jackson directed Manassas to be evacuated, after destroying all the Union stores found there, and setting the place on fire.

Jackson's position was now somewhat hazardous. Lee was approaching, but had not yet come up—(Longstreet's corps taking the same route that Jackson had)—and Pope was moving with his whole force to attack him. But it was necessary that the advanced ground should be maintained, and, accordingly, Jackson determined merely to fall back to within supporting distance of Longstreet, and hold on till the main body of the Confederate army arrived. This was done. He divided his corps, and sent Hill by way of Blackburn's ford to Centreville, so as to deceive the enemy, while he himself took up a position on the precise ground occupied by the right of the Federal army in the first battle of Bull Run. There he was joined by Hill, who, according to orders, had turned from Centreville back along the Warrenton road, and crossed the Stone bridge to Jackson's quarters.

Meantime, the enemy had followed Hill, and pursued him hotly until his rear-guard had passed over Bull Run, while Stuart attacked a portion of the Federals at Haymarket, and sent forward a dispatch to Longstreet, who was then fighting at Thoroughfare Gap.

It was now late in the day, August 28th, and the Union forces were seen advancing with the intention of crossing the stream at the Stone bridge and Sudley ford. Whereupon, Jackson immediately decided to attack them, and, pointing to the enemy in his front, he said, briefly, "Ewell, advance!" A fierce engagement followed, and at nightfall the enemy gave way, but remained, not far off, in line of battle waiting for daylight.

In this engagement, General Ewell was badly wounded in the knee, and his services were, consequently, lost in the subsequent battles.

At this time, a courier brought to Jackson the welcome intelligence that Longstreet had passed Thoroughfare Gap, and was rapidly pressing forward to join him : also, that Lee himself was near. The information was an immense relief to him,

and when the news came, he drew a long breath, and uttered a sigh of intense satisfaction.

The next morning, Friday, August 29th, Longstreet arrived and took position. General Lee was on the ground nearly at the same time, and immediately the order of battle was formed, though General Anderson's division had not yet come up, and the whole of the Confederate forces were overpowered by long marches and incessant encounters with their foe.

While Lee was thus getting his men into position, the Federals energetically attacked Jackson, and gradually the fight became general along his entire column. It continued very severe, and with changing success until the afternoon, when Hood's division, of Longstreet's corps, was ordered to attack the enemy's left. This was done with marked effect. Jackson, thus strengthened, fought with renewed vigor, and finally, about 9 P. M., the enemy was compelled to retire for nearly a mile. During the night, however, General Lee directed his troops to fall back to their old and better position of the morning, where they could again attack, with more advantage, next day.

The following morning, August 30th, the battle was renewed; but, as General Lee was now commanding in person, and as we have already briefly given the events of the fight in our sketch of that general, we may refer to it for details. Enough to say that the day ended in a complete victory for the Confederates, and another disastrous rout to the Union forces on the celebrated battlefield of Bull Run.

On the next day, Sunday, August 31st, Jackson's corps pressed the enemy towards Centreville, and on Monday afternoon his advance had a brief but severe engagement at Ox Hill, just above Germantown, the Confederates occupying Fairfax Court-house that same night.

It might be supposed that now, at last, some rest would be obtained by Jackson's iron-framed soldiers; but hardly had the victory been won, and Fairfax occupied, than a new movement commenced,—this time, for the purpose of crossing into Maryland. On the second day after the battle at Ox Hill, Jackson arrived at Leesburg, and was there joined by the other corps of the army. From Leesburg, in accordance with General Lee's plans, he marched straight across the country to

Williamsport, for the purpose of possessing Martinsburg, and intercepting the Federal retreat if the enemy moved up the river, while McLaws occupied Maryland heights; and this with a view to the surrender of Harper's Ferry, then garrisoned by a large force of Union troops, under General Miles. Jackson rapidly and most successfully performed his task, and Harper's Ferry, with " 11,000 troops, an equal number of small-arms, seventy-three pieces of artillery, and about 200 wagons, surrendered, on the 15th of September. This accomplished, Jackson, leaving General A. P. Hill to hold Harper's Ferry, hastily marched to join Lee, who had fallen back to Sharpsburg, after a heavy encounter with McClellan on the 14th, at South Mountain.

By a severe night's march, Jackson reached the vicinity of Sharpsburg on the morning of the 16th, and, by direction of Lee, he immediately advanced on the enemy, taking position to the left of Longstreet, near a Dunkard church, Ewell's division (General Lawton commanding) forming the right, and his own divison (General J. R. Jones commanding) forming the left. Major-general Stuart, with the cavalry, was also on his left.

That night the troops slept upon their arms, and on the following day, Wednesday, September 17th, the battle of Antietam was fought. The result has already been related (see page 77), and, on the morning of the 19th, the Confederate army having recrossed the Potomac, Jackson, with his troops, was again on the way to Martinsburg. The next day, a Federal force crossed in pursuit, but was routed by a portion of Jackson's corps, under A. P. Hill. On the evening of the 20th, the command moved to the Opequon river, in the vicinity of Martinsburg, and encamped there for a week. At the end of that time, Jackson went a little further on to Bunker Hill, and there, at length, gave to his weary troops that rest they so much needed.

In connection with this period, the following incident is related of Jackson. A correspondent states, that "on the morning of a recent battle near Harper's Ferry, after a sermon by one of his chaplains, Stonewall Jackson, who, by the way, is an elder in the Presbyterian Church, administered the sacrament to the church-members in his army. He invited all

Christians to participate in this ceremony. A Baptist, the straitest of his sect, thoroughly imbued with the idea of close communion, was seen to hesitate; but the occasion, and the man who presided, overcame his scruples: and thus it has happened that the prospect of a fight and the eloquence of Jackson made a Baptist forget that baptism is the door into the Church. In all Jackson's army an oath is rarely uttered. A religious enthusiasm pervades it which makes every man a hero. Conscious of the justice of our cause, and imbued with the strongest convictions of patriotism, his men are irresistible. In this incident we have an explanation of General Jackson's invincibility, and we are thus enabled to understand why his men are all heroes, and why they endure without a murmur the severest hardships to which any troops have been subjected during the war. When peace is restored, it will be honor enough for any man to say, ' I belonged to the army of Stonewall Jackson.' "

In the month of November, 1862, the Confederate army was once more on the move towards the Rappahannock, and Jackson, with his hardy veterans, accompanied it, forming the rearguard, as far as Millwood, where he remained until the 1st of December, watching the enemy and retarding his movements. He was then sent for to join Lee at Fredericksburg, which he did, by a rapid march, on the 10th, and his corps encamped beyond the Massaponnax, entirely out of sight, but ready for prompt work when called upon. This was not long unrequired. The battle of Fredericksburg may be said to have commenced on the 11th, and ended on the night of the 15th–16th, but the principal engagement was on the 13th, and in it Jackson, as usual, had a goodly share. We have, however, already given an account of this (see page 82), and therefore pass on to succeeding events.

After the battle of Fredericksburg, Jackson retired to Moss Neck for winter-quarters, with his corps hidden in the woods, and for a while devoted himself to the task of preparing his official reports. In this work it is said that he was exceedingly careful not to have any thing placed on record which was not established by irrefutable proof. *Truth* was with him the jewel beyond all price—and nothing discomposed him more than the bare suspicion that accuracy was sacrificed to effect.

He disliked all glowing adjectives in the narratives of his battles; and presented to the members of his staff and all around
him, a noble example of modesty and love of truth.   He
disliked all ostentation, self-laudation, or the attempts of others
to elevate him above his brother commanders.   He objected
to all popular ovations; and even refused, on several occasions,
to allow his portrait to be taken.   Thus, an account of the
battles wherein he fought may be relied upon as strictly truthful, if following his official reports, which are "the sworn
statements of a man who would have laid down his very life
before he would have attached his name to what was partial,
unfair, or aught but the simple, absolute truth."

The army now rested from its severe toils: the brave men
who had so long battled with an equally brave enemy, now
had months to recuperate, and gather fresh strength ere the
fierce cry of battle-strife was again likely to be heard, though
they were ever ready, should signs of any fresh encounter be
presented.   Jackson himself, at length, enjoyed some relief
from the anxieties and cares that had incessantly pressed upon
his mind ever since the war began.   With his headquarters in
a small outbuilding of the "Corbin House," situated on a crest
of hills running along the right bank of the Rappahannock,
he remained during the whole winter and spring of 1862-3,
watching the hills on the opposite side of the river, lest the
enemy should make a sudden advance, and at the same time
he enjoyed the social friendship of many who visited him.   Numerous incidents are related of his life at this period, but we
can only find space to mention one or two, as illustrating the
character of such a man.

"At his headquarters," says the pleasing writer we have so
often quoted from, "might be seen ornaments of the most
unique and surprising description.   On the walls of the apartment were pictures of race-horses, well known and dear in
former days to the planters of the neighboring region.   Then
there was a portrait of some celebrated game-cock, ready
trimmed and gaffed for conflict to the death.   A companion-
piece of these was the picture of a terrier engaged in furious
onslaught upon an army of rats, which he was seizing, tearing, and shaking to death as fast as they came.   These decorations of headquarters excited the merriment of the general's

associates; and one of them suggested to him that a drawing of the apartment should be made, with the race-horses, game-cocks, and terrier in bold relief, the picture to be labelled, 'View of the winter-quarters of General Stonewall Jackson, presenting an insight into the tastes and character of the individual.' Hearty laughter, on the part of General Jackson, greeted this jest from the distinguished brother soldier who had stood beside him upon so many bloody fields—whom he loved and opened his whole heart to—and to whom, when struck down by the fatal ball at Chancellorsville, his mind first turned as his successor.

"The children of the house and in the neighborhood will long remember the kind voice and smile of the great soldier—his caresses and affectionate ways. A new military cap had been sent him just before the battle of Fredericksburg, which was resplendent with gold braid and all manner of decorations. Jackson did not admire this fine substitute for that old, sun-scorched head-covering which had so long served him; and when, one day, a little girl was standing at his knee, looking up from her clustering curls at the kindly general, whose hand was caressing her hair, he found a better use for the fine gold braid around the cap. He called for a pair of scissors, ripped it off, and joining the ends, placed it like a coronet upon her head, with smiles, and evident admiration at the pretty picture thus presented.

"These are trifles, let us agree, good reader," adds the author who narrates them, "but, is it not a pleasant spectacle to see the great soldier amid these kindly simple scenes,—to watch the stern and indomitable leader, whose soul has never shrunk in the hour of deadliest peril, passing happy moments in the society of laughing children?"

It was during the time of his resting in winter-quarters that the following interesting letter was written:

GUINNEY'S DEPOT, CAROLINE COUNTY, VA.,
Dec. 10, 1862.

MY DEAR COLONEL—Yesterday I heard that Governor Letcher and yourself were coming to visit the army, but the arrival of the cars without you doomed me to disappointment. I hope you will come before long. Please give my

kindest regards to the governor, and remind him of his long standing promise to visit me. Colonel Linedi says he heard distant artillery, and others agree with him. The direction is towards Port Royal.

I have heard with great interest the reports of the Congressional Committee, recommending the repeal of the law requiring the mails to be carried on the Sabbath, and I hope that you will feel it a duty, as well as a pleasure, to urge its repeal. I do not see how a nation that arrays itself by such a law against God's holy day can expect to escape his wrath. The punishment of national sins must be confined to this world, as there is no nationality beyond the grave. For fifteen years I have refused to mail letters on Sunday, or to take them out of the office on that day, except since I came into the field; and so far from having to regret my course, it has been a source of true enjoyment. I have never sustained loss in observing what God enjoins, and I am well satisfied that the law should be repealed at the earliest practicable moment. My rule is to let the Sabbath mails remain unopened, unless they contain a dispatch; but dispatches are generally sent by couriers, or telegraph, or by some special messenger. I do not recollect a single instance of any special dispatch having reached me, since the commencement of the war, by the mails. If you desire to repeal the law, I trust that you will bring all your influence to bear in its accomplishment. Now is the time, it appears to me, to effect so desirable an object. I understand that not only our president, but also most of our colonels, and a majority of our congressmen, are professing Christians. God has greatly blessed us, and I trust He will make us that people to whom God is the Lord. Let us look to God for an illustration in our history that righteousness exalteth a nation, but sin is a reproach to any people.

Please send me a copy of the staff bill, as I may have something to say respecting it in my letter to Colonel Miles.

Very truly, your friend,
T. J. JACKSON

Colonel A. R. BOTELER, Richmond, Va.

In March, 1863, General Jackson moved his headquarters to a point near Hamilton's crossing, not far from General Lee

and, soon afterwards, his peaceful quietude was broken by the notes of war. On the 17th of the month the first movements of the Federals took place, by Hooker sending General Averill on an extensive raid in the direction of Gordonsville. But, it was not until the end of the month of April, when the Union forces had crossed the Rappahannock with a view of flanking Lee, that Jackson's active services were again in request. As we have seen in the account of the battle of Chancellorsville (page 90), Jackson was ordered, on Thursday evening, the 29th, to leave one division of his corps in front of the enemy at Fredericksburg, and proceed towards the field of action. His after movements we have already recorded,—how, after a consultation with General Lee, he attempted a flank movement on the enemy's right, stationed at the Wilderness, and how successfully it was executed. We have also hurriedly mentioned that it was on the evening of that first day's engagement he met his death-wound. But it is now our province to go into a few details explaining this mournful occurrence.

It was during the latter part of the day, May 2d, when the Federals were hurriedly retreating before Jackson's impetuous charge, that he directed certain movements to be made in the front, and then, being anxious to personally see them executed, he rode forward with his staff to the advanced line of skirmishers. The field of battle was, as we have before stated, amidst much of the thick scrub and wood of the "Wilderness," and it was with the utmost difficulty Jackson's party could proceed. They arrived, however, at the front, and, as night had now approached, Jackson, desirous of seeing more of the enemy's movements, rode on some distance ahead of his skirmishers, exposing himself to a dangerous fire from the enemy's sharpshooters posted in the timber. "So great was the danger, that one of his staff said, 'General, don't you think this is the wrong place for you?' He replied quickly : 'The danger is all over ; the enemy is routed. Go back and tell A. P. Hill to press right on!'" Soon after this order, General Jackson turned, and, accompanied by his staff and escort, rode back at a trot, on his well-known "Old Sorrel," towards his own men. Unhappily, in the darkness—it was now nine or ten o'clock at night—the little body of horsemen was mistaken for Federal cavalry charging, and the regiments on the right and left or

the road fired a sudden volley into them with the most la
mentable results.   Jackson was struck by three balls, one
through the left arm, two inches below the shoulder-joint
shattering the bone and severing the chief artery ; another
ball passed through the same arm between the elbow and
wrist, making its exit through the palm of the hand ; a third
ball entered the palm of the right hand about its middle, passing through, and breaking two bones.   He was wounded on
the plank-road, about fifty yards in advance.   Captain Boswell,
of Jackson's staff, was killed, and borne back into the Confederate lines by his own horse.   Colonel Crutchfield, chief of
artillery, was wounded by his side; and two couriers were
killed.   Major Pendleton, Lieutenants Morrison and Smith,
escaped uninjured.   As Jackson fell from his horse, he was
caught by Captain Wormley, to whom he remarked, " All my
wounds are by my own men."   He had previously given
orders to fire at any thing coming up the road, and probably
had forgotten, in his more important thoughts, to notify his
own movements.

Jackson was at once placed upon a litter, and started for the
rear ; but, now, the firing had attracted the enemy's attention,
who responded and made a slight advance.   The consequence
was that one of the litter bearers was shot down, and the
General fell from the shoulders of the men, receiving a severe
contusion, adding to the injury of the arm, and hurting his
side severely.   At the same time, the Federals charging, they
actually passed over his body, with a heavy fire going on from
both sides, and, for about five minutes, he was left thus, until
the enemy had been driven back.   An ambulance was then obtained, and he was immediately carried to the field hospital at
Wilderness Run.   There he was promptly attended by the
army surgeons, but he had already lost so large an amount of
blood, that for two hours he was nearly pulseless, and thought
he was dying.   A consultation immediately took place, and
amputation was decided upon.   The operation was performed
under the influence of chloroform, and was borne well.   But
he expressed an earnest desire that his troops should not know
he was wounded, and, while he was being carried from the
field, hearing the soldiers ask, " Who have you there ?" he
told the doctor not to tell them.   In moments of relief he ex

pressed anxiety concerning the battle, and movements of his corps, with a desire that General G. H. Stuart (Hill and Rodes being wounded) should command. After amputation, Jackson slept well through the night, and when he awoke requested that his wife should at once be sent for. He spoke of the attack which had been made on the previous evening, and felt confident of victory. A note now came from General Lee, expressing deep regret at the misfortune. The contents were: "I have just received your note informing me that you were wounded. I cannot express my regret at the occurrence. Could I have directed events, I should have chosen, for the good of the country, to have been disabled in your stead. I congratulate you on the victory which is due to your skill and energy."

Sunday evening he slept well; and on Monday he was carried to Chancellor's house, near Guinney's depot. He was cheerful, and talked about the battle, asking after all his officers, and especially about the "Stonewall Brigade." On Monday night he rested well, and next morning ate with a relish. On Tuesday and Wednesday, his wounds were doing very well. On Thursday, he suffered some pain; but now, to his great joy, Mrs. Jackson had arrived, and she assiduously nursed him to the end. But, from the following day, he gradually sunk. On Sunday morning, a week from the night of his being wounded, it was evident he had only a few hours more to live. Mrs. Jackson told him so, and in that tender and sacred converse between man and wife, which, at such times of extreme sadness, becomes more hallowed than ever, he said: "Very good! Very good! It is all right!" He then sent messages to all his friends, the generals and others, and murmured in a low voice his wish to be buried at "Lexington, in the valley of Virginia." His mind then began to wander, and he issued various orders to his officers,—among the last, being, "A. P. Hill, prepare for action!" After this, he speedily sank, and at a quarter past 3 P. M., Sunday, May 10th, he breathed his last, surrounded by weeping friends.

Immediately upon his death being made known, General Lee issued the following official announcement to his army:

GENERAL ORDERS—No. 61.

HEADQUARTERS, NORTHERN VIRGINIA, May 11, 1863.

With deep grief, the commanding general announces to the army the death of Lieutenant-general T. J. Jackson, who expired on the 10th instant, at quarter past 3 P. M. The daring, skill, and energy of this great and good soldier, by an all-wise Providence, are now lost to us. But while we mourn his death, we feel that his spirit still lives, and will inspire the whole army with his indomitable courage, and unshaken confidence in God as our hope and strength. Let his name be a watchword to his corps, who have followed him to victory on so many fields. Let the officers and soldiers imitate his invincible determination to do every thing in the defence of our beloved country.

R. E. LEE, General.

The body of General Jackson, embalmed, was conveyed to Richmond, where a great and solemn pageant marked the universal sense of loss. Laid in state, in the governor's reception-room, the dead hero was visited by thousands, tender women covering the pall with bouquets of flowers and wreaths; and when borne to the hall of the House of Representatives, the ceremony was grand in the extreme. Besides special regiments appointed to attend, there were members of his old brigade, the President of the Confederate States, members of the Cabinet, Generals Longstreet, Elzey, Garnett, and others, with Commodore Forrest, representing the navy, and the judges, citizens, and an immense concourse of persons, following in the train,—the general's old horse, caparisoned for battle, being led by a groom. Truly it was a grand, though mournful spectacle, and well might the Southern press, under such feelings, exclaim: "It would have been better for us to have lost a thousand ordinary men, than one 'Stonewall' Jackson!"

The honors bestowed upon Jackson's remains were of no common kind. During the great procession, his cold corse was carried by some of the bravest and most eminent military and naval commanders of his own South. Ewell, Winder, Corse, Kemper, Elzey, Forrest, Garnett, and Stuart—the chiv-

alrous, bold, and dashing Stuart—were the pall-bearers; and when the body was sent to its last resting-place at Lexington, Governor Letcher himself attended it thither.   Previous to its arrival, and shortly after his death, the superintendent of the Virginia Military Institute,—the same General F. H. Smith who, eleven years before, had submitted his name to the Board of Visitors for the vacant professor's chair,—officially announced the painful circumstance to the cadets, in a general order, embodying a brief *résumé* of his valuable services, and passing a high eulogy on his character.   "The military career of General Jackson," said the superintendent, "fills the most brilliant and momentous page in the history of our country, and in the achievements of our arms, and he stands forth a colossal figure in this war for our independence.   His country now returns him to us—not as he was when he left us.   His spirit has gone to God, who gave it.   His mutilated body comes back to us—to his home—to be laid by us in his tomb. Reverently and affectionately we will discharge this last solemn duty.   And,

> " Though his earthly sun has set,
> Its light shall linger round us yet,
> Bright—radiant—blest !"

When his remains arrived from Richmond, equally high was the honor shown to them at Lexington.   The cadets' battery, which he had so long commanded, fired half-hour guns, from sunrise to sunset; the flag of the State and the Confederacy was hung at half-mast; his lecture-room was draped in mourning, to remain so for six months; and the officers and cadets of the Institute wore the usual badge of mourning for thirty days.

The journals report that some loving hand planted on his grave a piece of laurel brought from the tomb of Napoleon at St. Helena; and it has been said by an intelligent Union chaplain, that "if any man whom this war has developed resembled Napoleon, it was Stonewall Jackson."   In this remark there is some reason, says a writer in the Tribune.   "Like Napoleon, Jackson had daring, originality; and like him, he taught his enemy that if they would beat him, they must imitate him."   But, by many competent judges, quite a different

estimate is held.   The character of Jackson being considered more assimilated with that of the stern Puritans or Covenanters ; not—even in a military point of view—with such a unique and master mind as Napoleon's.   However, the Southern general has and will have many great admirers, who almost deify him, through the deserved respect and admiration his countrymen have evinced towards such a brave and Christian man, as well as patriotic soldier.

O'Neill N.Y.

G. T. Beauregard
Gen. Comd'g

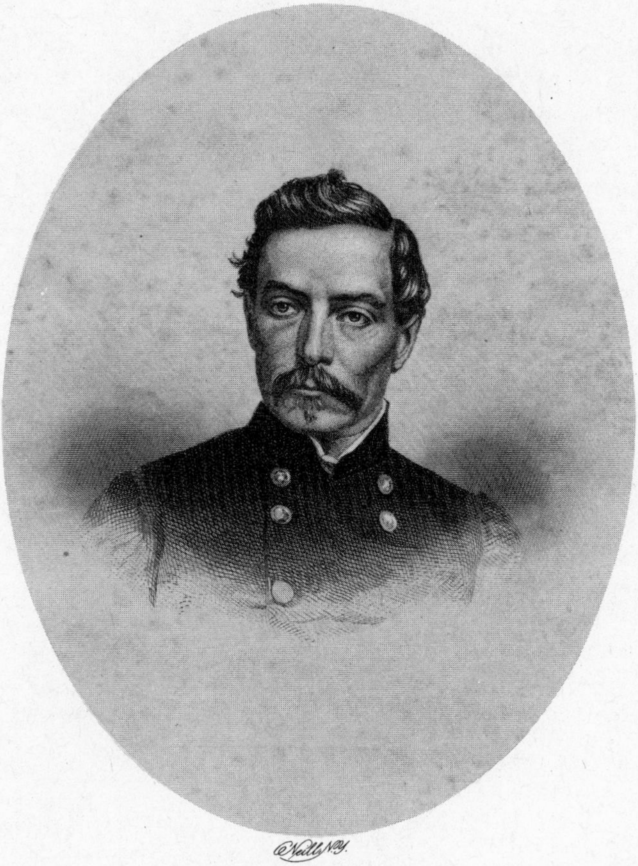

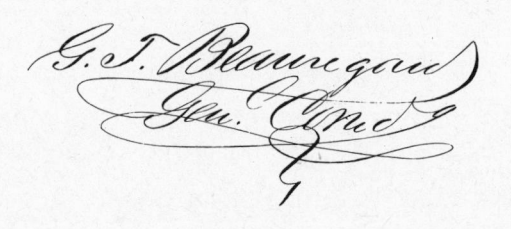

GENERAL PETER G. TOUTANT BEAUREGARD.

CHAPTER I.

SHORTLY after four o'clock in the dull gray of the morning of Friday, April 12th, 1861, unusual signs of excitement and agitation were seen among the citizens and residents of Charleston, South Carolina. Though at an hour when very few persons, under ordinary circumstances, are astir, and though the day was hazy and moist, yet every house appeared to be emptying its occupants and sending a living stream through all the streets leading to the wharves and battery. Not men, alone, but ladies of all ranks and grades, wended their way eagerly to the point of attraction. No gala-day had before witnessed so large a number of the fair sex gracing that public promenade; nor had any previous occasion awakened in their breasts so much anxiety, hope, and fear. With palpitating hearts and pallid faces, the more tender portion of that excited people stood facing the sea, watching tiny wreaths of white smoke curling upwards, in the soft twilight, from one point of view on the right, and quickly afterwards from another on the left, at James and Sullivan islands. Soon a dull, heavy sound fell upon the ear. Then came the whiz and the whirl of fiery implements of destruction; and, anon, the fury of a terrible cannonading, directed towards one solitary spot situated in

the bay, which, to the amazement of all, appeared as quiet as though death already tenanted it. For more than an hour no answering note replied to the iron messengers of slaughter hurled at it; but as daylight fully revealed the scene, the excited gazers on the battery promenade beheld, floating to the morning breeze from that one spot, which showed itself to be a fortress of great strength and importance, a large banner, elevated proudly aloft, and displaying on its folds the stars and stripes of the United States! Silence reigned around it, except in the battering it now received on either side from the assault. Another hour passed, and yet no answer came to the attack without; so that those who watched, began to augur results favorable to their own wishes, and to say that the tenants of that fort were going to yield. But they were mistaken. They knew not the character of those brave men—absolutely alone amidst surrounding foes, yet heroically bent on doing their duty, as true soldiers and loyal men, to the flag they served, and whose folds waved over them. They fancied that these men were about to succumb, without one note of fierce reply in honor of their name and country's reputation. But, not so. At half-past six, and while the spectators on the Charleston battery still looked on with varied emotions, suddenly, from casemate and parapet of that solitary fort, there darted forth sharp sheets of flame, and a storm of iron hail went hissing forward, in the direction of the assailing foe! The scene of carnage had, at last, begun, and the angry pieces of war on both sides were now dealing what destruction they could upon the opposite party. The atmosphere soon became charged with the smell of burnt powder, and the sky clouded, not only by the natural gloomy aspect of the day, but also by the smoke of the numerous guns now at work in deadly conflict.

Standing near one of these guns is General Beauregard, apparently in the prime of vigorous manhood, and having an eminently martial bearing. Spirit and determination may be seen in his glance, and a clearness of perception beyond that of ordinary men. Directing the heavy firing now going on against that solitary fort, and surrounded by members of his staff, he sends forth various orders in terse, abrupt tones, in the language of a man well used to, and fitted for command. Called

to the high and important post of General-in-chief of the Provisional Army of the State, and feeling the great responsibility attached to his position at that serious moment, when the first gun of open opposition to Federal power was fired, he could not be otherwise than keenly alive to the necessity for exercising every faculty of his experienced mind in the part he was now enacting. A few hours more—a day of gallant defence on the side of those heroic men in that solitary fort—and Beauregard was the victor over Sumter fallen!

We have no space here to give all the details of the attack on Fort Sumter, its sturdy defence by the brave Anderson and his comrades, and its ultimate surrender, when it was impossible to hold it longer under such an overwhelming fire. Our task now, must be merely to sketch the career of him who was destined to be the first military chief in active arms against the Government of the United States.

Beauregard was born on his father's plantation, in the Parish of St. Martin, Louisiana, in the year 1816. His great grandfather sprang from a noble family in France, which emigrated to this country during the reign of Louis XV., and settled in Louisiana. The name of the family was Toutant *de* Beauregard, until James, the father of Pierre Gustave, threw off the titular portion of it, for the reason, as some say, that it was repugnant to the old gentleman's republican tastes, or, as others state, that the name was often confounded with that of another family of Beauregards in his immediate neighborhood. From that time the family name has been simply *Toutant*,—no one but the subject of the present sketch having since used the original surname of Beauregard. There is, however, still another explanation of this change of name. It is said, by a writer in a New York paper, that " the family had an estate called Beauregard, and the elder Toutant—which was the rightful name—had been in the habit of signing himself Toutant *of* Beauregard. Thus, when he made an application to the member of Congress from the district in which he resided in Louisiana, for a cadetship at West Point for his young son, he signed himself in this way—Toutant de Beauregard—and the assumed title was taken for the surname. The appointment for the lad was therefore made out for Pierre G. T. Beauregard,

and the name was retained from a little vanity, perhaps, in its sonorous quality. Beauregard, however, is still known among his relations in Louisiana as Pierre Toutant."

James Toutant, the father, intermarried with Helene Reggio, whose earliest American ancestor came to this country about the time of the Beauregards. The family of Reggio is also of noble origin, being an Italian branch of the House of *Este.* The fruit of this marriage was three sons, of whom Peter Gustave is the second, and three daughters, married respectively to Mortimer Belly, Esq., of New Orleans, R. S Proctor, Esq., of St. Bernard, and M. Legendre, of New York

Pierre Gustave Beauregard entered West Point as a cadet, in 1834, and graduated June 30th, 1838, taking the second honors in a class of forty-five graduates. He was then appointed second-lieutenant in the First Regiment of artillery, which commission he only held for one week, being transferred to the corps of Engineers on July 7th. On June 16th, 1839, he was promoted to a first-lieutenancy, and in that capacity served with great distinction during the Mexican War. Of the several incidents wherein he made himself conspicuous, we have but to refer to General Scott's official reports, and his Autobiography, for ample testimony to the merits of the brave young officer. But the following illustrations of his career at that period deserve to be especially mentioned. The first occurred before Vera Cruz, as follows :

Lieutenant Beauregard was sent out by his colonel with a party of sappers to dig and prepare a trench, according to a profile and plan made by the colonel. No sooner had Beauregard examined the ground, than he discovered great objections to the plan. To assure himself, he climbed into a tree, and with the aid of the marine glass, the engineer's *vade mecum,* he made a reconnoissance, and saw plainly that the trench, as planned, would be enfiladed by the enemy's cannon. Here was a difficult position for a subaltern ministerial officer. He decided promptly, and returned to headquarters without sticking a spade. The colonel met him, and expressed surprise that he had so soon performed his task. Beauregard replied that he had not touched it. The colonel, with the astonishment military men feel in hearing their orders have not been obeyed, inquired the reason. He was soon informed of it. He was in-

credulous ; " the ground had been examined ;" " the reconnoissance was perfect," etc. The young lieutenant was satisfied,
however, that the reconnoissance of his old chief had not been
made like his, " from up in a tree." The colonel, like a sensi
ble man, concluded to make another examination : the plan
was changed in accordance with the young lieutenant's views.
The work done from these trenches is matter of history, but its
pages nowhere inform us to whom the credit is due.

A second incident occurred before the city of Mexico. A
night or two before the attack, a council of war was held.
There were assembled all the great folks, from Lieutenant-general Scott, Worth, Twiggs, etc., down to our friend Beauregard,
the youngest officer in the room. The debate went on for hours
Scott was solitary in his opinion. Every other officer present,
except one, had spoken, and all concurred in their views. The
silent one was Beauregard. At last General Pierce crossed
over and said, " You have not expressed an opinion." " I have
not been called on," said Beauregard. " You shall be, however," said Pierce ; and soon resuming his seat, announced
that Lieutenant Beauregard had not given his opinion. Being
then called out, he remarked, that if the plan which had received the consent of all but the commanding general was carried into effect, it would prove disastrous. It would be anothei
Churubusco affair. He then detailed the objections to it at
length ; and taking up the other, urged the reasons in its favor,
with equal earnestness. The council reversed their decision.
The city of Mexico was entered according to the plan urged
by the young lieutenant ; and it would seem that his reasons
influenced the decision. A few days afterwards General Scott,
in the presence of a number of principal officers, alluded to
Lieutenant Beauregard's opinion at the council, and the consequences which had followed from it.

On August 20th, 1847, Beauregard was brevetted captain,
for gallant and meritorious conduct in the battles of Contreras and Churubusco ; and again as major, for the battle of
Chapultepec, to date from September 13th, 1847. At the
Belen gate, Mexico, he was wounded ; and, afterwards, upon
his return home, he was presented with an elegant sword.
Subsequently he was placed by the Government in charge of
the construction of the Mint and Custom-house at New Or-

leans, as well as of the fortifications on and near the mouth of the Mississippi.

At the beginning of the year 1861, Major Beauregard was appointed superintendent of West Point Military Academy, "but was relieved by President Buchanan within forty-eight hours, as a rebuke, it is alleged, to the secession speech of Senator Slidell, who is a brother-in-law of Beauregard." Subsequently he resigned his commission in the service of the United States, and was appointed by Governor Moore, of Louisiana, Colonel of Engineers in the Provisional Army of the South. Soon afterwards, he was made Brigadier general in the forces of his native State, which appointment was confirmed by President Davis, on March 3d, with official directions to proceed to Charleston and assume command of all the troops in actual service in and around that place.

On arriving there, he immediately examined the fortifications, and put the city and defences in military array. Fort Sumter, at that time, was garrisoned by Major Anderson, of the regular army, and a force of officers and men; and it was hoped, by the State Convention of South Carolina, that it would be surrendered to the South without compulsion. But, every effort to induce such a course failed. The Federal commander could not and would not yield, while a shadow of hope remained of being able to hold out. That hope much depended upon receiving supplies from the government at Washington. Without those supplies the heroic little garrison could not exist, for all communication between Sumter and the city of Charleston was, on the 7th of April, cut off. Previously, the wants of the garrison had been supplied through the city, but now the time had come when General Beauregard and the authorities deemed it necessary to stop all further intercourse, except of a purely military character as between belligerents. Thus, Major Anderson had to look to Washington for immediate relief, sending a special messenger thither, stating his condition, and asking for official instructions what to do. Neither the relief, nor the instructions, however, came until too late, though notice had been sent the 8th of April, by an envoy from President Lincoln to Governor Pickens and General Beauregard, that "provisions would be forwarded to Fort Sumter peaceably, or otherwise by force."

The message of President Lincoln was immediately tele-graphed by Beauregard to the Confederate War Department at Montgomery, and the following reply came back:

"If you have no doubt of the authorized character of the agent who communicated to you the intention of the Washing-ton government to supply Fort Sumter by force, you will at once demand its evacuation, and if this is refused, proceed, in such manner as you may determine, to reduce it."

To this, Beauregard responded: "The demand will be made to-morrow at twelve o'clock." Whereupon, Secretary Walker again telegraphed: "Unless there are especial reasons con-nected with your own condition, it is considered proper that you should make the demand at an earlier hour." Beaure-gard replied: "The reasons are special for twelve o'clock."

This correspondence was on the 10th of April, and on the following day, Thursday, April 11th, at 2.20 P. M., General Beauregard sent two of his aids with a communication to Major Anderson, demanding the evacuation, with an offer to transport himself and command to any port in the United States he might select, to allow him to move out of the fort with company arms and property, and all private property, and to salute his flag on lowering it. To this communication Major Anderson refused to accede, but, as the messengers were leaving, he remarked, that if the fort was not battered to pieces, he would be starved out in a few days.

At 5.10 P. M. Beauregard received Anderson's answer, which, in writing, was as follows:

HEADQUARTERS, FORT SUMTER, S. C., April 11th, 1861

GENERAL—I have the honor to acknowledge the receipt of your communication, demanding the evacuation of this fort; and to say in reply thereto, that it is a demand with which I regret that my sense of honor and my obligations to my Gov-ernment prevent my compliance.

Thanking you for the fair, manly, and courteous terms pro-posed, and for the high compliment paid me,

   I am, General, very respectfully

     Your obedient servant,

(Signed)   ROBERT ANDERSON,

       Major United States Army, commanding

To Brigadier-general G. T. BEAUREGARD,

   Commanding Provisional Army, C. S. A.

This was telegraphed to Montgomery, and the following communication received at 9.10 P. M. in reply :

MONTGOMERY, April 11th, 1861.

To GENERAL BEAUREGARD:

Sir—We do not desire needlessly to bombard Fort Sumter If Major Anderson will state the time at which, as indicated by him, he will evacuate (be starved out), and agree that in the mean time he will not use his guns against us, unless arms should be employed against Fort Sumter, you are authorized thus to avoid the effusion of blood. If this or its equivalent be refused, you will reduce the fort as your judgment decides to be the most practicable.

(Signed)   L. P. WALKER.

At 11 P. M. Beauregard sent his aids with another letter to Major Anderson, based upon the instructions he had received. The contents of the letter ran thus:

HEADQUARTERS PROVISIONAL ARMY C. S. A.,
Charleston, April 11, 1861—11 P. M.

MAJOR—In consequence of the verbal observations made by you to my aides, Messrs. Chesnut and Lee, in relation to the condition of your supplies, and that you would, in a few days, be starved out if our guns did not batter you to pieces—or words to that effect—and desiring no useless effusion of blood, I communicated both the verbal observation and your written answer in my communication to my Government.

If you will state the time at which you will evacuate Fort Sumter, and agree that, in the mean while, you will not use your guns against us, unless ours shall be employed against Fort Sumter, we will abstain from opening fire upon you. Colonel Chesnut and Captain Lee are authorized by me to enter into such an agreement with you. You are therefore requested to communicate to them an open answer.

I remain, Major, very respectfully,

Your obedient servant,

(Signed)   P. G. T. BEAUREGARD,
                            Brigadier-general, commanding.

To Major ROBERT ANDERSON,
     Commanding at Fort Sumter, Charleston Harbor, S. C.

At forty-five minutes past midnight, Major Anderson had this letter placed in his hands, and, after consultation with his officers, at half-past two in the morning, April 12th, he returned the following reply :

GENERAL—I have the honor to acknowledge the receipt of your second communication of the 11th instant, by Colonel Chesnut, and to state, in reply, that cordially uniting with you in the desire to avoid the useless effusion of blood, I will, if provided with the proper and necessary means of transportation, evacuate Fort Sumter by noon on the 15th instant, should I not receive, prior to that time, controlling instructions from my Government, or additional supplies ; and that I will not, in the mean time, open my fire upon your forces, unless compelled to do so by some hostile act against this fort or the flag of my Government, by the forces under your command, or by some portion of them, or by the perpetration of some act showing a hostile intention on your part against this fort or the flag it bears.

I have the honor to be, General,
          Very respectfully, your obedient servant,

(Signed)   ROBERT ANDERSON,
                   Major United States Army, commanding.

This reply General Beauregard did not consider sufficiently to the purpose, inasmuch as information had come to hand (and after-events proved its truth) that an attempt would be made, by force, from a United States fleet then lying off the entrance of the harbor, to relieve the fort; and, in that case, Major Anderson would still feel himself bound to hold possession. Prompt measures, therefore, were necessary, and Beaugard immediately adopted them. He quickly sent back his aides, with instructions how to act, and at 3.20 A. M. of that eventful Friday, April 12th, the following declaration of hostility was delivered to Major Anderson :

SIR—By the authority of Brigadier-general Beauregard, commanding the provisional forces of the Confederate States,

we have the honor to notify you that he will open the fire of
his batteries on Fort Sumter in one hour from this time.

We have the honor to be, very respectfully,

Your obedient servants,

(Signed)   JAMES CHESNUT, Jr., Aid-de-camp.

STEPHEN D. LEE, Captain S. C. A. and Aid-de-camp.

Major ROBERT ANDERSON,

United States Army, commanding Fort Sumter.

What immediately followed has already been mentioned at
the opening of our chapter; but, as no event in the history of
America has had so important a bearing upon its present and
future, since the great day of her independence was acknowledged, we deem it best to give an official report of the occurrences that took place, so far as relating to the subject of our
present sketch.

General Beauregard says:

" At 4.30 A. M. the signal shell was fired from Fort Johnson;
and about five o'clock the fire from our batteries became general. Fort Sumter did not begin until seven o'clock, when
it commenced with a vigorous fire upon the Cummings' Poin
iron battery. The enemy next directed his fire upon the en
filade battery on Sullivan's Island, constructed to sweep the
parapet of Fort Sumter, to prevent the working of the barbette
guns, and to dismount them. This was also the aim of the
floating battery, the Dahlgren battery, and the gun-batteries
at Cummings' Point. The enemy next opened fire on Fort
Moultrie, between which and Fort Sumter a steady and almost constant fire was kept up throughout the day. These
three points, Fort Moultrie, Cummings' Point, and the end of
Sullivan's Island, where the floating battery, Dahlgren battery,
and the enfilade battery were placed, were the points to which
the enemy seemed almost to confine his attention, although he
fired a number of shots at Captain Butler's mortar battery,
situated to the east of Fort Moultrie, and a few at Captain
James' mortar batteries, at Fort Johnson. During the day
(12th inst.) the fire of my batteries was kept up most spiritedly;
the guns and mortars being worked in the coolest manner, pre-
serving the prescribed intervals of firing. Towards evening it
became evident that our fire was very effective, as the enemy

was driven from his barbette guns, which he attempted to work in the morning, and his fire was confined to his casemate guns, but in a less active manner than in the morning, and it was observed that several of his guns *en barbette* were disabled.

"During the whole of Friday night our mortar batteries continued to throw shells, but, in obedience to orders, at longer intervals. The night was rainy and dark, and as it was confidently expected that the United States fleet would attempt to land troops upon the islands, or to throw men into Fort Sumter, by means of boats, the greatest vigilance was observed at all our channel batteries, and by our troops on both Morris' and Sullivan's islands. Early on Saturday morning all of our batteries reopened upon Fort Sumter, which responded vigorously for a time, directing its fire specially against Fort Moultrie. About 8 o'clock A. M., smoke was seen issuing from the quarters of Fort Sumter: upon this, the fire of our batteries was increased, as a matter of course, for the purpose of bringing the enemy to terms as speedily as possible, inasmuch as his flag was still floating defiantly above him. Fort Sumter continued to fire from time to time, but at long and irregular intervals, amid the dense smoke, flying shot, and bursting shells. Our brave troops, carried away by their naturally generous impulses, mounted the different batteries, and at every discharge from the fort, cheered the garrison for its pluck and gallantry, and hooted the fleet lying inactive just outside the bar. About 1.30 P. M., it being reported to me that the flag was down (it afterwards appeared that the flag-staff had been shot away), and the conflagration from the large volume of smoke being apparently on the increase, I sent three of my aides with a message to Major Anderson, to the effect that seeing his flag no longer flying, his quarters in flames, and supposing him to be in distress, I desired to offer him any assistance he might stand in need of. Before my aides reached the fort, the United States flag was displayed on the parapets, but remained there only a short time, when it was hauled down, and a white flag substituted in its place. When the United States flag first disappeared, the firing from our batteries almost entirely ceased, but reopened with increased vigor when it reappeared on the parapet, and was continued until the white flag was raised, when it ceased entirely. Upon the arrival of my aides at Fort Sumter,

they delivered their message to Major Anderson, who replied that he thanked me for my offer, but desired no assistance. Just previous to the arrival, Colonel Wigfall, one of my aides, who had been detached for special duty on Morris' Island, had, by order of Brigadier-general Simons, crossed over to Fort Sumter from Cummings' Point in an open boat, with private William Gourdin Young, amidst a heavy fire of shot and shell, for the purpose of ascertaining from Major Anderson whether his intention was to surrender, his flag being down and his quarters in flames. On reaching the fort, the colonel had an interview with Major Anderson, the result of which was, that Major Anderson understood him as offering the same conditions on the part of General Beauregard, as had been tendered him on the 11th instant; while Colonel Wigfall's impression was, that Major Anderson unconditionally surrendered, trusting to the generosity of General Beauregard to offer such terms as would be honorable and acceptable to both parties; meanwhile, before these circumstances were reported to me, and, in fact, soon after the aides whom I had dispatched with the offer of assistance had set out on their mission, hearing that a white flag was flying over the fort, I sent Major Jones, the chief of my staff, and some other aides, with substantially the same propositions I had submitted to Major Anderson on the 11th instant, with the exception of the privilege of saluting his flag.

"The major (Anderson) replied, 'it would be exceedingly gratifying to him, as well as to his command, to be permitted to salute his flag, having so gallantly defended the fort, under such trying circumstances, and hoped that General Beauregard would not refuse it, as such a privilege was not unusual.' He further said, 'he would not urge the point, but would prefer to refer the matter to General Beauregard.' The point was, therefore, left open until the matter was submitted to me. Previous to the return of Major Jones, I sent a fire-engine, under Mr. M. H. Nathan, chief of the fire department, and Surgeon-general Gibbes, of South Carolina, with several of my aides, to offer further assistance to the garrison of Fort Sumter, which was declined. I very cheerfully agreed to allow the salute as an honorable testimony to the gallantry and fortitude with which Major Anderson and his command had defended

their posts, and I informed Major Anderson of my decision about half-past seven o'clock, through Major Jones, my chief of staff. The arrangements being completed, Major Anderson embarked with his command on the transport prepared to convey him to the United States fleet, still lying outside the bar, and our troops immediately garrisoned the fort, and before sunset the flag of the Confederate States floated over the ram parts of Sumter."

During the bombardment several incidents occurred that showed how the gallantry displayed by Major Anderson and his heroic band was fully understood and appreciated, even by those fighting against him. But we have not space, here, to record them. One circumstance, however, relating to the interchange of such courtesies as could be extended, may be mentioned. When the news arrived in Paris, a French gentleman said to an American there : " Quelle idée chevalresque ! On voit que vous avez profité, vous autres Américains, de l'exemple Français. Ce Général Beauregard porte un nom Français !"*

Immediately after the surrender of Fort Sumter, General Beauregard issued a complimentary order to his troops for their bearing, and the success which had attended their arms ; and, at a later period, he himself and his officers received the thanks of the Southern Congress, "for the skill, fortitude, and courage" displayed; and the commendation of Congress was also expressed in view "of the generosity manifested by their conduct towards a brave and conquered foe."

About this time General Beauregard was visited by a gentleman somewhat well known, both in the North and South, from his letters to the London Times. We allude to Mr. W. H. Russell, who says, under date of April 16th :

"I was taken after dinner and introduced to General Beauregard, who was engaged, late as it was, in his room at headquarters, writing dispatches. . . . He received me in the most cordial manner, and introduced me to his engineer officer, Major Whiting, whom he assigned to lead me over the works next day. After some general conversation, I took my leave;

---

* "What a chivalric idea! It is easy to see that you Americans have profited by French example. This General Beauregard bears a French name !"

but, before I went, the general said, ' You shall go everywhere and see every thing; we rely upon your discretion, and knowledge of what is fair, in dealing with what you see.   Of course you don't expect to find regular soldiers in our camps, or very scientific works.'   I answered the general, that he might rely on my making no improper use of what I saw in this country, but, ' unless you tell me to the contrary, I shall write an account of all I see, to the other side of the water; and if, when it comes back, there are things you would rather not have known, you must not blame me.'   He smiled, and said, ' I dare say we'll have great changes by that time.'

"The next day I went over and saw General Beauregard, again, at his quarters.   He was busy with papers, orderlies, and dispatches, and the outer room was crowded with officers. His present task, he told me, was to put Sumter in a state of defence, and to disarm the works bearing on it, so as to get their fire directed on the harbor approaches, as ' the North, in its madness,' might attempt a naval attack on Charleston.* His manner of transacting business was clear and rapid.   Two vases filled with flowers on his table, flanking his maps and plans; and, by way of paper weight, a little bouquet of roses, geraniums, and scented flowers lay on a letter which he was writing as I came in.   He offered me every assistance and facility, relying, of course, on my strict observance of a neutral's duty." . . . . "April 24th, I saw General Beauregard in the evening; he was very lively and in good spirits, though he admitted he was rather surprised by the spirit displayed in the North. ' A good deal of it is got up, however,' he said, ' and belongs to that washy sort of enthusiasm which is promoted by their lecturing and spouting.'

"Beauregard is proud of his personal strength, which, for his slight frame, is said to be very extraordinary, and he seemed to insist on it that the Southern men had more physical strength, owing to their mode of life, and their education, than their Northern ' brethren.' . . . . "He is apprehensive of an attack by the Northern ' fanatics' before the South is prepared, and he considers they will carry out coercive measures most rigorously."

---

* This, after events verified.

On the 4th of May, General Beauregard was again met by Mr. Russell, on his way to Montgomery. The latter gentleman says: " At one of the junctions, General Beauregard, attended by Mr. Manning, and others of his staff, got into the car, and tried to elude observation, but the conductors take great pleasure in unearthing distinguished passengers for the public, and the general was called on for a speech by the crowd of idlers.   The general hates speech-making, he told me; and, besides, he had been bored to death at every station by similar demands.   But, a man must be popular, or he is nothing."

From Montgomery—where he had personally reported to President Davis—it is variously stated that he went to Richmond and consulted with General Lee, and was afterwards at Norfolk with a large force.   But the reports of his movements at this time were, not only confused, but contradictory, and, under present circumstances, it is difficult to give any exact statement, until we find him, on May 12th, again at Charleston, departing in the steamer *General Clinch* on a tour of inspection.

On the 22d of May he was still at Charleston, as the following letter shows:

HEADQUARTERS PROVISIONAL ARMY C. S., }
CHARLESTON, S. C., May 22, 1861.   }

DEAR MAJOR—I send you, through Mr. T. K. Wharton, a piece of the flag-staff of Fort Sumter, which was struck nine times by the balls and shells of our batteries, and finally came down with the flag attached to it.   The piece sent you is intended as the staff of your battalion colors, and I have no doubt that when thus honored, and under the protection of our gallant comrades, it will meet with better success.

With the assurance of my high consideration, I remain, dear major, yours very truly,

P. G. T. BEAUREGARD,
Brigadier-General Commanding.

Major NUMA AUGUSTIN, Commanding Orleans Battalion, New Orleans.

A few days after, General Beauregard was appointed to a fresh command, supposed, at first, to have been Corinth, Mississippi; and several statements in the papers asserted he was there, or on his way; but if so, he must have speedily returned to Richmond, as he was at that place in the early

part of June. However, it was on the 27th of May he bade farewell to Charleston, in the following letter, addressed to General Martin.

CHARLESTON, May 27, 1861.

MY DEAR GENERAL—I sincerely regret leaving Charleston, where the inhabitants have given me such a welcome that I now consider it as my second home.

I had hoped that when relieved from here it would have been to go to Virginia, in command of the gallant Carolinians, whose courage, patience, and zeal I had learned to appreciate and admire. But it seems my services are required elsewhere, and thither I shall go, not with joy, but with the firm determination to do more than my duty, if I can, and to leave as strong a mark as possible on the enemies of our beloved country, should they pollute its soil with their dastardly feet.

But rest assured, my dear sir, that whatever happens at first, we are certain to triumph at last, even if we had for arms only pitchforks and flint-lock muskets, for every bush and haystack will become an ambush and every barn a fortress. The history of nations proves that a gallant and free people, fighting for their independence and firesides, are invincible against even disciplined mercenaries, at a few dollars per month. What, then, must be the result when its enemies are little more than an armed rabble, gathered together hastily on a false pretense, and for an unholy purpose, with an octogenarian at its head? None but the demented can doubt the issue.

I remain, dear general, yours sincerely,

P. G. T. BEAUREGARD.

At the beginning of June, General Beauregard was in consultation with President Davis and General Lee, at Richmond, while, by means of couriers, they held frequent communication with General Johnston, then in command near Harper's Ferry. The result was, that a military campaign was decided upon, embracing defensive operations in North Virginia and the Shenandoah valley, and concentrating an army, under Beauregard, at the Manassas Gap railroad junction, and immediate locality.

Beauregard immediately assumed command, and on the 5th of June issued a proclamation, earnestly inviting and enjoining

the people of the counties around " to rally to the standard of
their State and country." At the same time no strangers
were allowed to go North without a passport.

The following account of Beauregard and his army, at this
period, from a gentleman writing to a Southern paper, may
be found interesting.

Dating his letter from Manassas Junction, July 7th, he says :
" This place still continues the headquarters of the army ot
the Potomac. By nature, the position is one of the strongest
that could have been found in the whole State. About half
way between the eastern spur of the Blue Ridge and the Potomac, below Alexandria, it commands the whole country between, so perfectly that there is scarcely a possibility of its
being turned. The right wing stretches off towards the head-
waters of the Ocoogan, through a wooded country, which is
easily made impassable by the felling of trees. The left is a
rolling table-land, readily commanded from the successive ele-
vations, till you reach a country so rough and so rugged that
it is a defence to itself. The key to the whole position, in fact,
is precisely that point which General Beauregard chose for his
centre, and which he has fortified so strongly, that, in the
opinion of military men, five thousand men could there hold
twenty thousand at bay. . . . . .

" As might be expected from the skill with which he has
chosen his position, and the system with which he encamps and
moves his men, General Beauregard is very popular here. I
doubt if Napoleon himself had more the undivided confidence
of his army. By nature, as also from a wise policy, he is very
reticent. Not an individual here knows his plans, or a single
move of a regiment before it is made, and then only the
colonel and his men know where it goes to. So close does the
general keep his affairs to himself, his left hand hardly knoweth
what his right hand doeth ; and so jealous is he of this preroga-
tive of a commanding officer, that I verily believe if he suspected his coat of any acquaintance with the plans revolving
within him, he would cast it from him.

" The general's headquarters is a little farm-house, about
fifteen feet by twenty, fronting one of the roads leading to
Alexandria. The ground-floor is divided into two rooms. The
front one is filled with desks at which clerks sit writing, or

engaged in business of a varied character. The back one ap
pears to be used as a storeroom or kitchen. Above, the same
division continues, and the front room is the general's apartment. It is about fifteen feet long by ten wide, and hung with
maps of the State and country around. In the centre is a plain
pine table, on which lie, neatly folded up, what the visitor
would naturally take to be plans, specifications, surveys, geo-
metrical drawings, etc., and by their side military reports.
Every thing has the air of neatness, coolness, and mathematical calculation. Of course there is nothing in the room but
what pertains to the office, and to most eyes it would appear
somewhat bare; but what there is, is arranged with so much
taste, that the general impression is by no means unpleasing.

" The general is in his room the greater part of the day, apparently occupied with his plans and reports. Then, hour after
hour he sits alone by his neat little pine table, maps, plans, and
specifications before him, and large windows open behind and
around him—at first sight the cold, calculating, unsympathiz-
ing mathematician. Every now and then an aide enters with a
report or a message, which is delivered in military style,
deliberately examined in silence, the corresponding order
promptly written out or delivered in as few words as possible,
and our mathematical iceberg is alone again. When a visitor
drops in, however, at a leisure moment, the formality of the
officer readily gives way to that easy interchange of civilities
which characterizes our people at home, but nothing more.
Even at the table, where the general is daily surrounded by
the most distinguished gentlemen of the country, there appears
to be a distance which I suppose is natural to his position, but
which is rarely found elsewhere.

"The leading characteristic of General Beauregard's mind is
clearness and perception. Superadded to this is a strictly
mathematical education. This you see in every word and
look, even in the expression of his face. Sines, cosines, and
tangents stick out everywhere. In person he is slender and
compactly built, and extremely neat. Add to this a precision
of manner, slightly modified by the ease which characterizes
the well-bred man of the world, and you have a correct idea of
the man whose word is law and gospel throughout one of the
largest, most intelligent, and best-appointed armies ever as-

sembled on the American continent. In his personal staff the general has been peculiarly fortunate. They are principally from South Carolina, the same he had with him at the siege of Fort Sumter; all of them accomplished, discreet gentlemen, of the most pleasing manners. Among them I have been happy to meet Colonel Preston, so long a resident and so well known in Louisiana, whose genial society must be a happy relief to the severe labors of the day.

"The general's mess is very much in keeping with his character, and simple enough for Napoleon himself. It is served on a long pine table, set in an open piazza of the farm-house, and all his friends are hospitably welcomed to it three times a day. The general sits nearly in the middle, his aides immediately on one side, and his latest guests on the other; the rest of the company as they may choose or chance to seat themselves. The viands are such as the country around affords; only the rice was 'imported,' and with it, I suspect, a South Carolina cook, for every kernel was as independent as the State from which it came."

The author of "Battle-fields of the South," who was, himself, not only a close observer and fluent writer, but one of those brave soldiers who promptly volunteered at the Southern call for troops, and was in the Confederate army under Beauregard at the time, gives us some interesting sketches of the general; but we have not space to transcribe them.

On the 18th of July took place that engagement between a portion of the Northern army, under General McDowell, and the Southern forces, under Beauregard and Johnston, which, by the former, has been called the fight at Blackburn's ford, and, by the latter, the battle of Bull Run—terming the great battle of Bull Run, that of Manassas.

The particulars of this engagement, and the great battle of Bull Run, fought on July 21st, are too well known to need repeating here, and, moreover, have been briefly described in our sketch of General Jackson's life. The following, however, not generally known, nor to be found in official documents, deserves to be introduced here.

At a select dinner party, some time after this, General

Beauregard, in a speech having reference to the new Confederate flag, made the following remarks concerning this portion of the battle of Manassas.   He said:

"On the 21st of July, at about half-past three o'clock, perhaps four, it seemed to me that the victory was already within our grasp.   In fact, up to that moment, I had never wavered in the conviction that triumph must crown our arms.   Nor was my confidence shaken until, at the time I have mentioned, I observed on the extreme left, at the distance of something more than a mile, a column of men approaching.   At their head was a flag which I could not distinguish.   Even with the aid of a strong glass, I was unable to determine whether it was the United States flag, or the Confederate flag.

"At the same moment, I received a dispatch from Captain Alexander, in charge of the signal station, warning me to look out for the left; that a large column was approaching from. that direction, and that it was supposed to be General Patter- son's command, coming to reinforce McDowell.   At this moment, I must confess, my heart failed me.   I came, reluctantly to the conclusion, that, after all our efforts, we should at last be compelled to yield to the enemy the hard-fought and bloody field.   I again took the glass to examine the flag of the approaching column ; but my anxious inquiry was unproductive of result—I could not tell to which army the waving banner belonged.   At this time, all the members of my staff were absent, having been dispatched with orders to various points. The only person with me was the gallant officer who has recently distinguished himself by the brilliant feat of arms— General, then Colonel, Evans.   To him I communicated my doubts and my fears.   I told him I feared the approaching force was in reality Patterson's division ; that if such was the case, I should be compelled to fall back upon our reserves, and postpone till the next day a continuation of the engagement.

"After further reflection, I directed Colonel Evans to proceed to General Johnston, who had assumed the task of collecting a reserve, and to inform him of the circumstances of the case; and to request him to have the reserves collected with all dispatch, and hold them in readiness to support our retrograde movement.   Colonel Evans started on the mission thus intrusted to h'm.   He had proceeded but a short distance,

when it occurred to me to make another examination of the still approaching flag. It had now come within full view. A sudden gust of wind shook out its folds, and I recognized the stars and bars of the Confederate banner. It was the flag borne by your regiment [here the general turned to Colonel Hay, who sat beside him], the gallant Seventh Louisiana, and the column of which your regiment constituted the advance was the brigade of General, then Colonel, Early.

" As soon as you were recognized by our soldiers, your coming was greeted with enthusiastic cheers, regiment after regiment responding to the cry ; the enemy heard the triumphant huzza; their attack slackened ; these were in turn assailed by our forces, and within half an hour from that moment commenced the retreat, which afterwards became a confused and total rout. I am glad to see that war-stained banner gleaming over us at this festive board, but I hope never again to see it upon the field of battle."

A few days after the battle of Bull Run, General Beauregard received a letter from the bereaved sister of Colonel Cameron, who had been killed ; and surely we cannot err if, amidst the fierce scenes we are obliged to bring more prominently forward, we occasionally introduce touching incidents of natural affection like the one here named.

WASHINGTON, July 26th, 1861

GENERAL BEAUREGARD, Commander of the Confederate Army:

DEAR SIR—With a grieved and torn heart I address you. If it is in your power will you give a word of comfort to a distressed spirit? I allude to the death of the gallant Colonel Cameron, of the Federal army, on last Sunday, 21st July. We are all God's creatures, alike in his sight. It is a bereaved sister that petitions. Colonel Cameron received two shots, immediately following each other, that destroyed his life. The fate of his body is the grief, to know what has become of it. Think of a distress of a like nature in Southern families, and let us forgive as we hope to be forgiven.

All that we have been able to learn is, that Colonel Cameron was carried to a farm-house near the scene of battle. He had letters in his pocket declaring his name and station. He was rather a large man, with sandy hair, somewhat gray,

dressed in gray clothes. Have mercy on the bowed spirit that laments for the beloved lost—that would be comforted to know that he received decent burial. Notwithstanding the war, we are all brothers. "God prosper the righteous cause." In pity, have inquiries made, for the love a sister bears a brother, and may God show you mercy in time of trouble.

Should your noble spirit grant my request, and if by inquiry you can receive any information, please have a letter addressed to Mrs. Sarah Z. Evans, No. 553 Capitol Hill, Washington city, care of Adams' Express Company.

Very respectfully, your well-wisher,

SARAH Z. EVANS.

Please favor me so far as to have the letter acknowledged as received.   S. Z. E.

HEADQUARTERS, FIRST CORPS, ARMY OF THE POTOMAC, }
MANASSAS, August 5, 1861. }

MADAM—Your letter of the 26th ult. has been received, making some inquiries relative to the body of your late brother, Colonel Cameron, United States army, killed at Manassas on the 21st ult. In answer, I will state that, upon inquiry, I find he was interred, with several other bodies, in a grave about two hundred yards from the house of a Mrs. Dogan, on the battlefield, who attended herself this sad duty. . . . Indeed, I fully agree with you : may all the distress of this unholy war be visited upon the heads of those who are responsible for it, and may the Almighty Ruler of the Universe, in his infinite goodness and wisdom, (continue to) prosper the righteous cause!

A gentleman of this State, Mr. Kinlaw Fauntleroy, a private in Colonel Stuart's cavalry brigade, has in his possession a miniature portrait of Colonel Cameron and wife, which he intends to return to their friends after the war; for at present no intercourse of the kind is admissible between the two contending parties.

With much respect, I remain your most obedient servant,

P. G. T. BEAUREGARD,

General Commanding

Mrs. S. Z. EVANS, No. 553 Capitol Hill, Washington, D. C.

Other attempts were made by Colonel McCunn and Senator Harris, to obtain Colonel Cameron's body, but they failed :

and it was not until the following March, nearly eight months after the battle, that the place of his burial was found by a party of friends visiting the scene, and his body exhumed for the purpose of conveying it to Washington for reinterment.

It has often been asked by some, why Beauregard did not immediately advance on Washington, while the enemy was in confusion? But, independent of what he himself says, and what we conceive to be one fact, viz., the exhausted condition of the Confederate troops at the time, the following has been stated by an officer in the Southern army. He says: " I do not know what was the reason. Johnston, Beauregard, and President Davis held a consultation. Beauregard was in favor of advancing immediately, but Davis and Johnston both opposed the movement. Whether it was right or wrong, I shall not pretend to say. If we had advanced, we might now have Washington in our possession. But then what would Washington be worth to us after we had taken it, and how difficult would it have been to hold it? I think we ought to have advanced on Alexandria and driven the enemy from the soil of Virginia, but President Davis said not, and I am willing to risk him in every thing."

Other reasons have also been given, attributing the cause to political and personal jealousies, but we have no need, here, to bring them forward.

On Thursday, August 8th, Prince Napoleon, who had but a short time before arrived in the United States, paid a visit to General Beauregard, at Manassas. The Prince had a special escort and pass from the Federal authorities; and, on entering the Confederate lines near Fairfax, was received by the officer on guard there, who accompanied the party to Colonel Stuart, in command of the post. There, dinner was served, and immediately afterwards they continued their journey *via* Centreville to Manassas, crossing over the Stone bridge at Bull Run, and part of the battlefield. A courier was dispatched, in advance, to apprize General Beauregard, and shortly afterwards a member of his staff met the party about a mile from headquarters. Upon approaching the latter, a salute was fired, and Generals Beauregard and Johnston came forward to receive the Prince. He was conducted into the rather primitive frame structure serving as headquarters, and at once commenced

a lively conversation, in French, with both generals. It is stated that the Prince showed great caution and reserve in all he said, and preserved it throughout his stay. General Beauregard soon found occasion to suggest to the Prince an extension of his tour to Richmond; but although he and General Johnston were exceedingly intreating, the Prince declared that it would be impossible for him to go any further south. It being already late in the evening, and the imperial party being considerably fatigued, but a short tour was made through the camps after supper, which is said to have been of a decidedly frugal character. The Prince sought the plain couch, surrendered to him by General Beauregard, at an early hour. Shortly after five o'clock in the morning, the Prince was up, and after partaking of a breakfast as plain as the supper of the previous evening, he sallied out with his suite, under the guidance of Generals Beauregard and Johnston, upon a tour of inspection through the fortifications and encampments, and about the Junction. The crack regiments of the rebels, forming a division of about six thousand men, were drawn up in line and reviewed by the Prince. The troops cheered him lustily when he passed along the lines.

After the review, the field-officers of the several regiments were introduced by General Beauregard to the Prince, who exchanged some complimentary phrases with them.

The Prince then started upon his return, and arrived in Washington again the same evening.

After the battle of Bull Run, the two armies of Johnston and Beauregard were united in one, and styled the "Army of the Potomac." Both the generals still retained their respective commands, Beauregard being permitted to keep the military direction of all the troops, while Johnston—though his senior in rank—took charge of details. This was done to avoid confusion of any kind while before the enemy, or while there was any probability of another battle. The advanced brigades of the army were already bivouacked in full view of Washington, and daily had some conflict with the enemy, but, with that exception, quiet was maintained for some time. The policy of acting on the defensive was that enjoined by the Confederate authorities, and thus the army remained inert at its old quarters, from Manassas to Centreville, until October.

It was at the latter part of August, General Beauregard received an application for permission to the Jews in his army to absent themselves on furlough, to attend the services of their religion at the great celebration of the year.   This application he was compelled to refuse, and the following extract from his adjutant-general's reply, gives his opinion on the subject:

"To grant your application to give furloughs to the soldiers of the Jewish persuasion, from 'the 2d to the 15th day of September, so that they may participate in the holy service' of your ancient religion for this period of the year, is impossible, as you, and all Hebrews serving with this army, will surely understand.

" It would seem, indeed, the Ruler of nations and God of battles is guiding and aiding us, as certainly and visibly in these days as when, of old, He released your people from Egyptian bondage; and the general sincerely believes that all Israelites now in this army will do quite as acceptable service to Jehovah, at this momentous juncture, in standing here, at their posts, ready to battle for their homes, their liberties, and their country, as if their time was passed in the strictest observance and celebration of the sublime rites of Judaism for this period of the year.

" Confidently trusting in this, and assured that on reflection such must be the conclusion of all of your religion,

I have the honor to be, respectfully, your obedient servant,

THOS. JORDAN, A. A. General.

To M. I. MECHELBACKER, Rabbi Preacher.

On the 21st of October, a portion of the Confederate army, under General Evans, attacked and defeated the Federals at Ball's Bluff, near Leesburg. This engagement elicited from General Beauregard an official order, expressed, not only in strong terms of commendation towards General Evans and his troops, but in language significant of condemnation as regarded the defensive policy still adopted by the authorities at Richmond.   With reference to this, and to certain passages in the official report of the battle of Bull Run, which President Davis disapproved, and, for some time, would not allow to be printed, there arose a controversy between the friends of the general and the President, of a somewhat sharp and unpleasant na-

ture.' The subject was even taken up in the Southern Con gress, during a secret session ; the President having sent Beauregard's report in to that body, accompanied by comments of his own on some of its preliminary passages.   The order eventually taken by Congress, however, was to have the document published, after expurgating the portion referred to, and the President's comments thereon.   What was Beauregard's own feeling upon the subject, may be judged by the following letter, which, at the beginning of the controversy, he sent to the Richmond press for publication :

CENTREVILLE, WITHIN HEARING OF THE ⎫
ENEMY'S GUNS, Sunday, Nov. 3, 1861. ⎭

To EDITORS RICHMOND WHIG :

GENTLEMEN—My attention has just been called to an unfortunate controversy now going on relative to the publication of a synopsis of my report of the battle of Manassas.   None can regret more than I do this, from a knowledge that, by authority, the President is the sole judge of when, and what part of the commanding officer's report shall be made public.   I, individually, do not object to delaying its publication as long as the War Department thinks proper and necessary for the success of our cause.   Meanwhile, I entreat my friends not to trouble themselves about refuting the slanders and calumnies aimed against me.   Alcibiades, on a certain occasion, resorted to an extraordinary method to occupy the minds of his traducers—let, then, that synopsis answer the same purpose for me in this instance.   If certain minds cannot understand the difference between patriotism, the highest civic virtue, and officeseeking, the lowest civic occupation, I pity them from the bottom of my heart.   Suffice it to say, that I prefer the respect and esteem of my countrymen to the admiration and envy of the world.   I hope, for the sake of our cause and country, to be able, with the assistance of kind Providence, to answer my calumniators with new victories over our national enemies ; but I have nothing to ask of the country, Government, or any friends, except to afford me all the aid they can in the great struggle we are now engaged upon. *I am not either a candidate, nor do I desire to be a candidate, for any civil office in the gift of the people or executive.*   The aim of my ambition,

after having cast my mite in the defence of our sacred cause,
and assisted, to the best of my ability, in securing our rights
and independence as a nation, is to retire to private life, my
means then permitting, never again to leave my home, unless
to fight anew the battles of my country.

Respectfully, your most obedient servant,

P. T. BEAUREGARD."

Early in the year 1862, it was determined by the Confederate
authorities to speedily evacuate the position held at Manassas ;*
and accordingly, in January, General Beauregard was transferred to the department of the Mississippi.   On the 30th of
January he issued the following address to the troops at Manassas :

HEADQUARTERS FIRST CORPS, ARMY OF THE POTOMAC,}
NEAR CENTREVILLE, January 30, 1862. }

SOLDIERS OF THE FIRST CORPS, ARMY OF THE POTOMAC—My
duty calls me away, and to a temporary separation from you
I hope, however, to be with you again, to share your labors and
your perils, and in defence of our homes and rights, to lead
you to new battles, to be crowned with signal victories.

You are now undergoing the severest trial of a soldier's
life ; the one by which his discipline and capacity for endurance are thoroughly tested.   My faith in your patriotism, your
devotion and determination, and in your high soldierly qualities, is so great, that I shall rest assured you will pass through
the ordeal resolutely, triumphantly.   Still, I cannot quit you
without deep emotion, without even deep anxiety, in the moment of our country's trials and dangers.   Above all, I am
anxious that my brave countrymen, here in arms, fronting the
haughty array and muster of Northern mercenaries, should
thoroughly appreciate the exigency, and hence comprehend
that this is no time for the army of the Potomac—the men of
Manassas—*to stack their arms, and quit, even for a brief period,
the standards they have made glorious by their manhood.*   All
must understand this, and feel the magnitude of the conflict
impending, the universal personal sacrifices this war has en-
tailed, and our duty to meet them as promptly and unblench-
ingly as you have met the enemy in line of battle.

---

* It was not evacuated, however, until March.

To the army of the Shenandoah, I desire to return my thanks for their endurance in the memorable march to my assistance, last July, their timely, decisive arrival, and for their conspicuous steadiness and gallantry on the field of battle.

Those of their comrades, of both corps, and of all arms of the army of the Potomac, not so fortunate as yet to have been with us in conflict with our enemy, I leave with all confidence that on occasion they will show themselves fit comrades for the men of Manassas, Bull Run, and Ball's Bluff.

P. G. T. BEAUREGARD,
General commanding.

At midnight of Friday, the 30th, he left by a special train to Lynchburg, and thence proceeded rapidly to the West, taking with him fifteen thousand men. On the 3d of February he was at Nashville, Tennessee, consulting with Generals Pillow and Cheatham, and immediately afterwards began to strengthen the defences of the city. On the 13th of February, after visiting Bowling Green, and consulting with General A. S. Johnson, Beauregard went to Columbus and inspected the fortifications. It was, however, deemed unadvisable to defend it: "the works, therefore, were blown up, and all the cannon and stores transferred to Island No. 10, which it was thought might be converted into a little Gibraltar, and successfully beat back the enemy's flotillas on the Mississippi."

At this time, so high was the opinion entertained of Beauregard's military skill, that when it was known at New Orleans he wanted reinforcements, one of the crescent brigades promptly volunteered for ninety days' service. The offer, sent by telegraph, was immediately answered by Beauregard as follows:

"JACKSON, February 28th.

"To GOVERNOR THOMAS O. MOORE:—I will accept all good equipped troops, under Act of 21st of August, that will offer, and for ninety days. Let the people of Louisiana understard that here is the proper place to defend Louisiana."

On the 5th of March he publicly assumed command of the Confederate forces in the Valley of the Mississippi, as second to General A. S. Johnson, with his headquarters at Jackson. He then issued the following address to his soldiers:

" SOLDIERS :—I assume, this day, the command of the army of the Mississippi, for the defence of our homesteads and liber ties, and to resist the subjugation, spoliation, and dishonor o our people. Our mothers and wives, our sisters and children expect us to do our duty, even to the sacrifice of our lives.

" Our losses, since the commencement of the present war, in killed, wounded, and prisoners, are now about the same as those of the enemy.

" He must be made to atone for those reverses we have lately experienced. Those reverses, far from disheartening, must nerve us to new deeds of valor and patriotism, and should inspire us with an unconquerable determination to drive back our invaders.

" Should any one in this army be unequal to the task before us, let him transfer his arms and equipments at once to braver, firmer hands, and return to his home.

" Our cause is as just and sacred as ever animated men to take up arms ; and if we are true to it, and to ourselves, with the continued protection of the Almighty, we must, and shall triumph."

A few days afterwards he issued a general order for the guidance of his troops in battle, wherein the following passage relating to sharpshooting occurs :

" Officers in command must be cool and collected ; hold their men in hand in action, and caution them against useless, aimless firing. The men must be instructed and required each one to single out his mark. It was the deliberate sharp-shooting of our forefathers in the revolution of 1776, and New Orleans in 1815, which made them so formidable against the odds with which they were engaged."

About the same time, Beauregard sent an appeal to the planters of the Mississippi valley for bells, to be cast into cannon. He said: " More than once a people fighting with an enemy, . . . for homes and a land not more worthy of resolute and unconquerable men than yours, ... have not hesitated to melt and mould into cannon the precious bells surmounting their houses of God, which had called generations to prayer. We want cannon as greatly as any people who ever, as history tells you, melted their church bells to supply them ; and I, your general, intrusted with the command of the army em-

bodied of your sons, your kinsmen, and your neighbors, do now call upon you to send your plantation bells to the nearest railroad depot, subject to my order, to be melted into cannon for the defence of your plantations.

"Who will not cheerfully and promptly send me his bells under such circumstances? Be of good cheer; but time is precious."

In response to this, we find that many of the plantation bells used for indicating the time and calling the negroes together—each bell weighing from 100 to 500 pounds, and composed of the best metal,—besides other bells, were freely offered.*

Meanwhile, the necessity for superintending the works on Island No. 10, compelled Beauregard to be personally there, and, for some time, he successfully defended the place against the Federal attacks, in their gunboats, under Flag-officer Foote. "On the 1st of April, General Beauregard telegraphed to the War Department at Richmond, that the bombardment had continued for fifteen days, in which time the enemy had thrown 3,000 shells, and expended about 100,000 pounds of powder, without injuring the batteries, and only killing one man." But the movements of the Federal troops on the Tennessee river were now so rapid and serious in their nature, that it was deemed advisable for General Beauregard to proceed thither without delay. Accordingly, on the 3d of April, he gave over the command of Island No. 10 to General Mackall, and immediately started for Corinth. Four days later, Island No. 10 was captured by the combined land and naval forces of the North, under General Pope and Commodore Foote.

---

* On July 30th, 1862, there was a curious auction sale of 418 of these bells, captured at New Orleans. One of them had painted on it, "G. T. Beauregard; from the Baptist Church of Durhamville, Tenn."

CHAPTER II.

On arriving at Corinth, Beauregard at once concentrated all his forces in the immediate neighborhood, with a view of cutting off the enemy's communication with the South and East. The Federal army, under General Grant, was then at Pittsburg landing, on the field of Shiloh, and along both sides of the river Tennessee, toward Savannah, Tennessee. Grant, it was supposed by Beauregard, had not been reinforced by General Buell, his second in command, and, therefore, it was deemed advisable by the Confederates to attack him without delay. General A. S. Johnson had promptly moved forward to unite his forces with those of Beauregard, and General Polk had also arrived with his command from Columbus. General Bragg's army was likewise there; and, in order to avoid all confusion, General Beauregard was proclaimed, in orders issued by General Johnson, to be in command of the whole force. Never had the South seen, on a single battlefield, a more magnificent army assembled, " in numbers, in discipline, in the galaxy of the distinguished names of its commanders, and in every article of merit and display;" and, on Thursday the 3d of April, this splendid array of soldiers began the march to the battlefield. But, on that day, not much progress was made, owing to bad roads; and, therefore, it was not until Saturday afternoon that the Confederate forces reached

the immediate vicinity of the enemy. What followed is best described in General Beauregard's own words, as published in the following official report :

HEADQUARTERS ARMY OF THE MISSISSIPPI, }
CORINTH, MISS., April 11th, 1862. }

"GENERAL—On the 2d ult., having ascertained conclusively, from the movements of the enemy on the Tennessee river, and from reliable sources of information, that his aim would be to cut off my communications in West Tennessee with the eastern and southern States, by operating from the Tennessee river, between Crump's landing and Eastport, as a base, I determined to foil his designs by concentrating all my available forces at and around Corinth.

At the same time, General Johnson being at Murfreesboro, on the march to form a junction of his forces with mine, was called on to send at least a brigade by railroad, so that we might fall on and crush the enemy, should he attempt an advance from under his gunboats. The call on General Johnson was promptly complied with. His entire force was also hastened in this direction, and by the first of April our united forces were concentrated along the Mobile and Ohio railroad, from Bethel to Corinth, and on the Memphis and Charleston railroad, from Corinth to Iuka.

It was then determined to assume the offensive and strike a sudden blow at the enemy in position, under General Grant, on the west bank of the Tennessee, at Pittsburg and in the direction of Savannah, before he was reinforced by the army under General Buell, then known to be advancing for that purpose by rapid marches from Nashville *via* Columbia. About the same time General Johnson was advised that such an operation conformed to the expectations of the President.

By a rapid and vigorous attack on General Grant, it was expected he would be beaten back into his transports and the river, or captured, in time to enable us to profit by the victory, and remove to the rear all the stores and munitions that would fall into our hands, in such an event, before the arrival of Buell's army on the scene. It was never contemplated, however, to retain the position thus gained, and abandon Corinth, the strategic point of the campaign. . . . .

On the following morning the detailed orders of movement were issued, and the movement, after some delay, commenced, the troops being in admirable spirits. It was expected we should be able to reach the enemy's lines in time to attack them early on the 5th inst. The men, however, for the most part, were unused to marching, the roads narrow, and traversing a densely wooded country, became almost impassable after a severe rain-storm on the night of the 4th, which drenched the troops in bivouac; hence our forces did not reach the intersection of the roads from Pittsburg and Hamburg, in the immediate vicinity of the enemy, until late Saturday afternoon. . . . . Thirty minutes after five o'clock, A. M., on the 6th, our lines and columns were in motion, all animated evidently by a promising spirit. The front line was engaged at once, but advanced steadily, followed in due order with equal resolution and steadiness by the other lines, which were brought successively into action with rare skill, judgment, and gallantry, by the several corps commanders, as the enemy made a stand, with his masses rallied for a struggle for his encampments. Like an Alpine avalanche our troops moved forward, despite the determined resistance of the enemy, until six o'clock P. M., when we were in possession of all encampments between Owl and Lick creeks, but one. Nearly all of his field artillery, about thirty flags, colors, and standards, over three thousand prisoners, including a division commander (General Prentiss) and several brigade commanders, thousands of small-arms, an immense supply of subsistence, forage, and munitions of war, and a large amount of means of transportation—all the substantial fruits of a complete victory—such, indeed, as rarely have followed the most successful battles; for never was an army so well provided as that of our enemy.

Our loss was heavy. Our commander-in-chief, General A. S. Johnson, fell mortally wounded, and died on the field at half-past two in the afternoon, after having shown the highest qualities of the commander, and a personal intrepidity that inspired all around him, and gave resistless impulsion to his columns at critical moments.

The chief command then devolved upon me, though at the time I was greatly prostrated, and suffering from the prolonged sickness with which I had been afflicted since early in Febru-

ary. The responsibility was one which, in my physical condition, I would have gladly avoided, though cast upon me when
our forces were successfully pushing the enemy back upon the
Tennessee river, and though supported on the immediate field
by such corps commanders as Major-generals Polk, Bragg, and
Hardee, and Brigadier-general Breckinridge, commanding the
reserve.

It was after six o'clock in the evening, as before said, when
the enemy's last position was carried, and his forces finally
broke and sought refuge behind a commanding eminence,
covering the Pittsburg landing, not more than half a mile distant, and under the guns of the gunboats, which opened on our
eager columns a fierce and annoying fire with shot and shell
of the heaviest description.   Darkness was close at hand.
Officers and men were exhausted by a combat of over twelve
hours without food, and jaded by the march of the preceding
day, through mud and water; it was, therefore, impossible to
collect the rich and opportune spoils of war scattered broadcast
on the field left in our possession, and impracticable to make
any effective dispositions for their removal to the rear.

I accordingly established my headquarters at the church of
Shiloh, in the enemy's encampment, with Major-general Bragg,
and directed our troops to sleep on their arms, in such positions
in advance and rear as corps commanders should determine. . .
. . During the night the rain fell in torrents, adding to the dis-
comfort and harassed condition of the men; the enemy, moreover, had broken their rest by a discharge, at measured intervals, of heavy shells thrown from the gunboats; therefore, on
the following morning the troops under my command were
not in condition to cope with an equal force of fresh troops,
armed and equipped like our adversary, in the immediate possession of his depots, and sheltered by such an auxiliary as the
enemy's gunboats.

About six o'clock on the morning of the 7th of April, however, a hot fire of musketry and artillery, opened from the
enemy's quarter on our advanced line, assured me of the junction of his forces, and soon the battle raged with a fury which
satisfied me I was attacked by a largely superior force. . . .
Again and again our troops were brought to the charge, in
variably to win the position at issue, invariably to drive back

their foe.   But hour by hour, thus opposed to an enemy constantly reinforced, our ranks were perceptibly thinned under the unceasing, withering fire of the enemy; and by twelve meridian, eighteen hours of hard fighting had sensibly exhausted a large number, my last reserves had necessarily been disposed of, and the enemy was evidently receiving fresh reinforcements after each repulse.   Accordingly, about 1 P. M., I determined to withdraw from so unequal a conflict, securing such of the results of the victory of the day before as was then practicable."

General Beauregard now retired to Corinth, "in pursuance of his original design to make that the strategic point of his campaign," and the Federals, flushed with victory, and reinforced by troops from Missouri, and the army of Pope, marched forward under Major-general Halleck, who had now arrived and assumed entire command.   On the first day of May it had reached halfway to Corinth; but, meanwhile, the armies of Van Dorn and Price had come from Arkansas and Missouri, and united with that under Beauregard.   The forces under General Lovell, that had been at New Orleans—captured by the Federals on the 28th of April—had also joined the troops at Corinth; and thus, again, was there another splendid army ready to do battle with the enemy.

On the day after the battle of Shiloh, the following correspondence took place between the two opposing commanders :

LETTER OF GENERAL BEAUREGARD.

HEADQUARTERS ARMY OF THE MISSISSIPPI, }
MONTEREY, April 8, 1862. }

SIR—At the close of the conflict of yesterday, my forces being exhausted by the extraordinary length of time during which they were engaged with yours on that and the preceding day, and it being apparent that you had received, and were still receiving reinforcements, I felt it my duty to withdraw my troops from the immediate scene of conflict.

Under these circumstances, in accordance with usages of war, I shall transmit this, under a flag of truce, to ask permission to send a mounted party to the battlefield of Shiloh, for the purpose of giving decent interment to my dead.

Certain gentlemen wishing to avail themselves of this oppor

tunity to remove the remains of their sons and friends, I mus request for them the privilege of accompanying the burial party; and in this connection I deem it proper to say, I am asking only what I have extended to your own countrymen under similar circumstances.

Respectfully, General, your obedient servant,
P, G. T. BEAUREGARD,
General Commanding.

To Major-general U. S. GRANT, U. S. A.,
Commanding U. S. forces near Pittsburg, Tenn.

GENERAL GRANT'S REPLY.

HEADQUARTERS ARMY IN THE FIELD, }
PITTSBURG, April 9, 1862. }

GENERAL P. G. T. BEAUREGARD, Commanding
Confederate Army of the Mississippi, Monterey, Tenn.

Your dispatch of yesterday is just received. Owing to the warmth of the weather, I deemed it advisable to have all the dead of both parties buried immediately. Heavy details were made for this purpose, and it is now accomplished.

There cannot, therefore, be any necessity of admitting within our lines the parties you desired to send on the grounds asked

I shall always be glad to extend any courtesy consistent with duty, and especially so when dictated by humanity.

I am, General, respectfully, your obedient servant,

U. S. GRANT,
Major-general Commanding.

Shortly after, when the reinforcements had arrived, General Beauregard visited their encampment and inspected them, and was received with the warmest greeting and loud hurrahs.

On the 8th of May, Beauregard issued the following address to his army :

HEADQUARTERS OF THE FORCES AT CORINTH, MISS., }
May 8, 1862. }

SOLDIERS OF SHILOH AND ELKHORN—We are about to meet once more, in the shock of battle, the invaders of our soil, the despoilers of our homes, the disturbers of our family ties, face to face, hand to hand. We are to decide whether we are to be freemen, or vile slaves of those who are only free in name, and who but yesterday were vanquished, although in largely

superior numbers, in their own encampments, on the ever memorable field of Shiloh.   Let the impending battle decide our
fate, and add a more illustrious page to the history of our revolution—one to which our children will point with noble
pride, saying, "Our fathers were at the battle of Corinth."   I
congratulate you on your timely junction.   With our mingled
banners, for the first time during this war, we shall meet our
foe in strength that should give us victory.   Soldiers, can the
result be doubtful?   Shall we not drive back in Tennessee the
presumptuous mercenaries collected for our subjugation?   One
more manly effort, and trusting in God and the justness of our
cause, we shall recover more than we lately lost.   Let the
sound of our victorious guns be re-echoed by those of the army
of Virginia on the historic battlefield of Yorktown.

P. G. T. BEAUREGARD,
General Commanding.

At this time, the Federals had advanced to within a few
miles of Corinth, and on the 9th, the Confederates, under Van
Dorn and Price, drove back a part of their advance near Farmington, and compelled General Pope, in command of that portion of the army, to retire.   On the 21st, Halleck's batteries
were within three miles of Corinth, and daily skirmishing now
took place, with occasional firing from the artillery.   Gradually
the Federal troops advanced still nearer, employing all the
cautious skill and strategy that General Halleck was so eminently master of.   Corinth was strongly fortified, having
batteries or redoubts at every road or assailable point.   Between the fortifications and a marshy stream covering the
whole front, the dense timber had been cut down to form a
very strong abattis, through which no cavalry or artillery
could have passed, nor even infantry, except as skirmishers.
Thus, it was considered by the Federal commanders that a
hotly contested siege must take place, and when, day after
day, it was found that the slightest movement of the Federals
in advance was instantly and vigorously met, no doubt remained that Corinth would become the field of another heavy
battle.   Great, therefore, was the surprise of the beseigers
when, on the morning of Friday, May 30th, it was discovered
that Beauregard had withdrawn his whole army and evacuated

the place. For several days previous, the Confederate troops had been slowly and cautiously sent further South, and, finally, on the night of Thursday, the 29th and 30th, the whole were safely withdrawn, taking with them all they could, and destroying the remainder.

As much comment, and some controversy between officers of rank on opposite sides arose from this evacuation of Corinth by Beauregard, it is but just that some few particulars should be given.

An independent writer, himself in the army at the time, says:

"It soon became obvious that if Halleck would not advance from his works, we should either be compelled to retreat at no distant day, or be massacred at discretion by the enemy's guns, which were daily advanced nearer and nearer, with apparent impunity. The Federals were sorely afraid we would retreat, and in that case their mammoth trenches and laboriously constructed roads would but ill repay them for their patience and long suffering. This affliction, however, we could not spare them. Immense roads had been dug and levelled through miles of timber, unheard of supplies of shot, shell, and mammoth mortar batteries had been brought to the front with infinite labor, and much sacrifice of life and money, when, early one morning, our whole army quietly decamped towards Tullahoma, and ere the mists had risen, were beyond sight or hearing! . . . The result does Beauregard infinite credit. Halleck had stored his camp with immense supplies; he had destroyed hundreds of horses, wagons, mules, and carts in the work of transportation; had prepared for a bombardment of an indefinite period; built magazines and barracks, repaired railroads, and erected bridges, *thus occupying the whole spring in preparation;* and now, in one moment, all these plans were thwarted, and the hot season too far advanced for his troops to move a mile further into the interior!"

It must be remembered that at this especial time, Richmond, the Southern capital, was being closely besieged by McClellan; and, on the very day after Beauregard evacuated Corinth, the first of the series of battles near and around Richmond, was fought on the Chickahominy. Thus, there may have been other, and more secret reasons than those gen-

erally known, for resigning important positions in the West while the seat of government in the East was in danger.   Cer tain it is, that the authorities at Washington also deemed i advisable to call both General Halleck and General Pope soon afterwards, to their side—the first as commander-in-chief and the latter as general of the army of Virginia; and, when we know the state of doubt and anxiety in Richmond, at the time, it is not too much to suppose that Beauregard might have been thought of in like manner by his friends.   How ever, there was quite enough in the circumstances of the case itself, as some urge, for Beauregard to adopt the course he did. That ideas, similar to those we have mentioned were enter tained in the North, may be gathered from referring to some of the New York papers about June 1st, 1862.

At this time the health of Beauregard was such, that his physicians " urgently recommended rest and recreation ;" and accordingly, he addressed a letter to the authorities at Rich mond on the subject.

On the 15th of June he turned over his command to Gen eral Bragg, and left for Montgomery, where he arrived on the 17th, accompanied only by his personal staff.   Public report then stated that he had gone on to Richmond in consequence of the feeling still existing on the part of some of the author ities against him, and to explain the reason of his evacuating Corinth.   It was even said, that General Price had been sum moned to the War Office before Beauregard had left his army, and that strong animadversions upon his conduct had been made.   But, whether so or not, it is certain that great misrep resentations concerning him were abroad on all sides.   On the part of the North, there was either distinct and barefaced falsehood or gross error in some of the official reports, unless the testimony of all writers and personal witnesses on the side of the South must be considered as blindly mistaken, emanating from carelessly following each other's statements.   The whole affair, however, resolved itself into something like a personal matter between Generals Halleck and Beauregard, in which, it would seem, the veracity of each was on trial.   The question arose as to whether Halleck's official dispatch to Washington, dated June 4th, 1862, was correct.   This, General Beauregard denied, in a letter dated the 17th of June, and published in the

Mobile Advertiser. That statement elicited from General Granger, of the Northern army, a very strong reply, published in the New York papers, July 11th, and also, a similar response from an anonymous writer in the *Cincinnati Gazette.* Both of these asserted Beauregard to be wrong in his statements; but, as the correspondence is too long, we leave the subject without further comment.

For some time after General Beauregard retired from Corinth, he resided with his family at Mobile, and at Bladon Springs, Alabama, at which latter place he rapidly regained his health. His mind, however, was still active in the work of military operations, and two important letters, to be found in the *New York Tribune* of October, 1862, show the bent of his ideas.

In the month of August, 1862, General Beauregard was appointed to the command of the department of South Carolina and Georgia, relieving General Pemberton; and on the 24th of September he issued the following announcement:

HEADQUARTERS DEPARTMENT OF S. CAROLINA AND GEORGIA, }
CHARLESTON, September 24, 1864. }

I assume command of the department pursuant to paragraph XV., Special Orders, No. 202, Adjutant and Inspector General's Office, Richmond, August 29th, 1862.

All existing orders will remain in force until otherwise directed from these headquarters.

In entering upon my duties, which may involve, at an early day, the defence of two of the most important cities in the Confederate States, against the most formidable efforts of our powerful enemy, I shall rely on the ardent patriotism, the intelligent and unconquerable spirit, of the officers and men under my command, to sustain me successfully. But to maintain our posts with credit to our country and to our own honor, and avoid irremediable disaster, it is essential that all shall yield implicit obedience to any orders emanating from superior authority.

Brigadier-general Thomas Jordan is announced as Adjutant and Inspector-general and Chief of Staff of the department.

G. T. BEAUREGARD, General commanding.

Official—THOMAS JORDAN, Chief of Staff, and A. A. G."

A few days afterwards, he proceeded to Savannah, and at once commenced an inspection of the batteries and fortifications on the river. But, whatever might have been *his* opinions, it seems that the citizens had no hopes of the city being able to hold itself against any attack of the Federals, when once fairly commenced. This, as we now know, has been verified, by its capture, in December, 1864, by the Federal forces, under General Sherman.

In October, the Federals, at first under the command of General O. M. Mitchell, but upon his death, under General Brannan, temporarily commanding, made an attempt to destroy the railroad and bridges on the Charleston and Savannah line. This was planned by General Mitchell some time previous, but his illness prevented its execution, until the 22d of October, when they were met by a part of Beauregard's forces, and repulsed. The following is Beauregard's official report of the affair :

"CHARLESTON, S. C., October 23.

"The Abolitionists attacked in force Pocotaligo and Coosahatchi yesterday. They were gallantly repulsed to their gunboats, at Mackay's point and Bee's Creek landing, by Colonel W. S. Walker, commanding the district, and Colonel G. P Harrison, commanding the troops sent from here. The enemy had come in thirteen transports and gun-boats. The Charleston and Savannah Railroad is uninjured. The Abolitionists left their dead and wounded on the field ; and our cavalry are in hot pursuit."

In the middle of December, General Beauregard recommended all non-combatants in Charleston to leave the city, in view of the expected attack, threatened by the Federals. Indeed every thing about this time had the appearance of something serious again about to take place at Charleston ; and though it would seem that few availed themselves of the hint to go, yet military preparations continued with an earnestness that warned the citizens of what might be expected if they remained.

On the 28th of December, a general order was issued by Beauregard, for all the troops to be mustered for payment on the last day of the month, in accordance with army regulations. This closed his military labors that year ; but the exi-

gencies of the service, however, appear to have been such that he was unable to leave Charleston to visit his wife, who was seriously ill at New Orleans. General Butler, previous to leaving his command there, had, it is stated, "sent a polite note to General Beauregard, inviting him to visit his dying wife, assuring him of every courtesy and protection possible." If this be really so, it is most gratifying to record it, for such is rather the reverse of what has been the public reputation of the Federal general, in all matters relating to the opposite sex, during his administration at New Orleans.

On the 30th of January, 1863, there occurred, at Charleston, one of those daring naval exploits which have made the name of sailors famous throughout the war, though opportunity for many great deeds has rarely been met. Of this spirited affair, our space does not admit of any detailed account, but the following official notices explain it:

HEADQUARTERS, LAND AND NAVAL FORCES, }
CHARLESTON, S. C., January 31, 1863. }

At about five o'clock this morning, the Confederate States naval force, on this station, attacked the United States blockading fleet off the harbor of the city of Charleston, and sunk, dispersed, or drove off and out of sight, for the time, the entire hostile fleet.

Therefore, we, the undersigned commanders, respectively of the Confederate States naval and land forces in this quarter, do hereby *formally declare the blockade by the United States of the said city of Charleston, South Carolina, to be raised by a superior force of the Confederate States from and after this 31st day of January, A. D.*, 1863.

G. T. BEAUREGARD,
General Commanding.

D. N. INGRAHAM,
Flag officer commanding naval forces in South Carolina.

Official,—THOMAS JORDAN, Chief of Staff.

In the afternoon, General Beauregard placed a steamer at the disposal of the foreign consuls to see for themselves that no blockade existed.

The French and Spanish consuls, accompanied by General Ripley, accepted the invitation. The British Consul, with th

commander of the British war steamer Petrel, had previously gone five miles beyond the usual anchorage of the blockaders, and could see nothing of them with glasses.

Later in the evening, however, four blockaders reappeared, and next day several more; but the consuls, meeting again in the evening, were " unanimously of the opinion that the blockade had been legally raised," and drew up a report in accordance with that view. This was promptly met by the Federal commanders issuing a counter statement, in official form, denying the result of the engagement as given by the Confederate officers, and positively asserting that the blockade had *not* been broken. This statement was signed by six naval commanders, and sent to Washington by Admiral Dupont, and, of course, calmed the uneasiness that had been somewhat felt on hearing of Beauregard's proclamation. With regard to the correctness of either side—supported as each was by equal testimony—we have nothing to do at present.

A few days afterwards, intimations were received at Charleston, that a combined land and naval attack—long in preparation—would be made by the Federals on the city, and, accordingly, General Beauregard issued the following proclamation:

HEADQUARTERS, DEPARTMENT OF SOUTH CAROLINA,
GEORGIA, AND FLORIDA, February 18, 1863.

It has become my solemn duty to inform the authorities and citizens of Charleston and Savannah, that the movements of the enemy's fleet indicate an early land and naval attack on one or both cities, and to urge that persons unable to take an active part in the struggle shall retire.

It is hoped, however, that the temporary separation of some of you from your homes will be made without alarm or undue haste, thus showing that the only feeling which animates you in this hour of supreme trial is the right of being able to participate in the defence of your homes, your altars, and the graves of your kindred.

Carolinians and Georgians! the hour is at hand to prove your country's cause. Let all able-bodied men, from the seaboard to the mountains, rush to arms. Be not too exacting in the choice of weapons. Pikes and scythes will do for exterminating your enemies, spades and shovels for protecting your

firesides. To arms, fellow-citizens! Come to share with us our danger, our brilliant success, our glorious death.

G. T. BEAUREGARD, General Commanding.

Official,—J. M. OTEY, A. A. G.

At the same time, he ordered that "all furloughs to officers, non-commissioned officers, and privates belonging to this department, not based on surgeon's certificates, are revoked, and both officers and soldiers will repair without delay to their respective stations, to be ready to meet the enemy. Patriots and brave soldiers will not linger by the wayside."

The expected attack was, however, delayed, as the Charlestonians alleged, until the highest spring tides, in April, would enable the enemy's ships to float off in the case of any of them going aground.

In the month of March, various minor engagements took place, in the department under Beauregard's command, but we must pass them over to come to the more important matters connected with the attack upon Charleston. Great preparations had been completed, under Beauregard's supervision, and the immediate direction of General Ripley, who had made the study of heavy ordnance a specialty for years, and whose excellence in that particular branch of military knowledge was generally admitted. It was well known that the enemy was making the most formidable preparations, and it was considered, at Charleston, that when the struggle came, it would certainly be of a fearful character. It was to be a trial between new forces of tremendous powers, never before brought into use. The long mooted question of the fighting value of ships against batteries was to be brought to a test more conclusive than any to which human warfare had previously subjected it. In other words, monitor ironclads, which were claimed to be the most impenetrable vessels ever constructed, would necessarily come within point-blank range of the most numerous and powerful batteries that had ever been used in a single engagement. The more important of these batteries were manned by the South Carolina regulars, who were considered the most expert and practical heavy artillerists in the Confederate army. The forts were well officered, and it was thought scarcely possible that any floating thing could breast,

unharmed, the concentrated storm of heavy metal from the guns of Sumter, Moultrie, and Battery Bee, the three principal works commanding the throat of the harbor.

At length, to use the words of the Charlestonians themselves, the long delayed hour arrived. The attack on the city, threatened for more than a year, was imminent. Charleston was the heart, as she was the head and front of all the offence against the North. Through her closely blockaded port a hundred vessels had borne to the hands of the young Confederacy the means and material of war. To effect the absolute destruction, therefore, of that port was the natural wish of its enemies. But, as the people said, with the loftiest hope, the sternest courage, and the unconquerable resolve never to submit or yield, they were determined to go forth to the struggle conscious of, and equal to the great duties before them.

That it may be understood what was the force employed by the North in the attack upon Charleston, we append the following brief statement of the actual number of officers, men, and guns engaged in the attack on Charleston. The ironclads were all Ericsson Monitors, save the New Ironsides and Keokuk:

	Tuns.	Guns.	Officers and Men.
Ironsides............................	3,486	18	350
Montauk............................	884	2	100
Passaic.............................	884	2	100
Catskill............................	884	2	100
Weehawken.........................	884	2	100
Patapsco...........................	884	2	100
Sangamon..........................	884	2	100
Nahant.............................	884	2	100
Nantucket..........................	884	2	100
Keokuk.............................	740	2	100
Total......................	11,298	36	1,250

The officers of these vessels were natives of the following States: Captain Thomas Turner, Virginia; Captain John S. Worden, New York; Captain Percival Drayton, South Carolina; Captain John Rogers, Maryland; Captain John Downs, Massachusetts; Captain G. W. Rodgers, New York; Captain Daniel Ammen, Ohio; Captain D. M. F. Fairfax, Virginia; Captain A. D. Rhind, New York.

These vessels, and their brave commanders, were all ready

for the attack on Sunday, April the 5th, and the grand en
gagement took place on the next Tuesday, April 7th. The
following account of it deserves insertion here, as giving the
history from the Southern point of view, and as not materially
contradicted by the official accounts in the North :

"At two o'clock on Tuesday afternoon, a dispatch from Fort
Sumter announced that these ten vessels had crossed the bar,
and were cautiously steaming inward—the foremost one having at that time reached a point about three thousands yards
from the Fort. The next news was brought to us, an hour
later, by the dull detonation of the first gun from Fort Moultrie, which was immediately answered by a heavy report, and
a cloud of white smoke from the turret of one of the monitors.
At ten minutes after three, the enemy having come within
range, Fort Sumter opened her batteries, and, almost simul-
taneously, the white smoke could be seen puffing from the low
sandhills of Morris and Sullivan's islands, indicating that the
Beauregard battery on the left, and Battery Wagner, on the
extreme right, had become engaged. Five of the ironclads,
forming in line of battle in front of Fort Sumter, maintained a
very rapid return fire, occasionally hurling their fifteen-inch
shot and shell against Fort Moultrie and minor batteries, but
all directing their chief efforts against the east face of Fort
Sumter. Gradually, but visibly, the distance between the
attacking vessels and the fort was lessened, and as the enemy
drew nearer, the firing became hot and almost continuous.

"About half-past four o'clock, the battle became fierce and
general. The scene at that hour, as viewed from the battery
promenade, was truly grand. Battery Bee had now mingled
the hoarse thunder of its guns in the universal din, and the
whole expanse of the harbor entrance, from Sullivan's Island
to Cummings' Point, became enveloped in the smoke and constant flashes of the conflict. The ironclads kept constantly
shifting their position; but, whichever way they went, their
ports, always turned towards the battlements of Sumter, poured
forth their terrible projectiles against the walls of that famous
stronghold. Ever and anon, as the huge shot went ricochet-
ting towards the mark, the water was dashed up in vast sheets
of spray, towering far above the parapet of the fort, while the
wreaths of smoke constantly ascending from the barbette guns,

showed how actively the artillerymen of the post were discharging their duties. In the foreground our own staunch little ironclads—the Palmetto State and Chicora—could be seen steaming energetically up and down their chosen fighting position, evidently impatient to participate in the fray."

Next morning the Keokuk sunk, having been kept afloat during the night by means of her pumps; and during the day, Admiral Dupont, feeling convinced of the "utter impracticability of taking the city of Charleston with the force under his command," determined not to renew the fight. He, therefore, recrossed the bar, and, on the 12th, the whole fleet, except the New Ironsides, returned to Port Royal.

Immediately after the engagement, Beauregard issued the following congratulatory order to his troops:

HEADQUARTERS, DEPARTMENT OF SOUTH CAROLINA, GEORGIA, AND
FLORIDA, CHARLESTON, S. C., April 10, 1863.

The commanding general is gratified to have to announce to the troops the following joint resolutions unanimously adopted by the Legislature of the State of South Carolina:

"Resolved, That the General Assembly reposes unbounded confidence in the ability and skill of the commanding general of this department, and the courage and patriotism of his brave soldiers, with the blessing of God, to defend our beloved city, and to beat back our vindictive foes.

"Resolved, That his Excellency, the Governor, be instructed to communicate this resolution to General Beauregard."

Soldiers! the eyes of your countrymen are now turned upon you on the eve of the second anniversary of the 13th of April, 1861, when the sovereignty of the State of South Carolina was triumphantly vindicated within the harbor which we are now to defend. The happy issue of the action on the 7th instant—the stranded, riddled wreck of the iron-mailed Keokuk, her baffled coadjutors forced to retire beyond the range of our guns, have inspired confidence in the country that our ultimate success will be complete. An inestimably precious charge has been confided to your keeping, with every reliance on your manhood and enduring patriotism.

                    By command of   GENERAL BEAUREGARD.
THOMAS JORDAN, Chief of Staff.
JOHN M. OTEY, A. A. G.

It is a curious coincidence of war, says the *Charleston Cou rier*, that the commanders—Generals Beauregard and Ripley, Colonel Rhett, and Lieutenant-colonel Yates—with nearly all the garrison of Fort Sumter, are the same men who were the chief actors in the bloodless reduction of Fort Sumter in 1861, and who have now so gloriously and successfully repelled a formidable attack upon this famous fortress, while in their keeping.

In the month of April, there was some question in the Confederate Congress about changing the form and arrangement of their flag, and in reference to it, Beauregard, on the 24th of April, wrote to a friend: "Why change our battle-flag, consecrated by the best blood of our country on so many battle-fields? A good design for the national flag would be the present battle-flag as Union Jack, and the rest all white or all blue." This idea was adopted by the Congress, on the 1st of May, and thenceforth the Confederate flag was a white field,—the length double the width, with the union to be a square of two-thirds the width of the flag, having the ground red, thereon a broad saltire of blue, bordered with white, and emblazoned white mullets or five-pointed stars, corresponding in number to the Confederate States.

The month of May passed without any important movements calling for General Beauregard's personal supervision. He went on a tour of inspection along the coast and in Florida, and returned to Charleston on the 11th of June. At that time he was visited by an English military officer of distinction, Lieutenant-colonel Fremantle, then having a three months' run through the Southern States, and, from the published account given by that gentleman, we extract the following:

"General Beauregard was extremely civil to me, and arranged that I should see some of the land fortifications to-morrow. He spoke to me of the inevitable necessity, sooner or later, of a war between the Northern States and Great Britain; and he remarked that, if England would join the South at once, the Southern armies, relieved of the present blockade, and enormous Yankee pressure, would be able to march right into the Northern States, and, by occupying their principal cities, would give the Yankees so much employment, that they would be unable to spare many men for Canada. He acknowl-

edged that in Mississippi General Grant had displayed un-
common vigor, and met with considerable success. . . . . He
considered the question of ironclads *versus* forts as settled.
especially when the fire from the latter is plunging. If the
other monitors had approached as close as the Keokuk, they
would probably have shared her fate. He thought that both
flat-headed rifled 7-inch bolts, and solid 10-inch balls penetrated the ironclads when within 1200 yards. He agreed
with General Ripley that the 15-inch gun is rather a failure;
it is so unwieldy, that it can only be fired very slowly, and
the velocity of the ball is so small that it is very difficult to
strike a moving object. He said that Fort Sumter was to be
covered, by degrees, with the long green moss which, in this
country, hangs down from the trees; and his opinion was that
when this was pressed, it would deaden the effect of the shot
without being inflammable. He added that, even if the walls
of Fort Sumter were battered down, the barbette battery
would still remain, supported on the piers. . . . A caricature
in a New York Illustrated paper, wherein President Davis and
General Beauregard were depicted shoeless and in rags, contemplating a pair of boots, which the latter suggested had
better be eaten, excited considerable amusement when shown
to him and a party, at an excellent dinner one day. . . . General Beauregard told me he had been educated in the North,
and used to have many friends there, but that now he would
sooner submit to the Emperor of China than return to the
Union. . . . Before parting, he told me that his official orders,
both from the government and from the town council, were,
that he was to allow Charleston to be laid in ashes sooner than
surrender it; the Confederates being unanimous in their determination that, whatever happened, the capital of South
Carolina should never have to submit to the fate of New Orleans. But he did not at all anticipate that such an alternative was imminent. In answer to my thanks for his kindness
and courtesy, he said that the more Europeans that came to
the South, the more the Southerners were pleased, as *seeing*
was the only way to remove many prejudices. He declared
every thing here was open and above board, and I really believe this is the case."

In the month of June renewed preparations were made by

the Federal authorities to take Charleston and a change of naval and military commanders was made in the forces sent to work. Admiral Dahlgren was appointed to command the sea expedition, and General Gilmore the troops on land. These latter, since April, had established themselves on Folly Island, south of, and next to Morris Island, which is a strip of land fringing the ocean, and having a battery at its northern point, bearing directly on Fort Sumter, and the channel leading to the city. This battery was the goal aimed at by the enemy, and though several attempts had been made by the Confederate forces to dislodge him from the footing he had gained, they were unsuccessful.

At Charleston, the force there had been greatly reduced by the Confederate authorities, under the idea that all was safe from further attacks of the enemy, and thus General Beauregard was left with inadequate means to provide against assaults in no less than five different directions. For a number of weeks the Federal troops had been busily engaged on Folly Island, working under cover of the night, and screened by carefully arranged brushwood during the day. In this manner, batteries were thrown up, and guns and mortars put in position.

The attack upon Morris Island was at last made by the enemy on July 10th, and " after an engagement of three hours and a quarter all the strongholds upon that part of the island were captured, and the infantry pushed forward to within six hundred yards of Fort Wagner," while four monitors, under Admiral Dahlgren, engaged that fort, and the battery at Cummings' Point.

The following is General Beauregard's official announcement of it:

CHARLESTON, July 13, 1863.

To GENERAL S. COOPER, Adjutant and Inspector-general:

There is nothing new since yesterday. The enemy is engaged in establishing batteries for long range-guns on the middle of Morris Island, being aided by five monitors. Their wooden gunboats are firing on batteries Wagner and Gregg on the north end of Morris Island.

G. T. BEAUREGARD.

The *Richmond Enquirer* of the 13th gives the following of ficial dispatches from General Beauregard:

CHARLESTON, July 10, 1863.

To GENEAL COOPER, Adjutant and Inspector-general:

At dark on the 10th, the enemy obtained possession of the southern portion of Morris Island. Four monitors engaged Battery Wagner and the battery at Cummings' Point all day without damage or casualties, but the losses in opposing the landing were severe. Three hundred were killed and wounded, including sixteen officers. The enemy's loss is evidently heavy.

G. T. BEAUREGARD.

CHARLESTON, July 10—11:30 P. M.

To GENERAL COOPER,—

The enemy has a threatening force on the lower front of James Island, along the Stono, and an attempt was made to destroy the Savannah Railroad bridge, but was foiled with the loss of one steamboat.

G. T. BEAUREGARD.

The events of the next four weeks may be summed up in a few lines; for, to give any thing like details of what occurred during this remarkable siege of Charleston, would be to fill an entire volume by itself; and, moreover, can not be done consistently with the purpose of this biographical sketch. We can only, therefore, throw in occasionally some striking incidents that will serve to illustrate our subject.

The remainder of the month of July, and the early part of August, were employed by the enemy in erecting siege-works, and mounting heavy siege-guns, preparatory to the bombardment of Fort Sumter, as it was found that Fort Wagner did not interfere with the engineer corps at work. Meanwhile General Beauregard and the Mayor of Charleston issued another urgent appeal to the landed proprietors and others to send in their negroes for work on the fortifications; and the Governor of the State made an even stronger appeal. There was, however, much indifference shown in promptly responding; and though an act of the Legislature had been passed, involving a penalty on refusal, many of the planters preferred paying it to allowing their negroes to be so employed.

On the 17th of August General Gilmore opened his fire from about sixty pieces on Fort Sumter, while the fleet attacked Forts Gregg and Wagner. The latter was completely silenced, and the former nearly so. Throughout the day this furious bombardment continued, and the shock of the rapid discharges trembling through the city, called hundreds of citizens to the battery, wharves, steeples, and various look-outs, where, with an interest never felt before, they gazed on a contest that might decide the fate of Charleston itself. Above Battery Wagner, bursting high in air, striking the sides of the work, or plunging into the beach, and throwing up pillars of earth, were to be seen the quickly succeeding shells and round shot of the enemy's guns. Battery Gregg, at Cummings' Point, and Fort Sumter took part in the thundering chorus. As the shades of evening fell upon the scene, the entire horizon appeared to be lighted up with the fitful flashings of the livid flames that shot out from monster guns on land and sea.

Meanwhile some sharp correspondence had taken place between Generals Beauregard and Gilmore, on the mode of carrying on the war in that department, but it is too long to insert here.

On the 21st of August, General Gilmore addressed to General Beauregard a demand for the evacuation of Morris Island and Fort Sumter, and threatening, if not complied with, " in less than four hours, a fire would be opened on the city of Charleston, from batteries already established within easy and effective reach of the heart of the city. In the following night, and without further notice, fire was opened on the city from the Morris Island batteries. Twelve eight-inch shells fell in the city ; and several flew in the direction of St. Michael's steeple ; but fortunately no one was injured."

To the demand of General Gilmore, General Beauregard replied at length, refusing to surrender.

On the 24th of August, General Gilmore announced in dispatches to Washington, that " Fort Sumter was a shapeless and harmless mass of ruins." This appeared to be partly the case ; but the following brief accounts of events, a few days afterwards, show that it was still in possession of the Confederates, though Morris Island, Fort Wagner, and Battery Gregg had to be abandoned.

CHARLESTON, Sept. 7, 1863.

The bombardment was kept up without intermission all day yesterday, and far into the night. About one hundred and fifty of our men were killed and wounded at Batteries Wagner and Gregg.

The attempt to assault Battery Gregg was repulsed before the enemy had completed their landing. Great havoc is supposed to have been made in the enemy's boats by our grape and canister.

At dark on Monday, the enemy having advanced their sappers up to the very moat of Wagner, and it being impossible to hold the island longer, General Beauregard ordered its evacuation, which was executed between 8 P. M., and 1 A. M., with success. We spiked the guns of Wagner and Gregg, and withdrew noiselessly in forty barges. Only one barge, containing twelve men, was captured.

The enemy now holds Cummings' Point, in full view of the city.

All quiet this morning.

CHARLESTON, Sept. 7, Noon.

A dispatch from Major Stephen Elliot, commanding at Fort Sumter, announces that a flag of truce, demanding the immediate surrender of that fort, has just been received from Admiral Dahlgren by Lieutenant Brown, of the steamer Palmetto State.

General Beauregard has telegraphed to Major Elliot to reply to Dahlgren that he can have Fort Sumter when he takes it and holds it, and that in the mean time such demands are puerile and unbecoming.

CHARLESTON, Sept. 7, 8 ½ M.

At 6 o'clock P. M. the ironclads and monitors approached Fort Sumter closer than usual and opened a hot fire against it. Our batteries on Sullivan's Island, including those of Fort Moultrie, replied heavily. The firing is still going on.

CHARLESTON, Sept. 9, 1863.

GENERAL COOPER—Last night thirty of the launches of the enemy attacked Fort Sumter. Preparations had been made for the event. At a concerted signal, all the batteries bearing on Sumter, assisted by one gun-boat and a ram, were thrown

open. The enemy was repulsed, leaving in our hands on hundred and thirteen prisoners, including thirteen officers We also took four boats and three colors.

G. T. BEAUREGARD.

CHARLESTON, Sept. 9, 1863.

The enemy is silent to-day. General Beauregard refuses to have any communication with the Yankee flag of truce until an explanation is given of their firing on our truce boats.

We took the original flag of Fort Sumter which Major Anderson was compelled to lower, and which Dahlgren had hoped to replace.

CHARLESTON, Sept. 10, 1863.

There was no firing last night except from our batteries. The enemy is working hard on Morris Island. All is quiet this morning.

After this repulse of the Federals in their last attack upon " the shapeless and harmless mass of ruins" of Fort Sumter, but little more was done during the year by the enemy, except bombarding the forts, and shelling Charleston at intervals during day and night, until such became so customary to the citizens, says a foreign writer visiting the place, that it no longer produced the fear and dismay it formerly did.

During this period, Beauregard paid a just tribute to the Confederate navy, in an official order, as follows :

HEADQUARTERS, DEPARTMENT OF SOUTH CAROLINA,
GEORGIA, AND FLORIDA,
CHARLESTON, S. C., Oct. 28, 1863.

The commanding general feels it his duty to publish to the forces and to the country the names of the stout-hearted officers and men of the Confederate States navy, who, on the night of the 5th inst., assailed and so nearly destroyed the United States ironclad steam frigate, New Ironsides, at her moorings off Morris Island. Lieutenant Wm. T. Glassell, Acting Assistant Engineer J. H. Toombs, Pilot Wm. Cannon, Fireman James Sullivan, were volunteers for the service, which they executed with a skill and coolness commensurate with their daring. Their country cannot forget their brave

endeavor, though unsuccessful, and it will surely inspire officers and men of both arms of the service to emulate them.

They have shown what four resolute men can accomplish. The example must not be barren.

By command of
General BEAUREGARD.

THOMAS JORDAN, Chief of Staff.

The year 1863 now closed with nothing more of importance to record concerning Beauregard's movements. Carefully attentive to the duties of his post, he appears to have been always present at official headquarters, unless away visiting other portions of his department. In February, 1864, he was at Savannah; and, in the early part of March, in Florida, where he issued a proclamation, dated from near Baldwin, having reference to deserters from the Confederate army, and ordering all others who were bound to give military service, and yet evaded it on account of their families needing their personal attention, to do such work, for just pay, in the district, as would be of material help to the cause.

At this time occurred the death of his wife at New Orleans, on the 2d of March, 1864, and in referring to her, the New Orleans papers pay a very high tribute of respect and esteem to her memory.

It appears that General Beauregard was not able to attend the funeral; but the following letter was afterwards sent by him to express his obligations for the general sympathy shown:

CHARLESTON, March 28, 1864.

GENTLEMEN :—Accept for yourselves, and for the other officers and soldiers from Louisiana, who met with you at Mobile, on the 19th instant, my heartfelt thanks for the lofty and touching sentiments expressed in the resolutions you were pleased to pass on the occasion of the sad event which has torn from me a most dear and beloved wife, and from the State to which she belonged, one of its brightest jewels and ornaments. Mrs. Beauregard died a martyr to our cause. Her continued and long separation from the chosen one of her heart, under the trying circumstances she had to pass through, was more than her careworn and enfeebled condition could

endure. Yet she departed not from life without giving utter-ance to her undiminished devotion to that noble cause, and to her unshaken faith in its ultimate triumph. She was a true and fervent patriot. The foul breath of even the most vile among the vilest of our enemies never could taint the pure atmosphere that surrounded her.

How bright, how glorious I would deem the day on which it were given to me, at the head of my brave, and so hard-tried compatriots, to rescue, with her hallowed grave, the noble State that bestowed such honors upon her remains, from the footsteps of the foe who pollutes them by his presence. With sincere esteem, and sincere acknowledgments,

I remain yours, very truly,

G. T. BEAUREGARD.

Major Hy. St. Paul, Captain J. T. Purves,
     Lieutenant Charles Arroyo, Committee, Mobile, Ala.

In the month of April, the Confederate authorities deemed it advisable to strengthen their forces in North Carolina and around Richmond, and accordingly the valuable services of General Beauregard were called into requisition from Charles-ton. On the 21st he passed through Wilmington with a large body of troops, and assumed command of the district on the south and east of Richmond. General Butler, at the same time, prepared to advance upon Richmond by the James river, and on the 5th of May landed a large body of troops at City Point, and Bermuda Hundred. On the 7th, he struck for the Petersburg and Richmond railroad, and succeeded in destroy-ing a bridge seven miles from the former place, thus giving some hopes to the Federals that they had effectually got into the rear of the Confederate capital. But, on the 16th of May, General Beauregard, from Petersburgh, suddenly fell upon his forces, in a fog, and drove him back to his original position on the James river. In speaking of this fight the *Rich-mond Examiner* says, " *It was, during the time it lasted, one of the most terrific combats that has been known.* Confederate valor never had a more splendid illustration." This was fol-lowed up, in a few days, by renewed attacks on the enemy's lines, especially when it became known to Beauregard that General " Baldy " Smith's corps, and a part of Gilmore's, had

left Butler to reinforce Grant, then advancing towards the Chickahominy.

On the 2d of June, at 3 A. M., Beauregard made a heavy attack upon the Federals' advanced line of rifle-pits, near Warebottom Church, and succeeded in capturing the position, with about one hundred prisoners. A few days afterwards, however, the Northern army, under Grant, Meade, and Butler, were all across the James river, and Petersburg besieged. Beauregard had already taken measures for its sure defence; but on some of the first shells from the enemy entering the town, and striking a private dwelling, he sent a flag of truce to know why shelling was commenced without giving due notice to the non-combatants. General Grant replied, as is reported, that he did not know he was so near the city, and would cease shelling until further notice. If this be correctly stated, it displays an instance of great humanity on the part of General Grant, which we feel pleasure in recording.

Towards the end of June, the Confederate army was posted in every part of the outer and inner defences of Petersburg, and thence to Richmond; Generals Hill and Longstreet camped in front of the enemy's advanced lines,—General Lee as commander-in-chief, acting on the left—and General Beauregard holding the town. And here we can well leave him for the incidents of the next few weeks, as our space forbids dwelling upon them in detail; and, moreover, they are related, principally, in the sketch already given of General Lee.

On the 3d of October, General Beauregard was assigned to the command of two military departments, and the troops therein, known as the department of Tennessee and Georgia, and the department of Alabama, Mississippi and East Louisiana.

He immediately proceeded to the West, first visiting Governor Brown, at Milledgeville; and then, via Columbus, Georgia, on the 7th, Opelika, and Montgomery the next day, Talladega, Alabama, on the 10th, and Jacksonville on the 14th, where he joined Hood's army, and then issued an earnest appeal to the people to come forward and support renewed efforts to drive the enemy from the South.

It would, however, appear that Beauregard's position now was not so much that of a general in the field, as a military

director, and commander-in-chief over the western depart
ments. In some correspondence to the *Charleston Mercury*
we find it stated that he could not take direct control of either
Hood's or Taylor's armies, but merely order them from one
point to the other, as he deemed advisable. What those movements were is of so recent a date that we need not refer to
them more than to say, that their great object was frustrated
by General Schofield's victory over the Confederates at Nashville, Tennessee, and Sherman's grand march through Georgia,
towards Savannah. This latter, probably induced the authorities at Richmond to recall Beauregard from the West, to su-
perintend the defences at that place; for we find it stated in
the *Richmond Dispatch*, December 12th, that he was there in
conjunction with Generals Hardee, G. W. Smith, and R. Taylor; and about that time official orders extended his department so as to include South Carolina and the Atlantic sea
board of Georgia.

When Savannah was surrounded by the Federal forces, a
flag of truce was, on December 17th, sent in by General Sherman, demanding the surrender of the city, and, on the next
day, a reply was given by General Beauregard, refusing to
comply with the demand. But, on Monday, the 19th, the city
was evacuated; and on the 22d we find Beauregard again at
Charleston, notifying the Confederate authorities at Richmond,
that "the enemy, eight hundred strong, had occupied Pollard,"
an important station at the junction of the Mobile and Great
Northern and Alabama and Florida railroads, about seventy
miles north of Mobile.

On the 7th of January, 1865, he was at Macon, Georgia, and
sent to Richmond, Hood's official report of the last battle in
front of Nashville, on December 16th; also additional reports
from that general, dated Tupelo, January 6th.

Beauregard afterwards personally commanded the Southern
Army of Tennessee, retreating before Sherman in the successful advance of that general through South Carolina, until, on
February 23d, 1865, he was relieved by Johnston, though
remaining as second in command.

When the truce was agreed upon between Sherman and
Johnston, Beauregard addressed the following letter to Howel
Cobb, then commanding the Confederate forces at Macon,

besieged and nominally captured by General Wilson of the Union army :

" GREENSBORO', April 19, 1865.

" Major-General H. COBB, *via* Columbia, 19th, *via* Augusta, 20th :

" Inform general commanding the enemy's forces in your front, that a truce, for the purpose of a final settlement, was agreed upon yesterday between Generals Johnston and Sherman, applicable to all forces under their commands. A message to that effect from General Sherman will be sent him as soon as practicable. The contending forces are to occupy their present position, forty-eight hours' notice being given on the event of resumption of hostilities."

When Johnston surrendered, Beauregard was included among the principal generals, with staffs attached to them, who were paroled ; and it appears that he then went to Mobile, and afterwards to New Orleans. Here he quietly remained, cultivating his plantation, till, in the beginning of August, his house was suddenly surrounded by the military, under the idea that Kirby Smith was concealed there. Beauregard was confined in a cotton-press until the morning. He then complained to General Sheridan, who was greatly annoyed at the occurrence, and immediately righted the matter with Beauregard.

On the 16th of September he took the oath of allegiance, and in November was appointed president of the New Orleans, Jackson, and Great Northern Railroad.

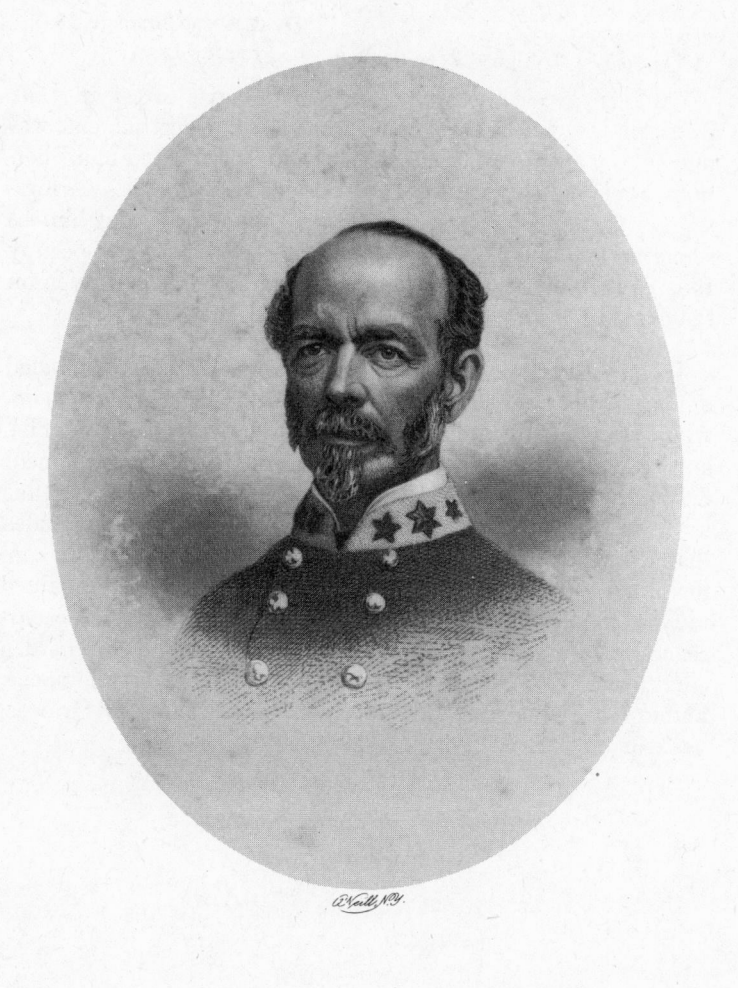

GEN. J. E. JOHNSTON.

GENERAL JOSEPH EGGLESTON JOHNSTON.

CHAPTER I.

Johnston.—Scotch Descent.—His Family.—Early Life.—Cadet at West Point.—Military Career.—Services in Florida.—Anecdote.—In the Mexican War.—Wounded.—Promoted.—Chief of Quartermaster's Department.—Resigns, and gives his Services to the South.—Commands in the Shenandoah Valley.—Unites with Beauregard.-Manassas.—Characteristics.—Evacuation of Manassas.—March to Peninsula.—McClellan.—Prince de Joinville.—Yorktown.—Battle of Williamsburg.—Letter to Jackson.—Battle of Seven Pines.—Johnston Wounded.—Sickness.—Recovery.—Assigned to Command of the West.—His Movements.—Delicate Position with regard to General Bragg.—Correspondence on the Subject.—Vicksburg.—Infirm Health.—On the Field at Jackson.—Grant's Movements.—Battle of Baker's Creek.—Jackson Camped at Vernon.—Incide..ts.—Order to Evacuate Port Hudson.—Fall of Vicksburg.—Evacuation of Jackson.—Visits Mobile, etc.—Commands the Army in the Field.—Sherman in Georgia.—Resaca.—Sherman's Advance.—Atlanta.—Johnston Superseded by Hood.—High Estimate of Johnston.

In the Confederate army there have been several officers or rank bearing this name, or a similar one, with merely the letter *t* omitted. The subject of our present sketch, however, is Joseph Eggleston Johnston, of Scotch descent, and, formerly, Quartermaster-general in the United States service, but, afterwards, in conjunction with Beauregard, commanding the Southern forces in the first battle of Bull Run, 1861.

This brave and skilful officer was born about the year 1808, in Prince Edward County, Virginia. His father was the late Judge Peter Johnston, of the general court of Virginia, distinguished alike at the bar, and on the bench, for sound practical sense and solid legal acquirements. In youth, he had been serving as an officer under Greene, in the campaign of 1781, and had borne himself honorably at Eutaw, Camden, and other places. After the war of the Revolution, Judge Johnston married Miss Polly Wood, a niece of Patrick Henry, and " one of the most accomplished ladies of her day." They had a large family of sons and daughters, to whose education

they paid the greatest attention, and thus brought them up to be persons of superior understanding. Among the sons, Joseph was the youngest, receiving the rudiments of education in Abingdon district, where his father had been appointed iudge. At school, he was noted as a boy of quick parts and a bold, enterprising disposition. He was, also, possessed of great fortitude, and calm endurance, as was evinced at one time, when, by an accident, his arm was broken, he submitted to the setting of the limb with the most stoical composure, and with equal patience bore the after confinement necessary to his situation. These traits of character, coupled with his father's past reminiscenses of a military life, no doubt led to his adoption of the army for a profession. In 1829, he graduated at West Point with great credit, and was immediately assigned to the Fourth Artillery, as brevet Second-lieutenant. He remained there until 1836, when he was appointed First-lieutenant and Assistant Commissary of Subsistence. In 1838 he was made First-lieutenant of Topo graphical Engineers, and, in that capacity, served throughout the Florida war. There he greatly distinguished himself by his coolness and bravery, during the whole time. It is related of him that, "on one occasion having been sent, under the escort of a party of infantry, to make a survey or reconnoissance of a region which lay around a lake, and having crossed the lake in boats, the party was waylaid by an ambuscade of Indians, and all its officers killed or disabled at the first fire. The men were thrown into complete confusion, and were in imminent danger of destruction, when Lieutenant Johnston took command, and by his coolness and determination succeeded in rescuing them. He laid hold of a small tree with one hand, and, standing boldly out in face of the whole fire of the savages, called upon the men to rally and form upon him. They immediately returned to their duty and resumed the action, a perfect volley of balls sweeping around. At last one struck Johnston immediately above the forehead and passed backward over the skull, without fracturing the brain, and he fell, but the troops had caught so much of his spirit that they repulsed the enemy and carried off the wounded in safety." For this, and other good service during the Florida war, he was brevetted captain, and in September, 1846, became a full

captain by seniority. On February 16th, 1847, he was brevetted a lieutenant-colonel of voltigeurs and sailed with the expedition of General Scott to Mexico. After the capture of Vera Cruz, on the advance to Cerro Gordo, he made a most daring reconnoissance, wherein he was severely, and, as was thought at the time, mortally wounded. He recovered, however, sufficiently to resume his command, and bear part in the concluding battles of that war. He distinguished himself at Molino del Rey, and was again wounded at Chapultepec. In this latter engagement, General Scott says of him : " Besides Generals Pillow, Quitman, Shields, Smith, and Cadwalader, the following are the officers and corps most distinguished in those brilliant operations : the voltigeur regiment, in two detachments, commanded, respectively, by Colonel Andrews, and Lieutenant-colonel Johnston—the latter mostly in the lead, accompanied by Major Caldwell (etc.)—the former the first to plant a regimental color, and the latter among the first in the assault." It is reported that General Scott should further say of him " Johnston is a great soldier, but he has an unfortunate knack of getting himself shot in nearly every engagement." This was undoubtedly a high testimony to his merits as a brave soldier ; and, for his gallant and meritorious conduct, he was several times brevetted.

At the close of the Mexican war he was retained as captain in the Topographical Engineers, and, at a later date, was made a full colonel in the regular army. In June, 1860, he was placed at the head of the quartermaster's department, with the rank of brigadier-general, and was in that post when the present national strife commenced. At that time he had a great reputation for capacity and probity, and was highly esteemed ; but he felt bound to join the service of his native State, when Virginia seceded, and was immediately appointed to a high command by Governor Letcher. When, however, the Virginia forces became absorbed in the general army of the Southern Confederacy, he received a direct commission from President Davis as Major-general, and proceeded to take command of the forces at Harper's Ferry, then temporarily under the control of Colonel " Stonewall" Jackson.

On the 23d of May, 1861, General Johnston assumed command of what was then called the army of the Shenandoah,

and, after a complete reconnoissance of Harper's Ferry and environs, he decided that the place was untenable, and, therefore, determined to withdraw his troops to Winchester. At this time General Patterson was advancing, with a strong Northern force, from Pennsylvania and Maryland, into Virginia, and it was supposed that an attempt would be made by that general to form a junction in the Shenandoah valley with General McClellan, then advancing towards Winchester from the western parts of Virginia. To prevent this junction, therefore, was most desirable, and, accordingly, on the 13th of June, General Johnston abandoned Harper's Ferry, after first burning the railroad bridge and such buildings as were likely to prove most useful to the enemy. On the 14th, while on his march up the valley, he learned that Patterson's forces had crossed the Potomac at Williamsport, and, consequently, it would be necessary to arrest the onward movement by taking up a strong position between the Federal army and Winchester. This was done at Bunker's Hill, on the Martinsburg turnpike, and with what result we have already seen in our sketch of General Jackson's life. Patterson fell back across the river, and Johnston pursued his way unmolested towards Winchester.

In the early part of July, Patterson made other attempts to entangle Johnston, and, by feints, to detain him in that part of the valley, so as to prevent the union of his forces with those of Beauregard, then strongly encamped on the plains of Manassas. But Johnston saw through this, and skilfully avoided being caught. Keeping his own designs very secret, he made several feint movements, completely deceiving the enemy to the last moment; and, when, on the 18th of July, he received a dispatch from Richmond stating that the Northern army, under McDowell, was advancing upon Manassas, he acted upon the discretionary power given him, and immediately advanced to join Beauregard. His own words are, "It was found to be necessary either to defeat General Patterson, or to elude him." The latter course was the most speedy and certain, and was, therefore, adopted. The sick were provided for in Winchester; and for the defence of that place, should the enemy follow, as was expected, the militia of Generals Carson and Meem, seemed ample. Colonel Stuart, with the cavalry, was

sent on in advance to guard the way, and on the 19th, the whole army (except a portion under Kirby Smith, that followed quickly after) moved through Ashby's gap to Piedmont, a station of the Manassas Gap railroad. Hence, the infantry proceeded by the cars,—the cavalry continuing the march by road,—and reached Manassas about noon of July 20th. There, though ranking Beauregard, he very considerately and generously yielded the seniority, so as not to disturb any of the plans of battle already formed, and, consequently, Beauregard retained supreme command on the field, while Johnston cordially and effectively supported him. The following day, July 21st, was fought the great battle which has been already alluded to and described in previous sketches. *Bull Run* will exist forever, on historic ground, as memorable for more than one severe conflict between the forces of the North and South, in which the former have been defeated. But we can only touch upon it now to say that, in all the dispositions of the battle, Beauregard submitted them first for approval to Johnston. At half past eight in the morning, General Johnston moved his headquarters to a more central position, where he could watch the course of events, but soon after ten o'clock,—no longer able to remain in the background,—he set out for the advanced lines, gallantly charging to the front with the colors of the Fourth Alabama by his side, all the field officers of that regiment having been previously disabled. Beauregard, however, earnestly persuaded him to retire, and this, reluctantly, he did, afterwards so directing and ordering the reserves, that his valuable services proved most effectual towards the successful issue of the day. When Brigadier-general Kirby Smith arrived about 3 P. M., with the remainder of his troops, he personally directed them to the right of the enemy where they could be most efficient, and where, indeed, their arrival produced that final repulse of the enemy which resulted in a total defeat.

After the battle of Manassas, the army remained in camp, with nothing of importance concerning it to relate, as connected with General Johnston, until the following March.

The personal appearance and characteristics of General Johnston, at this time, have been thus described: "He is about five feet eight or nine inches in height, of good form,

very erect, a handsome face, thick moustache and beard, some what sprinkled with white. His hair is slightly gray. His organs of benevolence and veneration are extremely large; and his eye is very full and large. He should talk well, and speak fluently. He has the decided advantage over Beauregard in appearance. Every thing about him—his bearing, style of dress, and even his most careless attitudes—betoken the high-toned and spirited soldier, who loves his profession, and whose soul revels in the din and uproar of the battlefield. Intellectually, he is the equal of any of the generals in the army. His reports are written with great vigor and a degree of elegance which shows that, in the turmoil of the camp, he is not unmindful of the graces of literature. As a strategist, he enjoys a very high reputation among military men. He is also considered one of the best fighters in the army; but his general manners are rather quiet and dignified."

In the early part of February, 1862, General Johnston issued a stirring appeal to the soldiers, on the re-enlistment question, which had much of the effect desired, and filled the ranks that had been thinned by expired service. A portion of that appeal, incidentally, referred to some new movement of the army; and the next month saw the plains of Manassas evacuated for the purpose of taking up another position further south, on the line of the Rappahannock and the Rapidan. The reasons publicly assigned for this, were that " it was a strategic necessity, and was the surest means of defeating the grand objects of the enemy, and insuring the success of the Confederate cause." The truth is, that it was known a large portion of the Northern army intended to try and reach Richmond by way of the Peninsula from Yorktown. General Johnston, therefore, having been left to his own discretion in the matter, wisely determined to change his base of operations on the Potomac, to one where he could be within supporting distance of the army around Richmond and on the Peninsula. His new line, therefore, was one purely defensive. It stretched from the Rappahannock, by a grand circle, to Cumberland gap, in the extreme southwestern corner of the State; embracing the Central and the Virginia and Tennessee railroads, the chief cities of Virginia, the valley of the James, with its canal and railroads, within the circumference. This position

was assumed in consequence of the great preparations made in the North to invade the South ; and the spirited address of General McClellan at that time, to his troops, clearly indicated a determination to carry on the war most vigorously and more energetically than had yet been done.

On the 14th of March, McClellan assumed command of the "Army of the Potomac," having been relieved from the general superintendence of all the military departments, and, in addressing his soldiers, he says: "The moment for action has arrived. The period of inaction has passed. . . . . In whatever direction you may move, however strange my actions may appear to you, ever bear in mind that my fate is linked with yours, and that all I do is to bring you, where I know you wish to be—on the decisive battlefield." What his plans were is well known, and has been ably spoken of by the Prince de Joinville, who accompanied McClellan, and afterwards published a small work on the campaign. To attack Richmond by the water line was his great desire; and it was this that General Johnston, with keen-sighted policy, prepared for. The authorities at Richmond also adopted every measure necessary to meet the enemy on his new battle-ground. The capital was, of course, the principal object to be considered, and General Lee was summoned from the South to take military control of all its defences.

On the 17th of March, General McClellan began to forward his troops from Alexandria, by transports, to Fort Monroe, and when he, himself, departed, it was with the expectation that General McDowell, with the rest of the great army would promptly follow. This, however, did not occur. It was found that, though Manassas had been evacuated by the Confederates, they were in far greater force in the Shenandoah Valley, where Jackson was heroically fighting, and in the front of the advanced Northern line of occupation in Virginia, than was before supposed. Consequently, some dread was entertained that Washington itself might be in danger, if left unprotected, and, accordingly, McDowell was detained for that purpose. All this was known to General Johnston, who, however, kept his own designs quite secret, even "shutting out his army from all intercourse with the public." Thus, when Yorktown was besieged in April, Magruder, in command there, was rein

forced from Johnston's army without delay or difficulty. John-ston himself went thither, and earnestly addressed the troops, calling upon them "to use every exertion to defeat the Northern invaders." But events proved that such was not to be done at Yorktown, nor, afterwards, at Williamsburg. On the 4th of May, Yorktown was evacuated by the Confederates, after, it is said, a unanimous opinion on the part of President Davis, General Lee (both having visited the place for the purpose), and General Johnston, that McClellan, by his ar-rangements, had made the place untenable. Magruder dis-sented from this view, but yielded to the judgment of the others.

General Johnston now retreated upon Williamsburg, hotly pursued by the victorious federals, but here he determined to impede their advance by giving battle. On the 5th of May was fought the battle of Williamsburg, and on the next day the city was occupied by the Federal troops, Johnston gradu-ally retiring towards Richmond. On the 8th he was at Bar-hamsville, and sent an official letter to Richmond, notifying the landing of the enemy at West Point, under cover of their gunboats. This movement appears to have been foreseen by Johnston, and is the key to his motives for withdrawing to the defences of Richmond, which now required all the available force that could be collected there. On the 19th, he occupied a line in the vicinity of the capital, so as to cover all the river batteries; and, a day or two afterwards, the advance of the Northern army came within seven miles of the city. The preparations now made to repel the enemy have already been touched upon in our sketch of General Lee. We will there-fore confine ourselves to what belongs merely to Johnston's personal doings.

On the 27th of May he sent a dispatch to General Jackson, (then in the Shenandoah Valley) wherein are the following important passages, having reference to the army movements at that time:

HEADQUARTERS DEPARTMENT OF NORTHERN VIRGINIA,
May 27, 1862, 9 o'clock 15 min.

To GENERAL T. J. JACKSON:

GENERAL—I have just received your letter of yesterday by Lieutenant Boswell. A copy of a dispatch telegraphed by

that officer from Staunton reached me this morning. After
reading, I wrote to you by a special messenger, suggesting a
movement threatening Washington and Baltimore, unless the
enemy still has in your vicinity force enough to make it rash
to attempt it. He has no force beyond the Potomac to make
it dangerous; only what he has on this side need be considered.

You cannot, in your present position, employ such an army
as yours upon any enterprise not bearing directly upon the
state of things here, either by preventing the reinforcements to
McClellan's army, or by drawing troops from it by divisions.
These objects might be accomplished by the demonstrations
proposed above, or by a movement upon McDowell, although
I fear that by the time this reaches you it will be too late for
either. The most important service you can render the
country is the preventing the further strengthening of McClel-
an's army If you find it too late for that, strike the most
important body of the enemy you can reach. You compel me
to publish orders announcing your success so often that you
must expect repetition of expressions.

Yours very truly,

J. E. JOHNSTON.

P. S.—It is reported this evening that McDowell is moving
this way from Fredericksburg. It is probable.

J. E. JOHNSTON.

On the day but one after, he issued an address to his army
" on the brilliant success won by the skill and courage of the
generals and troops in the Valley," and calling upon his own
soldiers " to emulate the deeds of their noble comrades there,
so as to make illustrious in history the part they would soon
have to act in the impending drama." Having ascertained
that the enemy was encamped on the inner side of the Chickahominy, near the Williamsburg road, not far from a place
called the Seven Pines, he determined to attack McClellan's
advance without delay. Written orders were dispatched to
the Confederate generals in command, and verbal instructions
given to General Longstreet, then near headquarters.

On Friday night, May 30th, a thunderstorm of unusual
violence shook the heavens, and rain fell so heavily that the

whole face of the country was deluged with water. The men in camp were exposed to all the violence of the storm, and the roads were rendered almost impassable with mud very deep. The enemy were even worse off, for the bottom lands at the head of the Chickahominy were flooded, and the stream itself was much swollen. Early in the morning of the 31st, however, it was rumored that Johnston intended attacking the enemy's left, and that because, as the bridges were washed away, it would prevent McClellan sending reinforcements to this portion of his army. The movement began between six and eight o'clock A. M., Longstreet and Hill in the advance, toiling through the mire on the Williamsburg road. The plan of operation was as follows:

"General Hill, supported by the division of General Longstreet (who had the direction of operations on the right), was to advance by the Williamsburg road to attack the enemy in front; General Huger, with his division, was to move down the Charles City road, in order to attack in flank the troops who might be engaged with Hill and Longstreet, unless he found in his front force enough to occupy the division. General Smith was to march to the junction of the New-bridge road and the Nine-mile road, to be in readiness either to fall on Keyes' right flank, or to cover Longstreet's left."

As the troops marched on, the heavens were surcharged with clouds, and raindrops fell thickly. In the front were dense woods, on marshy ground, the water in many places being two feet deep. Yet, "through all this, the regiments slowly advanced, while the artillery endeavored to follow. Horses were lashed and goaded. Artillerymen were up to their middle in mire, tugging at long ropes, and trying to get on, but their progress was very slow indeed. The gullies, holes, pools, and rocks, threatened to capsize them at every turn."

These, and other causes, delayed the attack on the enemy until about 2 P. M., when Longstreet, finding Huger's division had not come up as expected, opened the engagement, alone, with artillery and skirmishers. By three o'clock it became close and heavy. Meantime, General Johnston had placed himself on the left, with the division of General G. W. Smith, that he might be on a part of the field where good observation could be made of any counter-movement on the side of the

enemy. But, owing to the dense state of the atmosphere, the first sound of firing on the right did not reach him, and it was 4 P. M. when news came of Longstreet's vigorous attack. John ston then ordered forward the whole of Smith's division, and the battle now became general. What followed may be best related in General Johnston's own words, as given in his official report. He says:

"The principal attack was made by Major-general Long-street, with his own and Major-general D. H. Hill's divisions —the latter mostly in advance. Hill's brave troops, admirably commanded and gallantly led, forced their way through the abattis, which formed the enemy's external defences, and stormed their intrenchments by a determined and irresistible rush. Such was the manner in which the enemy's first line was carried. The operation was repeated with the same gallantry and success as our troops pursued their victorious career through the enemy's successive camps and intrenchments. At each new position they encountered fresh troops belonging to it, and reinforcements brought on from the rear. Thus they had to repel repeated efforts to retake works which they had carried. But their advance was never successfully resisted.

"Their onward movement was only stayed by the coming ot night. By nightfall they had forced their way to the 'Seven Pines,' having driven the enemy back more than two miles, through their own camps, and from a series of intrenchments, and repelled every attempt to recapture them, with great slaughter. The skill, vigor, and decision, with which these operations were conducted by General Longstreet, are worthy of the highest praise. He was worthily seconded by Major-general Hill, of whose conduct and courage he speaks in the highest terms.

"Major-general Smith's division moved forward at four o'clock, Whiting's three brigades leading. Their progress was impeded by the enemy's skirmishers, which, with their supports, were driven back to the railroad. At this point, Whit-ing's own and Pettigrew's brigades engaged a superior force ot the enemy. Hood's, by my order, moved on to co-operate with Longstreet. General Smith was desired to hasten up with all the troops within reach. He brought up Hampton' and Hatton's brigades in a few minutes.

"The strength of the enemy's position, however, enabled him to hold it until dark.

"About sunset, being struck from my horse, severely wounded by a fragment of a shell, I was carried from the field, and Major-general G. W. Smith succeeded to the command.

"He was prevented from resuming his attack on the enemy's position next morning, by the discovery of strong intrenchments not seen on the previous evening. His division bivouacked, on the night of the 31st, within musket-shot of the intrenchments which they were attacking when darkness stayed the conflict. The skill, energy, and resolution with which Major-general Smith directed the attack, would have secured success if it could have been made an hour earlier.

"The troops of Longstreet and Hill passed the night of the 31st on the ground which they had won. The enemy were strongly reinforced from the north side of the Chickahominy on the evening and night of the 31st. The troops engaged by General Smith were, undoubtedly, from the other side of the river.

"On the morning of the 1st of June, the enemy attacked the brigade of General Pickett, which was supported by that of General Pryor. The attack was vigorously repelled by these two brigades, the brunt of the fight falling on General Pickett. This was the last demonstration made by the enemy.

"Our troops employed the residue of the day in securing and bearing off the captured artillery, small-arms, and other property; and in the evening quietly returned to their own camps."

The wound General Johnston received, came while he was in the front, ordering some new attack. A battery opened from a thicket, and a piece of shell struck him severely; at the same time a minie ball entered his shoulder and passed down his back. He fell from his horse, and broke two of his ribs, thus compelling him to leave the field, at the time, with little hope of recovery. He was taken back to the city, to the residence of a celebrated physician, who carefully attended him, and the streets, for squares around, were kept clear of vehicles so as to prevent his being disturbed. It was some weeks, however, before he showed symptoms of recovery; and, at the end of July,

he left for Amelia Springs, to derive benefit from the pure country air.

For more than three months General Johnston was unable to attend to military duties. At length he was sufficiently restored to permit of his transacting business, though, apparently, not of resuming active duties in the field. In September he was at Gordonsville and Culpepper on some private matters, as reported, connected with the army; but not until the beginning of November did he again come forward in public life.

On the 24th of November he was assigned to the command of the West, in the following order:

ADJUTANT AND INSPECTOR-GENERAL'S OFFICE, }
RICHMOND, November 24, 1862. }

* * * * * * *

General J. E. Johnston, Confederate States army, is hereby assigned to the following geographical command, to wit: Commencing with the Blue Ridge of mountains, running through the western part of North Carolina, and following the line of said mountains through the northern part of Georgia to the railroad south of Chattanooga; thence by that road to West Point, and down the west or right bank of the Chattahoochie river to the boundary of Alabama and Florida, following that boundary west to the Choctahatchie river, and down that river to Chatahatchie bay—including the waters of that bay—to the Gulf of Mexico. All that portion of country west of said line to the Mississippi river is included in the above command. General Johnston will, for the purpose of correspondence and reports, establish his headquarters at Chattanooga, or such other place as in his judgment will best secure facilities for ready communication with the troops within the limits of his command, and will repair in person to any part of said command whenever his presence may, for the time, be necessary or desirable.

* * * * * * *

By command of the Secretary of War,

JOHN WITHERS, Assistant Adjutant-general.

His Excellency, the President, Richmond, Va.

On the 29th of November, General Johnston left Richmond with his staff, and arrived at Chattanooga on the 4th of De-

cember. The next day he proceeded to Murfreesboro, and as
sumed command of the army, though, from physical inability,
produced by his late wound, he was unable to do more than
direct movements. At this time, President Davis was on a
tour of inspection, and, in company with General Johnston,
visited Bragg's army.

The organization of the army, under General Johnson, at
the time he took command, was as follows:—General Bragg
in command of the army of the Mississippi, located at Murfreesboro, Tennessee, with Lieutenant-general Polk, commanding the
right wing, and under him, Generals Buckner, Cheatham, Breckinridge, etc.; Lieutenant-general Kirby Smith, commanding the
centre, located at Shelbyville, Tennessee; Lieutenant-general
Hardee, commanding the left wing, also located at Shelbyville.
Other detachments were under Generals R. Anderson, Pillow,
Wheeler, Morgan, Forrest, and Stearns; and the total amount
of force was about 65,750 men. General Johnston, however,
does not appear to have remained long at Murfreesboro, but
visited other portions of his department, leading to the infer-
ence that he was in command at Vicksburg. On the 26th of
December, 1862, while at Jackson, Mississippi, in company
with the President, who delivered an address before the legislature of Mississippi, General Johnston was called upon for a
speech. "The scar-worn hero," says a report of the proceedings, "looked a little nervous, while the house rang with loud
and prolonged applause. He rose and said: 'Fellow-citizens,—
My only regret is that I have done so little to merit such a
greeting. I promise you, however, that hereafter I shall be
watchful, energetic, and indefatigable in your defence.'"

At the end of the year (1862) was fought the battle of Murfreesboro, between Generals Bragg and Rosecrans, each claiming the victory, though the former retreated to Tullahoma. At
the time, General Johnston appears to have been at Jackson,
watching the movements of Sherman on Vicksburg, who had
to retreat after an unsuccessful assault upon the city. General
Grant had also to be carefully followed in his operations; but
General Johnston had some other duties now to perform,
which evidently placed him in a delicate position. President
Davis had returned to Richmond, and there, it would seem, h
was urged to remove General Bragg from his command. The

President, however, thought fit to consult General Johnston on the subject, and the following correspondence took place.

RICHMOND, Va., January 22, 1863.

General J. E. JOHNSTON, Chattanooga, Tenn.:

As announced in my telegram, I address this letter to you [explaining] the purpose for which I desire you to proceed promptly to the headquarters of General Bragg's army.

*   *   *   *   *   *

You will, I trust, be able by conversation with General Bragg and others of his command, to decide what the best interests of the service require, and give me the advice which I need at this juncture. As that army is a part of your command no order will be necessary to give you authority there, as, whether present or absent, you have a right to direct its operations, and do whatever else belongs to the general commanding. Very truly and respectfully yours,

JEFF. DAVIS.

TULLAHOMA, February 12, 1863.

MR. PRESIDENT,—Since writing to you on the 3d, I have seen the whole army. Its appearance is very encouraging, and gives positive assurance of General Bragg's capacity to command. It is well clothed, healthy, and in fine spirits. The brigades engaged at Murfreesboro are now stronger than they were on the morning of the battle—mainly by the return of the absentees brought back by the general's vigorous system.

*   *   *   *   *   *

My object has been to ascertain if the confidence of the troops in the ability of the army to beat the enemy is at all impaired.

I find no indication that it is less than when you were in its camps.

While this feeling exists, and you regard General Bragg as brave and skilful, the fact that some or all of the general officers of the army, and many of the subordinates, think that you might give them a commander with fewer defects, cannot, I think, greatly diminish his value. To me it seems that the operations of this army in Middle Tennessee have been conducted admirably. I can find no record of more effective

fighting in modern battles than that of this army in December, evincing skill in the commander, and courage in the troops, which fully entitle them to the thanks of the Government.

In the early part of January, the country north of Granada being considered impracticable, I directed Major-general Van Dorn to bring to General Bragg's aid the cavalry of the Mississippi army, except such as Lieutenant-general Pemberton considered necessary to him.

  *   *   *   *   *   *

I have been told by —— —— that they have advised you to remove General Bragg, and place me in command of this army. I am sure that you will agree with me, that the part I have borne in this investigation would render it inconsistent with my personal honor to occupy that position. I believe, however, that the interest of the service requires that General Bragg should not be removed. Most respectfully, your obedient servant,

J. E. JOHNSTON.

It appears, however, that there was a determination on the part of the authorities at Richmond, to have General Johnston in active command on the field, as will appear from the following extracts from his official reports. He says :

" While on my way to Mississippi, where I thought my presence had become necessary, I received, in Mobile, on March 12th, the following telegram from the Secretary of War, dated March 9.

" ' Order General Bragg to report to the War Department for conference. Assume yourself direct charge of the army of Middle Tennessee.'

" In obedience to this order, I at once proceeded to Tullahoma. On my arrival I informed the Secretary of War, by a telegram of March 19th, that General Bragg could not then be sent to Richmond, as he was ordered, on account of the critical condition of his family.

" On the 10th of April, I repeated this to the President, and added, ' Being unwell then, I afterwards became sick, and am not now able to serve in the field. General Bragg is, therefore, necessary here.' On the 28th my unfitness for service in the field was reported to the Secretary of of War.

" On the 9th of May I received, at Tullahoma, the following dispatch of the same date, from the Secretary of War :

' Proceed at once to Mississippi and take chief command of the forces there, giving to those in the field, as far as practicable, the encouragement and benefit of your personal direction.'

" It is thus seen, that neither my orders nor my health permitted me to visit Mississippi after the 12th of March, until the time when I took direct charge of that department."

From the time General Johnston arrived at Tullahoma, until the middle of April, communications by telegraph were received from General Pemberton, then at Vicksburg, indicating that all attempts on that place were apparently abandoned. But, on the 17th of April, news came that Grant had resumed vigorous operations, and that the Federal flotilla on the Mississippi was also actively engaged. These operations proved successful. Port Gibson was taken by the Federal forces on the first of May ; Grand Gulf was occupied, and General Grant began his march upon the Jackson and Vicksburg railroad. It was time, therefore, that Johnston himself, however sick he might be, should be personally present on the scene. Accordingly, he reached Jackson on the night of the 13th of May, and immediately assumed active command. On examination, he found matters very serious. His whole force there, even with expected reinforcements, would not amount to more than " eleven thousand," and Grant, with a powerful army, was rapidly approaching. Next morning, Thursday, May 14th, at an early hour, Johnston marched out some eight miles southwest of Jackson, and met the forces of Grant advancing by the main road. A battle was fought, lasting for some time, and ending in the repulse of the Confederates, and their evacuation of the city. At 2 P. M. Johnston retreated by the Canton road, by which alone he could form a junction with Pemberton, who was in the advanced front of Vicksburg. After marching six miles, the troops encamped, and General Johnston then sent a dispatch to Pemberton, advising and directing him what to do. But, on the morning of the 16th Pemberton was attacked by the enemy at Baker's creek, near Edward's station, on the Vicksburg railroad, and after nine hours' fighting, was compelled to fall back behind the Big Black river. On the 17th, Johnston

again tried to join Pemberton by marching in a direction intimated by that general, but that night it was ascertained he
had retired within Vicksburg.   The day after, General Johnston had his headquarters near Vernon, close to the Big Black,
and thence sent to Pemberton instructions to "hold out,"
until it might be seen if he could be relieved.   At the same
time he forwarded directions to General Gardner, at Port
Hudson, to evacuate that place ; and, after dispatching these
orders, he marched back to re-establish his line between Jackson and Canton.   There, for awhile, we will leave his military
movements, and introduce some notice of him from a visitor,
who had come across the Atlantic to see what was going on in
the Confederate States.   We allude to Lieutenant-colonel Fremantle, from whom we have already quoted, and who says, at
this particular time, after a difficult journey up the Mississippi :

"We left Jackson (Tuesday, 19th May) with the leading
troops (of Confederates proceeding to join Johnston—Grant
having gone to Vicksburg), and next day, about 6 P. M.,
reached General Johnston's bivouac. . . . . I presented my
letters of introduction, ... and to me he was extremely
affable, though he certainly possesses the power of keeping
people at a distance when he chooses, and his officers evidently
stand in great awe of him.   He lives very plainly, and at
present his only cooking utensils consisted of an old coffeepot
and fryingpan—both very inferior articles.   There was only
one fork (one prong deficient), between himself and staff, and
this was handed to me, ceremoniously, as the 'guest.'   He has
undoubtedly acquired the entire confidence of all the officers
and soldiers under him.   Many of the officers told me they
did not consider him inferior, as a general, to Lee, or any one
else.   He told me that Vicksburg was certainly in a critical
situation, and was now closely invested by Grant.   He said
that he, himself, had 11,000 men with him, hardly any cavalry, and only sixteen pieces of cannon ; but, if he could get
adequate reinforcements, he stated his intention of endeavoring to relieve Vicksburg. . . . . On the following day I was
received into his mess.   Major Eustis and Lieutenant Washington, officers of his staff, are thorough gentlemen, and did
all in their power to make me comfortable.   The first is a

Louisianian of wealth (formerly); and his negro always speaks French. . . . . I was presented to Captain Henderson, who commanded a corps of about fifty scouts. These are employed on the hazardous duty of hanging about the enemy's camps, collecting information, and communicating with Pemberton in Vicksburg. They are a fine looking lot of men, wild, and very picturesque in appearance. At noon a Yankee military surgeon came to camp. He had been left behind by Grant to look after the Yankee's wounded at Jackson, and he was now anxious to rejoin his general by flag of truce, but General Johnston very prudently refused to allow this, and desired that he should be sent to the North, via Richmond. By a very sensible arrangement, both sides have agreed to treat doctors as non-combatants, and not to make prisoners of war of them. . . . In the evening I asked General Johnston what prospect he thought there was of early operations, and he told me that at present he was too weak to do any good, and he was unable to give me any definite idea as to when he might be strong enough to attack Grant. . . . General Johnston is a very well read man, and agreeable to converse with. He told me that he considered Marlborough a greater general than Wellington. All Americans have an intense admiration for Napoleon; and they seldom scruple to express their regret that he was beaten at Waterloo. Remarking upon the extreme prevalence of military titles, General Johnston said, 'You must be astonished to find how fond all Americans are of titles, though they are republicans; and, as they can't get any other sort, they all take military ones. . . . In the course of our long conversation, he told me that the principal evils which a Confederate general had to contend against, consisted in the difficulty of making combinations, owing to uncertainty about the time which the troops would take to march a certain distance, on account of their straggling propensities. . . . He also said that Grant had displayed more vigor than he had expected, by crossing the river below Vicksburg, seizing Jackson by vastly superior force, and, after cutting off communications, investing the fortress thoroughly, so as to take it, if possible, before a sufficient force could be got to relieve it. . . . . In reference to himself, he said that altogether he had been wounded ten times. He was the senior officer of the old

army who joined the Confederates. . . . Saturday, May 23d, General Johnston, Major Eustis, and myself, left Canton at 6 A. M., on a locomotive for Jackson. On the way we talked a good deal about "Stonewall" Jackson, and he said that although this extraordinary man did not possess any great qualifications as a strategist, and was perhaps unfit for the independent command of a large army, yet he was gifted with wonderful courage and determination, and a perfect faith in Providence that he was destined to destroy his enemy. He was much indebted to General Ewell in the valley campaigns. Stonewall Jackson was also most fortunate in commanding the flower of the Virginia troops, and in being opposed to the most incapable Federal commanders, such as Fremont and Banks.

"Before we had proceeded twelve miles we were forced to stop and collect wood from the road side to feed our engine, and the general worked with so much energy as to cause his ' Seven Pines' wound to give him pain. We were put out at a spot where the railroad was destroyed, at about four miles from Jackson. A carriage ought to have been in waiting for us, but by some mistake it had not arrived, so we had to foot it. I was obliged to carry my heavy saddle-bags. Major Eustis very kindly took my knapsack, and the general carried the cloaks. In this order we reached Jackson, much exhausted, at 9 : 30 A. M. . . . I there took an affectionate farewell of him and his officers, and he returned to Canton at 3 P. M."

We have given the above extracts as significant of General Johnston's character as a courteous gentleman, and accomplished military officer of rank. And it is a somewhat striking fact, that he and many others, both North and South, have frequently shown similar kind and gentlemanly feeling to strangers even amid all their cares and anxieties. In the present case, and while his visitor was actually with him, he was receiving important communications, to which careful answers had to be returned. On the 23d of May, a dispatch came from Port Hudson, stating that the enemy was about to cross at Bayou Sara, and the whole force from Baton Rouge was in front of General Gardner. To this he sent renewed orders to evacuate Port Hudson. "You cannot be reinforced," said he. " Do not allow yourself to be invested. At every risk save

the troops, and if practicable, move in this direction." Dispatches also arrived from General Pemberton, dated Vicksburg, May 20th, and 21st. To these, on the 29th, he replied, "I am too weak to save Vicksburg. Can do no more than attempt to save you and your garrison. It will be impossible to extricate you, unless you co-operate, and we make mutually supporting movements. Communicate your plans and suggestions, if possible."

After this, much more correspondence with Pemberton, and also with the Secretary of War, at Richmond, took place, all having the same purport, viz., that he (General Johnston) was too weak to relieve Vicksburg, and had not at his disposal half the troops necessary. To the Secretary of War, on the 12th of June, he again said the same, adding, "To take from Bragg a force which would make this army fit to oppose Grant, would involve yielding Tennessee. It is for the Government to decide between this State and Tennessee."

At intervals, similar communications took place, and a movement of the army was made on the 29th of June, towards the Big Black, with a view of giving some relief to Pemberton. But, on the 5th of July, General Johnston learned that Vicksburg had fallen to the victorious Federal arms, and accordingly, he marched back, and encamped again at Jackson. There, however, he was not allowed to remain long in peace. On the morning of the 9th, General Sherman appeared, in heavy force, in front of the works thrown up for the defence of the place, and commenced intrenching, and constructing batteries. Next day some spirited skirmishing, with slight cannonading, occurred; and on the following day an assault was made on General Breckinridge's lines. On the 16th, General Johnston found that it would be impossible to hold the city, and, accordingly, that night evacuated it, and retired towards Brandon.

It is not to be denied, that these defeats and losses to the Confederates in the Mississippi department, produced much despondency and complaint. Upon the conduct of General Johnston many animadversions were cast, and an attempt was made to throw the whole blame upon him. In his official report he gives a long account of all his movements, and the orders he had issued, asserting, that in important ones, General Pemberton had not obeyed him. To this we must add, that, all

throughout, the wounds he had received, and his general ill health, made him less fit for the superintendence of active operations than might otherwise have been the case, and he himself constantly urged this upon the authorities at Richmond.

On the 27th of July, General Johnston went to Mobile to examine the fortifications there, leaving his army camped at Enterprise and Brandon, under the direct command of General Hardee. While there, he carefully inspected the works, and made a map of them, ultimately deciding that they required strengthening immediately, though, said he, "Mobile is the most defensible seaport position in the Confederate States." It is related, that when he was told there was an idea afloat in the city, of his coming there to order its evacuation, he replied, "Had that been my purpose, I should not have shown my countenance among you. I am here for the directly opposite purpose, of looking into your defences, and preparing to hold your city."

For the next few weeks General Johnston appears to have been visiting the principal posts of his department, and consulting with the several generals in command. It was supposed that he had superseded General Bragg, at Chattanooga, but this seems to have been a similar mistake to that made on a previous occasion, when he was seen there. However, on the 15th of September, he visited Atlanta, Georgia, and afterwards was actively engaged in collecting troops, directing their movements, and supporting Bragg and Longstreet, in Tennessee, as required. At the battle of Chickamauga, General Johnston held a force of 30,000 troops in reserve, at Kingston, fifteen miles from the scene of contest, besides 5,000 cavalry, under General Pillow, and 15,000 Georgia militia. This was done so as to keep a strong body of reinforcements ready, in case General Burnside arrived to join Rosecrans. As this did not occur, General Johnston had no occasion to use his men, General Bragg having effected what was desired, in driving the enemy back. In the early part of October, he so arranged the Confederate army in Tennessee and North Georgia, that one command, of some 58,000 men, occupied the centre from Lafayette to Look-Out Mountain, near Chattanooga: Longstreet on the left, from Bridgeport, on the Tennessee, to Trenton, with 44,000 men; and Bragg the right, from Dalton to Cleveland,

with 57,000 men. The cavalry was under General Wheeler, and numbered 15,000 strong.

At about the same time President Davis again visited the army, and on the 10th of October reviewed the troops, and examined the defences before Chattanooga; but General Johnston was away on an extensive inspection tour.

On the 4th he dates a dispatch from Meridian, north Mississippi; and after that we have little account of his movements until, when, in December, General Bragg was at last removed, in accordance with popular opinion, and General Johnston appointed to the field command of the army in Tennessee, then temporarily held by General Hardee. On the 27th of December he assumed command at Dalton, Georgia.

Commenting upon this appointment, and the correspondeuce between President Davis and General Johnston, concerning General Bragg, which we have already given in its proper date, though only made public at this time, the *Richmond Enquirer* remarks:

"The manly sentiments, and lofty sense of honor exhibited by General Joseph E. Johnston, in the correspondence with the President, recently published, relative to the removal of General Bragg, have given him a new claim upon the public sympathy and admiration, and are receiving their just praise. The *Atlanta Register*, while declaring that the announcement of the appointment of General Joseph E. Johnston to the command of the army of Tennessee will be hailed 'with delight by the army and the people,' adds, that 'he is an officer of generous and noble impulses, as is evidenced by his letters to the President in reference to the hero of Murfreesboro and Chickamauga.'"

There seemed, however, to be a cloud over the prospects of the Confederates at this time. Grant, Sherman, and Thomas were making rapid strides in successful encounters with the Southern forces; and again, was a retreat found necessary by General Johnston, who, the latter part of January, 1864, fell back from Dalton, and his advanced posts. On the 7th of February he was encamped at Rome, Georgia; but again advanced to Dalton shortly afterwards. At the same time the Federals made an attempt to get possession of the place, but were driven back.

In March, the movements of the Northern army indicated that a vigorous attempt would be made to penetrate through Georgia, and therefore General Johnston concentrated a strong force around Dalton, to oppose the enemy's advance. What the condition of his army was at this period may be gathered from the following letter, written to the *Mobile Advertiser*, in April. The writer says:

"I am happy to be able to say, that the condition of our army is splendid in every respect. It is well fed, well clad, in excellent health, and in high and hopeful spirits. For the first time in its history it has no barefoot soldier. . . .

"General Johnston is unquestionably a great captain in the science of war. In ninety days he has so transformed this army, that I can find no word to express the extent of the transformation, but the word regeneration. It is a regenerated army. He found it ninety days ago disheartened, despairing, and on the verge of dissolution. By judicious measures he has restored confidence, re-established discipline, and exalted the hearts of his army. The army of Tennessee, the most ill-starred and successless of all our armies, has seen its worst days.

"Let us hope, that it will have 'no more retreats, and no more defeats.' I have a firm faith now in the future of the army of Tennessee and its great captain. Let him but be unfettered, and furnished with adequate means, and all will be well. He is very fortunate in having such thorough soldiers as Hood, and Hardee, and Stewart, and Cleburne, to direct his columns, and execute his orders. With such leaders, it seems to me, that defeat is impossible. The intrepid dash, and the young, burning enthusiasm of Hood are directed by military genius, and controlled by a rare and high intelligence. Hardee is always prompt, ready, perfect, and successful. The calm, stoic Stewart, silent, stern, poised, imperturbable, never fails, never errs, and never dallies. He is ever at the right place, at the opportune moment. Cleburne is not merely, though he is altogether, a lion in battle, but he has the genius to 'ride upon the whirlwind, and direct the storm' of the mighty conflict. With these generals there will be no dallying, no blunders, no 'lost opportunities,' no disobedience of orders.

"General Johnston has two modes of stopping deserters.

One is, by liberal furloughs, allowing all to go home by turns, and the other is, by the inexorable doom of death to deserters. He has announced, in general orders, that he will grant no pardons, and the doomed must die. The court-martial have, at last, come to discover the necessity of punishing deserters with death, and few now escape. There are upwards of a dozen soldiers now awaiting execution of the death penalty for desertion. Some are to hang ; some to be shot."

At length, on the 2d of May, simultaneous with the onward movement of Grant in Virginia, Sherman began his grand march into Georgia. The Federal advance was in three columns—Thomas moving in front, direct upon Johnston's centre at Dalton, with his advance at Ringgold and Tunnel Hill ; Schofield, from Cleveland, thirty miles northeast of Chattanooga, *via* Red Clay, on the Georgia line, to unite with Thomas ; and McPherson, by a flank movement of some forty or fifty miles upon Johnston's line of communications at Resaca, a station on the Western and Atlantic railroad, at the crossing of the Oostanaula river, eighty-four miles from Atlanta, and fifteen miles south of Dalton.

The attack was made first on the 7th of May, by General Thomas, who drove Johnston's advance back to a place called Buzzard Roost, just north of Dalton. Johnston, knowing the importance of Resaca, and hearing of McPherson's movement, evacuated Dalton, and hastened to Resaca, which he reached just before the Federal advance.

On the 14th of May the two armies came into collision close to Resaca, at a place called Sugar Valley. General Sherman was determined to force his way, and General Johnston equally as determined to prevent him. In quick time he got up breastworks and gave the enemy battle. At first he appeared to be victorious, driving the Federals back some distance, but, eventually, he had to retire, and, after some desultory fighting on the 15th and 16th, he retreated to the Etowah river, passing through Kingston and Cassville. At both places fighting occurred, and Rome was occupied by a portion of Sherman's victorious troops. Johnston still retreated towards Altoona, where he made a stand, but with their inferiority of numbers, they were soon forced from this position by another movement of the enemy in their flank, by

which the Federal left reached the railroad near Marietta on Monday, May 30th.

It is with something of regret that we are compelled, from want of space, to omit most of those interesting details that are to be found connected with the movements of both armies during this celebrated advance through Georgia on the one side, and the masterly retreat on the other. It is quite impossible to do complete justice to such earnest and devoted men in a mere outline sketch of their eventful lives, or to narrate, within the limits of one volume, all the incidents of interest and importance connected with them.

A correspondent of the *Cincinnati Commercial*, dating from Resaca, May 26th, says :

"The designs of Sherman are now somewhat less mysterious. Last night Howard, Palmer, Hooker, Logan, and Dodge's corps were at, and slightly beyond, Dallas—a point on the flank of the rebel position in the Altoona mountains, in what is known as Hickory gap, ten miles southeast of Etowah, the station where the railroad crosses the Etowah river. At the point where the railroad pierces the Altoona mountains, forty miles from Atlanta, Johnston had halted for resistance, occupying a very strong, natural, and powerfully fortified position. Before we could attack him in front it was necessary to cross the Etowah river, and march up the steep and rugged slopes of the mountains which abut on the stream. When the army moved on Monday, Schofield's corps moved to Etowah, and succeeded in laying pontoons, making, the while, at several points, demonstrations leading the enemy to believe that we proposed to attack him directly in front.

"While Schofield was thus engaged, the rest of the army marched rapidly to the Etowah river, and crossed without serious opposition at a point about fifteen miles below the railroad bridge. Immediately resuming the line of march, and with but light skirmishing, reached Dallas last evening— about thirty miles from Atlanta, and within a short march of Marietta, a station on the railroad directly in the rear of the rebel position at Altoona. Schofield has crossed the river near Etowah station, and is moving down the ridge to join the main body, his rear guard skirmishing constantly with the enemy.

" Johnston is thus compelled to abandon his strong position in the Altoona mountains, and fight, if at all, in the open country south of there. Cannonading has been heard to-day, and the impression prevails that a battle is in progress to-day near Marietta.

" A courier from Johnston to his chief of cavalry, General Jackson, was captured day before yesterday, bearing a note of inquiry from the former, asking immediate information of Sherman's movements on his flanks. The courier was taken before General Thomas, who removed his clothes and dressed a trusty scout of his own in them, with an answer to Johnston's message. What this answer was is not generally known, but it is presumed that it did not communicate the movements of our forces with exactness."

Another correspondent says, after a graphic account of previous movements, " So far General Johnston has conducted his retreat in a masterly manner. He has finally succeeded in crossing the Etowah river, at the cliffs, eight miles from here, (Kingston) and there can be no more opportunities for forcing him to fight. . . . A great battle will undoubtedly be fought somewhere between here and Atlanta."

On the 28th of May there was an encounter between General Cleburne's division of Johnston's army and the advance of the enemy, under McPherson, at New Hope; and, after that, each party kept maneuvering for positions until near the end of June without another battle. At length, on the 27th of June, Sherman gave orders for an attack upon Johnston's position, then at Kenesaw mountain, near Marietta. At 8 A. M. General McPherson attacked at the southwest end of the mountain, and General Thomas at a point about a mile further south. At the same time, the skirmishers and artillery along the whole line kept up a sharp fire. Neither attack succeeded, though both columns reached Johnston's works, which were very strong. General McPherson lost about 500 men, and General Thomas about 2,000. The loss was particularly heavy to the Federals in general, and field officers. General Harker was one of those mortally wounded, while on the side of the Confederates the loss was trifling.

General Sherman, however, speedily rectified this by another

flank movement, which compelled General Johnston to abandon the mountain, and retreat towards Atlanta, leaving the
enemy to occupy Marietta.   This continued retrograde movement naturally produced considerable disappointment and
murmuring in the South.   Many were the comments made upon
it, and not a few sharp reasons referring, not only to General
Johnston, but to the authorities at Richmond, were given for
such repeated falling back.   A commander-in-chief of an army
is compelled to do many things that may appear to his command, and to the public, injudicious.   There are reasons and
causes never known to others, which cannot be fully explained,
and are only known by those to whom he is responsible, which
may compulsorily influence his actions ; and that general or
officer is quite unworthy of his high position who has not, in
addition to his military skill and personal bravery, that sound
and healthy moral courage which will enable him in need to
act independently of the opinions of irresponsible persons.
We do not say that all seeming errors can be thus excused,
nor do we venture this as an excuse for General Johnston, if
one be needed for him; the thought, however, should ever
serve to moderate sharp comments or severe criticism that
after events may possibly prove to be unjust.

The Confederate army had now fallen back to Atlanta, and,
on the 18th of July, the troops and the general public were
greatly surprised by an announcement that General Johnston
had been relieved, and General Hood assigned to the command
on the previous day.   The following address was then issued
by General Johnston to his army :

HEADQURTERS, ARMY OF TENNESSEE, July 17, 1864.

In obedience to the orders of the War Department, I turn
over to General Hood the command of the Army and Department of Tennessee.   I cannot leave this noble army without
expressing my admiration for the high military qualities it has
displayed so conspicuously—every soldierly virtue, endurance
of toil, obedience to orders, brilliant courage.

The enemy has never attacked but to be severely repulsed
and punished.   You, soldiers, have never argued but from
your courage, and never counted your fears.   No longer your
leader, I will still watch your career, and will rejoice in your

victories. To one and all I offer assurances of my friendship and bid an affectionate farewell.

J. E. JOHNSTON, General.

The suggestion made in the foregoing paragraphs was not, however, acted upon for months. Johnston was *shelved* by the executive authorities, until the state of affairs was such, under Sherman's successes in South Carolina, that the public voice almost *demanded* his recall. Accordingly, at the end of January, 1865, the Southern Congress signified to the President that it was the wish of the people that Johnston be restored to his original command. Still there was delay. A singular degree of opposition was manifested by certain members of the Senate and some of the official authorities. But the popular wish prevailed, and on the 23d of February he resumed command of the Army of the Tennessee in Sherman's front. His stay, however, in that position was only of short duration. Gallantly, but vainly, contesting the ground, as Sherman and his generals advanced, he finally reached Greensboro', N. C., on the 13th of April, where, having heard of Lee's surrender, with the previous fall of Richmond and Petersburg, he requested an armstice from the victorious Union commander. This was acceded to, and a meeting took place between the two generals, which, after more than one interview, resulted, on the 18th of April, in terms of agreement for the suspension of hostilities under certain conditions, subject to the approval of the President. Forty-eight hours' notice had to be given in the event of hostilities recommencing. The conditions, however, were not approved by the Executive authorities at Washington, and when a summons was shortly afterwards made to Johnston for the surrender of his army, he was compelled to yield. This was done on the 26th of April, 1865, at Bennett's House, near Durham's Station, North Carolina. Johnston and his army were paroled on the same terms as those given to General Lee, and thus the Confederate Army of the Tennessee ceased to exist.

The following orders were promulgated by Johnston on the occasion:

GENERAL ORDERS—No. 18.

HEADQUARTERS ARMY OF THE TENNESSEE, April 27, 1865.

By the terms of a military convention made on the 26th instant, by Major-General W. T. Sherman, United States Army, and General J. E. Johnston, Confederate States Army, the officers and men of this army are to bind themselves not to take up arms against the United States until properly relieved from the obligation, and shall receive guarantees from the United States officers against molestation by the United States authorities, so long as they observe that obligation and the laws in force where they reside. For these objects, duplicate muster-rolls will be made ; and after the distribution of the necessary papers the troops will march under their officers to their respective States, and there be disbanded—all retaining personal property. The object of this convention is pacification, to the extent of the authority of the commanders who made it. Events in Virginia, which broke every hope of success by war, imposed on its general the duty of sparing the blood of this gallant army and saving our country from further devastation, and our people from ruin.

J. E. JOHNSTON, General.

JOHNSTON'S FAREWELL TO HIS ARMY.

GENERAL ORDERS—No. 22.

HEADQUARTERS ARMY OF THE TENNESSEE }
Near Greensboro', May 2, 1865. }

COMRADES—In terminating our official relations, I expect you to observe the terms of the pacification agreed upon, and to discharge the obligations of good and peaceful citizens to the powers that be, as well as you have performed the duties of soldiers in the field. By such a course, you will secure comfort and restore tranquillity to your country. You will return to your homes with the admiration of our people, won by the courage and noble devotion you have displayed in this long war. I shall always remember with pride the loyal support you have given me. I part from you with regret, and bid you farewell with feelings of cordial friendship, and with earnest wishes that you may prosper.

J. E. JOHNSTON, General.

J. E. KENNARD, Colonel, etc.

On the 2d of May, General Johnston, in a letter which was published, explained his reasons for surrendering, and among several other causes which he alleges produced it, he says: " With such odds against us, without the means of procuring ammunition or repairing arms, without money or credit to provide food, it was impossible to continue the war except as robbers." To this he adds somewhat more concerning the useless destruction of their bravest men, besides great suffering and ruin to women and children on a desolating march.

It is generally conceded that General Johnston acted not only humanely but wisely in the matter of his surrender. In later letters he has given expression to sentiments that prove his sincerity. He says in one communication: " We of the South referred the question at issue, between us and the United States, to the arbitrament of the sword. The decision has been made, and is against us. We must acquiesce in that decision, accept it as final, and recognize the fact that Virginia is again one of the United States. Our duties and interest coincide."

In the beginning of last September, General Johnston was proposed as president of the Danville Railroad, but was rejected in favor of another party. He was, however, soon afterwards elected president of the National Express Company, and on the 31st of October, in response to an official notice of the action of the stockholders, spoke as follows:

" MR. CHAIRMAN AND GENTLEMEN—I have had no higher gratification in my life than my election to this position by the board of directors, and its confirmation by the stockholders. I hope that, six months hence, you may think and feel as you do now; but in the discharge of my duties I shall require much advice and assistance. I thank you, gentlemen, for the honor conferred upon me, and you, Mr. Chairman, for the kind manner in which you have informed me of my election."

On a business visit to New York lately, the general is reported to have said that the question of State-rights was now settled, and the Southern people regarded themselves as citizens of the United States; and as for slavery, if that institution had not existed, " Virginia would have been a richer State than New York to-day."

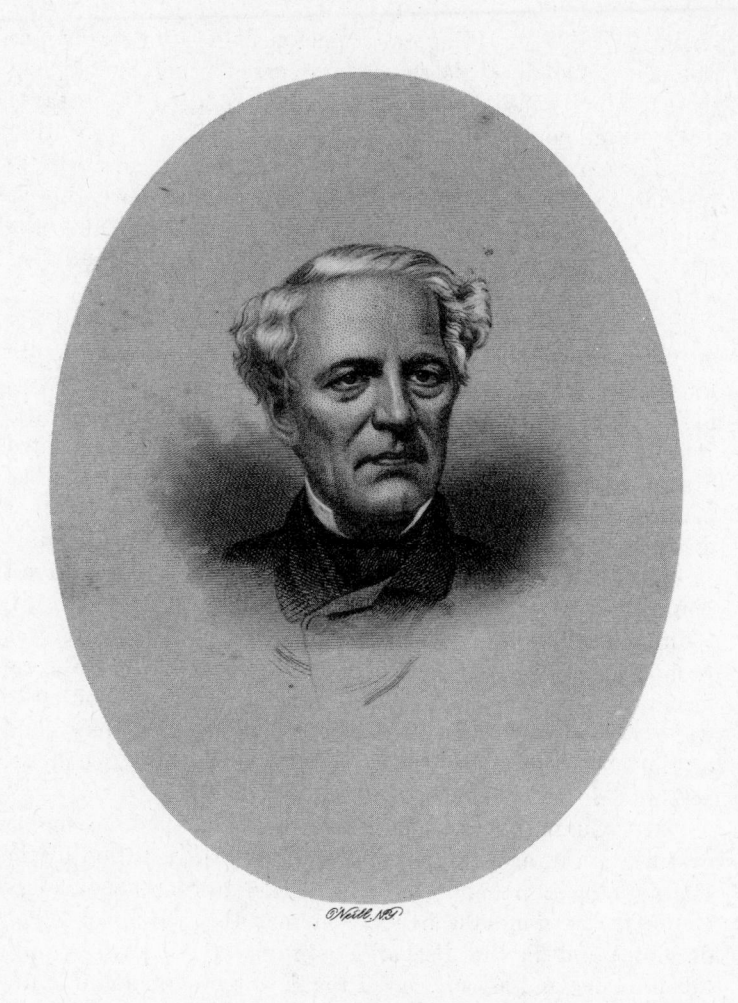

GEN. S. COOPER.

GENERAL SAMUEL COOPER.

THERE are some men whose career through life never displays itself by much public fame, and yet whose services are, and have been fully equal, in their real value, to those of generals and commanders, appearing more prominently on the scene of every-day life. Statesmen, high officials of the government, advisers of the constituted authorities, adjutants, commissariat officers, heads of departments, medical directors, and others, rarely come forward in the world's blazonry with that display common usage has affixed to the deeds of military or naval heroes. Yet those very men often deserve as much credit, and sometimes far more, than is awarded to commanders on the battlefield. Their astute, clear, calm, and penetrating minds—their wise judgment, and masterly ability, quietly plan, arrange, and direct, what is often brilliantly accomplished by the chief of a division, or the head of an army. Had General Lee retained his post as military adviser, or whatever it was, in the spring of 1862, it is very probable he would not have been so greatly noted as he is. Indeed, we hear but little of him during that period; and yet he was skilfully planning and directing important movements. So, with the subject of our present sketch, whose valuable services as adjutant-general, both in the North and South, have been generally admitted.

With any minute particulars of General Cooper's career, the public is not yet familiar, except through those ordinary official channels which give notices of appointments and dates of changes. Consequently, we can do little more at present than put such before the reader, to show who and what he is.

General Cooper was born in the State of New York, in the year 1798, and entered the Military Academy at West Point, when only fifteen years old. At that time, the period of study

was not so long as now, and, consequently, he graduated in
1815, receiving his commission as brevet second-lieutenant of
Light Artillery, on the 11th of December, in that year. He
obtained the full rank of a lieutenancy in 1817, and when, in
1821, the army was reorganized, he was retained in the rank
he then held. Shortly afterwards, he became first-lieutenant
of the Third Artillery, and in 1824, was transferred to the
Fourth. Here he remained four years, and then became aid-
de-camp to General Macomb, serving in that capacity until
the year 1830. These times were days of peace, and we see
little recorded of note to mark the military career of any man.
In 1831, Cooper was brevetted captain "for faithful service,
ten years in one grade." Five years afterwards, he became
full captain, and in 1847, he was made brevet major of the
staff (assistant adjutant-general). The following year, he was
brevetted colonel of the staff, "for meritorious conduct," particularly in the performance of his duties in the prosecution
of the Mexican war. These duties appear to have been the
onerous ones attached to the department of the adjutant-general, and so peculiarly skilled was he in that office that, in
1852, he was appointed head of the department, with the rank
of colonel in the army.

Adjutant-general Cooper was now at the summit of that
branch of his profession, in which he had labored so many
years to the satisfaction of the army, and approval of the
United States government, as well as the general public. At
that time, Charles M. Conrad, of Louisiana, was secretary of
war, under President Fillmore's administration; but, on the
5th of March, 1853, Jefferson Davis assumed control of the
war office, and thus the present head of the Confederate States
and Adjutant-general Cooper must have continually come in
contact with each other. How far this may have influenced
his after conduct, as regards the severance of the Union, we
cannot say; but, it is stated, that his political principles were
well known to be adverse to the present policy of the administration in the North, and though faithfully performing his
duties to the last moment of Buchanan's reign in power, he
immediately resigned when President Lincoln was installed.
He sent in his resignation on the 7th of March, 1861, at the
same time with Assistant Adjutant-general Withers, and both

were accepted, to be considered as taking effect on the 1st of March. Possibly, as General Cooper is a connection (we believe brother-in-law) of Mr. Mason, other than mere political reasons may have led to this great severance of his long association with the government, and with his native North.

It is singular that about the last official order signed by Adjutant-general Cooper, should have been the following:

WAR DEPARTMENT, March 1, 1861.

By the direction of the President of the United States, it is ordered that Brigadier-general David E. Twiggs, be, and is hereby dismissed from the army of the United States, for his treachery to the flag of his country, in having surrendered on the 18th of February, 1861, on the demand of the authorities of Texas, the military posts and other property of the United States in his department, and under his charge.

J. HOLT, Secretary of War.

By order of the Secretary of War,
  S. COOPER, Adjutant-general.

General Cooper immediately went to Montgomery, where he arrived on the 15th of March, and tendered his services to President Davis. These were cheerfully accepted, and the next day he was appointed Adjutant-general of the Confederate States,—a position, to some timid minds, the least enviable of any to be found. The president, and secretary of war, the commanding general, might, each and all, determine upon open strife with the North, and have great abilities for carrying it on; but where was the material to work with? Fighting could not be done without soldiers; soldiers could not be obtained without much careful thought as to the best method of procuring the men; and men could not be turned into an army of soldiers without skilful organization. The master mind to do this, however, for the new confederacy, came forward at the very moment such was wanted. With his perfect knowledge of all the intricate machinery necessary, and his long acquaintance with the inner workings of the regular army of the United States government, General Cooper stepped in to the precise place requiring to be filled, and undoubtedly must have been hailed as one of the most valuable aids to the cause, that could have been offered. He

must, however, have possessed a strong and determined will, fearless of all consequences, to have undertaken the duties of such a post. To the South, he gave more than himself;—he gave the vast energies of a capacious mind, fully stored with the knowledge and acquirements of many years experience in the duties of one of the most arduous and complicated services relating to the army. To the North, he made himself something, perhaps more to be dreaded, through the peculiar powers he possessed, than even a general in the field, for the latter, could, possibly, be beaten back, and his forces destroyed. An adjutant-general, however, such as Cooper, might speedily reproduce the whole, and thus in a measure, nullifying whatever of success the enemy of his cause may have attained.

The proceedings of General Cooper, after being appointed to his office, have not much individuality in themselves. Occasionally his name appeared, in reference to some important matter connected with the army, but his duties rarely brought him personally forward. In the latter part of July, 1861, he had some correspondence with General Johnston, respecting the alleged hanging by the Federals of two captives taken by them. The following letters explain the matter:

ADJUTANT AND INSPECTOR GENERAL'S OFFICE,
RICHMOND, July 29, 1861.

To General J. E. JOHNSTON, Commanding Army of Potomac, Manassas, Va.

SIR—Your letter of the 24th instant, inclosing one of the 26th from General Bonham, reporting the hanging of two sentinels of the South Carolina troops, who were captured on the 17th instant, by the enemy, near Centerville, has been received and submitted to the President, who instructs me to state, that you will send a flag to the general commanding the forces in front of you, report to him the case, and require that he deliver to you, as criminals, the persons who perpetrated the offence, or avow his responsibility for the act; and, in the latter case, that you will retaliate, retaining in your possession for that purpose, of the enemy, twice the number of those of our troops that were thus ignominiously executed.

Very respectfully, your obedient servant,

S. COOPER,
Adjutant and Inspector-general.

(Official)   R. H. CHILTON, A. A. G.

GENERAL JOHNSTON TO GENERAL COOPER.

HEADQUARTERS, MANASSAS, }
August 6, 1861. }

To General COOPER, A. and I. G.:

SIR—On the 21st ultimo, in obedience to orders received through your office, I addressed to Brigadier-general McDowell, commanding the department of Alexandria, a letter, a copy of which is inclosed herewith. A reply was returned to our outposts, but being addressed like one which I had a few days before refused to receive, on account of the superscription, Colonel Stuart refused to transmit it. He ascertained, however, that the alleged hanging of our two volunteers was denied by General McDowell.

Since then two other papers, inclosed, were sent under flags of truce, the bearer not being admitted. I send them merely to show the obstinacy with which the enemy avoids the established mode of communication.

Most respectfully, your obedient servant,

(Signed)   J. E. JOHNSTON, General.

(Official)   R. H. CHILTON, A. A. G.

Colonel Stuart was informed in reply to his references of the messages, that when properly addressed, we would give any aid in our power to Colonel Cameron's friends in their search.

J. E. J.

GENERAL JOHNSTON TO GENERAL M'DOWELL.

HEADQUARTERS ARMY OF THE POTOMAC, }
MANASSAS JUNCTION, July 21, 1861. }

SIR—Information has been given to me that two soldiers ot the army of the Confederate States, whilst under picket duty, were hung near Centreville, on the night of the 17th instant.

The object of this communication is to ascertain the nature of the offence which required this ignominious punishment, and upon what evidence the decision was based.

If done by your authority, I must demand that the perpetrators of this violation of the usages of civilized warfare, be

delivered to me, for such punishment as the nature of the of
fence demands, or be punished by yourself.

I have the honor to be your obedient servant,

(Signed)   J. E. JOHNSTON,

General Commanding C. S. Forces.

(Official)   H. H. CHILTON, A. A. G.

To Brigadier-general IRWIN MCDOWELL,

Commanding Department of Alexandria.

In March, 1862, martial law was proclaimed in certain coun
ties, and General Cooper at once put it in execution undei
charge of Generals Heth and Marshall, with an efficient military police.   All distillation of spirituous liquors was positively
prohibited, and the distilleries thenceforth closed.   Even the
sale of spirituous liquors was forbidden.

About the same time it was found necessary to call in to the
army all the soldiers who were absent, whether on furlough or
from any other cause, except well-attested sickness.   His general order on the subject, was dated March 24th, 1862.

Another of his orders, just after the battle of *Fair Oaks*, or
Seven Pines, and referring to officers in battle, may be worth
recording here.   It says :

Officers of the field are permitted to wear a fatigue dress,
consisting of the regulation frock coat, without embroidery on
the collar, or a gray jacket, with the designation of rank upon
the collar.   Only caps such as are worn by the privates of
their respective commands may be worn by the officers of the
line.

Mounted officers are ordered to dismount in time of action,
whenever they can do so without interference with the proper
discharge of their duties.

Officers of all grades are reminded that unnecessary exposure in time of battle on the part of commissioned officers is not
only unsoldier-like, but productive of great injury to the army
and infinite peril to the country.   They are recommended to
follow in this particular, to a reasonable extent, the excellent
xample set them by the enemy.

By command of the Secretary of War.

S. COOPER,

Adjutant and Inspector-General.

(Official)   GEO. F. FOOTE, A. A. General.

The several orders, issued by General Cooper, have been, however, so purely military, and have reference solely to details connected with the perfect working of the Southern army, that to repeat them here would be merely introducing a series of official documents. The preceding specimens are sufficient to give an idea of the work he has had to perform. That he executes it faithfully and vigorously is well known, and the service he has rendered the Confederate States, cannot be over-rated.

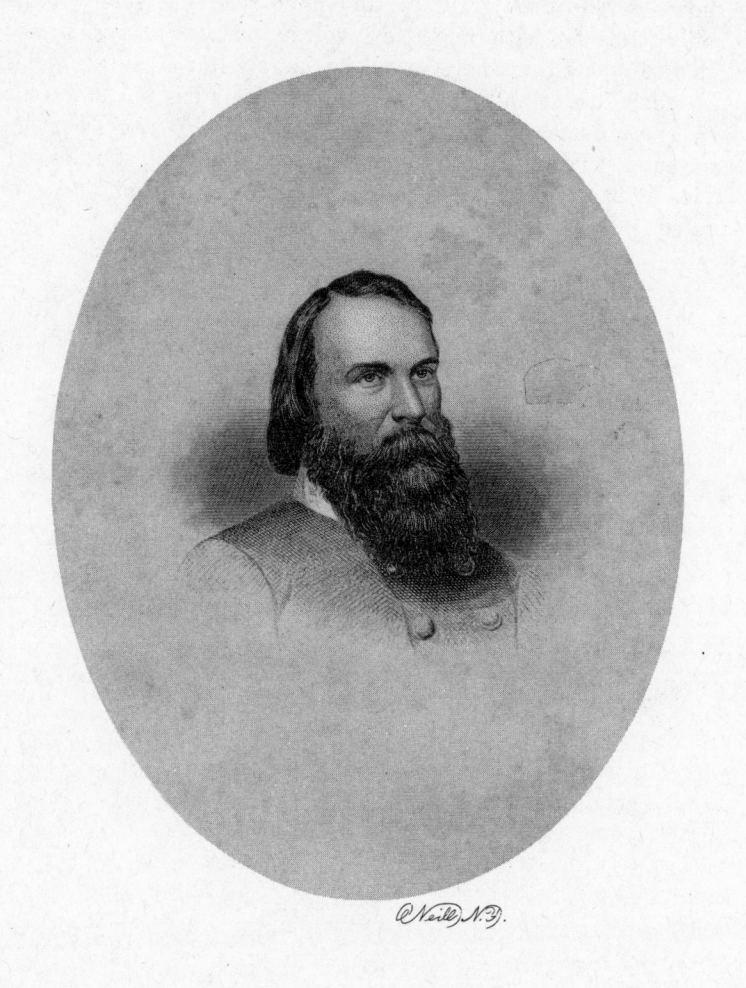

LT. GEN. LONGSTREET.

From a Photograph taken from life.

LIEUTENANT-GENERAL JAMES LONGSTREET.

A CALM, unobtrusive, self-possessed man, yet determined, and reckless of danger: such is the outer character of him whose public life we now bring forward in this sketch. Said a writer we have often quoted, "Every one deplores that Longstreet will expose himself in such a reckless manner. To-day he led a Georgian regiment in a charge against a battery, hat in hand, and in front of everybody."

Lieutenant-general Longstreet, though long a resident of Alabama, was born in South Carolina, about the year 1820, and entered the military academy, at West Point, in 1838. He graduated in 1842, and was brevetted second-lieutenant of the Fourth regiment of infantry. In March, 1845, he was transferred to the Eighth regiment, and was at the storming of Monterey, in Mexico. In a vivid account of this siege, written and published in 1847, by S. C. Reid, of Philadelphia, Longstreet is thus mentioned: "At three o'clock, on the morning of the 22d September (1846), the troops that had been detailed to storm the fort, on Independence Hill, were aroused from their slumbers. It was dark and cloudy, with a heavy, thick mist. The command consisted of three companies of the artillery battalion; three companies of the Eighth infantry, under Cap-

tain Screven, commanded by Lieutenants James Longstreet, T. Montgomery, and E. Holloway; and seven companies of the Texas Rangers. . . . As soon as the height was stormed. . . . Captain J. B. Scott's company, of the artillery battalion, and Company A, of the Eighth, under Lieutenant Longstreet, with a detachment of the Texas Rangers, were thrown forward, within musket range of the castle, to pick off such of the enemy as should give them a chance. Thirty minutes after this position was taken, their success caused the enemy to make a sortie with a large force, with a view to retake the hill. This attempt was opposed by our advanced party with great spirit, and the enemy was compelled to retire. . . The command now sustained a severe fire from the enemy's artillery, and a continued fire of musketry from the loop-holed walls, and parapets of the palace. . . . At length the critical moment arrived. . . Onward came the enemy in proud array, and most bravely were they met. One volley from the long line of bayonets which suddenly arose before them, with a deadly fire from the Texans, made them reel and stagger back aghast, while above the battle-cry was heard the hoarse command to 'Charge'! On rushed our men with shouts of triumph, driving the retreating enemy, horse and foot, who fled in confusion down the ridge, past the palace, and even to the bottom of the hill, into the streets of the city. The victory was won; the palace ours; and long, long did the cheers of the victors swell on the air, which made the valley below ring with the triumph of our arms."

It is a singular coincidence that the storming party, of which Lieutenant Longstreet was a conspicuous member, was conducted along its "dark and devious road" by Captain Sanders, and *Lieutenant George Meade*, of the topographical engineers, and a Mexican guide. Here, these two brave lieutenants—Longstreet and Meade—were fighting together, almost hand in hand—the one guiding the other, under a proud united flag, to storm a strong position:—seventeen years afterwards the two officers were battling against each other—Longstreet vainly striving to storm Meade's position, on his left, at the battle of Gettysburg!

In February, 1847, Longstreet was promoted to the rank of first-lieutenant, and from June of that year to July, 1849, he

served as adjutant of his regiment. He was brevetted captain
for "gallant and meritorious conduct" in the battles of Contreras and Cherubusco, August 20th, 1847, and major for
"gallantry" in the battle of El Molino del Rey, September
8th, 1847. In the assault of Chapultepec, September 13th,
1847, he greatly distinguished himself, and is thus spoken of
in General Scott's official report: "The following are the
officers most distinguished in those brilliant operations,— . . .
Lieutenant Longstreet, badly wounded—advancing, colors in
hand."

In December, 1852, he became a full captain; and, in July,
1858, he was made paymaster, with the rank of major. It was
in this position that he resigned his commission in the Federal
service, when the war broke out; and took sides with his native South. Then, for the first time, the public became acquainted with a name that has since maintained its *prestige* for
lofty daring and chivalrous courage throughout the war. But
not until the first battles of Bull Run was he conspicuously
brought forward. Appointed to command a brigade, he was
stationed at Blackburn's ford, when General Tyler, of the
Federal army, attempted to force a passage across, on the 18th
of July, 1861. Longstreet successfully resisted him, and compelled the Northern troops to fall back. Of his conduct on
this occasion, Beauregard, in his official report, says: "He
equalled my confident expectations, and I may fitly say, that
by his presence in the right place, at the right moment, among
his men—by the exhibition of characteristic coolness, and by
his words of encouragement to the men of his command, he in-
fused a confidence and spirit that contributed largely to the
success of our arms on that day."

During the great battle that followed, on Sunday, July 21st,
his position was still in the same place, with orders to move
"on the enemy's flank and rear at Centreville, taking due precaution against the advance of reserves from Washington."
This movement, however, was countermanded by Beauregard
and Johnston, at about half-past ten in the morning, when it
was fully ascertained what General McDowell's plans really
were. Instead of advancing on Centreville, Longstreet was
directed merely "to make a demonstration to his front, so as
to engross the enemy's reserves and forces." This was most

effectually done; during much of the day his men were exposed to an annoying, almost incessant fire of artillery, at long
range; but, by a steady, veteran-like maintenance of their
positions, they held virtually paralyzed, all day, two strong
brigades of the enemy, with their batteries (four) of rifle guns.
After the rout of the enemy on the main battle-ground, Longstreet's brigade was ordered to pursue in the direction of Centreville, but at night was directed to fall back upon Bull Run
again.

The author of "Battles of the South" says that, "on one
occasion, soon after this battle, his attention was arrested by
three horsemen galloping into camp, and saluting the colonel
of his regiment. These were none other than Evans, Longstreet, and Ewell—names now forever hallowed in the hearts
and history of our gallant army. From their style of riding
and peculiar seat in the saddle, I at first took them for dragoons, and was not mistaken. Evans was very restless, and
his horse reared and chafed, and plunged to the right and left
all the time he staid with us. . . . Longstreet is a powerfully-
built man, somewhat bald, about five feet ten inches high,
with sandy hair and whiskers—the latter allowed to grow un-
trimmed. He possesses a fine blueish gray eye, of great
depth, penetration, and calculation; seldom speaks unnecessarily, seems absorbed in thought, and very quiet in manner.
. . . . All three were dressed as citizens, with heavy black
felt hats on; and, except pistols in their holsters, were unarmed, and unattended."

After the battle of Bull Run, Longstreet was made a Major-
general under General Johnston, and remained with the army
in its quarters and skirmishing, until, in March, 1862, Manassas was evacuated.

At length, the army was moved to the Peninsula, and General Johnston, with D. H. Hill and Longstreet, joined their
forces to those of Magruder, at Yorktown. When this place
was evacuated by the Confederates, Longstreet was intrusted
with defending the rear of the army, and made every disposition to entice the foe into open ground. On the 5th of May,
a stand was made at Williamsburg, and General Longstreet
so arranged his forces, that the enemy was met a little on the
east side of the city. Generals Heintzelman, Hooker, and

Kearney, had approached by roads through thick woods, and these roads were made worse by a heavy rain, which commenced on Sunday afternoon, the 4th, and continued during the next day. It was a sore trial to men and officers to engage in battle on such a day. But it was to be; and, at early morn, the attack began. The Confederates were first located in the forest, beyond which was a space about a mile wide, partly so by nature, and partly cleared by the felling of trees, these being left prostrate on the ground, in order to obstruct the enemy's advance. On the opposite side of this cleared space was Fort Magruder, flanked by redoubts, and defended in front by rifle-pits. The day, as we have said, was stormy in the extreme, but the fighting was severe and effectual on both sides. Longstreet, according to his plan, allowed his advance to fall back so that the enemy should be enticed from the covering of the woods. This device proved successful, and boldly, and in beautiful order they came forward, immediately attacking the earthworks in front, but were instantly met by a portion of Longstreet's men, who rose up in the works, and poured vollies into their faces, compelling them to fall back to the woods, where, however, grapeshot mowed them rapidly down. Still they were not disheartened. Again and again did brigade after brigade of the Federals dash across the open space and assault the works. At length, about noon, Longstreet made a feint of retreating, which brought forth the enemy more boldly from the woods. "Quick as thought, they were attacked with great fury. Longstreet's artillery seemed to have acquired new life. Galloping into the open space, they commenced a fearful duel at short range." The Federals were again driven back, and for a time it seemed as though victory had been won by the Confederates. But now the gallant Kearney's brigade appeared in front, and Heintzelman, with characteristic energy, dashed up and down the field, urging the men to advance. Hooker also bravely holding his ground; and Hancock, on seeing his troops fall back, rode up and down the line, exclaiming, "Gentlemen, charge!" And charge, anew, they did. Rushing onward with an impetuosity that nothing could check, Longstreet's forces were compelled once more to give way, only, however, to rally again and resist the enemy, till night should put an end to the fearful struggle.

General McClellan had arrived with reinforcements, and the Federals that night bivouacked on the miry field, while the Confederates retired within their works. General Johnston, in chief command, being more on the advance towards Rich-mond.

It may be interesting to some to know that in this battle, sharing all the dangers, and even the discomforts of such a bivouac on the field, were the Prince de Joinville, the Count de Paris, and Duc de Chartres, volunteer aids to General McClellan.

At two next morning, General Longstreet commenced his retreat, all his forces marching away quite undisturbed. He had to hurry on, that he might overtake the main body of the army under Johnston, and came up with the rearguard of Hood's Texans, at West Point. A few days afterwards, they were all encamped around Richmond.

In the battles that followed, for the defence of Richmond, and which have been already described, General Longstreet bore an important part. Prior to the last series of seven days' successive engagements, on and about the Chickahominy, he issued a proclamation to his soldiers, couched in the language of a man feeling most deeply in regard to the invasion of Northern troops. One portion of it only, need we transcribe, wherein he says:

" Let such thoughts nerve you up to the most dreadful shock of battle, for were it certain death, death would be better than the fate that defeat would entail upon us all. But remember, though the fiery noise of the battle is indeed most terrifying, and seems to threaten universal ruin, it is not so destructive as it seems, and few soldiers after all are slain. This the commanding general desires particularly to impress upon the fresh and unexperienced troops who now constitute a part of this command. Let officers and men, even under the most formidable fire, preserve a quiet demeanor and self-possessed temper. Keep cool, obey orders, and aim low. Remember, while you are doing this, and driving the enemy before you, your comrades may be relied on to support you on either side, and are in turn relying upon you. Stand well to your duty, and when these clouds break away, as they surely will, the bright

sunlight of peace falling upon our free, virtuous, and happy land, will be a sufficient reward for the sacrifices which we are now called upon to make.

"JAMES LONGSTREET,
Major-general commanding."

Sentiments like these pervaded the minds of all the Con federate leaders and officers, and, generally, those of the men. With such feelings they went into battle, and with such determination to conquer, if possible, they bore every hardship, privation, and loss. General Longstreet, like many others, had given up much for the cause of his native South, and never once did he seem to despair of ultimate success. Always ready to do battle anywhere when duty called, he was much esteemed by General Lee, and looked upon as one of the hardest fighters in the war. His *soubriquet* of the "*War-horse*," was given him, we believe, on the occasion of the battles around Richmond.

The movements that took place after the events just referred to, have already been recorded, until General Longstreet, on the 24th of August, was dispatched by General Lee from Warrenton to reinforce Jackson, then in the rear of Pope's army, near the old battlefield of Bull Run. Longstreet proceeded by way of Thoroughfare gap, a pass in the mountains fifteen miles west of Centreville. This pass, which is a wild and romantic gorge, with frowning fir-clad battlements on either side—its narrow and winding road, and its rugged walls rising rock above rock to the summit, right and left—was defended by a force of the enemy under General Ricketts, who had judiciously posted some powerful batteries to take the eastern debouchement with shell and canister.

On Longstreet approaching the gap no enemy was at first visible, but, as the 7th and 8th Georgia were pushing forward in advance, the Federals suddenly opened several field-pieces, and commenced to sweep the road. "Oh! they are there, are they?" said Longstreet, laughing. "Well, we'll soon dislodge them, boys,' and immediately ordered up several pieces of artillery, which, galloping forward, commenced upon the assailing batteries so furiously, and with such accuracy, as to shelter the advancing infantry, and clear the summit of the road.

This was quickly accomplished, but the artillery were not con-
tent—they rushed up the rise and began to shell the foe, who
hastily retreated into open ground beyond. Their infantry,
then, finding themselves unsupported, fell back in disorder.

Longstreet continued his march, and next day his persevering and exhausted soldiers formed a junction with Jackson's
forces on their right wing. His arrival was hailed with loud
shouts of joy, and caused Jackson to draw a long breath, and
utter a sigh of great relief.

One incident connected with this march of Longstreet to
reinforce Jackson, must be mentioned. At that time a great
number of spies were about, and caused a considerable excitement in the different camps. Now it happened that while
Longstreet's advance was on its way, several brigades were observed to halt, thereby stopping all further progress of the
corps. Very angry at this, Longstreet trotted to the front,
and was informed that a courier had brought orders from
General Lee to that effect. "From General Lee ?" said he,
his eyes glowing with rage. "Where *is* that courier ?" he
asked. "There he goes now, General, galloping down the
road," was the reply. "Keep your eyes on him, overtake
him, and bring him here," he immediately responded. This
was soon accomplished. "By whose orders did you halt my
brigade ?" asked the brigadier in command of the advance.
The reply of the captured courier was, "As I have already
told you—by General Lee's! I have orders for Longstreet,
and must be off to the rear !" General Longstreet, himself,
then stepped forward, to the horror of the spy—for spy he was
—and said, "Here is Longstreet, where are your orders !"
The poor wretch was caught ! He turned red and pale, his lip
quivered—he was self-condemned. "Give this man ten
minutes, and hang him ! Let the columns push forward immediately !" In fifteen minutes the spy was lifeless, hanging
from a tree by the road-side; but before death he confessed
that although a Virginian, and a Confederate soldier, he had
been in communication with the enemy over ten months, and
was then acting for General Pope.

Some fighting of a severe character appears to have taken
place between Longstreet's forces, as he was going into position, about sunset on the 29th, and King's division of Mc

Dowell's corps, in which the former had been obliged to fall back.

Next morning, August 30th, the second battle of Bull Run began. " Part of Longstreet's corps was on the move early in the morning, and seemed to be cautiously taking up positions nearer the enemy's left. Presently the general advance was made, and it was a beautiful sight, as far as the eye could range, to see two parallel lines of glittering bayonets flashing in the sun. Then a gleam of sunlight told that the rifles had been brought to the ' ready,' and a moment after, a long flash could be observed, light curls of smoke arose, and the rattling echo of volleys of fire was carried on the wind. . . . . The cannonading was terrific, along the whole front, but, on the right the enemy's and Longstreet's artillery literally shook the earth. . . . Fiery Longstreet, with his impatient and gallant corps, rapidly pushed forward the right of the army, while shot and shell ploughed the ground in all directions around him."

The battle was once more won by the Confederates on the old ground of Bull Run, and the conspicuous part Longstreet played therein was honorably mentioned in General Lee's official report.

We have.not space to follow, in detail, the next movements that took place in the Confederate army wherein Longstreet figured. Enough to say that a rapid march was made into Maryland—Harper's Ferry taken with a large booty and many prisoners—and the battles of South Mountain and Antietam ensued. Wherever, in the exigency of the moment, and by order of General Lee, he was called, here, there, and everywhere amidst the fray was Longstreet to be found, moving with remarkable celerity, and always with a perfect *sang froid.* At Antietam, Longstreet commanded the Confederate right, and was thus opposed to Burnside who could not advance against him beyond the bridge he had so bravely gained. Night ended the gory contest, and the weary troops rested on another battlefield where victory was again claimed by both parties. The following day, fighting was not renewed; and, on the next, September 18th, at night, Longstreet accompanied the Confederate army back to Virginia, camping in the valley of Shenandoah, about Winchester and vicinity.

Longstreet's corps was clustered at a point ready to take position promptly whenever required. Daily drill was incessant and severe, discipline was at its highest pitch, and reviews were not unfrequent among the various brigades an divisions. At no period of the war were the soldiers more confident and gay. Extensive appropriations and purchases during their brief sojourn in Maryland and Pennsylvania had replenished their stores, and the government of the South had been so active in the clothing department that the army was quite comfortable, and many smiled to think how former friends would be agreeably disappointed in seeing them so transformed.

Thus passed away the months of September and October, without any active movement, the army taking its rest. Early in November, Longstreet's corps was rapidly marched to Fredericksburg, arriving there before any large body of the enemy had appeared—it being known that Burnside had relieved McClellan, and was intent upon the Lower Rappahannock. Then followed, in December, the great battle of Fredericksburg—Longstreet's position being on the left of the Confederate army, and having, under him, Ransom, McLaws, Picket, and Anderson. Cobb was posted on the rear right of Longstreet, and Hood, A. P. Hill, Early and others continued the line towards Jackson's corps on the right. Stuart's cavalry held the flanks, and D. H. Hill was in reserve. In this battle, General Longstreet was frequently with General Lee, occupying a post on the hill whence the enemy's movements could be seen. We know the result. Burnside had to retire after fearful slaughter; and once more the Confederate army, for a few months, rested in peace.

In February, 1863, General Longstreet, with two divisions of his corps, was detached for service, south of the James river. General Roger A. Pryor had, on the 30th of January, fought a battle at a place called the *Deserted House*, eight miles from Suffolk, Southeast Virginia—General Michael Corcoran, of the Federal army, being opposed to him. Victory was, as usual, claimed on both sides; but preparations were immediately made by the enemy to operate in that quarter more strongly. General Peck, under the vigorous control of Major-General Dix—then in command at Fortress Monroe—

personally came upon the field; whereupon Longstreet was sent to oppose him, and take the chief direction of affairs in that quarter. At this time he was made Lieutenant-general. He passed through Richmond with some 15,000 troops, about February 22d, and took up his headquarters at Petersburg, having for his military district South Virginia, and all between him and General Lee. In April he invested Suffolk, and stopped the navigation of the Nansemond river so as to prevent the Federals communicating with Norfolk. On the 14th he was within two miles of Suffolk, and firing commenced that evening. The next day, General Peck's right was attacked, but Longstreet's advance was gallantly met by General Foster's light troops. The fighting continued on the following days, until, on Sunday night, April 19th, a battery of five pieces, and some prisoners, were captured from the Confederates. On Monday the fighting was renewed, and then it relaxed for a few days; afterwards, on the 1st of May, commencing again, when the enemy attacked the rifle-pits formed along the banks of the river. This led to a sharp engagement during the day, the Federals being compelled to retire within their defences. But, at this time, the advance of General Hooker on Chancellorsville, called for a concentration of all the forces under Lee, and an order—intercepted, however, by the enemy—was sent to Longstreet, as also one to D. H. Hill, in North Carolina, to join the main army in North Virginia without delay. Accordingly, on the 4th of May, the siege of Suffolk was abandoned, and Longstreet, leaving a small force behind to hold the fortifications on the Blackwater, and keep the enemy in check, proceeded to join General Lee. This was done rapidly; and a short time afterwards, June 3d, the great movement for an invasion of Maryland began. On the 8th, General Longstreet's forces, with those of Ewell, arrived at Culpepper; the Confederate army, under Lee, having, at this time, been reorganized, and made to consist of three large corps, commanded by Lieutenant-generals Longstreet, Ewell, and A. P. Hill. Ewell was sent on from Culpepper, in advance, by the Shenandoah Valley, and suddenly came upon the Northern General Milroy, at Winchester, driving him out of that place and Martinsburg with considerable loss. Longstreet followed fast in Ewell's rear, to prevent any movement of the enemy upon it, and Hill

came swift upon Longstreet.   On the 26th of June, Longstreet accompanying General Lee, crossed the Potomac at Williams-port, and proceeded on to Hagerstown.   Thence, next day, he went to Chambersburg; and, on the 1st of July, the famous battle of Gettysburg began.   For an account of this battle we must refer to our sketch of General Lee, and will merely ob-serve that, on the 1st day, Longstreet did not reach the field until 4.30 P. M., too late to join in the fight.   He therefore re-turned to his headquarters, at *Cashtown*, for the night.   Speak-ing of him at this time, Colonel Fremantle says: "At supper that evening, he expressed himself to the effect that he con-sidered the enemy's position very formidable, and he thought they would intrench themselves very strongly during the night. Neither Longstreet nor Lee intended the fight to come off that day. . . Next morning, at seven o'clock, I rode over part of the ground with him, and saw him disposing of McLaws' di-vision for to-day's fight. . . . Ewell had the Confederate left, A. P. Hill the centre, and Longstreet was on the right. . . At 4.45 P. M. (July 2d), Longstreet suddenly commenced a heavy cannonading on the right; Ewell took it up on the left; and thus the battle of the second day was begun.   At dark it ceased, and, for that night, Longstreet bivouacked on the field. Next morning, at an early hour, he was up, and reconnoiter-ing.   By noon all his dispositions were made; his troops for attack were deployed into line, and lying down in the woods; and his batteries were ready to open.   He then dismounted from his horse, and went to rest for a short time."   Probably for an hour he thus slept, for at 2 P. M. he was at his post, while the roar of battle sounded in his ear, and shells carried destruction around him.   Seated on the top of a fence, at the edge of the wood, and looking perfectly calm, he was accosted by Colonel Fremantle, who said to him, in reference to the grand yet fearful scene before them, "I wouldn't have missed this for anything!"   Longstreet replied, laughing, "The devil you wouldn't!   I would like to have missed it very much; we've attacked and been repulsed: look there!"   The Con-federates were slowly and sulkily returning towards his posi-tion in small broken parties, under a heavy fire of artillery. "I could now," says Fremantle, "thoroughly appreciate the term bull-dog, which I had heard applied to him by his

soldiers. Difficulties seemed to make no other impression upon him than to make him a little more savage." He immediately set about making the best arrangements in his power to resist the Federal advance, by pushing forward some artillery, rallying stragglers, etc. One of his generals came up to him, and reported that he was unable to bring his men up again. Longstreet turned upon him and replied, "Very well, never mind, then, General; just let them remain where they are; the enemy's going to advance, and will spare you the trouble." Many of his wounded soldiers hearing a report that he was killed, anxiously inquired after him, and expressed very great pleasure on learning the safety of their chief.

"On the next day," says Colonel Fremantle, "a flag of truce came over from the enemy, and its bearer announced, among other things, 'that General Longstreet was wounded, and a prisoner, but would be taken care of.' General Longstreet sent word back that he was extremely grateful, but, being neither wounded nor a prisoner, he was quite able to take care of himself." The same writer observes: "The iron endurance of General Longstreet is most extraordinary; he seems to require neither food nor sleep. Most of his staff now fall fast asleep directly they get off their horses, they are so exhausted from the last three days' work."

Longstreet, in talking of the battle, said : "The mistake they had made was in not concentrating the army more, and making the attack on the 3d with 30,000 men instead of 15,000." That night, amid torrents of rain, the Confederate army retreated to the Potomac, and thence into the Shenandoah Valley again.

On the way to the Potomac, Longstreet's bivouac for the night was near a large tavern, and he had sent to order some supper there for himself and staff; but when he went in to devour it, General McLaws and his officers were found rapidly finishing the whole, apparently in ignorance who it was for, and too hungry to inquire. More, however, was soon procured, and the General sat down to a good meal. During supper, some women of the house came rushing in, exclaiming, "Oh, good heavens, they're killing our fat hogs. Which is the General? Which is the great officer? Our milch cows are now going." Longstreet at once replied to them, shaking his

head in a melancholy manner, "Yes, madam, it's very sad—very sad, and this sort of thing has been going on in Virginia more than two years—very sad!"

That night he, with his officers and men, slept on the open ground beneath a heavy, pouring rain, yet so wearied as to be almost unconscious of their uncomfortable position.

Next day there was a laughable spectacle in the afternoon. A negro dressed in the full uniform of a Northern soldier, with a rifle at full cock, was seen leading along a barefooted white man, with whom he had evidently changed clothes. General Longstreet stopped the pair, and asked the black man what it meant. He replied, "The two soldiers in charge of this here Yank have got drunk, so for fear he should escape I have took care of him, and brought him through that little town."

For the next two months nothing, except a splendid review of the whole army, occurred, of importance, connected with General Longstreet; but, in the beginning of September, it was found necessary to send reinforcements to Bragg's army in Tennessee and North Georgia, and he was detached from Lee to proceed thither. General Burnside had been appointed by the North in command of East Tennessee, and Cumberland Gap was surrendered to him on the 9th of September, by a Confederate force stationed there. On the same day, Chattanooga was occupied by Rosecrans, and Bragg's army fell back to Chickamauga. Thus it was important that Longstreet should bring his reinforcements into the field as speedily as possible, for the Confederates in that quarter were pressed sorely, and unanimity did not seem to pervade all their councils. Accordingly he pushed forward, by the way of Richmond and through Georgia, his advance arriving at the scene of operations just prior to the battle of the 19th of September.

The part Longstreet bore in this battle, which ended in the defeat of the Federals, after an heroic resistance under the gallant Thomas, is known to have contributed much to the fortunes of the day, and he strongly urged that advantage should be immediately taken by a forward movement of the whole army. But General Bragg deemed it advisable not to do so, much to the mortification of all his officers and troops.

The following particulars derived from the *Richmond Enquirer* of October 31st, will serve better to explain what occurred :

"When Longstreet took command of the left wing of the army on Sunday morning, the 20th, he found it helter skelter, with gaps a mile long between the brigades, and everything in confusion generally. The position chosen for the fight by General Bragg was most unfavorable in case of a repulse, and altogether in favor of the enemy. The order was for the right to begin the attack at dawn, but it was eleven o'clock before it opened, and then it rolled along until the left took it up. In a very short time, to use General Bragg's own words, "the right was disastrously repulsed, and had no fight in it," and Longstreet had to meet the enemy entirely alone. After some hours of hard fighting he drove him, in the wildest confusion, from every position, took from thirty to forty pieces of artillery, thousands of prisoners, and converted their army into a terrified, flying mob. It was then that he saw that by a forward movement of the whole army Rosecrans' whole force could be captured in twenty hours, and that no obstacle was between us and the Ohio, and perhaps peace. He therefore sent word to Wheeler, who was on his left, to dash forward between Chattanooga and the enemy, and cut him to pieces; but just as Wheeler was about to execute this movement he received an order from General Bragg directing him to pick up arms and stragglers. Longstreet had not heard from Bragg but once during the day, and then it was to say that he was beaten on the right. He now sent to beg him to advance, but the general-in-chief declined doing so."

On the 19th of October, General Grant arrived at Chattanooga and relieved General Rosecrans. The Confederates, at this time, occupied the south side of the Tennessee river, above Chattanooga to near Bridgeport below, and taking in the valley, Missionary ridge, and Lookout mountain. General Grant quickly determined to drive them from these positions, by uniting his forces, and, on the 26th, commenced operations by a series of excellent movements under Hooker, with the personal superintendence of General "Baldy" Smith, of the Engineer corps.

During Monday night the enemy crossed the Tennessee in

rear of Chattanooga, passed over the narrow peak known as
the Moccasin, again crossed the river, and intrenched themselves on the heights which align its margin. The movement
was designed to pave the way for the advance of a column
from Bridgeport, up the valley towards and, if necessary, into
Chattanooga. The latter must have commenced nearly simul
taneously with the one first mentioned, for on the night of
Tuesday our commanders learned of its approach in this
direction.

During Wednesday morning, the head of the column was
espied in the distance from Lookout Peak, and by dusk it had
effected a junction with the forces in the neighborhood of
Brown's Ferry. Subsequent developments showed that the
Eleventh and Twelfth corps of Meade's army—the former
under command of Howard, and the latter under command of
Slocum, and the whole under Joe Hooker—had taken this
method of reaching the Union army of Tennessee.

"On Lookout peak," says a writer, vividly describing the
affair, "gazing down upon the singular spectacle—a *coup
d'œil*, which embraced, in curious contrasts, the beauties of
nature and the achievments of art, the blessings of peace and
the horrors of war—were Generals Bragg, Longstreet, and
others, to whom this bold venture of the enemy opened at once
new vistas of thought and action. Infantry, artillery, and
cavalry, all glided silently by, like a procession of fantoccini in
a panorama, until among all the sundown's sumptuous pictures, which glowed around, there was not one like that of the
great, fresh, bustling camp, suddenly grown into view, with
its thousand twinkling lights, its groups of men and animals,
and its lines of white-topped wagons now strung, like a neck-
lace of pearls, around the bosom of the hills. The Federals
had succeeded in effecting a junction with their army of
Chattanooga."

An attempt on the part of the Confederates, to check this
movement, it is said, would have been impracticable, without
bringing on a general engagement, since an interposition of
their forces across the valley would have necessitated a fight on
both front and rear, and on both sides the enemy had the advantage of flanks protected. The first corps having passed,
and a portion of it gone into camp, there was still visible be-

low a considerable number of wagons, guarded, apparently, by an escort of from fifteen hundred to two thousand men. Hoping to capture these, General Longstreet determined, during the night, to make an attack, and accordingly ordered General Jenkins, commanding Hood's division, to take position for the purpose.

"The enemy occupied a line of hills parallel with the river in the neighborhood of Brown's Ferry; Law and Robertson the same line of hills, but nearer to Lookout Mountain, to prevent an attack on Bratton's rear, and Benning a position on the left of the two last named, being intended as a support to Colonel Bratton. These three brigades, as it were, covered the bridges across Lookout creek, over which they had marched, and threatened the line of the enemy at Brown's Ferry. Colonel Bratton, with Jenkins' brigade, now moved over to the left a mile or more up the valley, to attack the supposed rear-guard, and capture the wagon-train.

"Skirmishers being thrown out, the Federal pickets were soon encountered. These falling back, the enemy were found in line of battle, and, instead of being surprised, received our troops with a heavy volley. It was not long before it was discovered, that instead of a paltry body of men, who would yield as soon as discovered, we were fighting a whole division, belonging to the Twelfth corps, General Slocum, who had closely followed in the rear of the preceding column, and encamped after night. Nothing was to be done but to fight it boldly out, and make up in pluck and obstinacy what was lacking in numbers. On our part we had but six regiments—the First, Colonel Kilpatrick; Second Rifles, Colonel Thompson; Fifth, Colonel Coward; Sixth, Colonel Bratton; Palmetto Sharpshooters, Colonel Walker, and Hamptom Legion, Colonel Gary. Steadily as on a parade, these filed into position, and in a few moments artillery and musketry were playing with terrible effect through our ranks.

"The enemy in the neighborhood of Brown's Ferry discovering a battle in progress, had already thrown forward two columns, one of which advanced to attack the line occupied by Generals Law and Robertson, while the other moved steadily past that front, and aimed to penetrate the long interval between Bratton and Benning; in other words, to cut Jenkins

brigade off from the bridges over Lookout creek. The first column met with little success, being checked by the sharp fire of the Alabamians and Texans; but the second promised other results. The situation was a critical one; but General Jenkins, quickly divining the object of the movement, met the issue by ordering Bratton to return to the bridges, and the remainder of the division to hold its position at every hazard, until the safety of the former was assured. Lieutenant-colonel Logan, of the Hampton Legion, with fourteen companies whom he had relieved from picket, having reached the field, was ordered to the left of Benning, where, occupying a hill, he extended our line, and naturally contributed to the check of the enemy.

"Although we had not achieved a victory, we had, judging by results, been blessed with a providential success. The Federals encountered by Jenkins' brigade, were undoubtedly on the eve of a disastrous defeat, as is shown by the facts already set forth, namely, the breaking of the lines, and falling back in front, and on the right and left flanks, until wagon-trains and prisoners were captured in the rear. On the other hand, the pressure of the Yankee columns from Brown's Ferry, where it was known there were, at least, two corps, not distant more than a mile and a half, so threatened the integrity of our position, that it eventually became critical in the extreme. Probably from seven to ten thousand troops enveloped the line designed to protect Bratton from an attack upon his rear, and in a few moments they would have intersected the only road by which he could return.

"Being unable to counteract a movement on so grand a scale, with the small force at his command, General Jenkins did the next best thing, which was to recall Colonel Bratton, and to compel him, at the moment of success, to abandon all the fruits of his struggle, which had been so gloriously wrested from the enemy. Instead of censure, therefore, praise belongs to every officer and man concerned in the expedition. On the part of General Longstreet, the design was just like himself— bold, daring, dashing; and had it not been for the circumstances mentioned, it would have resulted in complete success."

In the beginning of November, Longstreet was dispatched

by Bragg up the valley towards Knoxville, where Burnside
was operating. Longstreet, however, was very ill provided
for his troops, and had to subsist them as best he could. "At
Lenoir station, he began by capturing a train of eighty-five
wagons, many of them loaded with valuable medical stores.
At Bean station, he captured thirty wagons, a quantity of
forage, and some horses; and in the Clinch valley forty other
wagons, laden with sugar and coffee." Several guns and a
number of prisoners were also captured; and at Loudon, he
had encountered General Burnside, compelling him to fall
back to Knoxville, which Longstreet immediately besieged.
This was on the 17th and 18th of November; and a constant
fire was thenceforth maintained, until the evening of the 28th,
when it was determined to make an assault upon one of the
forts commanding the approaches to the town. This fort was
on a hill near the Kingston road, and was called Fort Sanders.
It was a very strong work, and in front of it were felled trees,
with the tops turning in all directions, and making an almost
impassable mass of brush and timber. A space around the
fort was cleared, and the ditch in front was about ten feet
deep, with the parapet nearly twenty feet high.

At daylight of November 29, the assaulting column moved
up the slope, and was met by a heavy artillery fire, which
fearfully mowed down the advancing soldiers. Still onward
they pushed, struggling through the network of fallen timber
and other devices laid down to impede them. But, the intricate passage by which they had to mount, was too difficult for
them easily to master. The foremost parties stumbled and
fell over each other in confusion, at the same time the enemy's
fire poured fiercer and fiercer on their heads. The embrasures
of the fort, and the whole line of the parapet blazed forth at
once. Nevertheless, this did not effectually stop the advance.
Pushing on over every obstacle, they soon reached within
pistol-shot of the fort; then, suddenly, the enemy's guns
launched forth from every quarter, and the Confederate line
was shattered. Some, however, managed to spring into the
ditch, and clamber up the glacis, planting their flag almost
side by side with the Federal colors. The Confederate officers
boldly kept the lead, in front, to the very fort itself, but as
each head appeared above the parapet, a spatter of blood and

brains marked where the heroic assailants had met their doom. A Confederate captain succeeded in reaching one of the embrasures, and, "pushing his body through till he actually faced the very muzzle of the cannon, demanded the surrender of the garrison. The answer to him was the discharge of the piece, when, rent limb from limb, his mangled corse, or what was left of it, was hurled outward into the air." The brave men, thus at the very walls, seeing themselves now alone, surrendered and were hauled into the fort; but not until the trench was filled with the dead and dying. The assault, therefore, had failed, and the Confederates retired.

At this time, Burnside's forces within Knoxville were suffering much from short rations, and provisions were so scarce that only half allowance of bread could be issued. What the result might have been we cannot say; but General Sherman, who had been advancing from Chattanooga to Burnside's relief, arrived on the night of December 3d, and thus compelled Longstreet to raise the siege. He retreated at once towards Rutledge, up the valley, pursued next day by Burnside's (until relieved by Foster) and Sherman's forces combined. Longstreet, however, still fell back without battle, until he had reached Bear station, on the Cumberland Gap road, where, being hard pressed, he turned and attacked the enemy's advance, driving him back to Russellville. This was on December 13th, and next day, Longstreet firmly established himself for awhile, with his headquarters at Rodgersville, where he could carry on such operations, on either side, as circumstances might require. He had hoped to find his railroad communications with Virginia open, but, about this time, General Averill, of the Federal army, cut them off by destroying the track at Salem, Southwest Virginia. This compelled Longstreet to fall back upon his own resources; and, by the admirable arrangements he made, he succeeded in making his army self-subsisting in a tract of country where it was thought impossible for him to remain without external aid.

At the end of December, 1863, he was around Rutledge and Morristown, but unable to follow up advantages, in consequence of the large number of barefooted men in his command, at a time, too, when the weather was bitterly cold, and the mountains covered with snow. This, however, was reme-

died soon afterwards by a supply of shoes and blankets sent to his army in the early part January, while he was in winter-quarters at Morristown; his cavalry, meanwhile, daily skirmishing with the enemy. Still, for both armies, the rigors of the season, in that mountain region, must have been very severe; and, we can hardly conceive what the soldiers must have endured.

At this time, the following interesting correspondence passed between General Longstreet and Foster. We insert it, as indicative of the character of him whose life we briefly sketch:

LETTER FROM GENERAL LONGSTREET TO GENERAL FOSTER.

HEADQUARTERS, CONFEDERATE FORCES,
EAST TENNESSEE, Jan. 3, 1864.

To THE COMMANDING GENERAL, UNITED STATES FORCES, EAST TENNESSEE

SIR—I find the proclamation of President Lincoln, of the 8th of December last, in circulation in handbills among our soldiers. The immediate object of this circulation seems to be to induce our soldiers to quit our ranks and take the oath of allegiance to the United States government. I presume, however, that the great object and end in view is to hasten the day of peace. I respectfully suggest, for your consideration, the propriety of communicating any views that your government may have upon this subject through me, rather than by handbills circulated amongst our soldiers.

The few men who may desert under the promise held out in the proclamation, cannot be men of character or standing. If they desert their cause, they disgrace themselves in the eyes of God and of man. They can do your cause no good, nor can they injure ours.

As a great nation, you can accept none but an honorable peace. As a noble people, you could have us accept nothing less.

I submit, therefore, whether the mode that I suggest would not be more likely to lead to an honorable end than such a circulation of a partial promise of pardon.

I am, sir, very respectfully, your most obedient servant,

J. LONGSTREET,
Lieutenant-general commanding.

GENERAL FOSTER'S REPLY.

HEADQUARTERS, DEPARTMENT OF THE OHIO,
KNOXVILLE, EAST TENN., Jan. 7, 1864.

LIEUTENANT-GENERAL COMMANDING CONFEDERATE FORCES IN EAST TENN.

SIR—I have the honor to acknowledge the receipt of your letter, dated January 3, 1864.

You are correct in the supposition that the great object in view in the circulation of the President's proclamation is to induce those now in rebellion against the government to lay aside their arms and return to their allegiance as citizens of the United States, thus securing the reunion of States now arrayed in hostility against one another, and the restoration of peace.

The immediate effect of the circulation may be to cause many men to leave your ranks to return home, or come within our lines, and, in view of this latter course, it has been thought proper to issue an order announcing the favorable terms on which deserters will be received.

I accept, however, your suggestion that it would have been more courteous to have sent these documents to you for circulation, and I embrace, with pleasure, the opportunity thus afforded to enclose you twenty (20) copies of each of these documents, and rely upon your generosity and desire for peace to give publicity to the same among your officers and men.

I have the honor to be, General, very respectfully, your obedient servant,

J. G. FOSTER,
Major-general Commanding.

HEADQUARTERS, DEPARTMENT EAST TENNESSEE,
Jan. 11, 1864.

SIR—I have the honor to acknowledge the receipt of your letter of the 7th of January, with its inclosures, etc.

The disingenuous manner in which you have misconstrued my letter of the 3d, has disappointed me. The suggestion you claim to have adopted, was in words, as follows:

"I presume, however, that the great object and end in view was to hasten the day of peace. I respectfully suggest, for your consideration, the propriety of communicating any views

that your government may have on this subject through me, rather than by hand-bills circulated among our soldiers."

This sentence repudiates, in its own terms, the construction which you have forced upon it. Let me remind you, too, that the spirit and tone of my letter were to meet honorable sentiments.

The absolute want of pretext for your construction of the letter, induces me to admonish you against trifling over the events of this great war. You cannot pretend to have answered my letter in the spirit of frankness due to a soldier, and yet it is hard to believe that an officer commanding an army of veteran soldiers, on whose shoulders rest, in no small part, the destiny of empires, could so far forget the height of this great argument at arms, and so betray the dignity of his high station, as to fall into a contest of jests and jibes.

I have read your order announcing the favorable terms on which deserters will be received. Step by step you have gone on in violation of the laws of honorable warfare. Our farms have been destroyed, our women and children have been robbed, and our houses have been pillaged and burnt. You have laid your plans and worked diligently to produce whole-sale murder by servile insurrection. And now, the most ignoble of all, you propose to degrade the human race by inducing soldiers to dishonor and forswear themselves.

Soldiers who have met your own on so many honorable fields, who have breasted the storm of battle in defence of their honor, their families, and their homes, for three long years, have a right to expect more of honor, even in their adversaries.

I beg leave to return the copies of the proclamation, and your order.

I have the honor to renew to you the assurance of great respect, your obedient servant,

J. LONGSTREET,
Lieutenant-general Commanding.

Major-general J. G. FOSTER, Commanding Department Ohio.

Towards the end of January, 1864, Longstreet received large reinforcements, and early in February the lines of communication with Virginia were repaired. In March, sundry movements indicated a falling back up the valley, but, in real-

ity, these were only to cover the real object, which was to unite again with General Lee, in Virginia. This was done by April; and once more the hardy soldiers, under Longstreet, were on the old ground about Gordonsville. Here they rested a while, until, on the 4th of May, they were ordered forward to the battlefield of the Wilderness.

We have given particulars of these events in our sketch of Lee, and need only refer to Longstseet's share in them.

On the 3d of May he was in position, thirteen miles southwest of the Rapidan. On the 4th he took up marching orders; and on the night of the 5th, halted within twelve miles of the field of battle of that day. At midnight he was informed of the danger of Hill's corps, and immediately broke up his bivouac, commencing his march about two o'clock on the morning of the 6th. Directly his troops arrived on the battlefield, General Longstreet rushed forward, with his staff, to head the advance. Their faces glowing, the horses prancing, the cavalcade surrounding the Lieutenant-general had, however, not passed more than a hundred yards in advance of the column, when their mood was sobered into profound regret. One of the brigades of the flanking force, heated with the work of destruction that they had executed so splendidly, mistook the glad group of horsemen that came prancing along the plank-road, for a party of the flying foe. It poured into them, at short range, a deadly fire! General Jenkins fell instantly from his horse, with a bullet in his brain. Longstreet received a ball that entered his throat, and passed out through his right shoulder. Bleeding like an ox, he was helped from his horse, so prostrated, that fears were entertained of his immediate death. Major Walton, a gallant Mississippian, on his staff, threw open his vest and shirt-collar, and found great relief in discovering that he was mistaken in supposing that the. ball had cut the carotid artery.

Placed on a litter, the wounded general was removed from the field; but, feeble though he was, from the loss of blood, he did not fail to lift his hat, from time to time, as he passed down the column, in acknowledgment of its cheers of applause and sympathy.

General Longstreet was taken to his family, at Lynchburg, where he gradually recovered. On the 18th of May he wrote

to Judge Longstreet, that his wound was severe, but not dangerous. "It is," said he, "through the neck and shoulder; but I am improving." His corps, now under command of General R. H. Anderson, shared in all the after battles at Spottsylvania, Cold Harbor, and Petersburg, where it arrived on the 17th of June.

It was, however, nearly six months before Longstreet could report for duty. After staying a while at Lynchburg, he was removed further South, for the benefit of his health, and returned in October, sufficiently recovered to take up his command again. He then issued the following general order:

HEADQUARTERS, FIRST ARMY CORPS, Oct. 19, 1864.

The undersigned, with deep and grateful emotions, resumes command of his army corps.

Although separated from it since the first action of the past eventful campaign, the history of your share in that campaign is not unknown to him.

He has marked with pride and pleasure the success which has attended your heroic efforts under the accomplished commander who has so worthily led you.

Soldiers, let us not go backward. Let the First corps be always true to itself. We have in the past a brilliant, an unsurpassed record. Let our future eclipse it in our eagerness for glory, our love of country, and our determination to beat the enemy.

J. LONGSTREET, Lieutenant-general.

From that date, though many reports were spread abroad of his being appointed to the Shenandoah Valley, there is nothing important of his movements to relate, apart from what belongs to the army, as already mentioned in our sketch of General Lee. The following, concerning him, however, may be interesting.

The Richmond correspondent of the *London Times* writes: "I am happy to report that General Longstreet is at present quite free from the nervous sensibility in his right arm, from which for some time he suffered. The nerves of motion are still entirely paralyzed, and the arm is almost useless; but he is able slightly to move the fingers, and it is the opinion of

army surgeons, that he will regain plenary use of it in from
eighteen months to two years, when the nervous tissue shall
have time to repair itself. His general health and spirits are
excellent, and his confidence in the ability of his soldiers to
hold the Confederate line, and keep the enemy out of Richmond
for an unlimited period, is unabated. It is a strong testimony
to General Longstreet's value as a soldier, that each of the
three great captains of Secessia—Lee, Beauregard, and Johnston—esteem him equally, and desires his presence by his side.
Upon the 18th instant, Beauregard telegraphed from Jacksonville, in Alabama, soliciting Longstreet's company in the West,
but it was determined that he could not be spared from his
old army corps before Richmond."

The events following this date, as connected with General
Longstreet, are associated with those related under our sketch
of General Lee, up to the period of the surrender of the Army
of Virginia. We need not, therefore, again refer to them.
Longstreet was among those paroled, and after visiting various places in the South, came to Washington in November,
where he took the amnesty oath, and had an interview with
President Johnson.

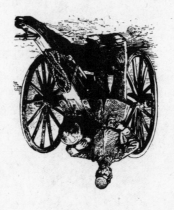

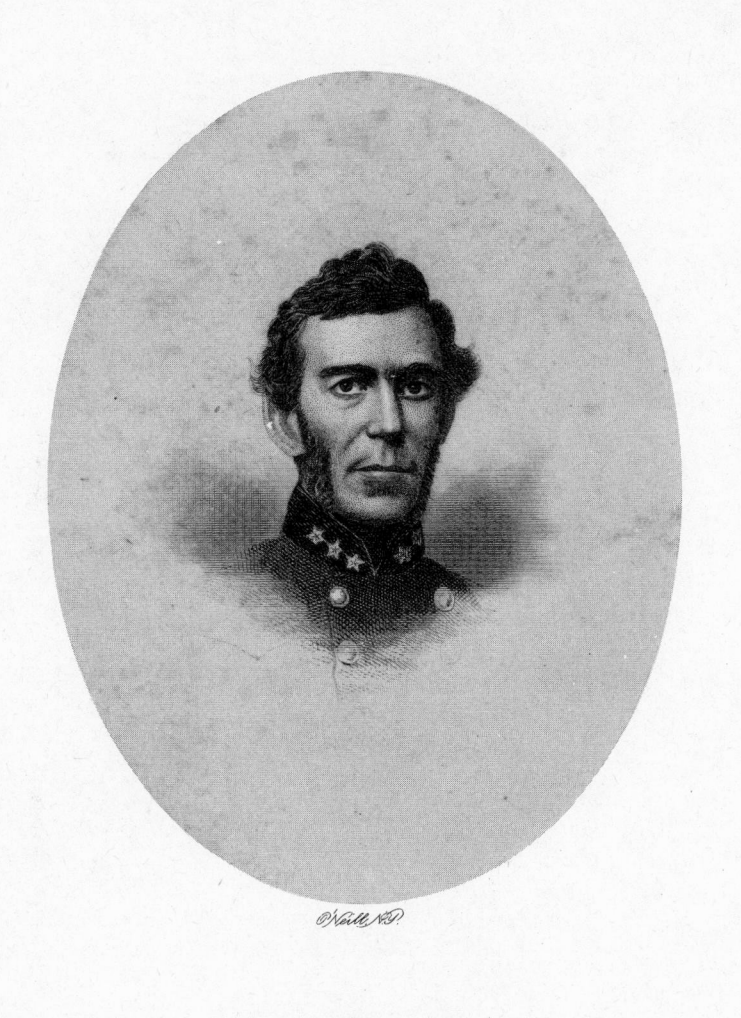

GEN. BRAXTON BRAGG.

GENERAL BRAXTON BRAGG.

His Birth and Early Services.—The Mexican War.—The Battle of Buena Vista.— An Attempt to Assassinate him.—Engaged on the Utah Expedition.—Settles in Louisiana.—Joins the Confederate Service.—Appointed Brigadier-general.—Commands at Pensacola.—Lieutenant Slemmer.—Commander Worden.—Bragg's Position.—Fort Pickens and Colonel Brown.—Colonel Wilson and his Zouaves.—General R. H. Anderson.—Surprise on Santa Rosa Island.—Bombardment of Pensacola.—Bragg Promoted.—Joins A. S. Johnson.—Battle of Shiloh.—General Gladden.—Bragg made a full General.—His Movement into Kentucky.—Munfordsville.—Arrival at Frankfort. —Battle of Perryville.—Retreat from Kentucky—Visits Richmond.—Returns to the Army.—Battle of Murfreesboro.—Generals Breckinridge and Hanson.—Retreat to Tullahoma.—Battle of Chickamauga.—Battles of Missionary Ridge and Chattanooga. —Retreat of Bragg.—Relieved of Command.—New Appointment as Military Adviser. —In Command at Wilmington.—Conclusion.

FEW generals in America are more widely known in connection with popular criticism upon their public life, than the subject of this sketch. "A little more grape, Captain Bragg,' is a saying that has become so hackneyed, from its repeated use in the mouths of all who refer to him, that we would fain omit it, but for the necessity of introducing a matter in his history that has been the subject of much comment. In our remarks, which must necessarily be very brief, we shall try to do justice to one who appears to have many strong and not always friendly opponents. Yet, whatever be the cause of this, it is certain that he has seen and done good service as a brave soldier in former times; nor should his military worth in the present be at all lessened. Let us, then, try to place him before our readers, void of all party feeling, and strictly as we find things honestly recorded.

Braxton Bragg was born in Warren county, North Carolina, in the year 1815, and is a brother of Senator Bragg, late a member of President Davis' cabinet. He entered West Poin as a cadet in 1833, and graduated on the 30th of June, 1837, receiving an appointment as Second-lieutenant of the Third Artillery. He was afterwards commissioned as Captain, and

was actively engaged throughout the Seminole war in Florida, and in duty along the coast. In 1838 he was at camp "Missionary Hill," two miles from Chattanooga, while General Scott was engaged in removing the Cherokees to the West. In the fall of that year he went to Fort Cummins, where he was for some time in command.

In the Mexican war, Captain Bragg was under General Taylor, and accompanied him to Corpus Christi. He was at the battle of Palo Alto, and Resaca de la Palma, and, for his vigorous defence of Fort Brown, opposite Matamoras, on the 9th of May, 1846, he was warmly commended to President Polk. At Monterey, Captain Bragg highly distinguished himself, as the following extracts from an account of the Mexican war will show. The writer says: " Captain Bragg's battery of light artillery having been sent for, the gallant captain came down the road at full gallop, exposed for nearly half a mile to the fire of the heavy guns of the citadel, and soon brought his battery into action in one of the narrow lanes on the outskirts of the city, directing his fire towards the barricades, and then proceeded to Captain Garland's assistance. . . . . Finally, he had to withdraw his battery from the narrow position he occupied in the lane, and in doing so he had to unlimber the gun carriages and reverse them. Four of his horses were killed, and seven wounded. These had to be replaced; and, in retiring, he was again exposed to the same deadly cross-fire. In this movement he lost two men killed and four wounded."

For his conduct in this engagement at Monterey, he was highly complimented by his superior officers. At Buena Vista he was likewise very conspicuous for his bravery, and it is reported of him that, in the final charge, when there was imminent danger of a defeat, he headed a gallant few, and succeded in hurling back the enemy at a most critical moment. It was during the hottest part of this engagement that General Taylor rode up to Captain Bragg's battery, and, as is currently reported, used the words we have already quoted: " A little more grape, Captain Bragg." The correctness of this has been, however, denied in a letter published more than five years ago, and which may be found in the *New York Herald* ot August 7th, 1859. However, that is immaterial to our present

purpose. Captain Bragg undoubtedly bore himse.f most bravely throughout the war, and for his gallant conduct he was brevetted Lieutenant-colonel.

"After the battle of Buena Vista," says a Southern paper, "two attempts were made to assassinate him." Of one of these he himself gives an account in a letter dated August 26th, 1847, from which the following is an extract:

An attempt was made, about 2 A. M., night before last, to assassinate me in my bed. I have no clue to the perpetrator, and can suggest no reason for the act. My escape without injury is almost miraculous. As exaggerated accounts may reach the press, the truth may interest you. A twelve-pound shell, heavily charged, was placed within two feet of my bed, just outside of my tent, and exploded by a slow match; the fragments literally riddling my tent and bedding, pieces passing above and below me, some through a blanket spread over me, and yet I was untouched. I was not aware that I had an enemy in the world, and at times feel disposed to believe now that it may have been intended as a practical joke by some fool ignorant of the effect of shells thus exploded. Be that as it may, my escape was almost miraculous, and I prefer not repeating the joke."

After the Mexican war, Lieutenant-colonel Bragg accompanied Colonel Albert Sidney Johnson on his expedition to Utah. On the 3d of January, 1856, he resigned his commission, leaving the United States military service, and devoted himself to a plantation he had in Louisiana. As appears by a letter made public at the time, he was a candidate for some local office in that State; but we hear little of him until the present war opened. He was then made commander-in-chief of the forces of Louisiana, by the legislature of that State; but, shortly afterwards, President Davis appointed him a brigadier-general in the Confederate army, and placed him in command of the forces at Pensacola, the Congress at Montgomery confirming the same in the early part of March, 1861.

General Bragg immediately went to his post, and fixed his headquarters at the Marine Hospital. He then issued a proclamation, forbidding all parties from furnishing supplies to the Federal war ships off Pensacola, and restricting communi-

cation of any kind between the people in the village and the vessels outside. The effect of this was severely felt by the crews afloat, for we find, from a letter dated March 18th, that " all the ships were out of provisions, and, only for the energy and enterprise of Captain Adams, of the Sabine, they would have been obliged to leave Florida altogether. The steamers could get no wood nor water, and a smuggler from Pensacola was actually selling water at four cents per gallon."

At this especial time, it must be remembered that open war had not broken out between the North and South ; but the state of things at Pensacola was similar to that which Charleston presented, though the latter, as a great city, had the higher importance, and is more publicly known. At Pensacola, the fine bay, and the splendid navy yard, forming the principal depot of the Gulf fleet, alone made the place of any note. The village itself was, otherwise, comparatively insignificant, but, in consequence of its nautical advantages, a small military force under Lieutenant Slemmer was, in the beginning of 1861, stationed there in charge of the forts. These forts were, Fort McRae, on the main land, with a lagoon behind it, and guarding one side of the harbor; Fort Barancas, directly facing the entrance of the harbor, and Fort Pickens on the other, or east side of the harbor entrance. This latter was on the extremity of the long, low, sandy Santa Rosa Island, which stretched away to the eastward, and formed an excellent breakwater to the bay. The Navy Yard was about a mile inside the bay, beyond Fort Barancas, and was thus in an admirably safe position.

Now, when Florida and Alabama seceded, State troops were immediately sent to secure these places. This was early in January, 1861. Forts Barancas and McRae, with the navy yard, were at once surrendered by the naval commandant ; but Lieutenant Slemmers, not approving such a course, secretly crossed over to Fort Pickens, as Major Anderson did from Moultrie to Sumter, and there heroically stationed himself and brave followers, to maintain the honor of his flag, until directed by his government what to do. In this, no honest-minded Southerner could justly blame him, but on the contrary, he should award the praise such conduct so well deserved. Hi position, however, was extrmely critical, and the Federal Gov

ernment determined to relieve him by sending reinforcements, in a steam transport; and the sloop-of-war Brooklyn was also dispatched for the purpose of affording protection.

Meanwhile, a secret agent, Lieutenant, now, Commander Worden—well known as connected with his gallant little *Monitor*—bravely ventured to take dispatches to the garrison, announcing this reinforcement and supplies; but in the attempt he was caught, and imprisoned.

We have no space, however, to relate the many interesting incidents that followed, and must, therefore, hurriedly pass them over, confining ourselves merely to the doings of him whose life we briefly sketch. But, the preceding information will give the reader an idea of the position of affairs when General Bragg took command.

General Bragg was well known to be a strict disciplinarian, and a very determined man. Certainly his position was very peculiar, and to maintain it required great nerve and energy, with a powerful and clear mind. The fearful burst of war had not yet been heard, and it was hardly possible to foresee what a day might bring forth. At length the news of Sumter-fallen, settled all doubts; and blood was thenceforth to stream through the length and breath of the land. Bragg's measures now became even more vigorous. Contraband information to the enemy, of any kind, was immediately punished. Newspaper correspondents were forbidden to promulgate news without permission; and one was sent to Montgomery under arrest for infringing the order. Postmaster Lamberton was also imprisoned for the same thing. Preparations were commenced for attacking Fort Pickens—now reinforced, and Lieutenant Slemmer relieved of his command by Colonel Harvey Brown; but General Bragg was officially notified by Colonel Brown, through Lieutenant Slemmer, that he should act simply on the defensive. Permission was asked by the Federals to send a messenger to Washington; but this was refused.

In the month of April the garrison of Fort Pickens was reinforced, and now numbered over one thousand men; and thus, through the early part of the summer, both parties remained looking at each other, but also strengthening their position. On June 24th, Fort Pickens was additionally reinforced by the arrival of Colonel William Wilson's Zouaves;

and these established themselves three quarters of a mile east of the fort, to guard against Bragg's threatened landing on that part of Santa Rosa Island.

July, August, and September passed, and, excepting a few minor occurrences, nothing of importance took place. At length, on the 8th of October, General Bragg sent a secret expedition by night, to break up Wilson's encampment. The force consisted of several companies of men, selected from regiments, for this special service, and were taken across in two steamers, a barge, and five or six launches, all under the command of General R. H. Anderson, of South Carolina, lately appointed under Bragg. They landed on the eastern part of the island—the night was very dark, and the enemy apparently wrapped in total security. Suddenly a wild cry of alarm from the outlying pickets is heard by the startled Federal Zouaves. Up from their couches they spring, in the garments of sleep, and rush out in amazement. Firing is heard, and before they can prepare for the attack, on come a host of foes, crushing in among them, slaying right and left!

It was a terrible sight—an awful moment! For the instant appalled, the surprized Federals are powerless; but their natural courage is soon recovered, and with the mad ferocity of entrapped men, they enter into the fight! The Confederates, however, are in a greater number than themselves, and drive them back to the very fort itself with fearful slaughter. Now, however, the tide of blood turns. The Federal commandant of Fort Pickens comes upon the scene; and the Confederates, having accomplished their main object, retreat to their boats, pursued by the enemy. Finally, General Anderson's command return to the main land, with some loss, and he himself, wounded. Thus ended General Bragg's night-surprise of the Federals on Santa Rosa Island.

A few weeks after this, in November, the bombardment of Pensacola was opened by the Federal fleet, and at night-time the scene was truly magnificent. This lasted, however, with variations, through the winter, but we can not here give space to its description.

Bragg was now made a Major-general, and as symptoms of serious Federal operations had shown themselves at the mouth of the Mississippi, he was often at Mobile to watch what was

going on, and to see to its defences. In the latter part of December he was thus away, when a little, unarmed propeller, employed between the Confederate forts and the village of Pensacola, was fired into from Fort Pickens, which led to a renewal of fire between the opposite parties holding possession at Barancas, and Santa Rosa. A spectator says: "Through almost the entire night our guns kept up, at regular intervals, their fire. The scene was grand beyond conception—the shells, in their screeching and screaming journey, resembling startled meteors coursing the heavens. About twelve o'clock several buildings in Warrington were fired, and flames, lighting up the yard, and the village, and forts, and batteries, presenting a scene grand as the bombardment which perpetuates the name of Anderson, and the birth-day of the new year. We have suffered no loss of life or limb, nor sustained any injury in guns. There is little likelihood of any more firing—no injury can be inflicted on the enemy, nor can he harm us."

In the beginning of February, 1862, General Bragg established his headquarters at Mobile; and shortly afterwards was sent, with his Second division, to join the army of the Mississippi, then under command of General A. S. Johnson, with General Beauregard as commander-in-chief of the department.

General Bragg's headquarters were now at Jackson, Tennessee; and on March 5th, 1862, he issued a stringent order with regard to all persons travelling without authority, and detailing a guard of one commissioned officer, and five men, to accompany each passenger train on the Memphis and Charleston, and Mobile and Ohio railroads. He also prohibited the sale of intoxicating liquors within five miles of any station occupied by the troops, or within one mile of any public highway used as a military road. Martial law was, likewise, proclaimed at Memphis; and all prisoners were to be sent to Mobile, whence a proper guard from that place was to transfer them to Tuscaloosa, Alabama. On the 6th of April occurred the battle of Shiloh, and here General Bragg commanded the centre of the army. In his official report, he says: "But few regiments of my command had ever had a day's march, and a very large proportion of the rank and file had never performed a day's labor. Our organization had been most hasty,

with great deficiency in commanders, and was, therefore, very imperfect. The equipment was lamentably defective for field service, and our transportation, hastily impressed in the country was deficient in quantity, and very inferior in quality. With all these drawbacks, the troops marched, late in the afternoon of the 3d of April—a day later than intended—in high spirits, and eager for the contest. . . . About 2 A. M., of the 5th, a drenching rain storm commenced, to which the troops were exposed, without tents, and continued until daylight, rendering it so dark, and filling the creeks and ravines to such an extent, as to make it impracticable to move at night. . . . It was seven o'clock in the morning before the road was clear, so as to put my command in motion. . . . At this juncture, the commanding general arrived at our position. My column moved on without delay, and, as promptly as could be, they were formed according to order of battle."

General Bragg then gives details of the battle in that portion of it under his command, speaking of Major-general Polk as his "senior," and, therefore, resigning to him authority in certain parts of the field, and concludes by mentioning the names of those who had specially distinguished themselves. He adds, "Brigadier-general A. H. Gladden fell early in the action, mortally wounded, whilst gallantly leading his men in a successful charge. No better soldier lived—no truer man or nobler patriot ever shed his blood in a just cause." His report embraces a few remarks on the results of the battle, and the causes which produced a state of things different from what might have been expected. "But," says he, "no one cause, probably, contributed so greatly to our loss of time, which was the loss of success, as the fall of the commanding general, A. S. Johnson."

The army fell back to Corinth, and about that time Bragg was made a full general, dating from April 6th, 1862. When it was expected another engagement would take place, he issued, on the 5th of May, a stirring address to his soldiers, and in allusion to the enemy said, "such a foe ought never to conquer freemen, battling upon their own soil." The evacuation of Corinth, however, and subsequent events, as already related, led to a change in the direction of affairs over the army, and General Bragg was appointed commander of the

department instead of Beauregard, who had been obliged to resign from ill-health.

Immediately afterwards, General Bragg began his movement from Tupelo, in Mississippi, through the states of Georgia, and Alabama, to Chattanooga, with a view to active operations in East Tennessee, and Kentucky. The Confederate army was now divided into three corps, respectively commanded by Major-generals Polk, Hardee, and Kirby Smith; the latter being at Knoxville, ready to push forward when Bragg should reach Chattanooga. General Bragg's forces, however, having arrived in that vicinity and finding Buell's army to the north of it, passed on a few miles higher up the Tennessee, and crossed at Harrison, on the 21st of August. Thence, Bragg proceeded by mountain roads to Dunlap—thus completely flanking General Buell on his left. From Dunlap he marched up the Sequatchie valley, and reached Pikeville on the 30th. From that place, Bragg sent a part of his forces to McMinnville, a place seventy-five miles southeast of Nashville, to attack some Federal cavalry thrown forward in advance, and meanwhile he proceeded on towards Crossville, having ascended the Grassy Cave road. Here the force that had been sent to McMinville rejoined the main army. On the 5th of September, General Bragg entered Kentucky, and marched to the right of Bowling Green, sending an advance on to Munfordsville to demand its surrender. Munfordsville is a large town on the Louisville and Nashville railroad, and Bragg was now between it and Buell's army at Bowling Green. The Federal commander, however, succeeded in getting ahead of the Confederates in the principal object they had in view. This, through some captured dispatches, was ascertained to be Louisville in Kentucky, and, as Buell's army received its supplies from there, depots being formed at Bowling Green and Nashville, that general wisely did all in his power to guard the line of communication thither by rail. Munfordsville at first resisted, but, on the 17th of September, it was captured by General Bragg's forces, and next day he issued an address to the people of Kentucky, in which he tells them that he has not come to injure, but to avenge them, and aid them in obtaining freedom. He invites them to join him in the struggle. "If," says he, "you prefer Federal rule

show it by your frowns, and we shall return whence we came
If you choose rather to come within the folds of our brother-
hood, then lend your willing hands to secure you in your her-
itage of liberty."

The Confederate force now moved to Bardstown,* and further towards the centre of the State, in many places, throughout the whole march, receiving kindly support. Detachments
were sent out to scour the country, and watch the Federals,
some of these detachments coming to within four miles of
Louisville and creating great alarm. Bragg, however, proceeded on to Frankfort, the State capital, and joined Kirby
Smith's forces, on the 4th of October, General Buell arriving
at Bardstown—evacuated by the Confederates—on the same
day. At Frankfort, a Confederate provisional governor was
elected on the day of Bragg's arrival, but even before the ceremony had well ended, intelligence of the enemy's approach
induced the newly appointed governor to fly. The Federals,
however, were not then intent so much upon Frankfort as
upon the army of Bragg, the rear of which was at Perryville,
a few miles south of Frankfort. General Buell had been constantly pressing the Confederate rear, and had now advanced
his three corps towards Perryville with the hope of surrounding Bragg's forces there. But, General Crittenden's corps of
the Federal army was somewhat delayed on a circuitous route,
and the other two corps of McCook and Gilbert, first came up
with the Confederates.

The battle which followed is best told in General Bragg's
official report. He says:

HEADQUARTERS, DEPARTMENT No. 2,
BRYANTSVILLE, KY., October 12.

SIR:—Finding the enemy pressing heavily in his rear, near
Perryville, Major-general Hardee, of Polk's command, was
obliged to halt and check him at that point. Having arrived
at Harrodsburg from Frankfort, I determined to give him battle there, and accordingly concentrated three divisions of my
old command—the army of the Mississippi, now under com-

* At this place, on September 26th, General Bragg issued another address
"To the People of the Northwest," but it is of too great a length even to give
a fair abstract.

mand of Major-general Polk—Cheatham's, Buckner's, and Anderson's, and directed General Polk to take the command on the 7th, and attack the enemy the next morning. Withers' division had gone the day before to support Smith. Hearing, on the night of the 7th, that the force in front of Smith had rapidly retreated, I moved early next morning, to be present at the operations of Polk's command.

The two armies were formed confronting each other, on opposite sides of the town of Perryville. After consulting the general and reconnoitering the ground and examining his dispositions, I declined to assume the command, but suggested some change and modifications of his arrangements, which he promptly adopted. The action opened at half-past 12 P. M., between the skirmishers and artillery on both sides. Finding the enemy indisposed to advance upon us, and knowing he was receiving heavy reinforcements, I deemed it best to assail him vigorously, and so directed.

The engagement became general soon thereafter, and was continued furiously from that time to dark, our troops never faltering and never failing in their efforts.

For the time engaged it was the severest and most desperately contested engagement within my knowledge. Fearfully outnumbered, our troops did not hesitate to engage at any odds, and, though checked at times, they eventually carried every position, and drove the enemy about two miles. But for the intervention of night, we should have completed the work. We had captured fifteen pieces of artillery by the most daring charges, killed one and wounded two brigadier-generals, and a very large number of inferior officers and men, estimated at no less than four thousand, and captured four hundred prisoners, including three staff-officers, with servants, carriage and baggage of Major-general McCook.

The ground was literally covered with his dead and wounded. In such a contest our own loss was necessarily severe, probably not less than twenty-five hundred killed, wounded, and missing. Included in the wounded are Brigadier-generals Wood, Cleburne, and Brown, gallant and noble soldiers, whose loss will be severely felt by their commands. To Major-general Polk, commanding the forces, Major-general Hardee, commanding the left wing, two divisions, and Major-generals

Cheatham, Buckner, and Anderson, commanding divisions, are mainly due the brilliant achievements of this memorable field. Nobler troops were never more gallantly led. The country owes them a debt of gratitude which I am sure will be acknowledged.

Ascertaining that the enemy was heavily reinforced during the night, I withdrew my force early the next morning to Harrodsburg, and thence to this point. Major-general Smith arrived at Harrodsburg with most of his force and Withers' division the next day, 10th, and yesterday I withdrew the whole to this point, the enemy following slowly but not pressing us. I am, sir, very respectfully, your obedient servant,

BRAXTON BRAGG,
General commanding.

To Adjutant-general, Richmond, Va.

After the battle of Perryville, General Bragg deemed it best to transfer the army back to Tennessee, giving up the plan of a longer campaign in Kentucky. What his reasons for this were, has been variously stated; but we need not stay to canvass them now. Suffice it that the retreat began, commencing on Sunday night, the 12th of October. It is said that when the Confederate troops abandoned Lexington, where the main part of the forces had been encamped, " the terror, dismay, and anguish of the inhabitants were extreme. The women ran through the streets crying and wringing their hands, while families hastily gathered their clothing, packed their trunks, and obtained wagons to depart, the greatest distress prevailing."

The conduct of this retreat across Kentucky, and through Cumberland gap, was left to General Polk, and, for the present, therefore, we need follow it no further. General Bragg, it appears, went to Richmond, where he arrived on the 27th October, and the next day had a conference with the President and his cabinet, on the conduct of the campaign. From the result of this consultation it seems that the course General Bragg had pursued was satisfactory, for he soon returned to the west with undiminished power, though General J. E. Johnston was appointed Department Commander.

Bragg's army returned into Tennessee by the middle of No-

vember, and was stationed at Lavergne, McMinville, and Murfreesboro. General Rosecrans, now in command of the Northern army, *vice* Buell relieved, was at Nashville, concentrating reorganizing, and disciplining his troops, preparatory to a forward movement. Bragg's forces were now estimated at 45,000 to 50,000 effective men. These were reviewed by President Davis on the 13th of December, when he paid a visit to the army, and " His Excellency expressed his gratification at their fine appearance and discipline—congratulating the commanders present upon the efficiency of their respective forces." President Davis returned to Chattanooga next day.

A day or two afterwards, some correspondence took place between Generals Bragg and Rosecrans, respecting an alleged violation by the Confederates of a flag of truce. The following reply of General Bragg deserves insertion, as showing his readiness to make the *amende honorable*, when justly due.

HEADQUARTERS ARMY OF TENNESSEE,
MURFREESBORO, TENN., December 16, 1862.

GENERAL:—I am in receipt of your communication of the 13th inst., in regard to the capture of three of your vedettes, under circumstances apparently implying disrespect to the flag sent by you.

Prior to the receipt of your letter, I had ordered an investigation of the case. From the report now before me, I am satisfied, and desire to assure you, that the party effecting the capture was wholly unaware that a "flag" had passed, and was acting under orders issued the day previous. It had left Lavergne at eight o'clock on the morning of the 13th, and pursued a circuitous route, coming upon the vedettes after the passage of the flag.

I take pleasure in informing you that I have ordered the men to be returned to your lines, together with their equipments, arms, etc.

I am, general, very respectfully, your obedient servant,
BRAXTON BRAGG,
General Commanding

Major-general W. S. ROSECRANS, Commanding
United States forces, Nashville, Tennessee.

The month of December was now passing away, and it

seems to have been expected that the Federals would not advance for some time. Christmas day, therefore, was spent at
Murfreesboro, and in the army with much festivity; yet, in
the midst of all the enjoyments of the hour, news came that
Rosecrans was marching direct upon them! General Bragg
immediately prepared his forces, and issuing instructions to
his army, the line of battle was thus formed : half of the army,
left wing in front of Stone river; right wing in rear of the
river. Polk's corps to form left wing; Hardee's on the right.
Withers' division to form first line on Polk's corps; Cheatham's the second; Breckinridge's the first line in Hardee's
corps, and Cleburne's the second. McCown was to be in reserve in rear of Cheatham, and Jackson the same in rear of
Hardee.

In a brief sketch like this, it is impossible to give any thing
like a minute account of the battle of Murfreesboro, or Stone
river, that followed. No justice could properly be done to it,
for the reports of both sides ought to be carefully examined
for the purpose. But, in this sketch it is enough to bring forward that which belongs especially to him of whom we write.
Therefore, the following independent account of the first day's
fight is introduced.

The enemy commenced the advance from Nashville on
Friday, by several different routes of march, driving in our
cavalry under Generals Wheeler and Wharton, who severally
fell back, gallantly contesting every foot of the way.

On Sunday our line of battle was formed about two miles
from Murfreesboro, stretching transversly across Stone river,
from the Lebanon pike on the right to the Franklin road on
the left. On Tuesday the enemy had deployed into line of
battle upon the ridge, whereon stands the residence of Mr.
Cowan, at a distance of something more than one thousand
five hundred yards from our first line, and considerably over-
lapping our left flank. During Monday they opened with
artillery at long range, and on Tuesday heavy skirmishing ran
up and down the line from the left to the centre, swelling
almost into a battle at one period, when the enemy attempted
two charges on Robinson's battery.

On the night of Tuesday it had become evident that the
attack in force would be upon our left, and Cleburne's division

was detached from the right for the purpose of strengthening that point and extending our line, which gave to the left wing four divisions—Cheatham's, Withers', McCown's, and Cle burne's.

On Wednesday the sun rose clear after several days of funeral gloom, drifting the mists which hung like silvery curtains o'er the field, dancing and glistening along the serried line of steel, which glittered in the morning light like the sparklings of countless diamonds, bathing the gay banners which floated in the front with a flood of refulgence, and drifting in golden showers through the emerald fringe of cedars which enclosed the field. Far as the eye could reach stood the two vast armies, silent and motionless; and it almost seemed instead of being drawn up for battle, to be some brilliant holiday parade; but at length a volley of musketry from the extreme left told too plainly that the work of death had in reality begun, and in an instant afterwards the strife had leaped from point to point, until the whole line, from left to center, was one unbroken blaze of fire.

About 8 o'clock A. M. the divisions of McCown, Cleburne, and Cheatham were ordered to charge. The enemy was strongly planted in a dense thicket where the outcropping of the limestone rocks formed a natural fortification. Swiftly, but with a perfect line, our troops emerged from the skirt of timber in which they had been sheltered, and moved across the open plain which intervened. The battle now became terrific. Crash upon crash of musketry stunned the ear; the ground trembled under the thunders of artillery; the cedars rocked and quivered in the fiery blast, and the air was rent with the explosion of shells. The enemy seemed determined to stake the fortunes of the day upon holding the position which they occupied, and offered a most gallant resistance; but nothing human could withstand the impetuosity of that charge. A spirit of fury seemed to possess our men, from the commanders down to the common soldier, and on they swept, shot and shell, canister, grape, and bullets, tearing through their ranks until the way could be traced by the dead and dying. Still on they went, overrunning infantry and artillery alike, driving the enemy like the hurricane scatters the leaves upon its course, capturing hundreds of prisoners and literally

blackening the ground with dead. Such a charge was never before witnessed. For two miles, through fields and forests, over ditches, fences, and ravines, they swept. Brigade after brigade, battery after battery, were thrown forward to stay their onward march ; but another round of musketry, another gleaming of the bayonet, and, like their predecessors, they were crushed into one common ruin. Meantime the brave Withers was not idle. His line of battle ran diagonally across an extended field, and the enemy had been pouring a tremendous fire into his position, until, driven almost to the verge of madness by the distraction of his men, he threw his division forward upon the ridge occupied by the enemy. Here was, perhaps, the bloodiest struggle of the day. The enemy was stronger at this point than any where else upon the field, and long and fiercely contended the position. Directly in front was a wide area of cleared land, and across this it was necessary to advance under the sweeping fire of six batteries ; but with dauntless hearts and a step as proud as though on parade his men sprang forward at the word, and marched on into the face of death. Once they wavered as the enemy poured a perfect hail of iron through their ranks ; but at this moment Bragg dashed by, the battle fires burning in his eyes, and the fate of nations in his hand. Again they rushed upon the foe, shot down the gunners at their pieces, and drove the supporting divisions far back to the rear.

That night, both armies rested as best they could among the cedars, or on the open plain. It was intensely cold, freezing severely. Upon the battlefield lay thousands of dead and wounded frozen stiff, and presenting a ghastly spectacle. The scene was fearful though picturesque. A brilliant winter moon shed its lustre amid the foliage of the forest of evergreens, and lighted up with silver sheen the ghastly battlefield. Dismounted cannon, scattered caissons, glittering and abandoned arms strewed the forest and field. The dead lay stark and stiff at every step, with clenched hands and contracted limbs in the wild attitudes in which they fell, congealed by the bitter cold. It was the eve of the new year. Moans of the neglected dying, mingled with the low peculiar shriek of the wounded artillery horses, chanted a *miserere* for the dying year. Amid the camp fires, feebly lighted to avoid

attracting the artillery of the enemy, groups of mutilated and shuddering wounded were huddled, and the kneeling forms of surgeons bending in the firelight over the mangled bodies of the dying, added to the solemnity of the night.

Next day there was little done but skirmishing. The enemy had taken up a stronger position than before, and both armies drew breath, for awhile, till renewed strength was obtained for the fight. On January 2d, no movement took place till about 4 P. M. when orders were given to assault the enemy's stronghold on the bend of river. General Breckinridge was directed to this duty. Hanson's, Palmer's, Pillow's, Preston's, and Gibbon's brigades formed the division, and, when the signal gun was given, onward they went to what seemed almost certain destruction. Through the thinned woods—into the open fields, the gallant leaders and their brave followers rushed. Then came the thundering fire of the enemy's artillery, and, expecting it, the men were ordered to lie down till it passed. But, directly the storm of shot and shell went by, —" Up, my men, and charge !" was the ringing cry of Breckinridge as he himself dashed on. With the impetuosity of a torrent they rushed forward. Wright's battery galloped up, and soon a fierce and bloody contest ensued. But, in vain ! In less than half an hour over 2000 brave soldiers on the Confederate side had fallen ! The task, therefore, was seen to be hopeless, and General Breckinridge ordered his division to fall back, when it was nearly dark.

In this attack, General Hanson fell mortally wounded, exclaiming, " Forward—forward, my brave boys, to the charge !" and afterwards, when brought from the field, he said with his flickering breath, " I am willing to die with such a wound, received in so glorious a cause." Captain Wright also fell at his guns mortally wounded.

General Bragg had sent General Patton Anderson with his brigade to the support of Breckinridge, and nobly did they bear themselves, receiving a high meed of praise from the commander-in-chief for their conduct.

The battle was over. General Bragg felt that prudence dictated a withdrawal ; and accordingly, on the following day, the Confederate army retreated towards Tullahoma.

Before we close this too hurried account of the great battle

of Murfreesboro, let us mention the names most pron.inentiy brought forward in laudatory terms by General Bragg. He says :

"Among the gallant dead the nation is called to mourn, none could have fallen more honored or regarded than Brigadier-generals James E. Rains and R. M. Hanson. They yielded their lives in the heroic discharge of their duties, and leave their honored names as a rich legacy to their descendents. Brigadier-general J. R. Chalmers and D. W. Adams received disabling wounds on Monday—I am happy to say not serious, but which deprived us of their valuable services. Having been under my immediate command since the beginning of the war, I can bear evidence to their devotion and to the conspicuous gallantry which has marked their services on every field.

"For the sacred names of the heroes and patriots of lower grades that gave their lives, illustrating the character of the Confederate soldiers on this bloody field, I must refer to the reports of subordinate commanders, and to the list which will be submitted. Our losses, it will be seen, exceeded ten thousand, nine thousand of whom were killed or wounded.

"Lieutenant-generals L. Polk, and W. J. Hardee, commanding corps, Major-generals J. M. Withers and P. R. Cleburne, commanding divisions, are specially commended to their government for their valor, skill, and ability displayed throughout the engagement.

"Brigadier-generals Joseph Wheeler and John A. Wharton, commanding cavalry brigades, were pre-eminently distinguished throughout the engagement, as they had been for a month previous in many successive conflicts with the enemy. Under their skilful and gallant lead, the reputation of our cavalry has been justly enhanced. For the just commendation of the officers, many of whom were pre-eminently distinguished, I must refer to their more immediate commendation."

On the 8th of January, General Bragg had his headquarters at Winchester, not far from the south border of Tennessee. He addressed the inhabitants of the district, calming their fears, and stating that he had fallen back to give his men repose. At the same time, he issued a congratulatory and complimentary address to his army.

From this date, for several months, nothing more was done by the main army, though detached commands were ever vigorously at work. The Confederates rested at Tullahoma and vicinity, while the Federals remained in the position they had moved to after the battle of Murfreesboro.

As regards General Bragg himself, there was, at this time, a great deal of unpleasant discussion concerning him. Like all men of a stern, unbending mind, he was not very popular, and it would appear that there were many who thought if he were removed from his post it would be to the advantage of the cause. But let us bear in mind that there are few men placed in a prominent position that are not subject to similar attacks, whether justly deserved or not; and, in General Bragg's case, it is certain that he was supported by the President and his cabinet; therefore, must have been deemed well fitted for his post. A foreign officer of rank, calling upon him at this time, May 29th, 1863, says, after describing his appearance, " He has the reputation of being a strict disciplinarian, and shooting freely for insubordination. I understand he is unpopular on this account, and also by reason of his occasional acerbity of manner. He was extremely civil to me, and gave me permission to visit the outposts, or any part of his army. He expressed regret that a boil on his hand would prevent his accompanying me. Rosecrans' position, he said, extended about forty miles, and Murfreesboro twenty-five miles distant from Bragg's headquarters, at Shelbyville, was Rosecrans' headquarters. The Confederate cavalry inclosed him in a semicircle extending over a hundred miles of country. . . He talked to me a long time about the battle of Murfreesboro, and said he retained possession of the ground he had won for three days and a half, and only retired on account of the exhaustion of his troops, and after carrying off over 6,000 prisoners, much cannon, and other trophies. He allowed that Rosecrans had displayed much firmness. . . . At 5 P. M., I was present at a great open-air preaching, at General Wood's camp. Bishop Elliott preached most admirably to a congregation of nearly 3,000 soldiers, who listened to him with the most profound attention. Generals Bragg, Polk, Hardee, Withers, Cleburne, and others were present. It is impossible to exaggerate the respect paid by all ranks of his army to Bishop Elliott; and.

although most of the officers are Episcopalians, the majority of the soldiers are Methodists, Baptists, etc. . . . I got back to Shelbyville at 4.30 P. M. (June 2d), just in time to be present at an interesting ceremony peculiar to America. This was a baptism at the Episcopal church. The ceremony was performed in an impressive manner, by Bishop Elliott, and the person baptized no less than the commander-in-chief. The bishop took the general's hand in his own (the latter kneeling in front of the font), and said, ' Braxton, if thou hast not already been baptized, I baptize thee,' etc. Immediately afterwards he confirmed General Bragg, who then shook hands with General Polk, the officers of their respective staffs, and myself, who were the only spectators."

We now turn again to the military operations under General Bragg's command.

With the exception of the minor affairs at Liberty, and Hoover's gaps, nothing particular occurred until the beginning of June, when Rosecrans advanced with a very powerful and numerous army. On the 27th, General Bragg fell back to Chattanooga, and established his headquarters first at Bridgeport, and then in the town. Round this place the Confederate army was now encamped, Rosecrans advancing upon it across the mountains on one side, and Burnside commanding the Federal forces in East Tennessee, coming down the valley *via* Cumberland gap on the other. Chattanooga was placed in a good state of defence, and works thrown up across the river as far as Blythe's ferry. Rosecrans, however, succeeded in moving well up to Chattanooga without molestation, and, on the 8th of September, the Confederates evacuated the place— retiring to the Chickamauga. Here, having been reinforced by General Longstreet, Bragg fought the Federals on the 20th of September, driving them back to Chattanooga. We have already given an account of this battle, and to it we refer.

Before this, President Davis had again visited Bragg's army, and, shortly afterwards, Longstreet had been detached to Knoxville. Then followed the disastrous battle of Missionary Ridge, Chattanooga, and the subsequent retreat to Dalton.

On the 2d of December, General Bragg was relieved from his command, and he took leave of the army in the following order

GENERAL ORDERS—NO. 214.

Upon renewed application to the President, his consent has been obtained for the relinquishment of the command of this army. It is accordingly transferred to Lieutenant-general Hardee. The announcement of this separation is made with unfeigned regret. An association of more than two years, which bind together a commander and his trusted troops, cannot be severed without deep emotion. For a common cause, dangers shared on many hard-fought fields have cemented bonds which time can never impair. The circumstances which render this step proper will be appreciated by every good soldier and true patriot. The last appeal the general has to make to the gallant army which has so long nobly sustained him is to give his successor that cordial and generous support essential to the success of your arms. In that successor you have a veteran whose brilliant reputation you have aided to achieve. To the officers of my general staff, who have so long zealously and successfully struggled against serious difficulties to support the army and myself, is due, in a great degree, what little success and fame we have achieved. Bidding them and the army an affectionate farewell, they have the blessings and prayers of a grateful friend.

BRAXTON BRAGG.

Immediately after his retirement from the army, General Bragg repaired to the Warm Springs, in Georgia, to recruit his health, and on the 5th of January, 1864, visited Columbus. The care and incessant labor of the past two years, it was stated, had left their traces upon his person; but he was still able for military duty, and, in February, received a new appointment in accordance with the following order:

ADJUTANT AND INSPECTOR-GENERAL'S OFFICE, }
RICHMOND, Va., February 24, 1864.   }

General Braxton Bragg is assigned to duty at the seat of government, and, under the direction of the President, is charged with the conduct of military operations in the armies of the Confederacy. By order.

S. COOPER, Adjutant and Inspector-general.

In this position, the general frequently visited the several

military posts and departments, often accompanied by the President. At the funeral of General J. E. B. Stuart he was one of the pall bearers; and in July and August he was at Columbus and Macon; and, when the army of Virginia assembled once more around Richmond, he examined their intrenchments and fortifications, preparatory to certain movements. But the post he occupied was one that we do not well comprehend; nor does it seem to have been rightly understood elsewhere. It was an anomalous one, and liable to much discordance of opinion in reference to it. However, towards the end of October, he was assigned to another department, and, in November, took command of the forces in North Carolina. In the beginning of December we find him at Augusta, sending in a report of Wheeler's operations; but he was at Wilmington, as his headquarters, when the Porter-Butler attack on Fort Fisher was unsuccessful. He then issued a congratulatory order, dated December 29th, 1864, to his troops; but, except the late achievements of the Federal arms, under General Terry, in that quarter, we have had little to record concerning him.

General Bragg has been long married, and his accomplished lady frequently visited him in camp, occasionally in the depth of winter. Of his family, we have no information at present, but, whatever be the fate of the Confederacy, it is certain that his name will be remembered as one of the principal of those brave and unselfish spirits, whose soul animated the cause, and whose mind and body ever fought heroically for its support.

General Bragg was blamed for the fall of Wilmington, though his friends attributed the loss of that place to the fact, that "he came into unpleasant collision with interests and persons, whose feelings could not, in the nature of things, be other than inimical to him." He was not, however, much longer before the public eye, except as to the battle of Kinston, N. C.; and when the Southern Confederacy ceased to exist, he quietly retired to Mobile, and thence to New Orleans, where he arrived on the 27th of June. On the 9th of October he took the oath of allegiance, and thenceforth quietly settled down to cultivate his plantation in Lowndes County, Ala., admitting the march of events, and using free labor on his fields.

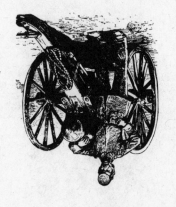

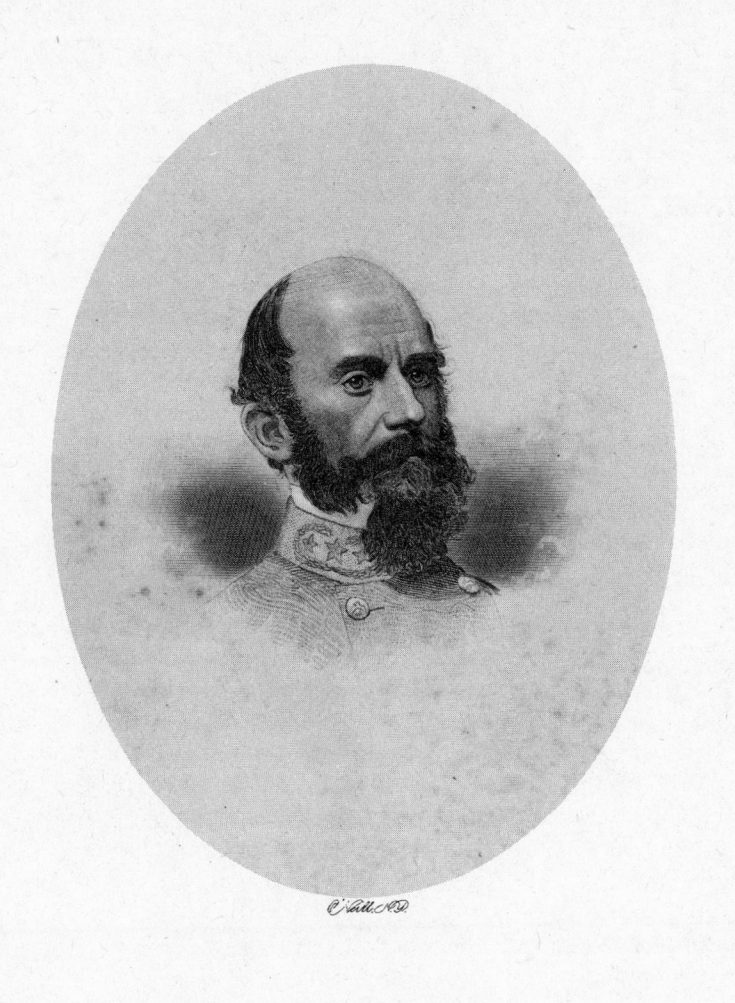

LT. GEN. R. S. EWELL

LIEUT.-GENERAL RICHARD STODDART EWELL.

THE early life of Lieutenant-general Ewell is not so much known as that of those whose career we have already sketched. So far as information can yet be obtained, he was born about the year 1817, in Prince William county, Virginia, though another account states his birth to have been in 1820, in the District of Columbia. In 1836 he entered the Military Academy at West Point, and graduated on the 30th of June, 1840, receiving an appointment as brevet second-lieutenant of cavalry, on the 1st of July. On the 10th of September, 1845, he was made first-lieutenant, and with that rank went into the Mexican war, serving in Colonel Mason's dragoons. He won his promotion to captain in the field, having received it for gallant and meritorious conduct in the battles of Contreras and Cherubusco.

In June, 1847, Captain Ewell was in New Mexico, greatly distinguishing himself against the Indians; and during the year 1858 he took charge of and commanded the troops that garrisoned Fort Buchanan in that territory. He was, however, suspended in 1859.

When Virginia seceded, Captain Ewell resigned his commis
sion in the regular army, and took sides with the South.*

The first time, as we believe, that Ewell came very promi
nently forward in the present war, was at Fairfax Court-house
on the night of May 31st. It must be remembered that Vir
ginia was the last State to secede, and thus many of the places
bordering the Northern States were but ill provided for defence. Among them was Fairfax Court-house, a village of
some few hundred inhabitants, eighteen miles from Washington. At the end of May, this place was guarded by the Warrenton Rifles, a company of infantry belonging to the Seven-
teenth Virginia, numbering, however, only eighty men (the
rest being sick or absent), and commanded by Lieutenant or
Captain John Quincy Marr. They had arrived there on the
30th of May, and the majority of the company were so young
that their female relatives had given them, in fond sport, the
name of the "Warrenton Babies," many of them being only
sixteen or seventeen years of age,—one, indeed, had attained
his sixteenth year only on the previous day. Two companies
of cavalry, however (the Rappahannock, and the King William counties cavalry), had previously arrived, under Colonel
Ewell. What followed may be best told nearly in the words
of a lady, the wife of Dr. M——, who was present on the occasion. She says, that about two o'clock in the morning she
was aroused by the tramp of horses and firing of muskets in
the village. Alarmed at the confusion that assailed her ears,
she awoke her husband. At the same moment their hostess
rushed into the room, exclaiming, "The Federalists are coming
in force; they have driven in our pickets (the two cavalry
companies) who are dashing through the town calling upon us
to fly for our lives."

"Where, then, are the Warrenton Rifles?" said Mrs. Dr. M——
"Scattering, in alarm," was the reply.

In a moment, the lady's husband—the doctor—who was
second-lieutenant of the company, apparelled and armed himself, and rushed out of the house to the quarters of his men,

---

* We find it stated in the *New York Herald* of May 18th, 1861, that a
"President Ewell, of William and Mary College,—a distinguished graduate of
West Point, and a classmate of General Lee—had been appointed a Colonel in
the Virginia army.

calling out, as he proceeded, for Captain Marr. But Captain Marr could not be found ; and meanwhile the Federal cavalry was pursuing the alarmed outposts through the place. All was confusion and dismay, and no one appeared who was pre pared to take command of the few infantry still remaining there. Suddenly a figure, only partly dressed, dashed forward and, placing himself at the head of forty-three members of the Warrenton Rifles—no babies did they show themselves, however—who were already drawn up to receive the enemy. Having deployed behind a fence, he advanced towards the Federals. These latter—company B, of the 3d cavalry, 1st brigade, commanded by Lieutenant Tompkins—were galloping back, and firing right and left in the darkness. In a moment they were called upon to " Halt !" by the new leader of the Confederates, who was, in fact, none other than the present Lieutenant-general Ewell. He had rushed from his bed, without stopping to complete his attire ; but, in the blackness of the night his white shirt proved a sure mark ; and, a shot in the shoulder was the only reply he received. This, for the time, disabled him, and Colonel Smith (" Extra Billy") took the command, being accidentally in the place. A firing was kept up for about half an hour, and, finally, Lieutenant Tompkins finding himself outnumbered, retreated with " five prisoners and two horses," his own loss being "three men missing, three wounded, and six horses."

We might have continued more of this interesting episode of the war, but our province here forbids. We must say, however, that Captain Marr had not slunk away. Rallying his company, and placing them in position, he went forward to reconnoitre, but never returned ! At eight o'clock next morning, his body was found lying in a field by the road-side. It appears that he must have hastily risen from his couch on the first sound of alarm and come out, for he had not given himself time to buckle on his sword, both sword and belt being grasped tightly in the hand of death,—a death most truly honorable, as being in defence of his native Virginia soil, and, moreover, as also being " the first who had shed his blood" in defence upon that soil. He was a single man, about thirty years of age, leaving a mother and two sisters dependent on him for support. The whole town of Warrenton afterwards

attended his funeral, and wept over his grave—a quiet uncb-trusive grave, with a simple square marble slab to mark his remains.

In the above striking incident, connected with General Ewell's life, we have adhered literally, and almost verbally, to the account printed in an interesting work before us, and which is verified by reference to the occurrence, in a Richmond periodical,* as also—in regard to Captain Marr being shot—borne out by the official report of the Federal commanding officer. That officer, could not then be aware who that other officer was contending with his party; but probably, ere this, he has known it was the present Lieutenant-general Ewell of the Confederate army.†

With the rank of colonel, we next find him in command of the camp of instruction for cavalry at Ashland, where his services were invaluable. His discipline was stern and rigid, but humane, and, out of raw mounted militia, he soon formed a most efficient body of troops. He was afterwards made a brigadier-general; and, at the battle of Blackburn's ford, July 18, 1861, was stationed on the extreme right, at Union Mills. In Beauregard's official report, he says: "Thanks are due to Brigadier-generals Bonham and Ewell for the ability shown in conducting and executing the retrograde movements on Bull Run, directed in my orders—movements on which hung the fortunes of the army."

General Ewell's position at the principal battle of Bull Run, on the 21st of July, was in the same place at Union Mills, and he was to have advanced on the enemy's flank and rear at Centreville, but the orders for such a movement miscarried. In the afternoon, however, he was directed to bring up his brigade into the battle on the left flank, and this was promptly executed, though, on arrival, the day had been won. He was, therefore, sent back, with all speed, to resume his original position, in order to prevent the possibility of its seizure by any force of the enemy in that quarter.

---

* Southern Illustrated News.

† This volume is a biographical sketch of conspicuous Southern Generals. Captain Marr, it is true, was not a general; but, may we not say, had he lived, he would assuredly have become one? We think so; and therefore hope to be excused for thus almost unavoidably bringing him forward.

Until April, 1862,* no movements of any importance brought General Ewell prominently forward, but in that month, he was directed to join "Stonewall" Jackson in the Shenandoah valley; and then commenced the brilliant career that has since marked his name. He left the vicinity of Gordonsville, and on the 30th, arrived with his division on the west of the Blue Ridge, marching directly forward to the position occupied by Jackson in Elk Run valley. Receiving orders there how to proceed, he went on to Newmarket, and then accompanied Jackson towards Front Royal.

It was on the 22d of May, that the army moved on, General Ewell in the advance. The next day Front Royal was captured, and Ewell proceeded on to Winchester, bearing a conspicuous part in the defeat of the enemy at that place. He then followed the retreating forces, under Banks, to the Potomac, and, on the return of Jackson's army from the pursuit, he was ordered to hold Fremont in check at Strasburg. This was successfully done, till Jackson, with the main body of his forces, had left Strasburg, on the evening of the 1st of June. Next day, General Ewell made a stand at Fisher's Hill, and impeded the progress of General Milroy. He then gradually retired towards Harrisonburg, forming the rearguard of the Confederate army. Passing to Cross Keys, on the road to Port Republic, he there had an engagement with General Fremont's forces, which he defeated, and next morning, June 9th, he marched to join General Jackson at Port Republic,

---

* When the Confederates evacuated Manassas in 1862, some interesting documents were found by the Federals, amongst others, the following, which explains itself:

October 18, 1861.

General G. T. BEAUREGARD:

SIR—The bearer, Charles Dillon, of the Twelfth Mississippi, has just brought some late papers, which may be interesting to you. He has a proposition to make in reference to watching the enemy, which I thought might be of importance to bring to your notice. They (he and three comrades) have been scouting around and about Springfield, and I have always found them reliable. He proposes now to go into Alexandria, and I advised him to see you, in order, if you wish him to do so, that his exertions may be properly directed.

Respectfully,   R. S. EWELL.

[Sequel—Charles Dillon was caught and killed as a spy.—March 19, 1862.]

leaving a small force behind to keep the enemy in check The battle here, between Jackson and Shields, was already raging hotly, but his arrival promptly arrested an advance of the Federals on General Winder, though he was soon afterwards driven back with some loss. His command, however, speedily rallied, and materially aided in the defeat of the enemy.

The movements of Jackson's army after this are well known, and have already been related. General Ewell accompanied it, with his command, to the battlefields around Richmond, and shared in the heaviest of the engagements.

On the way to Cold harbor, June 26th, Ewell was in front of Jackson's forces, and drove the enemy before him, surmounting every obstacle which they had placed upon the roads to bar his progress, and reaching Cold harbor about 5 P. M. In the battle that now followed, on June 27th, General Ewell was in the advanced centre of Jackson's corps, and maintained a hard fight with the enemy, " charging through the swamp, up the hill, in face of a terrible fire, and fighting with that daring which had so often excited the admiration of his commander." He continued the struggle until after dusk, when his ammunition being completely exhausted, he fell back. On the morning of the 28th, General Ewell was sent forward to Dispatch station, on the York river railroad, General Stuart being in advance, with his cavalry. Here Ewell tore up the track, and having ascertained that the enemy had not retreated, as was deemed possible, in the direction of the White-house and Pamunkey, he proceeded towards Bottom bridge, and thence, on the next day, rejoined the main corps. That evening, in company with D. H. Hill, and Whiting, all under the personal command of Jackson, he crossed the Chickahominy by the Grapevine bridge, and followed the enemy on their track, by the Williamsburg road, and Savage station. At White-oak swamp they were encountered, and driven back again. At Frazer's farm Jackson's corps was assigned to the front, and promptly followed the Federals to Malvern Hill, where, in that battle, General Ewell also bore a conspicuous part.

After the series of battles around Richmond had freed the capital from danger, it was found necessary to dispatch Jack

son's corps to arrest the movements of General Pope, then advancing in Northern Virginia. General Ewell's division was, therefore, forwarded thither within a fortnight after the engagement at Malvern Hill; and he arrived at Gordonsville on July 19th. On the 7th of August he led the advance, when Jackson moved forward ; and on the 9th, when near Cedar Run, was directed to diverge to the right, and pass along the slope of Slaughter's Mountain—the enemy, at that time, being posted in heavy force in the front. Ewell, with his command, reached the northwest termination of the mountain, and, upon an elevated spot, about two hundred feet above the valley below, planted a battery of guns, which opened with marked effect upon the foe. For some two hours, a rapid and continuous fire of artillery was kept up on both sides of the main armies, but Ewell was unable to advance as far as he desired, owing to the Confederate batteries in the valley sweeping his only approach to the enemy's left. At length, an opportunity presenting, he pushed on, under a heavy fire, and vigorously assisted in driving the Federals back.

The march towards Manassas then followed, by the circuitous route of the Thoroughfare gap, which we have already mentioned in our sketch of General Jackson ; and we need now only refer to the attack upon Bristoe station, made by General Ewell, on August 27th. Here General Hooker commanded the Federal army; and, after an obstinate struggle, Ewell retreated, in accordance with previous orders, to join the main body of the Confederate forces, at Manassas. Jackson and Ewell then fell back to the old battlefield of Bull Run, where, on the 29th, before the whole army had reinforced them, Ewell's corps was stationed behind the embankment of the intended line of railroad, passing from near Sudley Springs to beyond Groveton. In the afternoon, it was seen that the enemy was advancing in front, and after carefully reconnoitering, General Jackson gave Ewell orders to advance.

General Ewell immediately threw forward his own division and Jackson's, and attacked the enemy, then coming along the Warrenton turnpike. A fierce engagement ensued, lasting during the remaining two hours of daylight. Finally, the Federals gave way, and at nightfall were entirely repulsed.

In this engagement General Ewell was badly wounded in

the knee, and his valuable services were, therefore, lost in the momentous battle that took place next day. His division fell under the command of Brigadier-general Lawton—who ably sustained its reputation. The wound he had received was from a minie ball; and the bones were so shattered, that, in the opinion of his surgeons, at the time, amputation was deemed necessary; and he was accordingly removed, in a litter, to the hospital, near Aldie, where the operation was performed. He was, ultimately, taken to Charlottesville, to the house of Captain T. L. Farish, where he was carefully attended.

For several months afterwards, General Ewell was unfit for any active duty in the field. At length, on the 29th of May, 1863, he was able to rejoin his old corps, who were drawn up at Hamilton's crossing, near Fredericksburg, ready to receive him, his arrival being greeted with enthusiastic cheers. He had been made a lieutenant-general, and had now command of one of the three large corps (Jackson's old corps incorporated with his) into which the army under General Lee had been divided,—Generals Longstreet and A. P. Hill having command of the other two.

General Ewell, owing to the loss of his leg, had now to be always strapped on his horse, when on the field; and, when walking, moved with great difficulty on crutches. It was said of him, that his spirit was like the blast of that " wild horn on Fontarabian echoes borne," and would, as we find it did, act upon the veterans of Jackson's old corps, almost like a visitation of the dead warrior to his former comrades, from the realm of spirits.

It was at this time General Lee's plans began to be put in execution for invading Maryland, as we have already stated. General Ewell's corps was dispatched to Culpepper, reaching there on the 8th of June; and soon afterwards, in accordance with the orders received, he marched forward to attack General Milroy at Winchester, in the Shenandoah Valley. He rapidly passed through the gorges of the Blue Ridge Mountains, and then, by way of Front Royal, came upon Milroy on Sunday, the 14th of June, at 5 p. m. Getting his batteries swiftly into position, he massed his infantry, and then "charged across the field, to the very muzzles of the Federal guns, although the latter were fired vigorously. Without a pause, the

Confederates crossed the ditch, leaped over the breastworks, and planted their colors on the embankment. The Ohio regiment was driven from the works at the point of the bayonet. Some escaped back to the main fort, and the remainder were captured, or killed." Thus the fight continued until night— General Ewell fiercely assaulting the Federals, on the east, south, and west of the town. At one o'clock, General Milroy abandoned Winchester, and retreated to Harper's Ferry, leaving behind him an immense booty, in guns, ammunition, horses, commissariat stores, etc., to Ewell and his victorious troops.

General Ewell moved promptly up the valley—Martinsburg naving been taken about the same time by General Rhodes, while Jenkins, in the advance, with his cavalry, was crossing the Potomac, at Williamsport—and then marched on to Chambersburg, where he arrived on Tuesday evening, June 16th.

The whole army of General Lee was now rapidly marching into Maryland—General Ewell's corps in the advance. After crossing the Potomac it passed from Williamsport to Hagerstown, and at noon on the 22d of June, entered Greencastle, Pennsylvania. On the 23d, Ewell occupied Chambersburg, and next day he issued the following order :

"The sale of intoxicating liquors to this command, without written permission from a major-general, is strictly prohibited.

"Persons having liquor in their possession, are required to report the fact to the provost marshal, or the nearest general officer, stating the amount and kind, that a guard may be placed over it, and the men prevented from getting it.

"Any violation of part one of these orders, or failure to comply with part second, will be punished by the immediate confiscation of all liquors in the possession of the offending parties, besides rendering their other property liable to seizure.

"Citizens of the country through which the army may pass, who are not in the military service, are admonished to abstain from all acts of hostility, upon the penalty of being dealt with in a summary manner. A ready acquiescence to the demands of the military authorities will serve to lessen the rigors of war."

The same day a detachment from Ewell's corps was sent towards Carlisle, which was occupied by the Confederates on the 27th. Here, the limits of advance had been reached.

Meade, having relieved Hooker, on the 28th, marched the Federal army forward to meet the forces under Lee, and on the 1st of July the two armies met at Gettysburg.

Ewell's corps had been ordered to fall back 'on Gettysburg, and arrived there about an hour after the battle commenced. He took up his position on the left of the Confederate army, and immediately attacked the enemy with great vigor, so that, by night, Meade's right wing had fallen back, and the town of Gettysburg was in possession of General Ewell,—having been obtained by the divisions of Early, and Rhodes. The following day, and succeeding one, the battle was renewed, with what success has already been told. The Confederates retreated towards Virginia again, and on the 4th of July, Ewell, with the immense train of booty he had captured during the past few days, moved as rapidly as possible towards Hagerstown, and thence, crossing the Potomac, to Winchester.

The next movement of any importance was not until October, after the army had rested for some time on the Rapidan —General Ewell having the extreme left. On the 8th of October General Lee began operations anew, and General Ewell's corps marched towards and beyond Culpepper, which had been held by the Federals, but vacated on the approach of the Confederates. On the 13th, a skirmish took place between Ewell's advance and a body of Meade's troops at Bristow station, the latter falling back, but, on the next day, returning and giving battle to General A. P. Hill, who had arrived there. The result proved disastrous to the Confederates, and thus terminated the advance of General Lee's army. The Southern forces fell back to the Rappahannock, and was disposed on both sides of the Orange and Alexandria railroad, General Ewell's corps being on the right, and General Hill's on the left.

On the 7th of November, General Meade advanced again on the position of General Ewell, near Kelly's ford, and to the bridge over the river. This bridge was defended by a portion of Ewell's corps, and, at night, these were attacked by the enemy. A severe struggle ensued, resulting in the Confederates being defeated with the loss of four guns, eight battle-flags, and a number of men.

A few days afterwards General Ewell was obliged to absent himself on sick leave, in consequence of renewed trouble from his dismembered limb. He retired to Charlottesville, and we do not again find him on active duty until the following April, 1864, when he rejoined the army, then preparing for the vigorous campaign that ensued.

Here, however, we must again say that to enter upon details of battles and engagements, connected with each of the generals whose public life we sketch, would be so great a repetition as to become tedious and irksome to the reader. At the same time we wish to do justice to the brave men we write of; and, therefore, to meet the difficulty, we have given more full accounts in the history of the principal commanding officer on the field, to which all minor particulars are referred.

On the 4th of May, Ewell's corps having been encamped on Lee's right, moved easterly, a few of his brigades remaining behind for a day, guarding some of the fords across the Rapidan.   Johnson's division, having the advance, followed the turnpike, and encamped for the night within three miles of Wilderness Run. Rodes, next in the order of march, lay in his rear along the same route; and Early, who had moved from Ewell's left at Summerville ford, encamped for the night a little behind Locust Grove. Next day, Johnson moved with his division at the head of Ewell's corps, throwing out skirmishers as he advanced. These were driven in by the enemy, and the battle began.

We have already given details of this battle, and need only say that General Ewell was constantly engaged in directing and superintending the movements of his corps. On the evening of the first day's fight, assisted by General Smith, of the Engineers, he reviewed his position, and proceeded at once to cover his front with a line of field-works and an abattis of felled trees. Next morning, the 6th of May, the enemy attacked him with a heavy force, but, being repulsed, determined to make a movement on his flank. Ewell, however, " with the true instincts of military genius" was prepared at all points, and by a bold charge of Major Osborne upon the advancing column of Burnside's division, defeated the attempt so successfully that it was not again repeated. Finally, Ewell, giving directions to Early on the left of his corps, allowed General

Gordon, at his earnest request, to make a particular movement on the enemy's flank. The sun was now about to set, but Gordon's men, supported by R. D. Johnston's brigade of North Carolinians, moved briskly out of their works, and, rushing forward, drove everything before them. "A brilliant stroke thus closed, on Ewell's front, the second day of the battle of the Wilderness, in a crowning triumph."

To give some idea of the fearful nature of the slaughter in this battle we may add that, in front of Ewell's line, alone, were 1,125 Federal dead lying to the left of the turnpike.

On Saturday, May 7th, and the following day, Lee retreated towards Spottsylvania, to take up a new position, Ewell's corps in the rear. On Sunday, the engagement was renewed near Todd's tavern, and, Ewell having come up to the support of Anderson, the fighting was very heavy. The result was satisfactory in checking the enemy's advance, and Spottsylvania Court-house was successfully occupied by the Confederates before the Federals could arrive. Ewell held the town and heights on the north side, and kept the enemy at bay in every attempt made to take possession.

On Tuesday, May 10th, the battle was again commenced,— Ewell's corps being strongly posted in the centre,—and for three days' heavy fighting continued, resulting in the discomfiture of one of his divisions, under General E. Johnson and Brigadier-general G. H. Stewart, both of whom, with their men, were captured.

The next few days various movements took place, and on Thursday, the 19th, Ewell, with part of his corps, proceeded to make a reconnoissance in force on the enemy's right flank. The country through which he had to move is very diversified by woods and fields, and so much of forest, that it was quite possible to escape the observation of the enemy. General Ewell moved by a circuitous route, and struck the enemy's line of skirmishers at a point a little north and west of the road leading from Fredericksburg to Spottsylvania, and about eight miles from the former place. About 5 P. M. a sharp engagement ensued, and lasted till nine o'clock, when the fighting ceased, and the Confederates retired to their original position.

During the action, General Ewell's horse was shot under

him, and he received a severe fall.   He tried, on the next day, to again mount the saddle; but soon was obliged to relinquish the command of his corps to General Early, and retire.   He slowly recovered, and, in July, assumed command of the Department of Henrico, and finally, of the immediate defences of Richmond.

During the period of his command in this department, the following is related concerning him.   General Singleton, in January, 1865, was at Richmond, on a semi-official errand from Washington as to the question of peace.   On his return, President Lincoln asked him if he had seen General Ewell, and how he looked.   Singleton replied that, " while walking in Richmond, one day, he saw a general officer, driving a very poor-looking horse attached to a dilapidated sulky. The horse bolted across the sidewalk, and General Singleton seeing the officer was a cripple, carrying a crutch, took the animal by the head and turned him into the street.   This was the only time he had seen Ewell."

When Richmond was evacuated and a great portion of the city burnt, Ewell was accused of setting fire to it, but in a letter since published he indignantly denies the charge.

On the 6th of April, while on the retreat with Lee's army, he was captured at Burkesville, and ultimately sent as a prisoner of war to Fort Warren.   There he remained until released in August, when he left, with his wife, for their home in Nashville, Tenn.

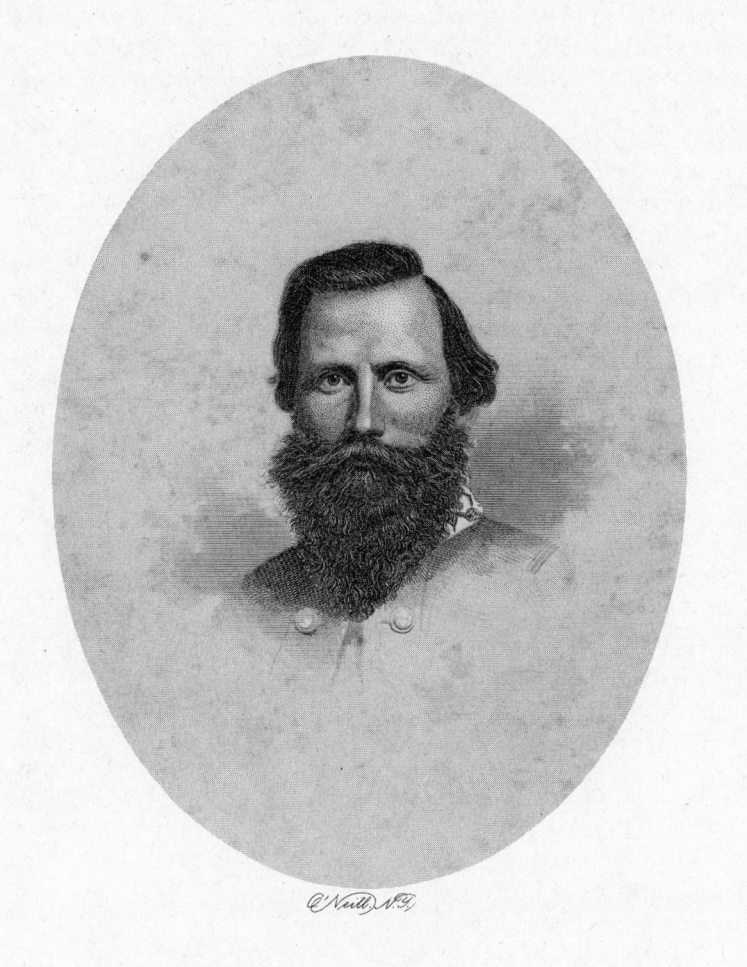

O'Neill N.Y.

GEN. J. E. B. STUART.

From a Photograph taken from life.

MAJOR-GENERAL JAMES E. B. STUART.

At the battle of Williamsburg, in 1862, while the enemy
were advancing on the redoubts from the Yorktown road, a
horseman dashed through the streets, and rode up to the headquarters of General Johnston, to report. He appeared much
fatigued and overworked, and would have served admirably
for a picture of Dick Turpin, when chased by officers on the
road to York. His horse was a splendid black, with heavy
reins and bit, cavalry saddle, and holsters: foam stood in a
lather upon him, and he was mud-splashed from head to hoof.
The rider, himself, bore no insignia of command : a common
black felt hat, turned down in front, and up behind : a heavy,
black overcoat, tightly buttoned : elegant riding-boots covering the thigh ; a handsome sabre, carelessly slung by his side,
and a heavy pair of Mexican spurs, that jingled and rattled on
the pavement as he dismounted, were all that could be noticed,
at a distance. A nearer view, however, showed a thick-set,
full-faced, ruddy-complexioned man, with close-cut hair, and
apparently some thirty years old. His eyes were bright, beaming, and, when lighted up, piercing, and full of deep expression. A stranger, unaccustomed to the war, would at first
have taken him to be a daring chief of some wild predatory
band ; and yet, a moment more would cause a change of opin-

ion, especially on hearing him speak, and noticing the high-toned, gentlemanly bearing he displayed.

As the horseman communicated with General Johnston, and mentioned something, both smiled, and presently it was known that he had been chased by "old Emory," of the Fifth United States Dragoons, whose light artillery could be heard blazing away, south of the town. In a moment more, he rode back again to the fight.

This horseman, whom we have thus described to introduce him, was James E. B. Stuart, then commanding the cavalry rear-guard of the Confederate forces at Williamsburg. Born about the year 1833, in Patrick county, Virginia, he very early displayed evidences of a quick and active turn of mind. His father, the late Archibald Stuart, formerly member of Congress, gave him a good academic education, and got him entered at West Point Academy in 1850. There, at the same time, were to be found A. P. Hill, Henry Heth, G. H. Stewart, N. G. Evans, J. H. Holmes, R. H. Robertson, S. M. Barton, and T. S. Rhett, all, of late, belonging to the Confederate army; and among his immediate classmates, were J. Pegram, G. W. Custis Lee, and J. B. Villepigue, also now fighting for the South. Of those in the academy with him, and now on the side of the North, were Burnside, Viele, Wilcox, Cogswell, O. Howard, and Lieutenant Greble of the artillery, who was killed at Great Bethel, in 1861.

Stuart graduated on the 30th of June, 1854, and next day received his appointment as brevet second lieutenant of the regiment of mounted rifles. On the 3d of March, 1855, he was transferred, with full rank, to the First Regular Cavalry, then having for its colonel, the late General Sumner, of the Union army, and for lieutenant-colonel, the present General J. E. Johnston, of the Confederate service. In July of the same year, he was made regimental quartermaster; and, the following December, received his appointment as first-lieutenant.

His regiment having been ordered to the wilds of New Mexico, he soon had an opportunity for indulging the bent of his inclination in riding and fighting with the boldest and fiercest among all the brave spirits that were there. Could we find space to narrate them, many stirring pictures might

be given of his roving, dashing, adventurous life in that region,—warring with the Indians, and bounding over the mighty plains. But we must pass over such scenes, and confine ourselves to a simple outline of his spirited career. One incident, alone, has to be related of this period. On the 29th of July, 1857, Colonel Sumner encountered a force of three hundred Indians of the Cheyenne tribe. They were strongly posted on the Solomon fork of the Kansas river, and after a sharp struggle, they were defeated and put to flight in great disorder. In this engagement Lieutenant Stuart was wounded, we believe, very severely.

Two years afterwards, Lieutenant Stuart was acting as aid to Colonel R. E. Lee, in the John Brown affair, at Harper's Ferry,—an account of which we have already given; and when the present war broke out, he resigned his commission on May 14th, 1861, and offered his sword to his native State. He immediately raised a company of cavalry, was soon afterwards elected colonel, and then acted as brigadier-general. At this time, he had a family, and many ties of kindred that might have influenced him, in the course he took. His wife was a daughter of Philip St. George Cooke, then colonel of the Second Dragoons (since a general) in the U. S. A., who was also a Virginian by birth, and a brother of the late J. R. Cooke, of Richmond. His mother, too, was alive in his native State; and several other associations bound him to her fortunes. There may have been, also, something in connection with his descent, which it is said was from David Stuart, of Inverness in Scotland, who claimed affinity with Queen Mary. This David Stuart was a follower of the elder "Pretender" to the British crown, and, in the rebellion of 1715, he was so implicated as to be obliged to fly. He emigrated to Virginia, and became tutor in the family of Mr. Brent, of Richland, Prince William county. The wife of Mr. Brent was a sister of Sir John Gibbons, Member of Parliament for Middlesex, and another sister being on a visit to Virginia at this time, ultimately became the wife of Stuart. Thus, all the connections of Colonel J. E. B. Stuart were Virginians, and combined with the inclination he had for a new and dashing life, no doubt led him to side with the South, independent of whatever patriotic feelings in that quarter he may have had.

Colonel Stuart was first stationed at Harper's Ferry, in command of the cavalry attached to Jackson's army, and his well-known bravery made him already conspicuous. It is said of him, at this time, by one who was competent to judge: "Stuart is characterized by untiring energy, clear judgment, and extra-ordinary powers of moulding and infusing his own brave spirit into the hearts of his men." General Johnston, who had assumed command of the army, also spoke of him as "the inde-fatigable Stuart;" and truly, this appellation seems deserved. While in the vicinity of the upper Potomac, he was on the alert, watching the enemy, riding from place to place with his men, and giving information to the general. From Point of Rocks to beyond Williamsport, he was constantly to and fro on duty; and, on the 15th of July, reported the advance of General Patterson. That general's movements he now incessantly watched "with lynx-eyed vigilance;" and, on one occasion, surprised a whole company, who were so much startled by his sudden command to throw down their arms, that they instantly submitted.

When General Johnston marched to unite with Beauregard at Manassas, Colonel Stuart, with his cavalry, covered the movement most effectually. Posting a cordon of pickets from Smithfield along by Summit Point and Rippon to the Shenandoah, he completely concealed the change of base, and thus enabled the army to wend its way without molestation.

In the battle of Bull Run, at the commencement, Stuart's cavalry, some 300 men, guarded the level ground extending along the stream from near Mitchell's ford to the Stone bridge, ready for employment as might be required, and during the day his impetuous spirit was permitted to have full vent. A dashing charge was made by him upon a regiment of Fire Zouaves, scattering them and riding them down against all opposition; and readers at all acquainted with the history of this battle, may remember how his daring horsemen startled the Federals in front of them, as they came, like a whirlwind, rushing forward. But, it was still more so in the disastrous panic that ensued among the Federal troops on the termination of the battle. Like the Black Hunstmen of the German forests in other times, or the wild horsemen of the Wolga, Stuart, with his men, dashed after the terror-stricken enemy. Over

the Stone bridge—across the fords—up the road—in and out of the woods where a passage could be found; on, on, slaughtering and cutting down, till they arrived near Centreville, did the Confederate cavalry pursue their way. But the rout was soon over. The foe had gone; hundreds of prisoners had been taken; many more human beings had been killed, and the victory was completely won.

In the official report of Beauregard, he thus mentions Stuart:

"Colonel J. E. B. Stuart likewise deserves mention for his enterprise and ability as a cavalry commander. Through his judicious reconnoissance of the country on our left flank, he acquired information, both of topographical features, and the positions of the enemy, of the utmost importance in the subsequent and closing movements of the day on that flank, and his services in the pursuit were highly effective."

Fairfax Court-house was occupied by Colonel Stuart the next day, and shortly afterwards he received a letter from Colonel McCunn, of the Federal army, on the subject of Colonel Cameron's body, left on the battlefield. This letter spoke in appealing terms on behalf of Cameron's wife and family, and alluded to Stuart's "kindness of heart, and high soldierly qualities;" but, of course, he could do no other than refer it to his commanding general, though he sent back a courteous reply.

A few weeks later, September 11th, Colonel Stuart successfully attacked and routed a party of Federals at Lewinsville, some six or seven miles from Washington. The affair was of no great importance, but it was the means of his being promoted to a brigadier-generalship, and this gave him more opportunity for the performance of several daring exploits. They are, however, so varied and numerous throughout his truly brilliant career, that we can only refer to minor ones, and give a little more space to those of most importance.

In the month of December, there was a fight between General Stuart's forces and the Federal troops at Dranesville, Va., in which the Confederates were defeated. Then followed a period of mere skirmishing, occasionally, between the detached parties of both armies; and, finally, in March, the Confederate forces moved southward to meet McClellan on the

Peninsula. The evacuation of Yorktown took place in the beginning of May, 1862, and the battle of Williamsburg occurred on the 4th. Here, as we have seen, General Stuart commanded the cavalry rear guard, and proved of great service in the after movements of the army on its way to Richmond.

But the affair which, more than anything else, first made his name so famous, was the bold reconnoissance conducted by him, through and around McClellan's army, in the middle part of June. This exploit borders so much upon the romantic, in its dash and gallant character, that it is almost impossible to compress it into a few lines of sober truth. It was one of those achievements that make men's blood warm up, even at the mere recital of it, more especially so to those who were participators in the stirring scene. With a force of 1,200 cavalry, and a section of the Stuart horse-artillery—having Colonel Fitz Lee, Colonel W. H. Fitzhugh Lee, Colonel W. T. Martin, and Lieutenant J. Breathed accompanying him in command—he first quietly rendezvoused beyond the Chickahominy, near Kilby's station on the Northern railroad, and then, without any one else knowing where they were bound, moved along the left of that road, scouts on the right, vedettes in advance, guards in the rear, and every precaution against surprise, or allowing the enemy to conceive their intention. Twenty-two miles of ground from Richmond did the bold raiders cover that day, and then silently bivouacked in the woods, near the South Anna bridge. A few hours' rest, and again, at sunrise, without flag or bugle-sound, they remount, and, turning sharply to the southeast, dash along the roads towards Old Church. This was held by the enemy; but Colonel Fitz Lee quickly made a detour, got behind their force, and induced them, under a false idea of numbers, to move rapidly away. Cleared from this, on went the horsemen to Howe's store, hastily captured some Federals stationed there, pushed forward to the Tolopotamy, crossed it without delay, and then, with Lieutenant Robins in the advance, skirted fields, leaped fences and ditches, rushed through woods, and suddenly came upon a party of the enemy's dragoons, reinforced, near Old Church. Instantly sabres were drawn; two squadrons went ahead at a gallop; a hand-to-hand conflict ensued; the Federals were quickly routed, though at a

cost to the Confederates of the brave Captain Latune,—and away went Stuart and his men as briskly as ever. Then went forward Colonel Fitz Lee, burning to have a brush with the enemy, now again collected near the home of his family. The country people cheered him on; they gave him information: "Hurry on, boys; hurry on; they're only a mile ahead," said one. "Four of them are prisoners here in the house," said another—a young girl with a gun in her hand. "Go in, boys; go into them," said a third; and thus it was the whole way. At the White House, Lee's squadron charged the foe; he dashed into their camp, took possession of horses, arms, stores of every kind which they burnt, captured prisoners, looked around for more, then halted for the rest of the band to join them. Now came the limits of their raid. Turn they must, and turn they did, but, not back by the way they came. No; they would try to pierce the enemy's lines, swim the Chicka-hominy, if need be, and so make the complete circuit back to their own camp. Briefly, Stuart mentioned this to his officers. Cheerfully they agreed; and then, once more, at a gallop along the road, now towards Tunstall station, did the daring horsemen go. Did they heed the danger? Did a man hesi-tate or complain? No; in good truth, not so. The gallant Stuart led them on; it was enough! Sublime in unshaken trust and confidence, the brave rank and file, not once nor for a moment faltered, though a huge army of well-trained sol-diers and skilful officers, under McClellan himself, was before them! Seemingly straight into the very jaws of the enemy, this heroic band dashed forward. But now the foe has be-come alarmed; still greater caution is needed; Colonel Martin is placed to guard the rear, but, instead of being attacked, a small outpost party voluntarily surrendered to him. On and on, however, Stuart and his followers urge their way. Tun-stall's station is reached; telegraph wires cut; the depot secured; five companies of cavalry escorting wagon trains, fly, and leave the stores; an infantry guard is captured; de-struction of the railroad is begun, when, lo! a heavy train of cars with troops aboard, comes thundering down from the Federal army! It is attacked, but the obstructions on the track are insufficient. Some loss, the troops in that train re-ceive, and away it rushed to the Pamunkey depot. Night

now comes on ; the burning stores illume the country around; the work is done; and once more Stuart and his brave command gallop forward. Moonlight helps them; but after a time they halt to close up their column. Then again at midnight the march is resumed. Day dawns : the Chickahominy is reached ; the stream is found unfordable; axes are used, trees felled ; a foot-bridge improvised under Lieutenant Redmond Burke's skilful hands; a friendly voice from some stranger gives good information ; an old bridge is mended, and cavalry, artillery, horses and men cross rapidly, and then, another dash along the Charles City road, and a mile or two more brings them near their main encampment. Faint, famished, worn out, utterly exhausted, the enemy now in full pursuit, this gallant band arrives within the Confederate lines, and draw rein, almost for the first time, except as mentioned, for more than sixty hours.

We may now only add that for this daring achievment Stuart was promoted to be a major-general of cavalry, and none of his officers or men failed to receive reward. The damage to the enemy was great, and perhaps more through the circumstance itself, than on account of stores and property destroyed.

A few days afterwards, General Stuart rode from camp into town, and was paying his respects to the authorities in a quiet way, at the executive mansion, when, as it became known to the large crowd of strollers in the Capitol square, that he was near by, the building was immediately surrounded by an enthusiastic multitude vociferating for Stuart. The gallant general in a few minutes made his appearance upon the portico and acknowledged the compliment paid him in a few remarks full of spirit and good cheer. Among other things he said he had been to the Chickahominy to visit some of his old friends of the United States army, but they, very uncivilly, turned their backs upon him. Seeing a manifest desire on the part of the people to make for him an ovation, the general then mounted his charger and galloped off amid the shouts of the crowd, which, by this time, had increased to more than a thousand persons.

The preceding illustration of one of Stuart's exploits will serve in a measure for the whole. After the same fashion did

he and his men traverse the whole region of the principal battlefields of Virginia, except the Shenandoah Valley, and, could we find space, many a stirring incident might be related.

At the time "Stonewall" Jackson was marching towards Pope's army, General Stuart arrived on a tour of inspection. He took command of the cavalry, and proceeded to reconnoitre, rendering most important service. After the battle of Cedar Run, during the short truce which followed for burying the dead, many officers of both armies met and conversed upon the field. Stuart was among them, and it was then that the following interesting incident occurred, as related by an eye witness:

"On a fallen gum-tree—the slain stretched around them—sat the officers of the parley; upon one side the Confederate cavalry leader, Stuart, and General Early; upon the other, Generals Hartsuff and Roberts. Stuart was lithe, gray-eyed, and tall; of an intense countenance, nervous, impulsive manner; and clad in gray, with a soft black hat. He wore, curiously enough, United States buttons, and his sword, which he exhibited, was made in Philadelphia. Early was a quiet, severe North Carolinian, who wore a home-spun civil suit, with a brigadier's star on his shoulder-bar. General Hartsuff was burly and good-humored; Roberts silent and sage, with white beard and distrustful eye. The former had been a classmate of the cavalry man, and he said, 'Stuart, old boy, how d ye do?' 'God bless my soul, Hartsuff,' replied the other, 'it warms my heart to see you!' and they took a turn together, arm in arm."

Shortly afterwards, Stuart, at the head of his cavalry, made another of those bold dashes, which so characterized him. General Pope then had his headquarters at Catlett's station, and, on a sudden, one night in the midst of a storm, Stuart got in the enemy's rear, and rushed upon Pope's quarters. That general escaped just in time, but with the loss of his coat and hat, besides many important documents, plans, maps, estimates, and returns of forces. In addition, there was much clothing found, including new full-dress suits for General Pope and his staff, also a quantity of private baggage, wines, liquors, etc. Some of the Union rifles had been stationed near the

headquarters, but they were quickly dispersed, and when Stuart's daring horsemen found that General Pope had escaped, they were so vexed that, instantly dividing into small parties, they galloped down every road with the hope of overtaking him, but in vain.

In the succeeding movements of the Confederate army, General Stuart was constantly engaged with a perfect net-work of scouting parties, and a cordon of pickets between Pope and Jackson. At Bristoe station he attacked a train of the enemy, and afterwards dashed upon Manassas, capturing a battery of New York artillery, and destroying an immense quantity of stores deposited there. He then galloped on to meet, and, if need be, assist Longstreet at Thoroughfare gap, capturing a party of Federals on the way, and engaging the Federal cavalry. Hearing the sound of a battle at or near Stone bridge, on August 29th, he hastily returned, and gallantly shared in the engagement going on; as also in the great fight of the next day. But hardly had the smoke of that second Bull Run victory to the South died away, than Stuart was off with his cavalry into Maryland — swimming fords — dashing through woods and fields—fighting where they could find an enemy—peaceably moving where there was a friend or non-combatant. The invasion of that State, and the events that occurred have already been told; but the following incident may be related.

On the retreat, a few of Stuart's cavalry were, on the morning of September 12th, at Frederick ready to depart. Some recruits had joined the bold legion under Stuart's command, and these were bidding tender adieus to some loved friends, when up rode a few squadrons of Federal cavalry, commanded by a Dutch major, with immense moustache. Halting before the city hall, he exclaimed, "Vere ish de Got tam repels? Vere ish de Got fur-tam Stuart—vere ish he mit his cavalrie? Let me shee him, unt I show him some tings!" A lady present, told him that a few of Fitzhugh Lee's cavalry had just left. "Goot! young voomans," said Meinheer, and immediately started in pursuit, saying, "Ve show de repels some tings." The major and his command had fairly got into the main street, when a company of Confederate cavalry met them, and both parties rushed together in strife. The upshot was, that the major's command was routed, and he himself,

shortly afterwards, pulled out of a cottage with a table-cloth bound round a slight wound in his head, and sent to the Confederate rear as a prisoner.

The retreat of the Confederate army into Virginia kept Stuart's force ever actively employed, and when other troops rested he found work elsewhere.   After a sharp affair at Sheperdstown with the Federal cavalry, he again started, on October 10th, upon another daring raid.   While the North were congratulating themselves that all the "rebels" had been driven away, General Stuart, with a force of some 1,300 troopers, under Hampton, W. H. F. Lee, and Jones, suddenly appeared before Chambersburg, in Pennsylvania, "took possession of the town, captured and destroyed much public property, mounted themselves anew on good horses, passed around the entire Federal army, and safely returned to their own camp, in Virginia, to recount their triumphs, without loss, or more than a few wounds received in skirmishes."*

Two or three skirmishes and minor engagements followed, between Stuart's cavalry and the enemy's under Pleasanton and others, but we must pass them over with this mere allusion to them.   Nothing that could be said in a brief space would do full justice to these rapid and remarkable exploits of Stuart, Hampton, the two Lees, and the brave officers and men under their command.

At the battle of Fredericksburg, in the following December, Stuart was on the right of Jackson's corps, and directed the batteries, fighting them with unyielding obstinacy, himself being everywhere in the thickest of the fight—"the target of artillery and sharpshooters alike."   His horse-artillery—including Captain Henry's, and the lamented heroic Pelham's—made sad havoc with Franklin's left flank; and "well did Stuart redeem his grim dispatch—that he was ' going to crowd them with artillery.'   The ceremony was too rough for them to stand, and when the voice of the general, in the darkness, ordered the last advance, the combat had terminated in the silence of the foe."

The battle of Fredericksburg was wholly concluded on December 15th, 1862, and immediately afterwards, away went

---

* Northern accounts, and see Stuart's official report.

Stuart and his men again, dashing about the country wherever
an enemy was found. The *scare* occasioned in the North at
this time, by his bold raids, is well remembered; but the following summary of what was done will be enough description.
Starting suddenly to the northward, around the Federal army,
he alarmed the whole district between Manassas and Washington by his rapid and successive attacks, and the captures he
made. A large force, in parties, was sent in vain to catch
him; but he was too sharp and keen for his pursuers. His object was to gain information of the position and movements of
the enemy, and the results were considered very important.
The only thing to be regretted was the loss of Captain John
W. Bullock, of the Fifth cavalry, one of the best and bravest
officers in the service. He was wounded at Dumfries, while in
command of the sharpshooters and gallantly charging a regiment of Federal infantry. While his friends were bearing him
from the field he was again hit in two places and mortally
wounded.

After scattering the enemy at Dumfries, General Stuart
went on to the Occoquan; but word having been sent out of
his approach, he found all the fords guarded. He determined,
however, to cross at Selectmen's ford, in the face of the enemy.
The advance was led by Colonel T. L. Rosser, of the Fifth
cavalry, who dashed into the stream, followed by Colonel
Drake, of the First, and some fifteen or twenty men. The
enemy had dismounted, and were drawn up in line of battle.
Colonel Rosser, placing himself at the head of the few men
near him, led the charge up in the face of a heavy fire, by file,
over a narrow and rocky ford. The Federals broke and were
pursued, several being captured. *General Stuart said he regarded this as the most gallant thing done by the cavalry since
the war commenced.* Colonel Rosser afterwards charged into
their camp and captured nine sutler wagons, loaded with the
best of liquor, clothing, boots, and luxuries of various kinds,
and burned their tents and army stores.

General Stuart then went towards Aldie, accomplishing many
of his characteristic feats. At Aldie, Colonel Rosser was sent
on a scout into the valley of Virginia to ascertain the state of
things there. Taking with him only fifteen men, he succeeded
in going around the most of Milroy's army, and passed nearly

ninety miles in front of General Jones. Although the country was full of bands trying to capture him, Colonel Rosser eluded them all, and after remaining inside of the enemy's lines as long as he pleased, started to return. At the Shenandoah he encountered the pickets of the enemy posted to catch him, but by a peculiar stratagem he captured them all, passed by their army at night, and returned safely to camp, bringing along with him all the Federal sentinels on the route.

This hurried sketch of what was done, would be incomplete if we did not mention that at one place he captured a telegraph station, and set the wires to work to deceive the enemy. The following letter from him refers to it.

HEADQUARTERS, Jan. 6, 1863.
DR. W. S. MORRIS, President Southern Telegraph Company, Richmond.

SIR—I have the honor to send, through the courtesy of Major John Pelham, my chief of artillery, an instrument captured at Burke's station, Ohio and Alexandria railroad, during my late expedition. I beg that you will accept it as a token of regard appropriate to your position. We surprised the operator, and my operator, Shepperd, took his place. I sat in the office some time while Shepperd read the wild alarms flashing over the wires about our operations, and ascertained the steps taken and the means at hand of resisting me, and then shaped my course accordingly.

Very respectfully your obedient servant,
J. E. B. STUART,
Major-general of Cavalry.

Later in the month of January, a detachment of Stuart's cavalry drove in the Federal pickets at Chantilly, but Colonel Wyndham afterwards routed them, and took prisoner, among others, the Rev. Mr. Landstreet, chaplain to General Stuart's force. But we must now again pass on. In the history of the war, yet to be written by some impartial pen, many pages will have to be filled with exploits of the cavalry on both sides, and it needs a volume by itself to give, in any sort of detail, those performed by Stuart and his companions. Speaking of the Southern Generals, an able writer says, "Each has his warm admirers, gained by such opportunities of intercourse as

have brought individuals within the said general's orbit   Each
has attached to him the prestige of entire absence of failure.
Il n'y a rien qui reussit autant que le succes.

"But while in the Shenandoah valley the achievements of
General Jackson aroused towards him a generous feeling of
gratitude for danger averted and prosperity preserved, it is
doubtful whether east of the Blue Ridge the twenty-nine years
of General Stuart, added to that indefatigable energy which
teaches him, after he has ridden fifty miles during the day, to
regard it as his highest happiness to ride a dozen more miles
at night 'to tread but one measure' in a Virginian country
house, do not incline the scale, especially if the balance be ad-
justed by fair hands, in favor of the younger general. There
have been many English officers, particularly in the East
Indian service, whose endurance in the saddle has been regarded as unequalled; but I doubt whether any Englishman
ever exhibited such superiority to bodily fatigue as is almost
nightly evinced by the gay cavalier who knows every hospitable. roof within a dozen miles of his headquarters (and what
roof is not hospitable?) and, accompanied by his banjo player,
visits them by turns, night after night, returning usually to his
hard-earned rest long after the midnight hour has flown.
With the earliest dawn of morning, the first ·voice, calling
gaily for breakfast, is that of the midnight merrymaker, who
rises the picture of health, good humor, and strength. It may
be noticed *en passant* that to the circumstance that he has
never touched tobacco in any form, or any wine, or other
liquor, General Stuart attributes much of his health and vigor.
Certainly so jovial and merry a company as is assembled at
General Stuart's headquarters it has never been my fortune to
see here."

Another account speaks of Stuart as being of a "free, socia-
ble, agreeable, and lively turn of mind," and as "a gentleman
of high-toned accomplishments, and rare genius;" "of more
than ordinary size, very handsome, fair complexion, with
bright beaming eyes, quick perception and deep expression."
He had with him, on his staff, "several odd and fantastic
characters. His cook was a Frenchman from one of the Café
houses in Paris, a ventriloquist and comical genius; the principal business man in his office was a Prussian, a man of dis-

tinction, education and wit; and in the musical department he had Sweeny, Jr., son of old Joe."

In the month of April, 1863, General Stuart was in com mand of the forces, respectively under Fitz Lee, and W. H. F. Lee, that successfully resisted the enemy's attempt to establish himself on the south side of the Rappahannock. On the 29th he reported to General Lee the movements of Hooker's army, and this enabled the Confederates to prepare for the coming battle.

Stuart did all he could to impede the enemy, and was ably seconded by the Lees. He crossed the Rapidan, hung upon Hooker's flanks, attacked his right at the Wilderness tavern, then marched by Todd's tavern to Spottsylvania Courthouse, to put himself in communication with the main army. In the movement of Jackson to the Wilderness, he was effectually covered by Fitz Lee's cavalry, commanded by General Stuart in person.

At dark, finding nothing else for him, as a cavalry leader, to do, he proposed to Jackson that the road to Ely's ford, in rear of the enemy, should be seized. Jackson approving, he went forward to this task, and had gained the heights when a messenger came with news of both Jackson and A. P. Hill being wounded, and urging him to come back and take command. He did so, and next morning vigorously pushed forward the corps now under his orders. The result is known; and we need only add to what we have before said, that he was very highly complimented in General Lee's official report, for " the energy, promptness, distinguished capacity, and vigor, added to his own personal example of coolness, and daring displayed."

In the grand movement of the Confederate army towards Pennsylvania, that followed upon the battle of Chancellorsville, General Stuart concentrated his forces at Culpepper, on the 8th of June, and next day was attacked by the enemy's cavalry and some infantry, at Brandy station. General Fitz Hugh Lee commanded the Confederates, and Generals Buford and Gregg the Federals. The battle commenced at 5 A. M., and lasted till 3 P. M., both parties fighting almost entirely with sabres. The result was claimed as a victory on both sides, but the enemy had to recross the Rappahannock, and

leave several prisoners, with some artillery, and colors in the hands of Stuart's command.

Of the march to Pennsylvania, and the succeeding campaign with the battle of Gettysburg, we have already given an account. General Stuart had his full share of that peril and adventure for which his temperament was so well adapted. As an eye witness well observes, "He roamed over the country almost at his own discretion, and always giving a good account of himself, turning up at the right moment, and never getting himself into any serious trouble."

The subsequent operations of General Stuart were now mostly those connected with the main army, as related in our sketch of General Lee. The flank movement of the Confederates, in October, gave Stuart ample work to perform; and, in December another raid was successfully undertaken upon the Orange and Alexandria railroad.

In the month of January, 1864, General Stuart was again at work on the Potomac, about Leesburg, and the Point of Rocks; and, with occasional visits to Richmond and his family, thus fully occupied his time.

On the 28th of February, he was encamped at Orange Court-house, and sent to Richmond a highly complimentary report of Colonel Mosby's daring exploit near Drainesville; and, in the early part of March occurred the affair already mentioned, between the Federals under General Custer, and the Confederate cavalry near Rio Mills.

The spring campaign then followed; the battle of the Wilderness had been fought, and, at last, the day came when the bold cavalry chief—the dashing raider—the kind and genial companion, as well as the skilful soldier—General Stuart—would be no more.

General Sheridan, of the Federal cavalry, had made a bold dash around Lee's flank, towards Richmond, and a portion of his command, under Generals Custer and Merrill, arrived at Ashland station, on the 10th of May, just before Stuart with his force reached there after them. The next day they were followed to a place called Yellow-tavern, where an engagement took place. Here, in a desperate charge, at the head of a column, the gallant Stuart fell, terribly wounded. He was immediately taken to Richmond, and every effort made to

save his life, but in vain. On the 11th he died, and the following account of his last moments, as related by those around him, may be interesting :

" About noon, President Davis visited his bedside and spent some time with the dying chief. In reply to the question put by the President, " General, how do you feel ?" he replied, " Easy, but willing to die, if God and my country think I have fulfilled my destiny, and done my duty.

" During the day, occasional delirium attacked him, and, in his moments of mental wandering, his faculties were busy with the past. His campaigns on the Peninsula, his raid into Pennsylvania, his doings on the Rapidan, and his several engagements, were subjects that quickly chased themselves through his brain. Fresh orders were given as if still on the battlefield and injunctions to his couriers to " make haste." Then he would wander to his wife and children, one of whom, his eldest boy, had died a year previous, while fighting on the Rappahannock, and in relation to whom he had said, when receiving a telegram that the boy was dying, " I must leave my child in the hands of God ; my country needs me here ; I cannot come." Then his mind would again carry him on to the battlefield ; and so it continued throughout the day. Occasionally his intellect was clear, and he was then calm and resigned, though at times suffering the most acute agony. He would even, with his own hand, apply the ice that was intended to relieve the pain of his wound.

" As evening wore on, mortification set in rapidly. In answer to his inquiry, he was told that death was fast approaching. He then said, ' I am resigned, if it be God's will, but I would like to see my wife. But, God's will be done.' Several times he roused up, and asked if she had come. Unfortunately, she was in the country at the time, and did not arrive until too late.

" As the last moments approached, the dying man, with a mind perfectly clear and possessed, then made a disposition of his effects. To Mrs. General R. E. Lee, he directed that the golden spurs be given as a dying memento of his love and esteem for her husband. To his staff officers he gave his horses ; and other mementoes he disposed of in a similar manner. To his young son, he left his sword. He then

turned to the Reverend Dr. Peterkin, of the Episcopal church, of which he was a strict member, and asked him to sing the hymn commencing :

> Rock of ages cleft for me,
> Let me hide myself in thee.

"In this he joined with all the strength of voice his failing powers permitted. He then prayed with the minister and friends around him; and, with the words, 'I am going fast now. I am resigned; God's will be done,' yielded his fleeting spirit to Him who gave it."

"The funeral of this much lamented and brave general took place on the 13th, at five o'clock, from St. James's church, corner of Marshall and Fifth streets.

"At the appointed hour the cortege appeared in front of the church, and the metallic coffin, containing the remains of the noble soldier, whose now silent voice had so often startled the enemy with his stirring battlecry, was carried down the centre aisle and placed before the altar. Wreaths, and a cross of evergreen, interwoven with delicate lilies of the valley, laurel and other flowers of purest white, decked the coffin.

"The pallbearers were General Bragg, Major-general Mc-Cown, General Chilton, Brigadier-general Lawton, Commodore Forrest, Captain Lee, of the Navy, and General George W. Randolph, formerly Secretary of War.

"The scene was sad and impressive. President Davis sat near the front, with a look of grief upon his careworn face; his cabinet officers were gathered around, while on either side were the senators and representatives of the Confederate Congress. Scattered through the church were a number of generals and other officers of less rank, among the former, General Ransom, commanding the department of Richmond. Hundreds of sad faces witnessed the scene; but the brave Fitz Lee and other war-wearied and war-worn men, whom the dead Stuart had so often led where the red battle was fiercest, and who would have given their lives for his, were away in the fight, doubtless striking with a double courage as they thought of their fallen general.

"The short service was read by Rev. Dr. Peterkin, a funeral anthem sung, and the remains were carried out and placed in

the hearse, which proceeded to Hollywood Cemetery, followed by a long train of carriages.

"No military escort accompanied the procession, but the hero was laid in his last resting-place on the hillside, while the earth trembled with the roar of artillery and the noise of the deadly strife of armies—the one bent upon desecrating and devastating his native land, and the other, proudly and defiantly standing in the path and invoking the blessing of Heaven upon their cause, to fight in better cheer for the memory of such as Stonewall Jackson and J. E. B. Stuart."

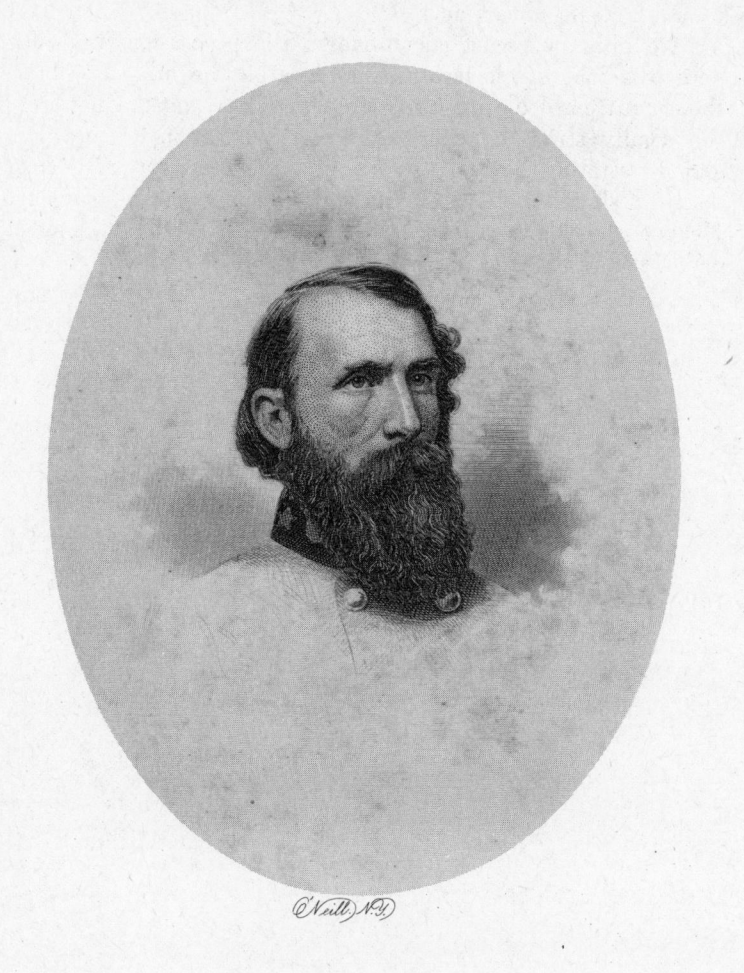

GEN. A. P. HILL

From a Photograph taken from life.

GENERAL AMBROSE POWELL HILL.

A New York paper, in speaking of the Confederate leaders,
says: "In all the battles of the war east of the mountains from
Bull Run to Antietam creek, five names have been conspicuous—Jackson, Ewell, Longstreet, A. P. Hill, and D. H. Hill.
All these men commanded brigades or divisions at the first
Bull Run contest. In all the fights in front of Washington,
last summer and fall, in all the terrible conflicts in the Peninsula, and before Richmond, in the recent bloody contests with
Pope along the Rapidan, and around Manassas, and in the
sanguinary engagements at South Mountain, and upon the
heights that overhang Sharpsburg, these five men have been
the leaders of the Confederates—with the single exception, that
Ewell, having been wounded in the battle near Centreville,
was unable to take part in those of Western Maryland. Many
of our readers have no doubt often inquired who are these
men, and whence came they? Beyond all doubt, they are
good generals, and have fought in a manner worthy of a better
cause."

Of the generals here named, we have already given a short
sketch of three, and now propose to furnish an account of the
fourth.

Ambrose Powell Hill was a son of Virginia. He was born about the year 1824, in the county of Culpepper, where his father, Major Hill, was, for many years, a leading politician, and merchant. In the year 1843 he entered West Point as a cadet, and graduated on the 3d of June, 1847, in the same class with General Burnside. On the 1st of July he was brevetted second-lieutenant of the First Artillery ; and on the 22d of August was made full second-lieutenant. On the 4th of September, 1851, he was promoted first-lieutenant of the First Artillery, and afterwards to a captaincy. In November, 1855, he was appointed an assistant on the United States Coast Survey. On the 1st of March, 1861, he resigned his position in the regular army, and when his native State seceded, received an appointment from the Governor, as Colonel of the Thirteenth regiment of Virginia Volunteers.

At the commencement of the war, Colonel A. P. Hill was stationed at Harper's Ferry, with the Confederate army assembled there. On the morning of the 13th of June, General Johnston having received information from Winchester, that Romney was occupied by two thousand Federal troops, supposed to be the van-guard of McClellan's army, dispatched Colonel Hill thither, with his own and Colonel Gibbon's (Tenth) Virginia regiments. He was directed to take the best position, and adopt the best measures in his power to check the advance of the enemy. But, immediately afterwards, it was ascertained, that McClellan was moving southward from Grafton, and therefore, Colonel Hill was withdrawn from Romney, leaving Colonel McDonald's regiment of cavalry to defend that region of country.

At the battle of Manassas, Colonel Hill arrived with his regiment, among those of General Johnston's command, who had been detained so long as only to come in time to share the last portion of the fight. But we find no mention of his name until, as a Brigadier-general, he fought at Williamsburg with such spirit and determination as to be especially noticed on the field. He was then made a Major-general ; and, on the 25th of June, 1862, formed one of the council-of-war, held in Richmond, at which were present Generals Lee, Jackson, Longstreet, D. H. Hill, Magruder, and others of high note in the Confederate army. At this time his division was on the

Meadow-bridge road, to the left of Longstreet, who was on the Mechanicsville road, close to the river Chickahominy. Hill, by this position, now united with, and became the right of Jackson's army that had just arrived.

Next day the fight began. Hugging the north bank of the river, Ambrose Hill maintained an unbroken line, and boldly held his position against the enemy, ultimately driving them from the bridge, which they had occupied, and thus cleared a way for Longstreet and D. H. Hill, to advance. He then re-formed his troops, and commenced an attack upon Mechanics-ville itself, which brought on a terrific fight.

This place had been strongly fortified by General Fitz John Porter, of the Federal army; and it is probable that, had not Ambrose Hill known that Jackson and Longstreet were near, he would have felt himself too weak to attempt its capture.

Artillery on both sides now opened with a terrible roar, and, as evening fell, the flash of guns, and long lines of musketry could be seen, in bright relief, against the blue and cloudless sky. A half hour of this deafening cannonade passed, with shells screaming through the air, and bursting upon the troops on either side, when the direct assault was ordered to be made. Then the enemy's artillery opened again, with great rapidity, upon the advancing men, "until it seemed as if every tree in the forest was cracking and shivering to pieces." The men under Hill's command, however, rushed on through this fearful fire, and swarmed into the breastworks. "In a little while the Federal guns were silent: a loud noise of many voices was heard; and then a long, wild, piercing yell, as of ten thousand demons, and the place was won!"

During the battle General Hill was ever in the front, regardless of danger; and although his coat was torn in several places, miraculously escaped.

The next day's work, General Ambrose Hill was in the centre of the army, bearing towards Cold Harbor, and proceeding with Longstreet, along the edge of the Chickahominy. When near Hogan's plantation, he halted a while to await the arrival of Jackson at Cold Harbor, and directly this was ascertained, he marched forward, in accordance with instructions from General Lee. His position was the centre of the whole army, but on the left of that portion of it which now advanced to

unite with Jackson. On arriving in front of the enemy he
vigorously pushed their centre; but his division, thoroughly exhausted by hard marching and previous fighting, was unequal
to the task, and was withdrawn in favor of Whiting's division
of Texans, Alabamians, and Mississippians. Hill marched to
the rear, and rested awhile. Here, when the enemy had been
driven back to the right, he suddenly rose up before them, and
attacked so severely, that, coupled with the assault of Jackson,
and the rest, they had to retreat most hastily.

For several days following, the pursuit of the Federals was
continued, Ambrose Hill's division being one of the foremost
in advance, on their left flank. The wretched, swampy
country through which both armies had to move, we have
already described, and it was with difficulty the troops could
proceed. Nevertheless, "onward" was the word, and amidst
a scene of carnage and destruction, Hill, with his heroic followers, "rushed forward to contend with the fresh and untouched divisions of the enemy. Now driven back, new troops
poured in to take their place, and General Hill continually
found himself opposed to several reliefs ere other regiments of
the Confederate army could come up." The fighting was most
determined and heroic on both sides; and at length the position of General Hill became precarious in the extreme. Fortunately, he collected some of the broken divisions of other
commands, and, together, he once more dashed towards the
foe, who thereupon retired; fortunately, perhaps, for him, as
he could hardly have withstood them longer, with his few
torn and wearied brigades. Gathering the remnants of his
gallant division, almost decimated by continual hard fought
engagements, he moved to the rear to recruit and reform.

In this engagement, General McCall, of the Federal army,
was captured.

It has been said, by a participant in this battle, that "had
not Hill's division been made of steel, rather than flesh and
blood, they could not have withstood the many hardships of
these trying days; for, after fighting desperately at Mechanicsville on Thursday, they marched to Gaines's Mills and
fought five hours on Friday; rested part of Saturday; travelled a circuitous route, and a terrible road of many miles, o
Sunday and Monday, achieving another brilliant victory

against great odds. Hill, however, is a military genius, and had it not been for the scientific handling of his men, few would have rested uninjured on the torn and bloody field of Monday night. All were prostrated with fatigue, and lay on the ground without fires, covering, or food, too weary to think of any thing but rest."

The pursuit of the enemy to Malvern Hill, and the engagement there, fell upon other portions of the army, and General Hill afterwards retired to the intrenchments around Richmond. Not long afterwards, however, he was sent to reinforce Stonewall Jackson, who had been dispatched to check the advance of Pope in North Virginia. At the battle of Cedar Run, General Hill gallantly maintained the prestige he had already gained, his division strongly supporting Ewell's position, and vigorously maintaining the fight. In the subsequent operations, as previously narrated, he bore a conspicuous part, marching with Jackson on his flank movement towards the Rappahannock and Manassas. His especial part in the work, after surprising the latter place, was to deceive the enemy by drawing their attention to his own movements, while Jackson proceeded to the old battlefield of Bull Run. Hill's division, with some cavalry, marched to Centreville, and thence suddenly turned back by the Warrenton road to the famous Stone bridge. Near this point, he rejoined Jackson, after being hotly pursued by the Federalists.

The battle that followed has already been told, with the part General A. P. Hill so ably played therein; but we may add, that his division fought so bravely, and fired so fast, that, having shot away all their cartridges, they set about collecting more from the bodies of fallen friends and foes, and thus continued the engagement. When the cartridges, so obtained, gave out, they then charged forward with a fierce yell, and the cold steel of the bayonet. The next morning, August 30th, General Hill's corps held the ridge of hills on the battleground, with Longstreet on the right, at an obtuse angle, so that if the enemy attacked the centre, they would have their flank exposed to Longstreet, and if they forced him back, their flank would be open to Hill. We need not repeat what followed. The second battle of Bull Run was fought, and the enemy again defeated. General Hill went forward in pursuit,

and on the 1st of September, he encountered a large body of the Federals of Germantown, a small village near the main road from Centreville to Fairfax Court-house. General Hill immediately ordered the attack, and after a brief, but hotly contested fight, the enemy withdrew.

The Confederate army then marched into Maryland; and General Hill accompanied that part of it under command of Jackson. On the 6th of September, Hill's division, with Ewell's, occupied a position near the railroad bridge, on the Monocacy, guarding the approaches from Washington; but when it was ordered to move on Harper's Ferry, he rapidly proceeded there by the road from Williamsport to Martinsburg, recrossing the Potomac, and taking the advance. Martinsburg was evacuated on his approach, and General Hill pursued his way unmolested, coming in sight of the enemy drawn up in force at Bolivar Heights, about 11 A. M. on September 13th. He then encamped near Hallstown, about two miles from the enemy's position. In the afternoon of the next day, General Hill was ordered to move along the left bank of the Shenandoah, turn the enemy's left, and enter Harper's Ferry. General Lawton, commanding the division of Ewell (absent on account of his wounded leg), was directed to move along the turnpike for the purpose of supporting General Hill, and otherwise operating against the enemy to his left. In execution of these orders, General Hill moved obliquely to the right, until he struck the Shenandoah river. Observing an eminence, crowning the extreme left of the enemy's line, occupied by infantry, but without artillery, and protected only by an abattis of fallen timber, Pender, Archer, and Brockenbrough, were directed to gain its crest, while Branch and Gregg marched along the river, and, during the night, to take advantage of the ravines, cutting the precipitous banks of the river, and establish themselves on the plains to the left and rear of the enemy's works. Thomas followed as a reserve. All this was effectively accomplished, Lieutenant-colonel Walker, chief of Hill's artillery, bringing up the batteries of Captains Pegram, McIntosh, Davidson, Braxton, and Crenshaw. On the 15th, at an early hour, the attack on the enemy began, and shortly afterwards General Hill, according to orders, ceased firing, as a signal for storming the works. The white

flag was, however, soon displayed, and the garrison capitulated. General Hill was left to receive the surrender of the Federal troops, etc., while Jackson moved forward to the main army under Lee.

General Hill having accomplished this, then proceeded to Antietam, where the battle was raging, and reached there at 4 P. M., on the 17th of September, taking his position on the Confederate right. His timely arrival materially aided in the fortunes of the day, and enabled General Lee to maintain his ground, though, as we have elsewhere shown, neither party left in a condition to renew the conflict.

The following night, September 18th, the army fell back to Virginia, recrossing the Potomac early on the morning of the 19th. General Hill, with General Early, had gone on, in the advance, towards Martinsburg, but a force of the enemy came over the river, and General Hill faced about to charge them. "His division," says Jackson, in the official report, "advanced with great gallantry against the infantry, in the face of a continual discharge of shot and shell from their batteries. . . The enemy were driven into the river, followed by an appalling scene of the destruction of human life." An eye-witness says, "With no stop or hesitation, using no artillery, sending his men in steadily, General A. P. Hill drove the enemy into and across the river, taking 300 prisoners, and *making the river blue with their dead.*"

The army now recuperated awhile, and generals, officers, and soldiers obtained that rest they so much needed. Again they took up the march, and crossed North Virginia to Fredericksburg. There, as we have before related, another great battle was fought, and General Hill was again conspicuous. His part in that battle we mentioned in the words of his gallant commander, General Lee; but we may add that the fighting was terribly severe at his position on the right, and nothing but the most determined bravery and endurance could have prevented his division from being annihilated by the impetuous charge of Franklin and Hooker.

From this date there is little to record of General Hill that has not already been stated in previous sketches. His individuality is merged in the glorious deeds of the army wherein he bore so high and important a position. To relate, in de-

detail, what was done by this brave and skilful officer at
Chancellorsville, and again in Maryland and Pennsylvania,
would involve useless repetition, and the reader must be
referred to the preceding more extended accounts of this
period.

In the spring of 1863, the Confederate army was in winter-
quarters at Fredericksburg, when, on the 28th of April, *at
midnight*, General Hill, in accordance with orders received
that evening, took up his march towards Chancellorsville. In
the battle that followed, his division formed the centre of Jackson's corps, on the old turnpike road, near the Wilderness.
General Rhodes was in front, and when Hill moved forward,
after Rhodes had gallantly charged, he had to form his men in
and on each side of the road leading through the thick wood.
It was at that time Jackson met his death wound, and his last
order was to his staff, "Go back and tell A. P. Hill to press
right on!" The command of the corps now, however, devolved upon General Hill, as the senior officer, but while
rushing forward to the assault he himself was wounded, and
had to retire from the field. For his gallantry in this battle,
Hill was soon after made a lieutenant-general, and had the
command of one of the three grand corps into which the army was
then divided. Fortunately his wound did not detain him long
from the saddle. On the 8th of June he was commanding his
corps, again on the march to new scenes of glory. Up the
Shenandoah, into Maryland, and at Gettysburg, his name
prominently appears with the other brave generals who figured
there. On the first day's fight (July 1st), at Gettysburg, the
corps of General Hill was mostly engaged, two of his divisions
driving the enemy back, and capturing a great many prisoners, some cannon and colors. In speaking to one looking
on at this engagement, he said, "The Yankees have fought
with a determination unusual to them;" and he pointed out a
railway cutting in which they had made a good stand. He
also showed a field, in the centre of which he had seen a man
plant the regimental colors, round which the regiment had
fought for some time with much obstinacy, and when, at
length, it was obliged to retreat, the color-bearer retired last of
all, turning round every now and then to shake his fist at the
advancing Confederates. The poor fellow, however, sacrificed

his life to his fearlessness, and General Hill said he felt truly sorry when he saw him fall.

On the following day, General Hill occupied the centre ot the Confederate army, and was seated, with General Lee, just below a tree, watching through his glass the progress of the fight. Two of his brigades gave way, and night closed upon the scene. Next day a portion only of his corps was engaged, with what result the reader already knows.

The next important movement of the army, after the retreat from Gettysburg, was in October, 1863, when General Hill was sent forward to Bristoe station in pursuit of Meade's army, which had fallen back from its advanced position on the Rappahannock. Hill had but two brigades in front, and these were repulsed with considerable loss in killed and wounded, besides five pieces of artillery. General Hill then returned to the Rappahannock, whither Meade followed, and routed a small force stationed there to guard the bridge over the river.

We must now pass on to the momentous campaign of the year 1864, in every battle of which General Hill bore a part. During the period of rest, from the preceding November until May, nothing occurred of importance to relate in this connection. Encamped with the army on the Rapidan, it was not till the 4th of that month he had again an opportunity to signalize himself, but this was conspicuously done when he marched rapidly from his quarters to the Wilderness, and shared in that hard-fought battle. Hill's corps behaved, on this occasion, with the most remarkable bravery, and the general himself was everywhere present, pressing on and encouraging his men. Spottsylvania, Cold Harbor, Petersburg, and every fight around Richmond, all bear witness to the heroism and determination of the Confederate generals and their officers and men. We have already told the tale, as fully as space would permit, in our sketch of General Lee, to which we refer. In all reports of those engagements, to the present time, a well-deserved tribute is paid to the skill and valor of Lieutenant-General A. P. Hill. On the 1st of April, 1865, during the attack of the Union forces on the works around Petersburg, General Hill, in trying to rally his troops, fell, pierced by three bullets, and his body was buried, next day, in the city He was a brave soldier and good officer.

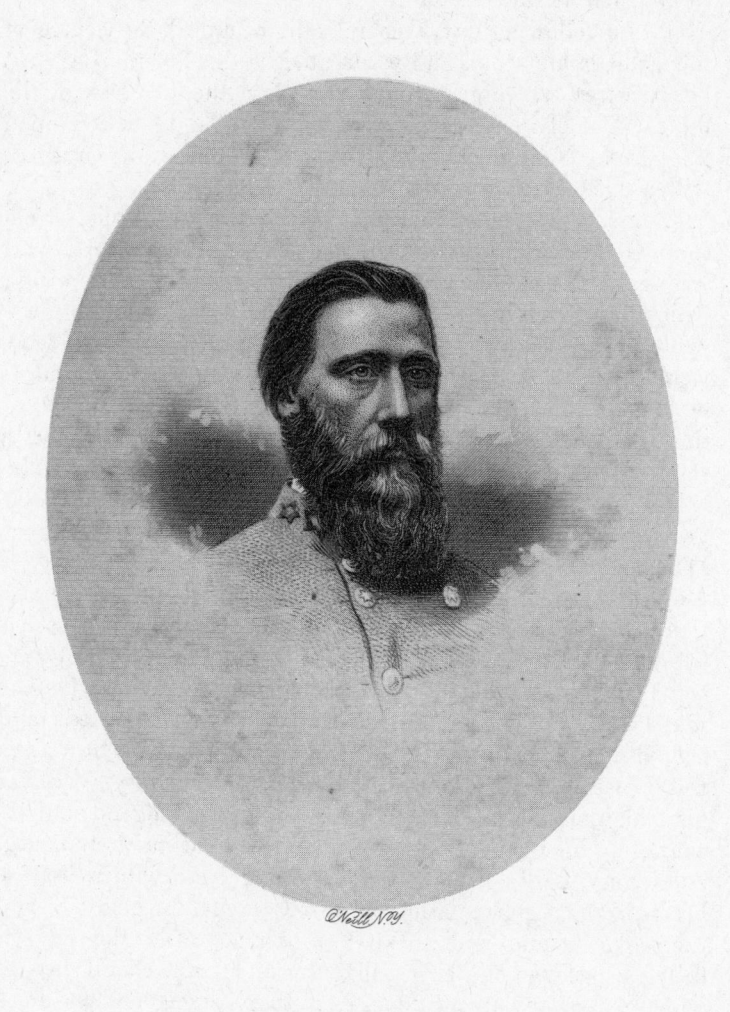

GEN. HOOD.

LIEUTENANT-GENERAL JOHN B. HOOD.

CONCERNING the subject of our present sketch, but very little, specially interesting, can be gathered bearing date prior to the opening of hostilities between the North and South. Of his family connections we are unable to obtain any information. But we find he was born a Kentuckian, at Owensville, Bath county, on the 29th of June, 1831. He was educated at Mount Sterling, entered West Point Military Academy in 1849, and, graduating at the end of the usual term, he joined the 4th regiment of infantry, in 1853. With this regiment he served nearly two years in California, and then was transferred, in July, 1855, to the 2d cavalry, already mentioned more than once, as that to which Albert S. Johnson and General Lee belonged, in the respective commands of colonel and lieutenant-colonel. With this regiment he did duty on the western frontier of Texas, and in July, 1856, was wounded in a fight with the Indians. No doubt it was here, in the wild service of the Texan west, that, in common with others we have to note, he derived that boldness and dash so conspicuous in him during the past four years of war. This is apparent from the fact that, some time before the civil strife began, he was ordered from Texas to report for duty as instructor of cavalry at West Point; but, afterwards, at his own request, was returned to his regiment, then at San Antonio.

It has been stated that he foresaw the present difficulties, and returned to Texas with a view of joining the South; but that statement is opposed to another account, from one who was with him on the battlefield at the Chickahominy. The latter specifies that Hood gave up his connection with the old army, and followed the legal profession in his native State, prior to

joining the Southern Confederacy. Be this as it may, we find him resigning his commission on the 16th of April, 1861, and entering the new army of the South with the rank of first-lieutenant, with the order to report to General Lee early in May, 1861. He was then appointed captain of cavalry, and sent to Magruder, then in command on the Peninsula. Several skirmishes and engagements occurred, of no particular note, however, except the fight at Great Bethel, wherein the cavalry figured; but we find no particular mention of Captain Hood's name until, on September 30, 1861, he was ordered to Richmond, and received the rank of colonel of infantry. There was, at the time, a regiment of Texas volunteers in camp near the city, and an attempt had been made to organize them by appointing Colonel Allen, of Texas, to the command; but, from some cause of dissatisfaction with him, this appointment was withdrawn, and Colonel Hood assigned to the post.

At this period Hood was in all the manly vigor of good health, and presented a fine, commanding appearance, with a powerful melodious voice, and a kindly though piercing eye; consequently his manners and look soon won upon his soldiers, and very speedily he obtained their cordial good-will. The men found him able and ready to give all the necessary instruction, not only in drilling them, but also in other minor technicalities of the field. Thus he succeeded in forming a somewhat rough, but hardy and daring set of recruits, into a fine and most effective regiment.

At the beginning of November, 1861, Hood and his men were ordered to Dumfries, in Virginia, and there, with another regiment, organized into a brigade under Senator Wigfall, who had been appointed a brigadier-general. When, however, Senator Wigfall had to take his seat in the Confederate Congress, on March 3d, 1862, Colonel Hood was assigned to his post, with a brigadier's rank. In this month the grand army of Virginia evacuated Manassas, and marched south. Hood's brigade then accompanied it to the Peninsula, and appears to have been attached to Longstreet's corps at Yorktown and Williamsburg, and when the army retreated to Richmond, he brought up the rear of the main force, though Longstreet was further behind him. On the 7th of May, the Union forces, under General Franklin, landed at West Point, on the York

river, and then Hood came prominently forward in attacking him. Posting his Texans in an advantageous position among the swampy woods, he suddenly fell upon the Federals as they advanced, and gave them battle. The fight was wild and confused for hours. The enemy then hurriedly fell back to the shelter of the gunboats, and General Hood followed the main army towards Richmond.

Particulars of the several battles around Richmond have already been related, but we may mention that the battle of Gaines's Mill was the first great fight in which Hood's brigade had participated. Previously they had been held in reserve, and placed where skirmishing or outpost work was carried on. Now, however, they were called upon to show of what stuff they were made, and a desperate part was assigned them. The Federal batteries had to be charged, and when the proper moment came, the word was given. Hood himself, on foot, led them forward, and, with a wild shout, at a run, they rushed on right into the redoubts and among the guns. A hand-to-hand conflict ensued ; their ranks were broken for a moment, but, rapidly closing, the Texans fought like fiends. The result is known. The enemy retired before the tremendous charge of Hood's brigade, while he, by his gallantry on this occasion, obtained promotion as a major-general.

From this time the movements of General Hood were so bound up with the grand army under Lee, that to relate them in detail, would only be repeating what we have already narrated, and, therefore, a few illustrations of the part he sustained in the several battles is all that need be given.

At the battles of Groveton and Bull Run, on August 29th and 30th, 1862, he was especially conspicuous for daring and skill in his movements. On the first day, it is related that " General Lee, seeing the moment had arrived for a demonstration on the enemy's left, about nightfall this was undertaken. Hood's division was ordered forward, and no sooner had these splendid troops thrown themselves with ardor into the contest, than the whole appearance of the field suddenly changed. Up to that moment the conflict had been obstinate, but the firing upon both sides had perceptibly decreased in intensity. It was just at that moment Hood's division advanced ; and the quick tongues of flame leaped from the muzzles of his muskets,

lighting up the gathering gloom with their crimscn light. . . .
Then, with one long roar of musketry, and a maze of quick
flashes everywhere, Hood's men charged forward, with wild
cheers, driving the enemy before them into the depths of the
forest."

In the next day's conflict, his division took the advance of
Longstreet's corps, and, pressing forward, "never yielded an
inch." Hood himself, equally with other generals, shared the
dangers of his men; and when the fight was won, could claim
a full share of the high praise bestowed by Lee upon all.

It is a singular coincidence, that the troops actually opposed
to Hood's division, at this battle, were the same he encountered
at Gaines' Mill; and, as there, after a gallant contest, they
had to retire before him.

The first invasion of Maryland, in September, again brought
General Hood prominently forward at Boonesboro, where, in
conjunction with D. H. Hill, he held the mountain pass against
McClellan until Lee came up. What occurred has already
been told, and we pass rapidly on, with Hood still accompanying the army, to the battle of Fredericksburg. Here Hood held
the right of Longstreet's corps, and was, consequently, on the
left of Jackson. The enemy had taken possession of a small
copse in front of Hood, but he quickly dispossessed them of it,
and drove them off with great loss.

In the month of February, 1863, Longstreet, with two of
his divisions, proceeded south, to the siege of Suffolk, in Southeast Virginia; and, as General Hood does not appear to have
participated in the battle of Chancellorsville, it is to be inferred that he accompanied his corps-commander, though very
little is to be found relating to this expedition. However, in
the month of June, we find both of them in Maryland again,
at the second invasion of that State by General Lee. Hood
was severely wounded in the arm, at Gettysburg; and, on the
retreat, he was borne in a carriage, suffering very much from
such a conveyance. It was, at first, thought his arm could not
be saved, but proper care and attention preserved it, though
ever afterwards it was shrivelled, and nearly useless. Still,
he did not absolutely forsake his command. Resting awhile
to recover from his wound, he was able to accompany Longstreet, at the end of August, into East Tennessee, and on to

reinforce Bragg, then preparing for the battle of Chicka-mauga.

In. this battle, previously described, Major-general Hood, with his division, was on the left, hotly engaged, and ultimately drove the enemy from the front of him. In the engagement of the second day, Sunday, September 20th, 1863, he was again wounded, making amputation of his leg needful, it being terribly shattered.

For his valuable services in this and other engagements, Hood was afterwards made a lieutenant-general; but six months elapsed before he could again take the field. In the beginning of March, however, he was at Richmond, and about the middle of the month proceeded to take command of his corps in North Georgia, under General Johnston. On the way to Dalton, an accident occurred to the train he was in, arising from a collision, and General Hood suffered in con-sequence, but was not prevented from continuing his jour-ney.

Soon after taking command, he issued a very excellent order with regard to troops attacking, when in line of battle. He said, "They must not be moved at the double-quick step, or be in any way unnecessarily fatigued, before engaging the enemy, that they may be in the best possible condition for pressing him, and improving any advantages which may be gained."

Of the subsequent operations connected with Sherman's ad-vance in Georgia, and Johnston's retreat, we have already spoken. At the battle of Resaca, Hood commanded the right, and as the army fell back, he was very effective in stubbornly disputing the enemy's progress. On the 18th of July, General Johnston having been relieved, Hood was appointed in his place, and assumed command in the following address:

HEADQUARTERS ARMY OF TENNESSEE, July 18, 1864.

SOLDIERS—In obedience to orders from the War Depart-ment, I assume command of this army and department. *I feel the weight of the responsibility so suddenly and unexpect-edly devolved upon me* by this position, and shall bend all my energies and employ all my skill to meet its requirements. I look with confidence to your patriotism to stand by me, and rely upon your prowess to wrest your country from the grasp

of the invader, entitling yourselves to the proud distinction of being called the deliverers of an oppressed people.

J. B. HOOD, General

The Confederate army was now before and in Atlanta, Sherman vigorously at work around it.   On the 20th Hood attacked the enemy's right, on Peach-tree creek, near the Chattahoochee, driving him from his works, and capturing colors and prisoners.   The day following, at night, the army shifted its position fronting on Peach-tree creek, and Stewart's and Cheatham's corps formed in line of battle around the city. Hardee's corps made a night march, and attacked the enemy's extreme left on the 22d, at one o'clock, and drove him from his works, capturing sixteen pieces of artillery and five stands of colors.   Cheatham attacked the enemy at four o'clock, P. M., with a portion of his command, and drove the enemy, capturing six pieces of artillery.   During the engagement the Confederates captured about two thousand prisoners.

Such is the account, in General Hood's hurried report of what was, in reality, a severe engagement, with great loss on both sides ; and we cannot pass it over without mentioning the death of the gallant, and now justly lamented, General McPherson, whose brilliant career in the Federal army is so well known.

On the 28th of July, Hood made another attack on Sherman, who was extending his line more to the right, and was thus compelled to fall back before the fierce assault of the Confederates.

At length, after various sharp encounters between the contending parties, Atlanta was evacuated, and General Hood sent the following report explaining the cause.

HEADQUARTERS, September 3, 1864.

On the evening of the 30th of August the enemy made a lodgement across Flint river, near Jonesboro.   We attacked them there on the evening of the 31st with two corps, but failed to dislodge them.

This made it necessary to abandon Atlanta, which was done on the night of the 1st of September.

Our loss on the evening of the 31st was small.

On the evening of the 1st of September, General Hardee's corps, in position at Jonesboro, was assaulted by a superior force of the enemy, and being outflanked, was compelled to withdraw during the night, with the loss of eight guns.

The enemy's prisoners report their loss very severe.

J. B. HOOD, General.

The above dispatch of the fall of such an important city as Atlanta, is, however, so brief, that we think it may be interesting to give some details, as related by a correspondent. The writer says:

" The position of the Federal troops on the 30th of April was as follows : General Howard's army of the Tennessee, which had the right of the line, having crossed the West Point railroad nearest to Fairburn, had pushed forward in an oblique direction, and was therefore near Jonesboro, twenty-two miles south of Atlanta, while his communicating force—the army of the Ohio, under General Schofield—passing over the railroad nearer to Red Oak, crossed the country in a more direct line, and found itself near to Rough and Ready, and on the extreme left of the Union army. Both of these places are stations of the Macon railroad, but about eleven miles apart. It was therefore necessary that the gap between those wings should be filled, and the army of the Cumberland, under General Thomas, and which had marched along the route in two columns, behind the armies of the Tennessee and Ohio, now came forward to the front and formed the centre of the main army. Sherman's line was therefore eleven miles in extent, and ranged along the Macon railroad from Rough and Ready to Jonesboro, with its centre at Couch's.

" The Confederate forces had, at this time, been divided into two main armies, separated by an interval of twenty-two miles.

" One part of the army was intrenched at Atlanta, and the other at Jonesboro, under General Hardee, and was also intrenched. The cause of this separation of the forces arose from the fact that Hood had found out by Kilpatrick's raid that it was necessary he should protect his communications at that point by a large force, to prevent a repetition of such a catastrophe as had taken place at that part of the line on the 20th instant. He certainly had not expected so speedy a move

ment of Sherman's whole army in the same direction. Sherman's army was, therefore, between the enemy's forces, and had, as was announced from the War Department, literally divided the Confederates in two.

" When General Howard found the enemy in force at Jonesboro, he at once intrenched his command, locating the salient or projecting angle within half a mile of the railroad. This the enemy did not approve of, and an attempt was made to drive off the Federal troops from the position, doubtless supposing the force to be merely a raiding party. The Confederates attacked General Howard's works at about three o'clock on the afternoon of the 30th of August, and were repulsed. Meeting with so unexpected a force, they fell back into their works at Jonesboro, leaving their dead and wounded in front of General Howard's lines.

" General Sherman soon perceived the advantages of his position, and determined to profit by Hood's mistake. Having the Confederate forces separated, the principal object was to keep them so, and thus conquer them in detail. He therefore ordered the advance of the left (Schofield) and centre (Thomas) rapidly to the railroad, where they made a good lodgment, and during the 31st of August, nearly the whole distance between Rough and Ready and Jonesboro was despoiled of its railroad track, ties, and other material. These two armies were also brought nearer to the intrenched positions at Jonesboro, and to the left of Howard's command. By this plan of operation, Sherman had interposed his whole army between Atlanta and Jonesboro.

" Having placed his troops in the desired position, Sherman, on the 1st of September, ordered a general attack on the enemy at Jonesboro. The movement was made with great gallantry, and after an amount of skirmishing and artillery fire, an assault of the works was ordered. The Fourteenth corps, under the command of Brevet Major-general Jefferson C. Davis, was selected to make the assault, and gallantly they charged upon the works amid a storm of grape and canister from the enemy's artillery. Nothing daunted, the brave boys who had held their own throughout the Georgia campaign, rushed upon the intrenchments and carried them handsomely, capturing about a thousand prisoners and ten pieces of artil-

lery. General Sherman speaks highly of the conduct of the men of the gallant Fourteenth, and officially awards to General Jefferson C. Davis the honor he has so bravely won.

"During the night the enemy, finding it impossible to hold Jonesboro, retreated along the Macon railroad in a southerly direction, and took up a position at Lovejoy's station, seven miles distant, and twenty-nine miles from Atlanta. Here they threw up hasty intrenchments to prevent the further pursuit of our cavalry, which had followed them to this point, inflicting damage on their rear, and causing confusion during the retreat.

"While Sherman was busily engaged in his attack upon Jonesboro, Hood, who had still remained in Atlanta, finding that he was outflanked, his line of supply cut off, and the Federal troops between him and a large portion of his army, became speedily convinced that his position was untenable. In order to save that portion of his command then with him, he determined to evacuate the fortified city, and on the night of September 1st he blew up his magazines, destroyed all his supplies that he could not remove, consisting of seven locomotives and eighty-one cars loaded with ammunition, small-arms, and stores, and left the place by the turnpike roads.

"General Slocum, who held command of the army of observation, soon discovered the position of affairs in Atlanta, and on the morning of September 2d moved his forces from the Chattahoochee river and occupied the place. He captured in Atlanta fourteen pieces of artillery, many of them in first-rate condition, and a large number of small-arms."

Various comments, as usual, were made upon this evacuation of Atlanta by Hood; but it was generally concluded that the evil, though great, was not so bad as might be inferred from the loss of such a city. It was said, by one reviewer of Hood's operations, during the period, that "the final loss of Atlanta was not by any means a test of his ability or capacity to command, for the holding of that city depended upon many contingencies that could not be controlled by him or anybody else;" and remarks were added concerning the various causes that had produced the course he took.

Upon the evacuation of Atlanta, a truce of ten days was agreed to, and at the expiration of that time, Hood, on the 19th of September, shifted his position to the West Point rail-

road, with a view of getting in Sherman's rear. Just previous, on Sunday, the 18th of September, President Davis arrived at General Hood's headquarters, and, the following day, reviewed the whole army. In the evening, the President addressed the soldiers in hopeful and encouraging tones. Turning to Cheatham's division of Tennesseans, he said: "Be of good cheer, for within a short while your faces will be turned homeward, and your feet pressing Tennessee soil."

President Davis was followed by General Howell Cobb, who, in a few remarks, made many happy hits, and convulsed the audience with laughter. General Hood was enthusiastically called for. Slowly rising from his chair, and dashing his hat down like a blushing school-boy, the general said: "Soldiers, it is not my province to make speeches: I was not born for such work; that I leave to other men. Within a few days I expect to give the command 'forward,' and I believe you are, like myself, willing to go forward, even if we live on parched corn and beef. I am ready to give the command 'forward' this very night. Good-night."

In reflecting upon the fall of Atlanta, and the want of success attending Hood's army at this time, we should not forget the bodily infirmities of the general in command, consequen upon the severe wounds he had received at Gettysburg and Chickamauga. But the spirit within was as powerful to will and to do as ever. He was evidently one of those whom no disasters or physical ailments—not even the partial dismemberment of his body—nor any amount of external trouble, annoyance, or ill-will can crush; and though his career was not so conspicuous at the beginning of the war, as that of some generals, yet he well and bravely bore his share throughout. His was no longer the fine commanding presence of earlier days, in the outset of his military life,—nearly four years of hard service having reduced his frame, and robbed him of much of his physical ability, leaving the vigor of his powerful mind alone unbroken. An eye-witness says of him, at this time:

"General Hood appears to be in as cheerful a flow of spirits as his brave and patriotic veterans. I saw him to-day, surrounded by a group of major-generals and brigadiers, in social converse under an oak-tree. Where the next campaign will be, is scarcely even discussed. At present there are no evi-

dences of a movement.   But I have reason to predict that before many moons have waned, the Federals will hear of Hood
and his army, through quite a novel and unexpected channel."

Towards the end of the month, Hood got well in the rear ot
Sherman at Atlanta.   He began his march on the 29th of September, and next day encamped for the night near the old
battle-ground of New Hope church.   Here he concentrated
his forces, bringing up the corps of S. D. Lee, and Wheeler's
cavalry.   Forrest was then at work on the left, and Wheeler
was now sent to the right, and to Marietta.   At a defile in the
Allatoona mountains, the Federals, under General Corse, attacked the advance of Lee's corps under S. G. French, and the
Federal general was there slightly wounded.   Hood, however,
went on, pursued by a part of Sherman's forces to Resaca,
where he arrived on October 12th, the enemy having retired
to Atlanta.   Leaving Wheeler in charge at Resaca, Hood
marched rapidly forward to Dalton, took possession, and then
went on to the gap, at Ringgold, with his right flank at Lafayette.   From here to Gadsden and Jacksonville, Ala. (the
latter place Beauregard's headquarters at the time—he having
become department commander), the army occupied the whole
ground by the 22d of October, in good condition, and ready
for the next grand movement.   On the 25th of October, Hood's
forces were at Tuscumbia and Florence, and on the 2d of November some of the enemy in Decatur were driven out, and
the place captured by the Confederates.   Resting his forces
awhile, Hood then crossed the Tennessee at Florence, on November 13th, General Thomas, with the Federal army, falling
back towards Nashville.   At first, the Confederate advance in
Tennessee seemed highly prosperous.   Pulaski was evacuated
by the Federal forces under General R. W. Johnston, on the
23d, and Hood marched on to Columbia.   Here, by a flank
movement, on the night of the 25th, he compelled Thomas's
forces to withdraw.   At Spring Hill, there was a slight engagement, but on the 30th of November, a battle was fought
at Franklin, Tennessee.   The following account of it is from
General Hood's dispatch :

HEADQUARTERS, ARMY OF TENNESSEE, near NASHVILLE }
Dec. 8, *via* MOBILE, Dec. 9, 1864. }

To HON. J. A. SEDDON:

About four o'clock P. M., November 30th, we attacked the enemy at Franklin, and drove them from their centre line of temporary works into the inner lines, which they evacuated during the night, leaving their dead and wounded in our possession, and retired to Nashville, closely followed by our cavalry. We captured several stands of colors and about one thousand prisoners. Our troops fought with great gallantry. We have to lament the loss of many gallant officers and men. Major-general Cleburne and Brigadier-generals John Williams, Adams, Gist, Strahl, and Granberry were killed. Major-general John Brown, and Brigadier-generals S. Carter, Manigault, Quarles, Cockerill, and Scott were wounded. Brigadier-general Gordon was captured.

J. B. HOOD, General.

A subsequent telegram from General Hood says: " Our loss of officers was excessively large in proportion to the loss of men."

Hood now advanced upon Nashville, and laid siege to it, on the 2d of December, closely investing it for a fortnight. At the end of that time, the Federal forces attacked the Confederates, and the battle of Nashville was fought, ending in the defeat of Hood's army, and his retreat to the Tennessee river, pursued by the victorious Federals. The following dispatch, from General Beauregard, gives a brief account of the affair:

MACON, Jan. 7, 1865.

To General S. COOPER, Adjutant and Inspector General:

General Hood reports from Spring Hill, December 27, 1864, that on the morning of the 15th instant, in front of Nashville, the enemy attacked both flanks of his army. They were repulsed on the right with heavy loss, but towards evening they drove in his infantry outposts on the left flank.

Early on the 16th, the enemy made a general attack on his entire line. All their assaults were handsomely repulsed with heavy loss until half-past six P. M., when a portion of our line to the left of the centre suddenly gave way, causing our lines to give way at all points, our troops retreating rapidly. Fifty

pieces of artillery and several ordnance wagons were lost by
us on that day. Our loss in killed and wounded heretofore
small—in prisoners, not ascertained. Major-general Edward
Jackson, and Brigadier-generals T. B. Smith, and H. R. Jack
son are captured.

G. T. BEAUREGARD, General.

General Hood recrossed the Tennessee at Florence, General
Forrest covering his retreat, and was at Tupelo on the 6th of
January, 1865, where, on the 23d, he took leave of the army
in the following order:

HEADQUARTERS, ARMY OF THE TENNESSEE,)
TUPELO, Miss., Jan. 23, 1865.)

SOLDIERS—At my request, I have this day been relieved
from the command of the army. In taking leave of you, accept my thanks for the patience with which you have endured
your hardships during the recent campaign. I am alone
responsible for its conception, and strove hard to do my duty
in its execution. I urge upon you the importance of giving
your entire support to the distinguished soldier who now as-
sumes command, and shall look with deep interest on all your
future operations, and rejoice at your success.

J. B. HOOD.

After General Hood was relieved, he visited Augusta, on the
3d of February, and made a speech at a serenade there given
him. He then published his official report of the Atlanta
campaign—in which he somewhat differs from General Johnston—and afterwards proceeded to his home at San Antonio,
in Texas. There he quietly remained, until, on the 25th of
September, he departed for the purpose of learning how his
case was disposed of by the authorities at Washington.

A gentleman who had an opportunity of talking with him
on board the steamer from Galveston, says that General Hood
stated to him it had been his advice, to every one with whom
he had any influence, to quietly accept the new order of
things ; and his intention now was to write, in the form of his
memoirs, some account of the operations in the late war.

GENERAL ALBERT SYDNEY JOHNSTON.

THE short career of this gallant officer, in the Confederate army, prevents the same extended notice of his life, that others of his rank have been considered entitled to, and which their services have demanded. He was born in the year 1803, in Macon county, Kentucky, and received his early education at the Transylvania University, in that State, under President Holley. At the age of nineteen, he entered West Point Academy as a cadet, and graduated on the 30th of June, 1826, standing number eight in his class. He was then brevetted second-lieutenant of the Second infantry, but was subsequently transferred, in 1827, to the Sixth infantry, and served as Adjutant to his regiment from 1828 to 1832. From the 8th of May to the year 1833, he was Aid to Brigadier-general Atkinson; and during a part of that time he was acting as Assistant Adjutant-general of Illinois Volunteers, in the Black Hawk War. With these forces, President, then *Captain* Lincoln, also served.

On May 31st, 1834, he resigned his commission in the regular army, and went to reside in Missouri. In 1836 he emigrated to Texas, arriving there shortly after the battle of San Jacinto. There, alone, and perfectly unknown, he determined to begin a new career. We may not stop to inquire what were the motives which induced him to leave the United States' service. In all ages, and throughout all forms of government, merit and perseverance, even when acknowledged, do not always find a reward. It is wise, therefore, in a world so wide, for a brave soul to rise above disappointment, and try new fields, where pent-up energies may have full play. There was, it is true, plenty of room even in his native State, for action; but

the lands of Texas, and its peculiarly romantic charms—its wild and daring life—probably presented greater inducement to a nature like Johnston's, which felt itself, perhaps, too cramped under the military control of a more settled government.

At the time when Johnston entered Texas, an intestine war was raging; and, without hesitation, he entered the Republican army, in General Rusk's division, as a private soldier. The general speedily discovered his abilities, and made him Adjutant-general of his command. Subsequently, he was made senior Brigadier-general of the Texan army, and was appointed to succeed General Felix Houston, in the chief command. This led to a duel between them, in which Johnston was wounded. In 1838, he was chosen Secretary of War of the new Republic, under President Lamar; and, the following year, he organized an expedition against the Cherokees, seven hundred strong, who were defeated at a battle on the Neuches.

In 1840 he retired from the service, and settled on a plantation, in Brazonia county, near Galveston. Here he remained quietly, attending to his new home, for two or three years, and during that time always advocating the annexation of Texas to the United States. At length, when the Mexican war broke out, he once more, in 1846, and, at the request of General Taylor, allowed his daring spirit to find its vent on the battlefield. He arrived in Mexico shortly after the battles of Resaca and Palo-Alto, and was elected Colonel of the First Texas regiment, serving as such from June 18th, to August 24th, 1846. After that regiment was discharged, he was appointed Aid, and Inspector-general to General Butler. In that capacity he was at the famous battle of Monterey, and, during the fight, his horse was three times shot under him. For his conduct on that day, he was recommended by General Taylor, for the appointment of Brigadier-general; but the position was bestowed upon Caleb Cushing.

After this he retired to his plantation, cultivating the earth with his own hands, in the truly honest and noble occupation of a farmer, on his own land. His circumstances, however, were not good; and when Taylor was made President, that gallant old general forgot not Johnston, but, on October 31st,

1849, bestowed upon him the appointment of Paymaster of the regular army, with the rank of major.

When the army was increased by four new regiments, the Texas Legislature asked that he should be appointed one of the colonels, and, accordingly, Jefferson Davis, then Secretary of War, gave him command of the Second Cavalry, with his headquarters at San Antonio, Texas. There he still further displayed his military talents, and won the confidence of the country, by the vigorous and successful warfare he initiated against the wild tribes of Indians, who were constantly engaged in marauding forays upon the early settlers.

In the latter part of 1857 he was appointed, by President Buchanan, to the command of the Utah Expedition, sent to quell the Mormons, who had shown much disturbance. It was in September that he started upon this expedition, and the perils which he and his followers encountered are well known. On the 6th of November, being in the Rocky Mountains, they were overtaken by a snow-storm of such fury, that it "racked the bones of his men, and starved the oxen, horses, and mules." The snow was from two to four feet deep, and the thermometer from sixteen to eighteen degrees below zero for ninety days afwards. But they pursued the march, making only thirty-five miles in fifteen days, and when they went into camp, subsisted on mules, without bread or salt, until provisions were sent by Government, in the following spring. The troops suffered from cold and hunger to a great extent; but the Colonel fared no better than his men during that period.

In the spring of 1858, he crossed the plains, and arrived at Salt Lake City, where the ability, zeal, and energy he displayed, caused him to be brevetted Brigadier-general (dating from November, 1847), and full commander of the military district of Utah.

When the Mormon troubles were ended, General Johnston was sent to California; and, on the death of General Clarke, assumed command of the department of the Pacific. There he remained until, hearing that his adopted State, Texas—where his home and his farm belonged—had passed the Ordinance of Secession, he resigned his position in the United States army, and at once prepared to remove South, to assist in repelling the threatened invasion by the North.

It is stated, that " on the inception of the war, General
Scott, fully aware of the great military genius of Albert Syd‹
ney Johnston, made a vigorous, but ineffectual effort, to secure
his services for the Federal Government, tendering him the
chief command, to which his seniority and rank, according to
army regulations, entitled him.   But Johnston nobly rejected
the offer : he would not sell his birthright and his home."
Measures were, therefore, taken to have him arrested before he
could join the South.   Vessels, with officials on board, were
directed to intercept his passage by sea ; but this coming to
his knowledge, he took the overland route, and thus avoided
an arrest.   Perhaps one secret reason for attempting to seize
him was, from the fact of his being a kinsman of Mr. Floyd,
who, it is said, had some influence in getting him placed in the
command at California.   General Sumner had already been
dispatched to supersede him, on the first signs of strife ; but
Johnston, with three or four companions, increased afterwards
to one hundred, on mules, proceeded by way of Arizona.   He
left Los Angelos the 2d of July, 1861, passed through Texas, and
arrived at New Orleans in safety.   This was in August, 1861,
and immediately proceeding, via Memphis, to Richmond, he
was assigned to the command of the department of Kentucky
and Tennessee, with the rank of General.   He being a native
of Kentucky, and his thorough knowledge of the Western country, coupled with his great ability, rendered his appointment
to this position specially appropriate.

General Johnston at once proceeded to his command ; and,
as Kentucky, though before professedly neutral, had now assembled troops to threaten the borders of Tennessee, he felt no
hesitation in making his headquarters at Bowling Green, already taken possession of by General Buckner, for the South.

The arrival of General Johnston in the west, gave great
pleasure to the upholders of the Confederate cause, and many
high expectations were formed of him.   But his own anticipa-
tions of success were far less sanguine.   As an experienced
military man, he well knew the immense advantages the North
possessed in resources and men, besides the long established
organization of army drill.   With him there was all to do, and
little to do it with.   Everything was new, and had to be
fashioned into shape, while in the field there were skilled cap-

tains on the side of the North, fully equal to those arrayed against them in behalf of the South. Buell was not far off, in a position of immense strength, with an army said to be 50,000 strong. In his rear was the Cumberland river, liable to rise at any moment, and to admit the largest class steamers as high as Nashville. Then there was the Tennessee, traversing the entire State, and capable of passing gunboats to Alabama; while, at the mouth of both these rivers—at Paducah and Smithfield—the enemy was collecting an enormous force, both naval and military. Thus there was much cause for anything but the exultant hope others appeared to entertain upon his arrival: his own failure to sympathize in this feeling being attributable, in great measure, to his peculiarly unpretending character.

Immediately upon assuming his command, General Johnston issued the following proclamation :

" Whereas, the armed occupation of a part of Kentucky by the United States, and the preparations which manifest the intention of their government to invade the Confederate States through that territory, have imposed it on these last, as a necessity of self-defence, to enter that State and meet the invasion upon the best line for military operations ; and, whereas, it is proper that the motives of the government of the Confederate States in taking this step should be fully known to the world ; now, therefore, I, Albert S. Johnston, general and commander of the Western Department of the Army of the Confederate States of America, do proclaim that these States have thus marched their troops into Kentucky with no hostile intention towards its people, nor do they desire or seek to control their choice in regard to their union with either of the confederacies, or to subjugate their State or hold its soil against their wishes. On the contrary, they deem it to be the right of the people of Kentucky to determine their own position in regard to the belligerents. It is for them to say whether they will join either the confederacy, or maintain a separate existence as independent sovereign State. The armed occupation of their soil, both as to its extent and duration, will, therefore, be strictly limited to the exigencies of self-defence on the part of the Confederate States. These States intend to conform to all the requirements of public law and international amity as be-

tween themselves and Kentucky, and, accordingly, I hereby command all who are subject to my orders to pay entire respect to the rights of property and the legal authorities within that State, so far as the same may be compatible with the necessities of self-defence. If it be the desire of the people of Kentucky to maintain a strict and impartial neutrality, then the effort to drive out the lawless intruders, who seek to make their State the theatre of war, will aid them in the attainment of their wishes. If, as it may not be unreasonable to suppose, these people desire to unite their fortunes with the Confederate States, to whom they are already bound by so many ties of interest, then the appearance and aid of Confederate troops will assist them to make an opportunity for the free and unbiased expression of their will upon the subject. But if it be true, which is not to be presumed, that a majority of those people desire to adhere to the United States, and become parties to the war, then none can doubt the right of the other belligerent to meet that war whenever and wherever it may be waged. But, harboring no such suspicion, I now declare, in the name of the government which I serve, that its army will be withdrawn from Kentucky so soon as there shall be satisfactory evidence of the existence and execution of a like intention on the part of the United States.

By order of the President of the Confederate States of America.

A. S. JOHNSTON,

General, commanding the Western Department of the Army of the Confederate States of America."

The work of General Johnston, for the remainder of the year, was to strengthen his position and ascertain the intentions of the enemy. His own forces had been considerably magnified, not only to deceive his foe, but to inspire hope among friends; but he constantly kept the war department at Richmond well informed of the truth. Had that truth really been known to the enemy, at the time, it is very probable that Buell could have easily ovewhelmed Johnston's army; but, it was so disguised that the Federal commander determined to try and take him on the rear, and, accordingly, measures were adopted to capture Fort Donelson. At this period, General Beauregard arrived in the west, and a conference was immediately held

between the two generals. Beauregard expressed surprise at
the small number of Johnston's forces, and fully agreed with
him in the plans he had formed. These were to try and
secure Nashville by fighting at Fort Donelson, and Johnston
sent the larger part of his army thither for the purpose, retaining only about 14,000 men, to cover his front, and of those,
3,000 were so enfeebled by recent sickness that they were unable to march. General Pillow, and afterwards General
Floyd, were placed in command of the fort, and General
Buckner in the field.

The details of the fall of Fort Donelson do not belong to this
sketch, but we may give the following extracts concerning it
from the official reports of Generals Floyd and Pillow.
General Grant was in command of the assailants, and, previous
to Floyd's arrival, General Pillow had made various preparations to resist Grant. The reports then mention the occurrences of the three days' fighting that ensued, and go on to say :

" We had now only about 12,000 troops, all told. Of these
a large proportion we had lost in the three battles. The command had been in the trenches night and day for five days,
exposed to the snow, sleet, mud and ice-water, without shelter,
and without adequate covering, and without sleep.

" In this condition the general officers held a consultation to
determine what he should do. General Buckner held it as his
decided opinion that he could not hold his position one half an
hour against an assault of the enemy, and said the enemy
would attack him next morning at daylight. The proposition
was then made by the undersigned to again fight through the
enemy's line and cut our way out. General Buckner said his
command was so worn out, and cut to pieces, and demoralized,
that he could not make another fight ; that it would cost the
command three-quarters of its present numbers to cut its
way through, and it was wrong to sacrifice three-quarters of a
command to save one-quarter ; that no officer had a right to
cause such a sacrifice. General Floyd and Major Gilmer I
understood to concur in this opinion.

" I then expressed the opinion that we could hold out another
day, and in that time we could get steamboats and set the command over the river, and probably save a large portion of it.
To this General Buckner replied that the enemy would cer-

tainly attack him at daylight, and that he could not hold his position half an hour. The alternative of the propositions was a surrender of their position and command. General Floyd said that he would neither surrender the command nor would he surrender himself a prisoner. I had taken the same posi- tion. General Buckner said he was satisfied nothing else could be done, and that, therefore he would surrender if placed in command. General Floyd said he would turn over the command to him if he could be allowed to withdraw his command. To this General Buckner consented. Thereupon, General Floyd turned the command over to me, I passing it instantly to General Buckner, saying I would neither surren- der the command nor myself a prisoner. I directed Colonel Forrest to cut his way out. Under these circumstances, General Buckner accepted the command and sent a flag of truce to the enemy for an armistice of six hours to negotiate for terms of capitulation. Before this flag and communication was delivered I retired from the garrison."

The fall of Fort Donelson made the evacuation of Bowling Green imperative on General Johnston. He had waited the result, opposite Nashville, and, on the 15th of February, *at midnight*, he received news of a great victory,—*at dawn* intel- ligence of a defeat! Thus situated, he determined to unite his forces with those under General Beauregard, and, as he con- ceived Nashville was incapable of defence under the circum- stances, he left a rearguard under General Floyd, and fell back to Murfreesboro. There he managed to collect an army able to offer battle; but the weather was so inclement, and the floods in the river such as to wash the bridges away, that nothing effective could be accomplished. He, therefore, marched on, and crossed the Tennessee, at Decatur, in Ala- bama, early in March, and soon afterwards a portion of his army joined the forces of Beauregard under Bragg's command.

In regard to Fort Donelson, it is but just to General John- ston to give place to a few words from himself, inasmuch as some severe remarks were made respecting him at the time. In a letter written to Mr. Barksdale, member of the Confed- erate Congress, from Mississippi, he says, after mentioning previous occurrences:

"I have given this sketch, so that you may appreciate the embarrassments which surrounded me in my attempts to avert or remedy the disaster of Fort Donelson.

"The blow is most disastrous, and almost without remedy. I, therefore, in my first report, remained silent. This silence you were kind enough to attribute to my generosity. I will not lay claim to the motive to excuse my course. I observed silence, as it seemed to me the best way to serve the brave and the country. The facts were not fully known—discontent prevailed, and criticism or condemnation were more likely to augment than to cure the evil. I refrained, well knowing that heavy censures would fall upon me, but convinced that it was better to endure them for the present, and defer to a more propitious time, an investigation of the conduct of the generals, for, in the mean time, their services are required and their influences useful. For these reasons, Generals Floyd and Pillow were assigned to duty, for I still felt confidence in their gallantry, their energy, and their devotion to the Confederacy.

"The test of merit, in my profession, with the people, is success. It is a hard rule, but I think it right. If I join this corps to the forces of General Beauregard (I confess a hazardous experiment), then those who are now disclaiming against me will be without an argument. Your friend,

"A. S. JOHNSTON."

General Beauregard had concentrated his men at and around Corinth, and the united forces were prepared, early in April, to strike a heavy blow at the enemy, which was attempted on the field of Shiloh.

The battle of Shiloh has already been mentioned, and we need now only allude to the manner of General Johnston's death. On the 6th of April, the army marched on the enemy. The ground was broken and undulating, and covered, in a great measure, by lofty trees, without any undergrowth. Mile after mile, the Confederates rushed on, sweeping the camps of the enemy before them. General Johnston was in the advance, before the troops of Breckinridge and Bowen. He had addressed them in a few brief words, and given the order to "Charge!" when at two o'clock, a minie ball cut the artery of his leg. Still he rode on until from loss of blood, he fell,

exhausted, into the arms of Governor Harris, who carefully bore him a short distance from the field, into a ravine, and reclined him in his lap. The general's staff had been mingled with others, but now rode up to seek for him. Stimulants were speedily administered, but in vain. The last words he uttered were, just after he was shot, "Governor, I believe I am seriously wounded!" Now, he was totally unconscious. A member of his staff, Colonel Wm. Preston, in an agony of grief, threw his arms around him, and called aloud to see if he would respond, or know who were around. But no sign, or reply came, and in a moment or two more, he quietly breathed his last, at half past two P. M. April 6th, 1862.

His body was borne from the field by his staff officers, and intrusted to Colonel Preston, by General Beauregard, to be taken to New Orleans, until directions should be received from his family. The fact of his death, however, was for some time concealed from the army; and a mistake arose on the part of the enemy in supposing that his body was found on the field. There was one General Geo. W. Johnston—the provisional governor of Kentucky—in the battle, and he also fell mortally wounded. This gentleman was met in his dying moments by General McCook, of the Federal army, as the latter was advancing, and, taking him up in his arms with that kindly feeling which few brave soldiers ever fail to show towards friend or foe at such a time, asked his name. The answer, probably, led to the mistake about General Johnston. As soon as it was deemed expedient to publish his death, the following general order was issued from headquarters, at Corinth, by General Beauregard:

HEADQUARTERS, ARMY OF MISSISSIPPI, ⎫
CORINTH, Miss., April 10, 1862. ⎭

SOLDIERS—Your late Commander-in-chief, General A. S. Johnston, is dead; a fearless soldier, a sagacious captain, a reproachless man, has fallen. One who, in his devotion to our cause, shrank from no sacrifice; one who, animated by a sense of duty, and sustained by a sublime courage, challenged danger, and perished gallantly for his country, while leading forward his brave columns to victory. His signal example of heroism and patriotism, if imitated, would make his army invincible.

A grateful country will mourn his loss, revere his name, and cherish his many virtues.

P. G. T. BEAUREGARD,
General Commanding.

At Richmond, on arrival of the news, President Davis sent into Congress a special message concerning the battle, and particularly referring to General Johnston's death. He says:

"But an all-wise Creator has been pleased, while vouchsafing to us His countenance in battle, to afflict us with a severe dispensation, to which we must bow in humble submission. The last long, lingering hope has disappeared, and it is but too true, that General ALBERT SYDNEY JOHNSTON is no more.

"My long and close friendship with this departed chieftain and patriot, forbid me to trust myself in giving vent to the feelings which this intelligence has evoked. Without doing injustice to the living, it may safely be said that our loss is irreparable. Among the shining hosts of the great and good who now cluster around the banner of our country, there exists no purer spirit, no more heroic soul, than that of the illustrious man whose death I join you in lamenting.

"In his death he has illustrated the character for which, through life, he was conspicuous—that of singleness of purpose and devotion to duty with his whole energies. Bent on obtaining the victory which he deemed essential to his country's cause, he rode on to the accomplishment of his object, forgetful of self, while his very life-blood was fast ebbing away. His last breath cheered his comrades on to victory. The last sound he heard was their shout of victory. His last thought was his country, and long and deeply will his country mourn his loss.

"JEFFERSON DAVIS."

When the remains of General Johnston reached New Orleans, then in possession of the Confederate forces, they were escorted to the City Hall by the military, attended by the governor of Louisiana, General Lovell, their staffs, and other prominent officers and gentlemen. The body was laid in state in the mayor's parlor, and the public admitted. Silence, and deep-

felt, unaffected grief marked the occasion. Ladies brought magnolias and other flowers with which they encircled his coffin simply, but beautifully. And thus, while gentle hands and weeping eyes moved softly around him,—his sheathed sword still by his side—the dead warrior—the hardy campaigner—the industrious farmer—the adventurous explorer—and the great commander, was borne to his final and eternal rest.

*   *   *   *

The appearance of General Johnston was well suited to his military character—in height, over six feet, and with a large, sinewy frame, his whole appearance was commanding, while his manners were, occasionally, very silent and reserved, and often abstracted. He was married, and had a son, who, in 1863, was on the staff of President Davis. His brother, Josiah Stoddard Johnston, a man of the most eminent abilities, was, by the Confederate cause looked upon as a great ally. He, however, met a violent death in the blowing up of a steamboat on the Red river, La. This brother had a son, J. S. Johnston, who resided near Georgetown, Kentucky, but was obliged to fly to Mobile, in August, 1862, on account of his sympathies with the Confederacy. Thus the fortunes of the whole family, like that of so many others, seem to have been interwoven with the cause of their native South.

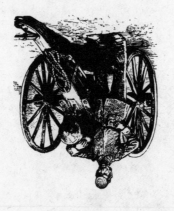

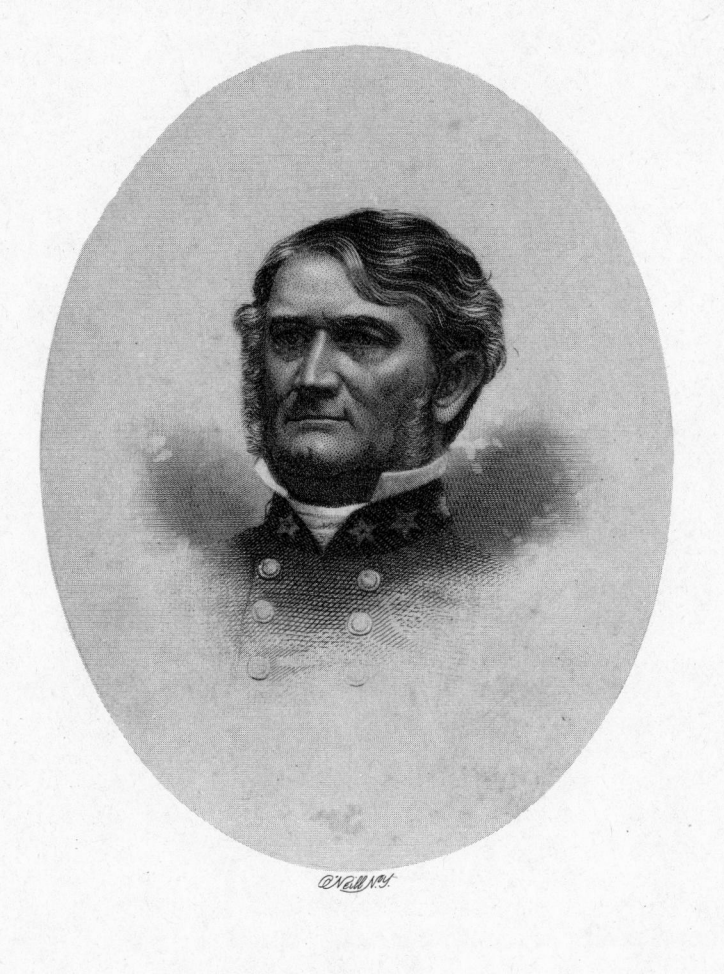

LT. GEN. POLK.

LIEUTENANT-GENERAL LEONIDAS POLK.

THE father of Leonidas Polk was Colonel William Polk, a highly distinguished soldier in the revolutionary war, and a near relative of Thomas Polk, who was one of the few that issued the famous Mecklenburg declaration of independence.

Young Polk was born about the year 1806, in Raleigh, North Carolina, and, after receiving the first rudiments of education in his native State, was admitted to West Point as a cadet in the year 1823. It was at his father's wish he commenced life in the military profession, though it would seem his own inclinations led him subsequently into a different calling. On the 30th of June, 1827, he graduated, standing No. 8 in his class. It is said that while going through his term at the academy, he was induced to turn from the military profession to that of the church, at the instigation of Bishop McIl vaine, of Ohio, who was chaplain of that institution at the time. Certain it is, however, that, though he was appointed a brevet second-lieutenant of artillery, and remained in the army a few months, he resigned, and commenced studying for the ministry, on the 1st December, 1827. After the usual examination, he was admitted to holy orders in the Protestant Episcopal church, and, in 1838, received an appointment as Missionary Bishop in Arkansas and part of the Indian territory, with a provisional charge of the diocese of Alabama, Mississippi, Louisiana, and the Republic of Texas.

His movements during this time we would fain record, did our space permit. The wilds of the frontier regions of the West embrace many scenes, giving to such a man as the travelling bishop, or itinerant Methodist preacher, abundant

material of interest and adventure, and Bishop Polk must have often gone through all the numerous and exciting incidents consequent upon the life of a Western missionary. In 1841, however, he was ordained regular Bishop of Louisiana, and held that post for twenty years.*

The events that occurred during this period are matters of general history. The Mexican war, the wars with the Indians, and the several changes made by the progress of civilization in the West, belong to that time; and no doubt Bishop Polk participated largely in much of what took place, for a mind like his could hardly have remained passive under such stirring events.

At length the note of war was heard in his own land. The deadly strife between North and South commenced, and a Southern Confederacy was formed. President Davis applied to Bishop Polk to know if he would rejoin the army, and, it is said first offered him the appointment of a brigadier-general, which was refused. Ultimately, however, he accepted a major-generalship, and laying aside the bishop's robe, donned the garments of a soldier. His reasons for this have been given as follows: Bishop Meade, on hearing of what he had done, told him that he already had a commission in a very different army to which he should still hold allegiance; but Polk replied, that while he accepted the major-generalship he did not intend to resign his right to the bishopric. " When," said he, " I accept a commission in the Confederate army, I not only perform the duties of a good citizen, but contend for the principles which lie at the foundation of our social, political, and religious polity."

In June, 1861, the new major-general, Bishop Polk, visited Richmond, and had a long conference with President Davis. He then returned to the West, and took up his command, which extended from the mouth of the Arkansas river, on both sides of the Mississippi, to the northernmost limits of the Confederate States, and took in the encampment at Corinth. His headquarters were at Memphis, and thence he issued his first

---

* We are not aware when Bishop Polk was married, but his wife was a Miss Devereux, of Raleigh, and possibly he was united to her before leaving for the West.

general order, dated July 13th, 1861, in which he gives some lengthy reasons for taking upon himself such a "grave respon sibility."

In commenting upon Bishop Polk's appointment, the *Memphis Appeal* remarks, "This is the first instance in the country's history of the appointment of a high church dignitary to a position of so much responsibility in the military service;' and, we may add, that it was an appointment far from being wise, where great military talent and experience were so much needed.

At this time, General Polk presented the appearance of a tall, well-built, good-looking man, bearing in every word and glance the impress of a soldier more than the divine. His hair was slightly gray, and his whiskers completely so. The eyes were gray, deep set, keen, and penetrating; nose, rather of the Roman order; his mouth sunken, with lips in general tightly compressed. Affable in manner; agreeable in conversation; yet determination expressed upon his countenance, such was the military bishop, General Polk.

One of the first events that occurred in his department, after taking command, was the capture, at Columbus, in Kentucky, of the steam packet *Cheney*. She had been conveying Federal troops up the river, and this becoming known, she was seized, and conveyed to Memphis, as a prize. A few days later, hearing that General Pillow, then at New Madrid, was likely to be in danger from the operations of large Federal forces, under Lyon and Fremont, General Polk immediately directed seven riverboats to be used for the purpose of conveying him and his troops away. This was promptly done; and the whole command of five thousand men, safely brought to Randolph, near headquarters, at Memphis. But, the first event here mentioned, was denied, by General Polk, as being under his authority. Columbus being in Kentucky, and that State not yet having openly espoused the cause of the North, this was made one of the subjects of correspondence between a committee of the Kentucky Senate, and General Polk. He had, however, now marched on to Columbus, and taken possession of the place, which still further increased the difficulty. The reasons he gave for so doing were, that it was a military necessity, arising from the fact, that Kentucky had herself dis-

regarded neutrality, by permitting Federal troops to organize companies, establish depots and camps, and erect military works. This was put forth in a proclamation he issued on the 4th of September, and also in a letter to Governor Magoffin, at the same time assuring him that he would withdraw the Confederate forces from Kentucky, if she would agree to make the Federals do the same. He also stated, that his proceedings were approved by President Davis. A lengthy correspondence followed, which produced no satisfactory result, and which we need not transcribe. Polk placed Columbus in a good state of defence, General Grant, at that time, being with his forces, at Cairo, a little higher up the river.

Not long after General Grant came down the river in force, with a design of attacking the Confederates, stationed at Bloomfield and New Madrid, under General Thompson. At 3 A. M., of November 7th, General Polk was informed, by a courier, that the enemy had landed on the Missouri shore, five or six miles above the small village of Belmont. This led him to expect that the attack would become general, and he immediately dispatched instructions to division officers. Colonel Tappan was in command of the small force at Belmont, and General Pillow was sent by Polk to his relief, across the river General Polk then examined other portions of his command, and found that General Cown, on his left flank, was already well prepared, and General Cheatham also in good position. This care was necessary, lest the Federals should attack him in the rear; but it was likewise needful to send more reinforcements to Belmont; and this was done under some difficulty. The fight, however, had now begun at Belmont, and, after a well-contested engagement, ended in a victory to the South, though this was denied by the North. General A. S. Johnston, who had then assumed entire command of the department, and was at Bowling Green, said officially, "This was no ordinary shock of arms: it was a long, and trying contest, in which our troops fought by detachments, and always against superior numbers. The 7th of November will fill a bright page in our military annals, and be remembered with gratitude by the sons and daughters of the South."

Polk's official dispatch to Richmond, and the answer received from President Davis are as follows :

HEADQUARTERS, FIRST DIVISION WESTERN DEPARTMENT, }
COLUMBUS, KY., November 7, 1861. }

To General Headquarters, through General A. S. JOHNSON:

The enemy came down on the opposite side of the river, Belmont, to-day, about seven thousand strong, landed, under cover of gunboats, attacked Colonel Tappan's camp. I sent over three regiments, under General Pillow, to his relief; then, at intervals, three others; then General Cheatham.

I then took over two others in person, to support a flank movement which I had directed. It was a hard-fought battle, lasting from 10.30 A. M., to 5 P. M. They took Beltzhoover's battery, four pieces of which were recaptured. The enemy were thoroughly routed. We pursued them to their boats seven miles, then drove their boats before us. The road was strewn with their dead and wounded, guns, ammunition, and equipments. Our loss considerable; theirs heavy.

[Signed,]   L. POLK,
                    Major-general commanding.

RICHMOND, November 8, 1861.

To MAJOR-GENERAL POLK:

Your telegraph received. Accept for yourself, and the officers and men under your command, my sincere thanks for the glorious contribution you have just made to our common cause. Our countrymen must long remember gratefully to read the activity and skill, courage and devotion, of the army at Belmont.

[Signed,]   J. DAVIS.

A few days after this, a serious accident occurred, which was nearly terminating with fatal results to General Polk. A large Dahlgren gun had been loaded during the above-mentioned battle, but not fired. It was discharged on the 11th, when it exploded, caught the magazine of the piece which was immediately below it, and killed eight men, besides seriously wounding five others. Among these latter was General Polk, who was knocked down senseless by the concussion, and had his clothes literally torn off him. Fortunately, he soon recovered, and without other injury.

Through the remaining part of the year 1861, nothing more

of importance connected with General Polk occurred. Jan
uary passed away in like manner; but, in February, Forts
Henry and Donelson fell, while General Polk was still at Columbus, compelled to remain and guard that post as long as he
could. But his situation soon became very critical. The Federals were collecting immense forces in Kentucky and Missouri,
and it was clearly seen by General Polk—General Johnson
having already commenced retreating south—that to hold Columbus any longer was hardly possible. Accordingly, " having received instructions from the War Department, through
General Beauregard, to evacuate the place, and select a defensive position lower down," it was done. On the 1st of March
the troops moved, General Stuart's brigade going by steamer,
to New Madrid, and the remainder marching by land, to Union
City, under General Cheatham. General Polk remained until
the next day, to supervise the completion of the work, and
then, at 3 P. M., himself and staff followed the rear column.
He retreated by the way of Humbolt, towards Corinth, where
the principal portion of the armies of the West, under Generals
Beauregard, Johnson, and himself, were to unite. This was
accomplished by the beginning of April; and General Polk was
placed in command of one of the three grand *corps d'armée*
into which the forces were divided.

The battle of Shiloh followed, on the 6th of April. It has
already been described in previous sketches, and all we need
say now is, that the commander-in-chief, General Beauregard,
very highly complimented " Major-general Polk for the zeal,
intelligence, and energy with which all orders were executed,
and for the foresight and military ability displayed, as well as
for his fearless deportment, in personally leading his command
against the adversary." The army now retreated to Corinth,
and, when that place was evacuated, the 30th of May, Polk's
corps proceeded, in accordance with orders, to Baldwin and
Tupelo. General Bragg was now appointed in command of
the department, and Polk's forces accompanied the army in
its movements through Tennessee, and into Kentucky, as previously described in our sketch of General Bragg. The march
was long, rough, and weary, but not without its charms, for it
was amidst some of the wildest and most magnificent scenery
to be found. Passing Chattanooga—crossing the Tennessee

at Harrison—on through the mountain passes of the North,—
the army finally reached Frankfort, in the beginning of October. At the same time the Federal forces arrived to attack
the rear of Bragg's army, stationed at Perryville; and on the
8th of October a battle took place. Polk's forces, under
Cheatham and Withers, formed the Confederate right wing,
and well did they sustain their previous reputation.

The following incident connected with this battle we will
give, as far as possible, in the words of General Polk, as he related it to a foreign military officer afterwards visiting him:

"Well, sir," said Polk, "it was at the battle of Perryville,
late in the evening—in fact, it was almost dark when Liddel's
brigade came into action. Shortly after its arrival, I observed
a body of men, whom I believed to be Confederates, standing
at an angle to this brigade, and firing obliquely at the newly
arrived troops. I said, 'Dear me, this is very sad, and must
be stopped,' so I turned round, but could find none of my young
men, who were absent on different messages; so I determined
to ride myself and settle the matter. Having cantered up to
the colonel of the regiment, which was firing, I asked him, in
angry tones, what he meant by shooting his own friends, and I
desired him to cease doing so at once. He answered with surprise, ' I don't think there can be any mistake; I am sure they
are the enemy.'

"'Enemy!' I said; 'why I have only just left them myself.
Cease firing, sir: what is your name, sir?'

"'My name is Colonel ———, of the —— Indiana; and
pray, sir, who are you?'

"Then, for the first time I saw, to my astonishment, that he
was a Yankee, and I was in rear of a regiment of Yankees.
Well; I saw there was no hope but to brazen it out. My dark
blouse, and the increasing obscurity befriended me; so I approached quite close to him, and shook my fist in his face, saying, 'I'll soon show you who I am, sir! Cease firing, sir, at
once.' I then turned my horse, and cantered slowly down the
line, shouting in an authoritative manner to the Yankees to
cease firing; at the same time I experienced a disagreeable
sensation, like screwing up my back, and calculating how
many bullets would be between my shoulders every moment.
I was afraid to increase my pace until I got to a small copse,

when I put the spurs in and galloped back to my men. I im
mediately went up to the nearest colonel, and said to him,
'Colonel, I have reconnoitered those fellows pretty closely, and
I find there is no mistake who they are; you may get up and
go at them.' And I assure you, sir, that the slaughter of that
Indiana regiment was the greatest I have ever seen in the
war."*

The army now moved from Kentucky into Tennessee again,
General Bragg leaving the whole conduct of the retreat to
General Polk. At early dawn of the 12th of October, the
troops had reached Bryantsville, and from this place the scene
presented was something extraordinarily picturesque and striking as the immense cavalcade passed on. "Ammunition
trains, and batteries of captured artillery had preceded; and
following them were trains of goods, wares, merchandise, provisions, army stores, captured muskets, escorts of cavalry, and
artillery drawn by oxen. Then came private trains of refugee
families, flying with their negroes for safety—ladies and children in carriages, stage-coaches, express wagons, omnibuses,
buggies, ambulances, Jersey-wagons, and every kind of vehicle
imaginable.† After this came the wagons of the different bri
gades of General Smith's army, with infantry, cavalry, and
artillery in the rear. Intermixed with the throng were thou
sands of cattle, horses, and mules."

The enemy was in pursuit, and it was necessary to urge on
the teams night and day for fear of capture. Part of the way
was along the bed of Dick's river, a miserable rocky branch,
which the troops had to cross and recross for six miles, during
one dark and hazy night. Terrible, then, was the scene of
confusion. Wagons broke down, or were overturned; teamsters bawled and screamed, and cracked their whips, and swore
in the most outlandish gibberish; and so it went on. Day
after day did the retreating army press towards the mountain
region of Cumberland gap; and day after day did the gallant
Wheeler, who covered the rear, perform all but superhuman

---

* Freemantle's Three Months in the South, p. 166; also see *Charleston
Mercury*, November 20th, 1862.

† The people of Kentucky, friendly to the South, were thus flying from the
Northern army invading their soil.

deeds to retard the enemy. From Altamount to Cumberland gap he encountered the enemy twenty-nine times, and, finally at Rock Castle, the pursuers abandoned the chase. The army of the Mississippi was saved! It took its way down the val ley, and thence to Murfreesboro, as already related.

It appears that at about this time, General Polk visited Richmond, and greatly surprised the public, one Sunday, by his presence in St. Paul's church at the morning service. His well-known, manly form was immediately recognized, and many would have gladly seen him ascend the pulpit. Ten days afterwards he left for the West, having acquiesced in the President's decision to sustain General Bragg.

At the battle of Murfreesboro, Polk, now a lieutenant-general, commanded the First corps, and well shared in the terrible struggle of those three days. After the retreat to Tullahoma, however, a few months of needful rest followed— during which no events of moment transpired worthy of record here. The same writer, whom we have so often quoted, relates the following. On a visit to the camp at this time, May, 1863, he says: "Lieutenant-general Polk is a good-looking, gentlemanlike man, with all the manners and affability of a 'grand seigneur.' He is fifty years old—tall, upright, and looks more like a soldier than a clergyman. He is very rich, and owns, I am told, seven hundred negroes. He is much beloved by the soldiers on account of his great personal courage and agreeable manners. He told me he was educated at West Point, and was at that institution with President Davis, the two Johnstons, Lee, Magruder, etc., and that after serving a short time in the artillery he had entered the church. He explained to me the reasons which had induced him temporarily to forsake the cassock and return to his old profession. He stated the extreme reluctance he had felt in taking this step; and said that so soon as the war was over he should return to his episcopal avocations, in the same way as a man, finding his house on fire, would use every means in his power to extinguish the flames, and would then resume his ordinary pursuits. . . General Polk told me an affecting story of a poor widow, in humble circumstances, whose three sons had fallen in battle one after the other, until she had only one left, a boy of sixteen. So distressing was her case that the general went

himself to comfort her. She looked steadily at him, and ro
plied to his condolences by saying, 'As soon as I can get a few
things together, General, you shall have Harry, too.' The
tears came into General Polk's eyes as he related this incident,
which he concluded by saying, 'How can you subdue such a
nation as this?'" . . General Polk's son, a young artillery
lieutenant, told me that he had been a cadet at the institute
where Professor "Stonewall" Jackson once taught, and at the
outbreak of the war, Jackson was called upon to make a
speech. He did so, in these words, "Soldiers, make short
speeches; be slow to draw the sword in civil strife, but when
you draw it, throw away the scabbard." Young Polk said
that the enthusiasm created by this speech of old Jack's was
beyond description."

General Polk was, as we have elsewhere mentioned, at the
battle of Chickamauga, where much of an unpleasant nature
occurred between General Bragg and himself. The result was,
that Polk, on the 30th of September, was deprived of his command,* for "dereliction of duty," and ordered to Atlanta,
where he arrived on October 3d. After reflection, however,
and examination into facts, convinced the President and
General Bragg that there had been some mistake; and, accordingly, General Polk was re-appointed, but sent to take
command of the paroled prisoners at Vicksburg and Port
Hudson, which he did in the latter part of November. The
following January, 1864, he was appointed to command the
department of Alabama, Mississippi, and East Louisiana. In
a previous address to his troops, on the last day of the year,
1863, he earnestly appealed to all good citizens to forget self,
and repair to the field that they might assist in the defence of
their country. He, himself, energetically applied himself to
the task of obstructing General Sherman's progress, in his
Mississippi expedition, and succeeded, to a great extent, in

* General Polk, in his farewell address to his command, says: " In consequence of an unfortunate disagreement between myself and the commander-in-
chief of this department, I have been relieved of my command, and am about
to retire from the army. Without attempting to explain the circumstances
of this disagreement, or prejudicing the public mind by a premature appeal to
its judgment, I must be permitted to express my unqualified conviction of the
rectitude of my conduct, and that time and investigation will amply vindicate
my conduct on the field of Chickamauga."

checking, though, as events have shown, not wholly frustrating his after plans. In February, General Polk so arranged his command as to place the Northern department of it under General Forrest, with his headquarters at Como; and the southern department, under General S. D. Lee, with head-quarters at Jackson. Various encounters with the Federals ensued, and, on the 26th of February, General Polk issued a congratulatory address to his troops, in which he considers the campaign, in that quarter, against Sherman, to have success-fully closed. He adds: "The concentration of our cavalry on his column of cavalry from West Tennessee formed the turning point of the campaign. That concentration broke down his only means of subsisting his infantry. His column was defeated and routed, and his whole force compelled to make a hasty retreat. Never did a grand campaign, inaugu-rated with such pretension, terminate more ingloriously. With a force three times that which was opposed to its advances, they have been defeated and forced to leave the field with a loss of men, small arms, and artillery."

When General Sherman carried his operations into North Georgia, and Johnson required all the force that could be brought to him, Lieutenant-general Polk was sent, with his troops, to form the left wing of the army. At Dalton, and again at Resaca, Polk placed his troops with great skill, and, in the retreat, "Loring's division of his corps brought up the rear and did effective service."

At length, the day came when the career of General Polk was to end. The Confederate army had retreated to Marietta, whither Sherman had closely followed it. It was a strong point on Kenesaw mountain, at which General Johnston had encamped. The Federal lines were well formed in front of him, and it was on the afternoon of June 14th, that Johnston, Hardee, and Polk, rode out from their quarters to make some telescopic observations of the Federal position. At the time, there was a brisk artillery fire going on between the two armies, but no engagement of the infantry. The generals, dismounting, walked to the front, where some of the enemy's artillerists, observing the party, fired. Their aim was too suc-cessful. One of the projectiles struck General Polk on the left arm, about the elbow, passed through his body, consider-

ably mangling it, and carried off the right arm. He died on
the spot, and his remains were immediately taken to Marietta
and thence to Atlanta, where funeral services were performed
on the 15th.   Thus ended the life of one whose character reminds us of the middle ages, when priest and monk forsook
the stole and cloister to join crusaders in the battlefield.   We
conclude by quoting the following tribute to his memory, as
found in *The Church Journal :*

   " Our strong condemnation of the bishop's course in voluntarily forsaking the exercise of his apostolic office in order to
take up the arms of earthly warfare, and bear his part in the
work of blood, has repeatedly been expressed during his life-
time, and neither justice nor generosity calls for a repetition of
the censure over his grave.   We would rather—now that
death has closed the account—recall the earlier days, when
the many noble traits of his personal character surrounded him
with friends, and made him second to none throughout all the
South, in his influence for good.   His manly bearing, his
frank and cordial manner, his high sense of honor, his real
tenderness and easily kindled sympathy of temperament—a
sympathy through which the fever of Revolution made of him
an early and an easy prey—his wise and eloquent labors in behalf of education, his splendid success in advocating and fur-
thering the 'University of the South,' his administrative
ability, his fatherly affection and firmness in the government
of the clergy and people of his diocese—these are the things
which we would most willingly recall, now that he is dead
and gone.   Or if his military career cannot be altogether
ignored—and alas! who can forget it?—we would rather remind our readers of the many acts of kindness and tenderness
shown by him to our sick and wounded men ; of the personal
dignity, and purity, and elevation of character, which he retained undiminished, even amid the thrilling excitements and
sharp temptations of the camp ; of his great success in winning
the confidence and love of his men, and in extending the spirit
of religion among the armies with which he served ; of his
open effort not altogether to sink the bishop in the general ;
and last, not least, of that striking scene in our little church at
Harrodsburg, when, after inspecting the building and deciding
that it should not be used as a hospital by his army, he laid

aside his sword, and entered the chancel, and knelt down at the altar, and aloud poured out his soul to God in a fervent prayer for peace.   When we think of all these things, we may well leave him to his Master, and our Master, to judge; nor feel it needful to mingle any earthly censure with the sincere expression of our sorrow at his fall."

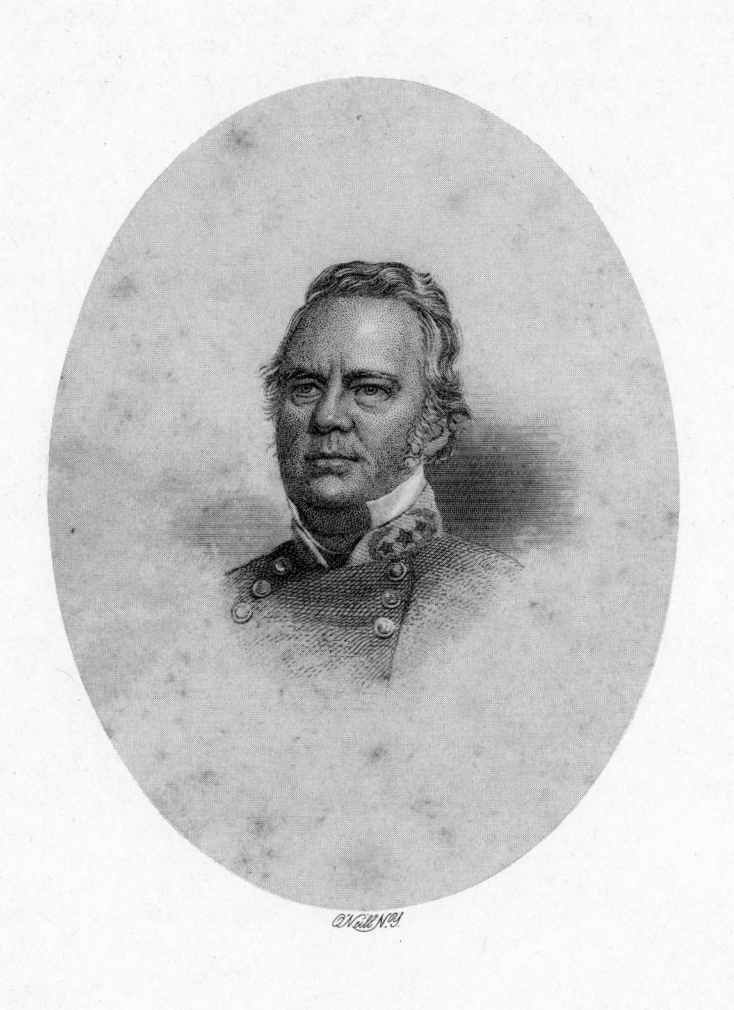

GEN. STERLING PRICE.

LIEUTENANT-GENERAL STERLING PRICE.

GENERAL PRICE is one of those extraordinary characters that troublous times always develope. Not a military man by education, nor, indeed, by actual profession, he possesses, however, many of the talents of a commander and a soldier. In strategy, he has frequently outmanœuvred several generals sent against him; and the success he has obtained, at any time, has mainly been the result of good sense and hard fighting. Yet he is as distinguished in the more peaceful walks of life, as he has been in those of war. As a politician, an orator, a citizen, a farmer, and a man, we find him praised by all who speak of him, while it also appears that he well deserves a place among the principal generals of the South.

Sterling Price was born about the year 1810, in Prince Edward county, Virginia, but emigrated to the west while very young. He settled at Charlton, in the State of Missouri, when he was twenty years of age, and there pursued the peaceful occupation of a farmer. For fourteen years thereafter we hear nothing of him; but it is evident that he had not been idle during the time, neither on his farm, nor amongst his fellow-men, for, in 1844, he was elected a member of Congress by a large majority. He took his seat in December, 1845, but, having failed to receive the party nomination in the following spring, he resigned and returned home. Just about this time the war broke out with Mexico. Several States—Mississippi, Tennessee, Illinois, Arkansas, and Louisiana—were sending volunteers, and Missouri followed the example by giving authority to Price for raising a regiment of cavalry, and appointing him colonel. This was on the 12th of

August, 1846, and the troops agreed to serve for twelve months.

Colonel Price's regiment was the 2d Missouri cavalry, and, with the 1st, Colonel Doniphan, two companies of Missouri infantry, and four of dragoons, was attached to that division of the grand army under Colonel (afterwards General) Kearney, uncle of the lamented General Philip Kearney, killed in 1862, at the battle of Chantilly, Va. Kearney's forces were to operate in New Mexico, and, in June, they proceeded, by separate detachments, from Fort Leavenworth, the place of rendezvous, towards Santa Fe. The distance thither is about 1,000 miles, nearly the whole of which is over boundless prairies, upon which are numerous herds of deer, antelope, and buffalo. The road between the two points was an old, but good, wagon-way, much travelled, with watering-places well-known. Fifty days it took for the army to reach Santa Fe, nothing of note occurring by the way. On the 16th of August, San Miguel had been taken, and thence the troops proceeded, through grand mountain scenery, to the city, which was found to be deserted by the Mexicans. General Kearney immediately took possession, and shortly afterwards, Colonel Price, with his regiment, arrived. General Kearney now proceeded to California with a portion of his command, sent Colonel Doniphan against the Navajos, and thence to unite with General Wool in Mexico; and left Colonel Price in charge of his own regiment, as the garrison force for New Mexico. In addition, there were 200 regular dragoons, under Captain Burgwin, and Fischer's company of St. Louis Light Artillery. This was the total of the force, numbering about 2,000 men, Colonel Price had with him, to take care of New Mexico, and, though this was his first military experience, he succeeded, as will be seen, in securing to the United States that valuable and extensive territory. A governor (Charles Bent) had been elected by General Kearney, but the military command of the province was entirely in the hands of Colonel Price, who must, undoubtedly, have shown rare qualities of mind and body, for such an able and experienced officer as General Kearney to have felt sufficient confidence in leaving him there.

Not long after Kearney's departure, an insurrection was planned against Price and the Americans, but was happily

discovered in time to prevent its complete, though not its partial, success. Governor Bent, and several of his officers, being absent, at the time, from Santa Fe, fell victims to it, and were brutally massacred. The garrison force, also, was obliged to live in detachments where forage could be obtained, and twenty of these were surprised and killed. This led the insur- gents to augur complete success, and, accordingly, they strongly posted themselves on heights, at a place called Cañada. This was on the 23d of January, 1847, and, on that day, Colonel Price, at the head of 400 men, marched against them. On the following day, he succeeded, after nearly two hours' engage- ment, in thoroughly routing them with some loss. The enemy then fell back to another strong position up a river, at the pass of Emboda ; thither, Colonel Price, now joined by Captain Burgwin and his dragoons, followed them. A gallant charge was made in a narrow gorge, and the enemy was again routed.

The insurgents, however, made yet another stand at San Fernando de Taos, where Governor Bent had been massacred, and there Colonel Price, with his command, pursued them. The country was mountainous, and the snow very deep, but the American force toiled over the steeps, crossed the valleys, marched through wild passes, and frightful-looking gorges, till, on the 3d of February, 1847, they entered San Fernando— evacuated by the foe—and went on to El Pueblo, where the Mexicans were more strongly posted than before. That after- noon the engagement began, ceasing at night, but renewed next day, and ended in the total defeat, and entire submission of the insurgents, after considerable loss on both sides.

We have not space to follow the after movements of Colonel Price, when he marched to Chihuahua, over the fearful, and previously impassable desert *Jornada del Muerto* (Journey of Death), nor can we detail his engagements with the Mexicans at Taos and Rosales. The services Price rendered in New Mexico raised his rank to that of Brigadier-general, and it was considered by every one, that " his campaign had been one of the most brilliant of the war, especially considering his slender force of volunteers ; and it forcibly displayed the extraordi- nary energy and enterprise of his character."

After his return from the Mexican War, in 1848, he settled down again upon his farm, though mixing more than before in

exciting political questions. Finally, in 1852, he was elected
Governor of Missouri, and his whole time was then devoted to
the welfare of the State. In 1860, he supported Mr. Douglas
for the Presidency. When it was found that Mr. Lincoln had
been elected, signs of strife were speedily manifested, though
no overt act was committed for some time. In January, ex-
Governor Price was chosen President of the State Convention;
and when the authorities decided upon resistance to the Federal Government, he was placed, by Governor Claib Jackson,
at the head of the Missouri State Guard, as Major-general.

From some skilful pen we have the following graphic description of General Price and his followers. Of his personal
appearance the writer says: "He is over six feet in height,
with a frame to match, full, but not portly, and straight as an
Indian. His carriage is marked with dignity, grace, and gen-
tleness, and every motion bespeaks the attitude and presence
of the well-bred gentleman. He has a large, Websterian head,
covered with a growth of thick, white hair, a high, broad, intellectual forehead, florid face, no beard, and a mouth among
whose latent smiles you never fail to discover the iron will that
surmounts all obstacles.

"The army of General Price is made up of extremes. It is
a heterogeneous mixture of all human compounds, and repre-
sents in its various elements every condition of Western life.
There are the old and the young, the rich and poor, the high
and low, the grave and gay, the planter and laborer, farmer
and clerk, hunter and boatman, merchant and woodsman—men,
too, who have come from every State, and been bronzed in
every latitude, from the mountains of the northwest to the
pampas of Mexico. Americans, Indians, half-breeds, Mexicans,
Frenchmen, Italians, Germans, Spaniards, and Poles—all mixed
in the motley mass who have rallied around the flag of their
noble leader. It is a ' gathering of the clans,' as if they had
heard and responded to the stirring battle-call of my poetical
friend, Harry Timrod."

"It has been a puzzle to many how Price, without govern-
mental resources, has managed to subsist a considerable army
in a country almost desolated. His system is not known in
the ' regulations.' He never complains of a want of transportation, whether he is about to move ten miles or a hundred

miles. He pays for what he takes, in Missouri State scrip. His men go into the cornfield, shuck the corn, shell it, take it to the mill, and bring it into camp, ground into meal. Or, should they have no flour, they take the wheat from the stack, thresh it themselves, or with horses or oxen, and as with corn, ask the aid of the miller to reduce it to flour. Such an army can go where they please in an agricultural country. His troops not only loved him, but were enthusiastically devoted to him. His figure in the battlefield, clothed in a common, brown linen coat, with his white hair streaming in the wind, was the signal for wild and passionate cheers; and there was not one of his soldiers, it was said, but who was willing to die, if he could only fall within sight of his commander."

Upon the outbreak of the present war, one of the first acts of General Price, May, 1861,* was to consult with General Harney of the Federal forces, as to the best mode of "restoring peace and good order to the people of the State, in subordination to the laws of the General and State Governments." Certain riotous demonstrations having appeared at St. Louis, Price having " full authority over the militia of the State," undertook, with the sanction of the Governor, to maintain order; and General Harney declared that he had no intention of using the military at his command, to cause disturbance. Both enjoined upon the citizens to keep quiet, and attend to their ordinary occupations.

Soon after this, when General Harney was removed by the authorities at Washington, General Price issued the following address, which, as it clearly defines his views and position, we insert :

HEADQUARTERS MISSOURI GUARD,￫
JEFFERSON CITY, June 4, 1861. ￫

To the Brigadier-generals commanding the
    several Military Districts in Missouri :

To correct misrepresentation, and prevent all misunderstanding of my opinions and intentions in reference to the military trust confided to me by the Government of Missouri, I desire to

---

* Just prior to this, the arsenal at Liberty had been seized; and, on the 10th of May, a brigade of Missouri militia had been forced to surrender, unconditionally, at the demand of Captain (afterwards General) Lyon, of the Federal army.

state to you, and the public generally, that my past and present
position as a private citizen, as a member of our State Convention, and as a military commander, and my influence, have
been exerted to prevent the transfer of the seat of war from the
Atlantic States to our own State. Having taken no steps towards dissolving our connection with the Federal Government,
there was no reason whatever for disturbing the peace and
tranquillity of Missouri. I have, therefore, desired, and such I
am authorized, has been, and still is, the desire of the Chief
Executive under whose orders I acted, that the people of Missouri should exercise the right to choose their own position in
any contest which might be forced upon them, unaided by any
military force whatever. The right to bear arms in defence of
themselves and of their State cannot be questioned, secured as
it is by both the Constitution of the United States and of this
State. For the purpose, therefore, of securing to the people of
Missouri a free exercise of their undoubted rights, and with a
view to preserve peace and order throughout the State, an
agreement has been entered into between General Harney and
myself, which I consider alike honorable to both parties and
governments represented. The Federal Government, however,
has thought proper to remove General Harney from the com
mand of the department of the West; but as the successor oɪ
General Harney will certainly consider himself and his government in honor bound to carry out this agreement in good
faith, I feel assured that his removal should give no cause of
uneasiness to our citizens for the security of their liberties and
property. I intend, on my part to adhere to it both in its
spirit and to the letter. The rumors in circulation, that it is
the intention of the officer now in command of this depot to
disarm those of our citizens who do not agree in opinion with
the administration at Washington, and put arms in the hands
of those who, in some localities of this State, are supposed to
sympathize with the views of the Federal Government, are, I
trust, unfounded. The purpose of such a movement could not
be misunderstood, and it would not only be a palpable violation of the agreement referred to, and an equally plain violation of our constitutional rights, but a gross indignity to the
citizens of this State, which would be resisted to the last ex
tremity.

My wish and hope is, that the people of the State of Missouri be permitted, in peace and security, to decide upon their future course, and so far as my abilities can effect this object, it shall be accomplished.

The people of Missouri cannot be forced, under the terrors of a military invasion, into a position not of their own free choice. A million of such people as the citizens of Missouri were never yet subjugated, and if attempted, let no apprehensions be entertained of the result.

I enjoin upon you, gentlemen, to see that all citizens, of whatever opinion in politics or religion, be protected in their persons and property.

STERLING PRICE,
Major-general commanding.

Events, however, were rapidly tending to serious collision between the respective forces; and, on the 20th of June, the first engagement occurred at Booneville, between the State troops, commanded by Captain Marmaduke and General Lyon. The Missouri men were defeated, though showing great bravery in this, their first pitched battle. Price therefore, was now compelled to come forward openly in favor of resistance to the Federal power. The day following the battle of Carthage, July 6th, General Price arrived at that city, accompanied by Brigadier-general McCulloch, of the Confederate army, who had been appointed by the authorities at Richmond to the command, under General Polk, head of the department.

On the 25th of July, the Missouri army, under Generals Price, McCulloch, and Pierce, began its march from Cowskin Prairie, near the Indian country, towards Springfield, where the Federals, under Lyon, Sturgis, Sweeney, and Sigel, were uniting their forces to overpower the State. But it soon became apparent that a division of the chief command would be inimical to the good of the cause, and, possibly, injurious to the troops. Price, therefore, with a truly unselfish and patriotic spirit, relinquished his post to McCulloch, expressing himself in substance as follows: "I seek not distinction; I am not fighting for that; but in the defence of the liberties of my countrymen. It matters little *what* position I hold. I am

ready to surrender, not only the command, but my life as a sacrifice to the cause." That his services and his presence among the men should not be lost, he took a subordinate position in the forthcoming contest. McCulloch assumed chief command, and Price was a division general under him; and thus the army marched forward to meet the foe.

On the 10th of August, the battle of Oak Hill, or Wilson's Creek, was fought, ending in defeat of the Federals, and death of their chief in command, General Lyon. Their forces, afterwards, first under Major Sturgis, and then Colonel Sigel, retreated to Springfield, and then to Rolla. Springfield was occupied by a part of the Confederates, under General Rains, on the 11th. The victory, however, was claimed by both sides, though the falling back of Sigel left the field undoubtedly to the Missouri men.

At this time, General Fremont had arrived to take chief command of the Western Department. On the 29th of July, he had reached St. Louis, and military preparations were immediately carried on with renewed vigor. But we cannot follow, in detail, the events of this stirring campaign in Missouri. Clearly, on the side of the State, General Price was the leading spirit, while McCulloch was the ruling authority among the Confederate forces. On the 20th of August, Price issued a proclamation " to the people of Missouri," exhorting them to maintain their privileges and rights against all persons, and especially against " any one claiming to be provisional or temporary governor of Missouri." This referred, no doubt, to the appointments made by the Federals; but it is evident that Price and the Missouri people were very jealous of any power —whether of the North or South—which might attempt to encroach in the least upon their perfect freedom. At this time, for some reason, Generals McCulloch and Hardee—who had been stationary at Greenville — withdrew, the former into Arkansas, the latter to join the forces under A. S. Johnson.

General Price, now again in full command, marched to the Missouri river with a force of about 4,500 men, and seven pieces of cannon. On the 7th of September, he encountered and fought General J. Lane, at a placed called Drywood, some fifteen miles east of Fort Scott. The conflict lasted nearly two·

hours, ending in Lane retreating, and some of Price's forces occupying the fort, the remainder, with their General, proceeding to Lexington.

On the 20th of September, 1861, Lexington, and all the United States forces there assembled, were surrendered to Price, by Colonel Mulligan, after a three days' siege. The Federal troops, and their gallant chief, held out bravely, but were at length obliged to yield. Immediately General Price issued an order, that the forces under Colonel Mulligan, having stacked their arms, " were not to be insulted by word or act, for they had fought like brave men." Colonel Mulligan, on giving up his sword, had it immediately returned to him by General Price, who said he "could not see a man of his valor without his sword." The Federal commander, however, would not give his parole, because " his government had not acknowledged the Missourians as belligerents." He was, therefore, a prisoner, though only such in name, for Price, with true chivalric courtesy, induced Colonel Mulligan and his wife to become his guests, and treated them with every possible hospitality : the same spirit being displayed by the victorious Missourians—officers and privates alike.

In his official report of this battle, General Price did not forget to bestow a very high meed of praise upon his troops. Said he, "No general ever commanded a braver or better army. It is composed of the best blood and bravest men of Missouri."

During the siege, quite a number of citizens came in from the neighboring country, and fought as they expressed it, " on their own hook." A participator in the battle tells an anecdote of an old man, about sixty years of age, who came up daily from his farm, with his walnut-stock rifle, and a basket of provisions, and went to work just as if he were engaged in hauling rails, or some other accustomed labor. He took his position behind a large stump upon the descent of the hill on which the fortification was constructed, where he fired with deadly aim during each day of the siege.

No sooner was Lexington taken than Price heard that Fremont, Sturgis, and Lane, were advancing with a heavy force, and in such a way as to cut him off. This he adroitly prevented by sending out cavalry, as if intending to attack each

of the enemy separately, and so covering his retreat. This retreat was executed in a most admirable manner, and amidst numerous obstacles. The Osage river was crossed in two flat-bottomed boats, constructed for the occasion by the Missouri soldiers; and then Price moved to Neosho, on the Indian frontier of the State. Here the Legislature had assembled, and here Price again formed a junction with McCulloch, at the head of 5,000 men. It was at this time, the State Legislature at length passed the Ordinance of Secession, and General Price had the satisfaction of firing a hundred guns to celebrate the event.

From Neosho, Price and McCulloch fell back to Cassville and Pineville, on the southern borders of the State. Fremont came on after him, and Springfield was taken from the Missouri forces stationed there, by Colonel Zagonyi, of Fremont's body guard. At Pineville, Price, however, was ready for another battle, but just then Fremont was recalled, and the Federals retreated to Osceola and Rolla. Price followed them to Osceola, and then returned to Springfield to forage his army and obtain supplies. This was about the 1st of December, 1861, and since the previous June, his gallant army had marched over eight hundred miles of ground, often in want, and yet fighting five battles and thirty skirmishes.

On December 4th, 1861, the Confederate Congress unanimously passed a resolution of thanks to "Major-general Sterling Price and the Missouri army under his command, for the gallant conduct they had displayed throughout their service in the present war."

About this time, Price had been appointed a major-general in the Confederate army—(holding this rank previously over State troops only)—but this was not confirmed, and Major-general Earl Van Dorn was assigned to the Department of Missouri and Arkansas, Ben McCulloch being over the forces further West. This appointment, though with the concurrence of General Price, did not succeed so well as anticipated. The two generals cordially united in resisting the advances of the enemy, but sufficient troops and material could not be found. The result was, that Price hearing of the Federals approaching in great numbers, determined, on the 13th of February to retreat, and gave orders accordingly. His army then moved

into Arkansas, arriving at Cove Creek, on the 25th of that month, and uniting with Van Dorn. Shortly afterwards, the Confederate forces were united with those under Ben McCulloch, and they then marched to attack the Federal army under General Curtis and Sigel, at Pea Ridge, Arkansas. The battle commenced on the 6th of March, 1862, after two days' long and dreary travelling through mud and snow. Gates's regiment of Price's body guard, and the Louisiana regiment, immediately attacked Sigel near Bentonville, but though that gallant German officer retreated to Curtis's main wing of the army, he did so in good order and without loss. This was on Thursday, March 6th, and on the next day the great battle raged in all its fury. Those who witnessed it, and were competent to judge, said it was the Buena Vista of the war, so far; and, certainly, we may infer it was more than ordinarily severe, from the separate accounts given of it. Van Dorn and Price were opposed to Curtis; while McCulloch and McIntosh faced Sigel. There were a number of Indians also engaged, and these were in McCulloch's command. Price pushed forward with his accustomed valor; and McCulloch did the same on his wing; but, during a terrible fusilade, the latter was killed. Van Dorn was not behind in cool daring and skill, and, as commanding officer, his testimony to the extraordinary valor of the Missourians under Price, is to be regarded. He said: "The Old Guard of Napoleon was not composed of braver men: I have never in battle seen their equals."

On Saturday, March 8th, the battle was renewed, and the cannonading was terrific. General McIntosh was killed, besides many other brave officers and men; and, finally, the Confederates fell back, leaving Curtis, Sigel, and Jefferson C. Davis, masters of the field.

The battle of Pea Ridge seemed to decide the question of Confederate rule in the State for a time, and it led to the retreat of Van Dorn with his army towards the Mississippi. Price, it is said, differed from Van Dorn about the attack on Curtis, when it was undertaken, but other circumstances also followed, which made General Price's position such as was not agreeable to him, nor so useful to his countrymen as he desired. He, therefore, resigned his commission in the State militia, April 6th, in an address to the "soldiers of the State

guard," which was full of patriotic fire, and generous enthusiasm. He then joined the Confederate army, having received his appointment, now confirmed, as major-general.

Immediately afterwards, Price and Van Dorn left the field in Arkansas to join the forces under A. S. Johnston and Beauregard; leaving Brigadier-general Pike on the Indian frontier, and Brigadier-general J. S. Roane in command of Arkansas, but without troops. On the 11th of April, Price, with his division, arrived at Memphis, and was most enthusiastically received. When called upon to speak, he said: "The time for speech-making had passed, and the time for action had arrived. He had commenced this service without men, money, or munitions of war; now he could boast of a gallant horde of true soldiers, not inconsiderable in numbers, and unsurpassed in valor and zeal, who would stand by him and he by them to the end—for weal or woe, come when that hour may. He had returned the arms and supplies he had borrowed to begin with, and still retained abundant supplies for the valorous sons of the West, won by them in the conflicts of the past for future use. He expected soon to be heard from in the thundering tones of the cannon, the roar of musketry, and the clashing of bayonets."

The battle of Shiloh was over when Price arrived with his forces, and joined Beauregard at Corinth; but on the 10th of May, he was with Van Dorn in the engagement at Farmington. There was, however, not a little ill feeling, among some in command, about General Price. Possibly, with the freedom that often pertains to men unaccustomed to the ordinary restraints of military life, when under strict discipline, he may have expressed himself too openly, as it is related he did. But whatever was the cause, his relations with the regular Confederate army, at this time, were not quite amicable. In June, he went to Richmond to consult with the authorities there, and, on his return, moved his division upon Iuka, Mississippi, taking possession on the 11th of September. His plan was to try and draw the Federal forces away from Corinth, and thus render its capture easy by General Van Dorn, who was to attack it during his absence. This plan failed through the promptitude of Generals Grant and Rosecrans, the latter personally moving on Price at Iuka. This battle took place on

the 20th of September, 1862, and ended in the defeat of General Price with great loss; General Little, a brave and much loved officer, being among the killed.

General Price now marched back and reunited with Van Dorn, both forces then moving on Corinth, held at the time by Rosecrans. The battles that ensued, on the 2d, 3d, and 4th of October, were ably fought, and with great obstinacy, but resulted in the defeat of the Confederates.

In this battle, General Price was again conspicuous for his daring, and also for his skilful arrangements. Van Dorn, being senior in rank, had the command, and Price ably seconded him. The other generals mentioned were Lovell, Maury, Herbert, and Villepigue. Had we space, some account of this battle, and the doings of the several commanders could well be given here.

In November, 1862, General Price sat on a court of inquiry to determine certain charges against General Van Dorn, who was, however, acquitted.

In December, the Confederate forces again fell back to Granada, before the advance of General Grant; but, on the 20th of the month, Van Dorn succeeded in getting behind the Federal commander, and, for a short time only, reoccupying Holly Springs, capturing the whole force stationed there, and destroying an immense quantity of stores and supplies. During the next month or two, however, we hear little of General Price, until, it seems, he arrived in Richmond to again confer with the authorities. The result was his appointment to a new command in the Trans-Mississippi department, where General Marmaduke was operating against Generals Blunt, and Herron. In March, 1863, Price arrived at Mobile, and proceeded thence to Little Rock, Arkansas. There, in conjunction with Marmaduke, he planned an expedition against Cape Giradeau, at that time the depot of supplies for a portion of Grant's army. The Confederate force left Little Rock about the middle of April, crossed into Missouri on the 20th, and was before Cape Giradeau—then held by General McNeil —on the 25th. McNeil had, just previously, removed the stores into Illinois, and obtained reinforcements from St. Louis. The result, therefore, was a disappointment to the Confederates, and after a sharp engagement, Marmaduke—who had the

command, for Price seems to have remained at Little Rock—retreated back to Arkansas, where he arrived on the 2d of May. From that date, various movements of no great importance occurred in Price's command, until July 4th, when an attack was made upon Helena, Arkansas, held by the Federal General Prentiss. A heavy engagement followed, and, finally, the Confederates again fell back to the middle of the State. General Steele now came on the field to aid in driving the Confederates out of the State; and, on the 10th of September, after an encounter with the forces of Marmaduke, Price, and Holmes, he entered Little Rock—the capital of Arkansas—and ultimately the Southern troops had to leave the Federals in possession. Price then crossed the border, and, in the early part of November, was at Marshall, Texas, not far from the confines of Louisiana.

On Christmas day, 1863, Price's command was at Longwood, twenty miles west of Coldon, and he had with him about 13,000 men. The majority of these, however, were new men. His old followers from Missouri—those who had served at Lexington and Pea Ridge under him—were nearly all in their graves, and only some 3,000 of his soldiers now hailed from the State of Missouri. The rest were principally Texans, and members of the adjoining territories.

In the early part of March, 1864, Price assumed command of all the Confederate forces then preparing to advance upon Arkansas, and, as he said in a proclamation, " chase the Union army from that State." The operations of General Banks on the Red river, in April, called for General Steele to join him, and Price at once moved forward to cut off his retreat. This he was unable to do completely, but so far impeded him that he was compelled to cut his way through Price's forces, to regain Little Rock. The following month, May, Price was at Camden, Arkansas, still watching for some opportunity to successfully engage the forces, but especially to accomplish his long desire of marching again into Missouri. He set about this in June, by flanking Little Rock, and marching to the northwest of the State, where, at Bayettsville, he halted to organize his forces. There, recruits, horses, provisions, ammunition, medicines, and other stores poured in abundantly from Missouri, in spite of all precautions on the part of General

Rosecrans, then in command of the department, to prevent it. Shelby, the General next to Price, was ordered to advance, and this he did, by crossing the border line in September. He then marched on to Doniphan and Bloomfield, Mobile, and finally proceeded towards Pilot Knob, Price quickly following, and reaching Bloomfield on the 24th of September, thus, once more entering the State for the purpose, as he alleged, of freeing it from Northern rule. The next day Frederickton was taken, and Price's forces, on the 27th, were in front of Ironton, then garrisoned by General Ewing. A skirmish ensued, which resulted in the capture of a small detachment of the Federals, and Price then marched towards Jefferson city. There he was met by a stout resistance, and compelled to move on Booneville. General Pleasanton pursued him with 8,000 cavalry, forcing him to leave his task unaccomplished. On the 23d of October he was attacked, and defeated with great loss—Generals Marmaduke and Cabell being taken prisoners, besides many officers and men. On the following day, Price was again attacked, near Fort Scott, and obliged hurriedly to retreat into Kansas. He then turned down to the South, and crossed the Arkansas river, above Fort Smith, in the Indian territory. On the 8th of December, his headquarters were at Washington, in the south part of Arkansas, his troops at that time greatly suffering from the weather. Later accounts, up to the end of

In January, 1865, General Price had a bitter controversy with ex-Governor Reynolds, of Missouri, about the failure of the last campaign. Price dates his letters from Shreveport, *Louisiana*, on January 6th, and from Washington, *Texas*, January 26th, thus indicating his locality at those dates. When, however, news arrived that the three great Southern armies east of the Mississippi had surrendered to the Federal power, General Price was sent by Kirby Smith to negotiate with General Canby for terms of surrender; which being settled on the 26th of May, he soon afterwards departed for Mexico. There he settled down under the auspices of the Emperor Maximilian as an agent for immigration, and to examine lands for colonization purposes. Cordova, in the State of Vera Cruz, was the place selected for the new colony; and, at the end of September, General Price was there actively engaged in his new duties.

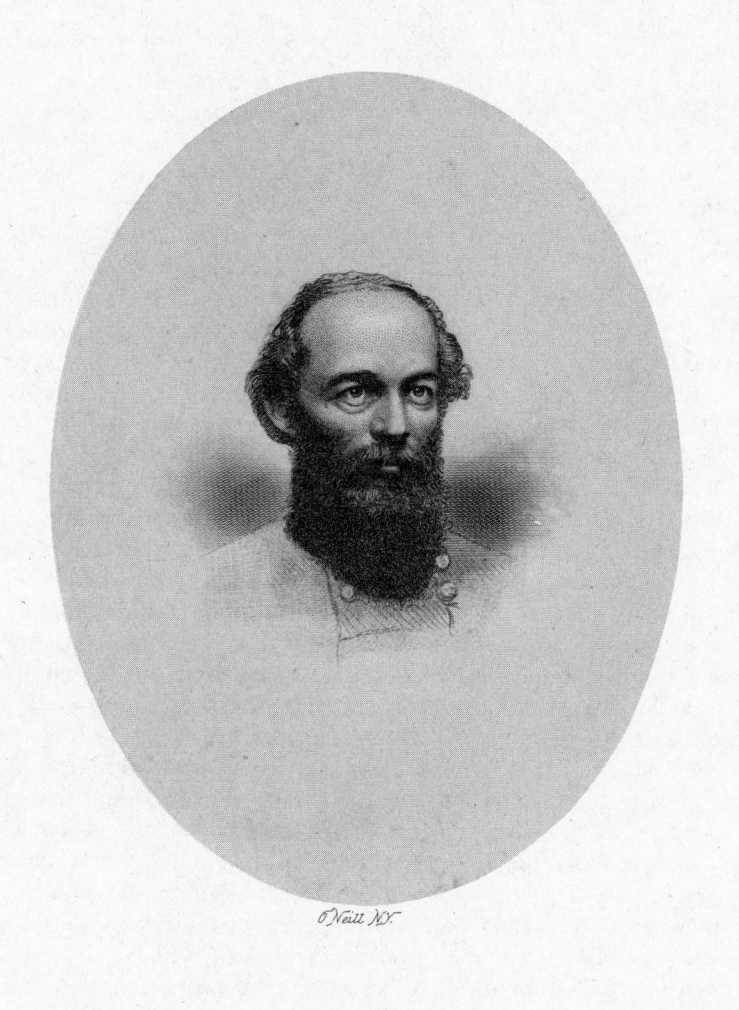

O'Neill N.Y.

LT. GEN. KIRBY SMITH.

LIEUTENANT-GENERAL EDMUND KIRBY SMITH.

LIEUTENANT-GENERAL E. KIRBY SMITH was born in Florida, about the year 1824, and is connected, by ties of blood, with others of his name in the Federal army, and in the State of Connecticut. His father was the late Joseph S. Smith, at one time a lawyer, residing in Litchfield, Connecticut. This father married Frances, daughter of Judge Ephraim Kirby, of that place—the author of "Kirby's Connecticut Reports." Lawyer Smith was appointed a major of the United States army in the early part of the war of 1812. He was afterwards promoted to Colonel, and served during the war on the Canada frontier. After the war he was appointed United States Judge for the district of Florida, and removed, with his family, to St. Augustine, where he died about the year 1841. He had two sons; the eldest, Ephraim Kirby, graduated at West Point, and was a captain in the regular army during the Mexican war. He was killed at Molino del Rey.

The second son, Edmund Kirby, graduated at West Point, on the 30th of June, 1845, and was made brevet-second-lieutenant of the 5th infantry, then with General Taylor in Mexico. Kirby Smith was at the battles of Palo Alto and Resaca; after which he was made full second-lieutenant, and assigned to the 7th regiment, with which command he participated in the taking of Monterey, highly distinguishing himself by his bravery. He was afterwards with Scott at Vera Cruz; and, at Cerro Gordo, obtained a brevet as first-lieutenant, for gallant and meritorious conduct, the brevet appointment dating April 18th, 1846. At Contreras, he had another brevet, as captain, given him for good service; and, throughout the

Mexican war his conduct was such as to merit and receive approbation from his superiors.

In 1849, Captain Smith was appointed Assistant Professor of Mathematics at West Point, and was afterwards captain in the same cavalry regiment with R. E. Lee and others already mentioned. Accompanying this regiment, he had much opportunity for developing his bravery in the various engagements with the Camanche Indians, and in a desperate battle with them, on May 12th, 1859, he was severely wounded. He was then promoted major in the regular army; but when his native State seceded, in 1861, he immediately resigned his commission, and gave his sword and services to the cause of the South.

At this time he had, as we have already intimated, several family ties in the North as well as the South. His nephew was the late Colonel J. L. Kirby Smith, of the 43d Ohio regiment, a brave officer, promoted from a lieutenancy of the topographical engineers, but who fell in the battle of Corinth.* It is also stated that a gallant young officer, Lieutenant Kirby, in command of Rickett's battery of regulars, late in the day at Bull Run, 1861, was a relation of his. His sister was the widow of the late Colonel L. B. Webster, United States army, and then resided at Geneva, New York. An aunt and a first cousin were also in New York; but his mother remained in Florida, at St. Augustine.

The private character of Kirby Smith is represented to have been "above reproach, as a gentleman and a Christian. He was a member of the Episcopal church, and, a few years since, entertained serious thoughts of giving up his profession and studying for the ministry." A writer, speaking of him, says, "he is a remarkably active man, and of very agreeable manners, wearing big spectacles and black beard."

Kirby Smith, upon offering his services, was immediately

---

* The following extract from General Stanley's report of the battle of Corinth, will show in what estimation Colonel Smith was held, as a soldier:

"Soon, in the battle on the 4th inst., Colonel J. L. Kirby Smith, of the 43d Ohio, fell with a mortal wound. I have not words to describe the qualities of this model soldier, or to express the loss we have sustained in his death. The best testimony I can give to his memory is the spectacle witnessed by myself, in the very moment of battle, of stern, brave men, weeping like children as the word passed, Kirby Smith is killed.'"

made colonel in the Confederate army, and was sent to serve with General Johnston, then at Harper's Ferry. He there had charge of a brigade, and was, in fact, a brigadier-general, though, it appears, his rank was not confirmed till after the battle of Manassas. In this engagement Kirby Smith, having been delayed (by some treachery, it is said) with his portion of Johnston's forces from the Shenandoah, arrived on the ground about half-past three, P. M., of the 21st of July, 1861. He had come, with his troops, by the cars, intending to go right on to Manassas as previously directed ; but, when near the battlefield, the firing told him that an engagement was in progress. Accordingly, he stopped the cars, and prepared his men to march, at once, to the scene of contest. Advancing through the fields, and receiving directions from General Johnston how to move, he came suddenly upon the enemy's right flank and rear, with what result is known. For himself, personally, however, there was not the opportunity to do much. In moving forward, he was struck by a ball and severely wounded. His command, threfore, had to be led by Colonel Elzey, who admirably accomplished, "with great promptitude and vigor," the movement so effectual in defeating the Federal army. In the official reports, however, full praise is given to General Smith for the able and rapid disposition of his forces he had displayed.

From the battlefield of Manassas, Kirby Smith was taken to Lynchburg, where his wound was effectually healed. Upon his recovery, he was married, on the 24th of September, to Cassie, daughter of Samuel S. Selden, deceased, of Lynchburg. He then appears to have visited his native home, and, after a short rest, returned again to the army of the Potomac. In the beginning of November, his brigade was stationed at Camp Wigfall, on the Orange and Alexandria railroad, near Bull Run, Van Dorn's being also close by.

Late in February, 1862, Kirby Smith, having been made a major-general, was appointed to command the Confederate forces in the neighborhood of Cumberland gap, and in East Tennessee, and during the following month arrived at his post. He immediately proclaimed martial law, in accordance with directions received from President Davis, and appointed Colonel Churchwell provost-marshal. This law was very stringent

as regarded the sale of spirituous liquors, and, on one occasion, at Jonesboro, Tennessee, a large seizure was made for infringing it.

In the summer of 1862, it was decided that General Bragg should advance into Kentucky, while Kirby Smith's forces were to operate more to the eastward, and seem to threaten Cincinnati. This great movement was followed out as previously related, and General Smith's army marched through the gaps in the Cumberland mountains, where they were joined, in August, by Claiborne's division. The troops then made forced marches to Barboursville, Kentucky. Here they halted long enough merely to get water, and then pushed on to the Cumberland ford. At that place, a few days' rest were given to the wearied men, who had been marching almost barefoot over stony roads, through mountain passes, and with green corn, garnished with a small supply of poor beef, for their food. Again moving forward, the forces of General Smith were descending the Big Hill, not far from Richmond, Kentucky, on the morning of August 29th, when the Federals were discovered in front, indicating a determination for battle. This Kirby Smith did not hesitate in giving them. Advancing two or three miles further, the enemy was found drawn up in line of battle near Mount Zion church, six miles from Richmond, and on the morning of the 30th, the leading division of the Confederates, under General Claiborne, commenced the action. The fight soon became general, and after a severe struggle, in which General Churchill and Colonel Preston Smith bore a conspicuous part, the enemy was defeated, and Kirby Smith held the field. Next morning, he ordered the cavalry to go round to the north of Richmond and attempt to cut off the enemy's retreat, and, while this was being done, the Confederates in front ceased firing. Mistaking this for a retreat, the Federals gallantly pushed forward, and charged upon the Texas and Arkansas troops under McCray. This heroic brigade stood the ground almost alone, but succeeded in driving back the enemy with terrible loss, and in great confusion, leaving knapsacks, swords, pistols, hats, and canteens scattered along the road, with the dead and dying.

The Federal army, now under command of General Nelson, —who had just arrived and relieved General Manson,—re-

treated to Richmond, swiftly followed by Kirby Smith. At the town, however, Nelson had determined to make another stand ; and, for the second time, that day—the third time since meeting each other—the Confederates and Federals again tried their strength. The result was, another victory to the Southern troops ; and on this, the 31st day of August, 1862, General Kirby Smith was completely master of the place. Next day, General Smith continued the march, and on the 4th of September he arrived at Lexington. There his reception by the inhabitants was very enthusiastic, and abounding in evidences of the most friendly welcome. It is related, that streets, windows, and gardens were filled with ladies and little girls, with streamers of red and blue ribbons and flags with stars. Beautiful women seized the hard brown hands of rough and ragged soldiers, and with tears and smiles thanked them again and again for coming into Kentucky and freeing them from the presence of those who had been of late in authority over them. For hours the enthusiasm of the people was unbounded. At every corner of the streets, baskets of provisions and buckets of water were placed for the refreshment of the wearied soldiers, and hundreds of the men were presented with shoes, hats, coats, and tobacco, from the grateful people, while private residences were turned, for the time, into public houses of entertainment. But, if the reception of the infantry was enthusiastic, the cheers of wild delight which greeted General John Morgan's cavalry as they came dashing through the streets, amidst clouds of dust, was without a parallel. The bells of the city pealed forth their joyous welcome, whilst the waving of thousands of white handkerchiefs and tiny flags attested the gladness and delight of every heart.

And thus the victorious forces of Kirby Smith marched on. From among the rocky passes of the wild Cumberland mountains to the town of Lexington, they had gone through much of that fearful toil of travel an army so often has to endure. But here was, at least, some partial recompense ; and hope led them on still further. Cincinnati was the desired goal, and rapidly from Lexington, on to Paris, next to Cynthiana, and finally to within a short distance of the Queen City of the West, did the joyous troops of the South wend their way. Then came fear, and something of a panic, among the startled

citizens of the place. Ohio was firm in allegiance to the North, and had skilful and brave commanders, besides its own heroic volunteer militia, in the frontier cities, to defend it—particularly in Cincinnati; but here was Kirby Smith right before them, and Bragg, with another army, marching swiftly forward, as was supposed, to the attack. It so happened, however, that such was not the intention of General Bragg. The orders given to Kirby Smith were, " to *menace*, not attack;" and the purposes of the campaign required that Smith's command, after making its demonstration on the Ohio, should fall back into the interior, to co-operate with the splendid army Bragg had brought into Kentucky. The consequence was that, in a few days, General Smith retired from before Cincinnati, and directed his march to Frankfort, where he arrived prior to Bragg, who reached there on the 4th of October.

The movements of the Federals now led General Smith to suppose that they would come upon him, and not upon Bragg's forces, then, mainly, with the rear at Perryville; and thus, in the battle which followed at the latter place, Smith's command was not engaged, he not having received orders to move there until too late. On the 9th of October he arrived at Harrodsburg, and joined the main army. In the retreat of the Confederates, as already related, General Smith's command took the advance, and in repassing those places where, but a short time before, such joy had been shown, it was painful as well as humiliating to witness the sorrowful expressions now displayed. However, there was nothing for him but to obey, and the army then proceeded by the way in which they had come. On the 10th of October there was an engagement of five hours, between a part of his command and the Federals, under Colonel E. A. Parrott, of the 1st Ohio Volunteers, and, after this, the army pursued its way unmolested, reaching Tennessee, October 24th.

Kirby Smith was now made a lieutenant-general, and, for a short time, was absent on leave, in consequence of ill health, but returned to his post again early in November, retaining command of the East Tennessee department, with a portion of his troops there, while the rest were in the vicinity of Murfreesboro. At the battle which there took place, his corps was, first, on the right, with Morgan's cavalry, and afterwards had

the centre. The result of the three days' fight we have already shown, and will now proceed to the after movements of General Smith.

Early in January, 1863, he arrived in Richmond, owing to recent changes made in the army, and in March he was appointed to the department west of the Mississippi. In the early part of April he arrived there, and assumed command through a general order, which named Alexandria, Louisiana, as his headquarters. In May, he was at Shrieveport, Louisiana, with his wife, and throughout the following months was occupied, in conjunction with the several military commanders under him, in resisting the advances of Banks from New Orleans to Alexandria, and beyond. His movements, however, have not been made well known, until, in the beginning of September, we find him at Arkadelphia, with the main Confederate army. The events that occurred in that department have already been recorded. Kirby Smith returned to his former quarters, and, in April, 1864, successfully resisted General Banks' renewed attempt up the Red river, beyond l'Ecore. At the beginning of the next month he was with Price, a Camden, Arkansas, and issued the following address to the army

HEADQUARTERS, TRANS-MISSISSIPPI DEPARTMENT, }
CAMDEN, Ark., May 3, 1864. }

SOLDIERS OF THE TRANS-MISSISSIPPI DEPARTMENT:

Once more, in the hour of victory, we are called upon to mourn the heroic dead.

Generals W. R. Scurry and Horace Randal have fallen upon the field of honor. At Jenkins' ferry they offered themselves up, precious victims on the altar of liberty.

Mouton and Green are gone; Scurry and Randal have followed on the same glorious path. Be it ours to emulate their virtues and valor, and to act as men not unworthy to associate with such heroes.

The colors of their respective brigades will be draped in mourning for thirty days.

E. KIRBY SMITH, General Commanding.

HEADQUARTERS, TRANS-MISSISSIPPI DEPARTMENT, }
CAMDEN, Ark., May 4, 1864. }

SOLDIERS OF THE TRANS-MISSISSIPPI DEPARTMENT:

The campaign inaugurated at Mansfield on the day of na-

tional fast and supplication has, under Providence, been crowned with most glorious and brilliant success. You have defeated a foe three times your own. The fields of Mansfield, Pleasant Hill, Cloutierville, Poison Spring, Marks' Mill, and Jenkins' ferry attest your devotion. Eight thousand killed and wounded, six thousand prisoners, thirty-four pieces of artillery, twelve hundred wagons, one gunboat and three transports, are already the fruits of your victories. The path of glory is still open to you—permanent security to your homes before you. Call together your comrades, and, shoulder to shoulder, we will yet free the soil of our beloved country from the invader's footsteps. Soldiers of Arkansas, Missouri, Texas, and Louisiana, you have the thanks of a grateful people. Your living will be respected—your dead honored and revered.

E. KIRBY SMITH, General.

There is little of real military importance to record concerning General Kirby Smith, after this date, until near the period when the South surrendered its temporary power. Various reports as to his movements and intentions were spread abroad. Some said he was negotiating for a transfer of his forces to the emperor of Mexico; others, that he was engaged in heavy cotton speculations, and defied alike the North and the South; and finally, that he was assassinated in a quarrel by an ex-officer of the Confederate army, whom he had badly treated. But to none of these reports have we any positive evidence. There appears, however, to have been a spirit of recklessness and self-will on the part of all under his command; for it was reported, in March, that his troops refused to cross the Mississippi when ordered, and that he himself was frequently coerced into measures not emanating from his own ideas. At length, news came of Lee's surrender, and Kirby Smith then issued a proclamation calling upon his troops still to resist. This was dated on the 21st of April, and five days later he attended a public meeting at Shreveport, where some very strong speeches of a similar tendency were made by various speakers. Just at that time General Grant's commissioners had arrived at the Red River, with a view to arrange for the surrender of the Trans-Mississippi forces; but not until the 26th of May did Kirby Smith—or rather his

army—yield. On the same day the surrender was formally made, General Smith arrived at Galveston, and on the 30th of May was at Houston, whence he issued a farewell address to the troops lately under his command. In this address he says:

"Your present duty is plain. Return to your families. Resume the occupations of peace. Yield obedience to the laws. Labor to restore order. Strive both by counsel and example to give security to life and property. And may God in his mercy direct you aright, and heal the wounds of our distracted country."

Later intelligence states that General Grant had written to say that Kirby Smith could return home on parole; and, accordingly, after visiting Havana, he arrived, in the beginning of November, at Lynchburg, and there took the amnesty oath, afterwards proceeding on to Washington.

As much to General Kirby Smith's prejudice has been said and written, it is but just to insert the following on the opposite side. A Galveston Union paper says:

"He was an able commander in the field, devoted to the cause he espoused, and essentially a warm-hearted, true man. However much we may condemn the policy he pursued latterly, as a commander, we have no hesitation in saying that we consider him one of the purest and best men, in a moral sense, connected with the Confederate service, and that the reports circulated prejudicial to his integrity are without foundation."

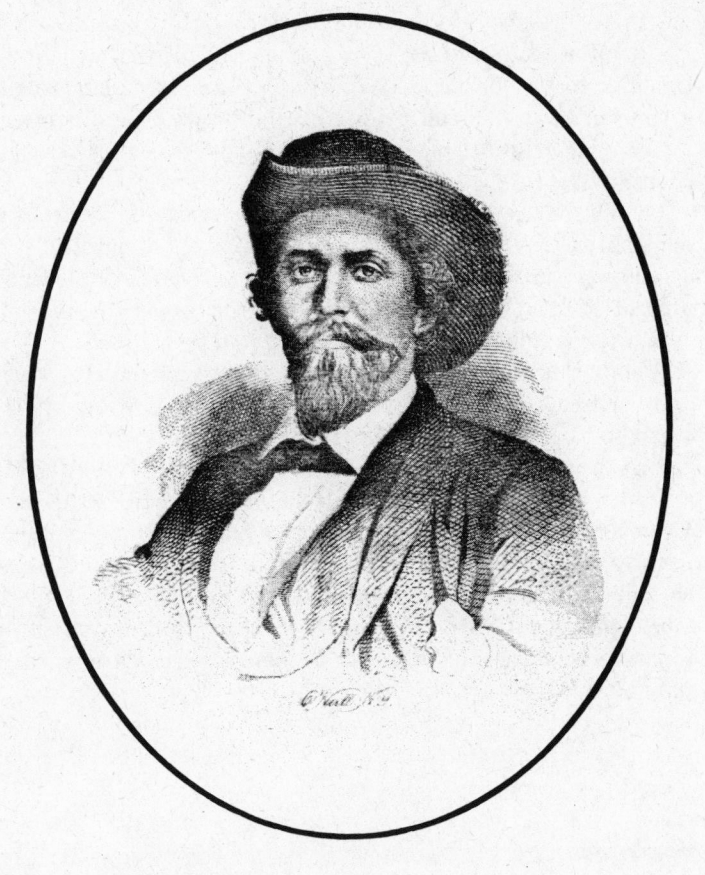

John H. Morgan

From a Photograph taken from life.

MAJOR-GENERAL JOHN H. MORGAN.

THIS bold and daring chief was born in Lexington, Kentucky, about the year 1827. His parents were of good repute, though not of the wealthy class, and they had a large family to maintain. John was the eldest of six brothers, all of whom, save one, have devoted themselves, their means, and all they possessed, to the cause of the South. Their names are Calvin, who always acted as agent, in Kentucky, for his brother John; Colonel Richard, who was adjutant-general to A. P. Hill; Major Charlton, who formerly represented the United States Government abroad, but lately was in his brother's command; and Lieutenant Thomas Morgan, also in the same command, and twice captured. There was, likewise, a cousin, whom we find mentioned serving as a private soldier.

When the Mexican war broke out, Morgan joined the First Kentucky regiment as a private, and went to share in some of those hard-fought battles so well known. For his bravery and good conduct, he was promoted from the ranks to a second-lieutenant, and returned home in that capacity.

About this time he purchased an establishment, and engaged in the manufacture of jeans, linseys, and bagging for the Southern market. About the same time, he married Miss Rebecca Bruce, who, after years of sickness, died at the commencement of the present war. Morgan then determined to take up arms for the South, and secretly collected a little band of followers, who elected him captain, and each provided his own arms, horse, and equipments. Escaping from Lexington, where they had been closely watched, they started forth in quest of adventure.

This was in the fall of 1861, when Buckner was at Bowling Green; and thither Morgan and his companions went. On the 30th of September they arrived at the Confederate camp, on

Green river, opposite Munfordsville, where they were cordially received. Captain Morgan not wishing to be united to any particular command, asked to be allowed to serve as a partisan ranger, but it was not deemed prudent to grant his request. He, therefore, moved to the north bank of the river, rented a vacant house for his men and, with this as his headquarters, made the country between Green river and Bacon creek the scene of many daring exploits.

Early in the year 1862, Morgan was promoted to the rank of Colonel—his men having already increased to the number of a regiment. Soon afterwards the Confederates retreated from Bowling Green to Murfreesboro, and the rear of the army was covered by Morgan's and Colonel Forest's cavalry. General Buell now occupied Nashville; and on the 15th of March, Morgan made a successful raid in the rear of the Federal army.

On the 19th of March, he again passed through Gallatin, at night, and the next day captured a train of cars, bound down the road. The up-train soon came in sight, and Morgan, individually, signalled it to stop. On board of this train was an old friend of Morgan, a physician in the Federal army, now residing at Louisville. From this fact alone, John permitted the locomotive, with his friend, to proceed North, shouting, as it started, "Tell Guthrie that you have saved him twelve thousand dollars!" Morgan's men then destroyed two water-tanks, and tore up about a mile and a half of the road. He immediately retired his forces, now fifteen hundred in number and located himself near Sparta, in the eastern part of the middle section of Tennessee.

His exploits, however, extended far and wide; and not a few dashing adventures had he and his men at this time. One day, in the vicinity of Nashville, while riding in advance of his command, he met a Federal colonel and his staff, trotting leisurely along. "Halt!" said Morgan. "I'll be d——d if I do," was the reply. "I have already been halted a half-dozen times since I left Nashville, and I'll submit to it no longer. Who are you, any how?" Quickly drawing out his pistol, and presenting it, he very quietly replied, "Morgan; and you are my prisoner." The Federal officer made no further resistance.

He and his escort, besides a considerable force in the rear, were captured; but Morgan was pursued, and had to hurry away.

On another occasion, with forty of his men, he dashed in among the enemy's pickets, and captured eighteen out of thirty. A few days after, he nearly succeeded, by an ambush, in capturing General McCook and his staff. Again, disguising himself as a wagoner from the country, and entering Nashville alone, he personally communicated with General Buell, and induced that officer to believe a shrewd tale, which ultimately led to the caputre of about seventy of the Federal cavalry. His next exploit was an expedition to Lebanon, where a small detachment of Federals was stationed. These were easily secured, the prisoners paroled, and their arms distributed among the captors, who, with their work accomplished, then lay down to rest. But at daylight an alarm was given: "The enemy is upon us," was the cry; and before they could prepare for a defence, General Dumont, with a strong force, appeared. Resistance was useless. "Save, who can," was the order from Morgan; and though a number were captured and killed— among the former, Morgan's younger brother—many more escaped. Morgan, mounted on his beautiful mare, dashed through the advancing ranks of the enemy, cutting his way right and left. His noble animal was shot under him, and it was only by the most reckless daring and courageous self-possession that he saved his life. Even parties opposed to the South acknowledged, in speaking of this engagement, that "the fight was a gallant one; Morgan's men resisting the attack of our force for nearly two hours."

The disaster attending this sudden surprise at Lebanon, made Morgan almost insanely determined to match it by a like return; and the following incident has been related as truthful concerning him.

In one of the telegraph offices on the line between Louisville and Nashville, was seated one day, the operator, looking very grum. He had just sent forward a dispatch relative to Morgan's captured men, and was making some very strong observations about the famous raider, when a horseman alighted at the door, and, with whip in hand, carelessly walked in. The intruder had on a butternut suit, all bespattered with

mud, and an old slouched hat, with rim partly torn off.
Stepping forward to a vacant chair, he seated himself, and
asked for news. "No news," was the curt reply. A morning
journal lying on the desk, the stranger, reaching out his hand
with the most perfect *sangfroid,* took the paper, opened it, and
began to read. Glancing down the first column, he presently
said "John Morgan at work again! Great pity that man can't
be caught—he plays the wild with every thing." At mention of
Morgan's name the operator, with great vehemence, remarked,
"If I had him here I would soon put a ball through his cursed
body. No more pranks from him, the mighty John Morgan, I
tell you!" "Why, you wouldn't kill him—would you?" asked
the stranger, quietly looking up from his paper, and lifting the
torn brim of his old hat. "Kill him?" was the response; "aye,
that I would, sooner than I'd shoot a mad dog. I just dare him,
at any time, to cross that door, and if he isn't a dead man in
five minutes, there's no truth in me."

The stranger rose, took off his hat, and, with a quiet mien
and gentle voice, said, "I am John Morgan, sir: execute your
threat. Here is a pistol; you are entirely welcome to use it." As
he spoke, he fixed his large, piercing eyes steadfastly upon the
operator. The latter, amazed, was hardly able to answer. He
fell back, pale, and trembling, and making numerous apolo-
gies, saying he had no idea that the stranger could be *Colonel*
Morgan; and he hoped he would forgive him. "You have my
pardon, sir," replied Morgan, in a firm, gentlemanly tone.
"Another time I would advise you to be less boastful of your
courage and veracity. I have but little time to stay. Seat
yourself, and send the messages that I shall dictate, to
Louisville. Make no mistake. If you do, your life is the forfeit.
I understand the operation, sir, therefore don't attempt to give
any information but what I instruct you." The command
being readily obeyed, Morgan then said, "Now, show me all
the dispatches that have passed through this office in the last
twenty-four hours." The poor victim again preferred compliance to the alternative, and delivered the documents to his
visitor, who, after reading them, said, "That will do, sir;—
Good morning:" and, going to his horse, mounted, and rode
swiftly away.

Immediately, and probably from the information thus

gained, Morgan, with some of his men, laid in wait for a train from Louisville bound to Bowling Green, where a Union mass meeting was going to be held. As the cars approached Cave City, half a dozen horsemen suddenly appeared in front of the locomotive, and sang out, "Halt," with a wave of the hands as a signal. But the engineer not stopping, some thirty others appeared, armed to the teeth, and ready to aim at him and the passengers. Immediately the alarmed cry arose, "Morgan! Morgan!" and the utmost confusion prevailed. The cars were stopped, the rails behind and before obstructed, and the horsemen immediately demanded the surrender of all soldiers and freight belonging to the Federal government. Morgan himself entered the ladies' car, and as he stood for a moment, every eye was fixed upon him with a look of terror. "Be quiet, ladies," said he, with a pleasant smile, "none of you shall be hurt; I only want the blue-coated gentleman." He then approached an officer seated by the side of his wife, who imploringly entreated of Morgan not to take him. "Spare my husband, Colonel Morgan! Don't take him from me," she cried. "For God's, sake don't take him. Have mercy—mercy on me, colonel, and spare him to me. I appeal to you as a gentleman; to your generosity; to your kindness; for my sake, don't take him away." Morgan replied, "I will not, madam. Take him yourself, and teach him better than to come down here to kill Southern people. That is all I ask. Will you promise me this?" The grateful woman did so, thanking him in the most passionate terms. In another part of the cars, however, a Major Helveti was taken, and some Government funds and stores. There was also in a safe some $30,000 of private funds belonging to a cotton firm at Louisville; and this, Morgan assured the agent, should not be touched. "My men are not thieves," said he, "and not a cent of private property shall be molested."

On the 11th of May, with his reorganized but diminished company, Morgan dashed into Oakland, capturing all Federals on duty, rode furiously on to Glasgow, which he entered next day, and then proceeded to Burksville. From Burksville, Morgan proceeded to Sparta, Tennessee, and arrived there on the Tuesday night, after riding through by-ways and bridlepaths, some 170 miles from Oakland.

A few days after the affair just mentioned, he was at
Chattanooga on a peaceful mission, and then moved up the
valley to Knoxville. Here he recruited his forces awhile,
strengthening and increasing them, and, receiving an appointment as acting brigadier-general, under Kirby Smith (who
was in command of East Tennessee), he started off again into
Kentucky.

Tompkinsville, Lebanon, Harrodsburg, Versailles, Cynthiana, Winchester, and many other towns, were favored with his
presence and some practical understanding of his peculiar
style of warfare, until, arriving at a point between Livingston
and Sparta, he encamped, after as bold a raid as could have
then been possibly conceived. At several of the places his
telegraph operator worked the wires effectually; and what the
command accomplished may be told in the conclusion of
Morgan's own report. He says:

"I left Knoxville on the 4th day of this month (July) with
about 900 men, and returned to Livingston on the 28th inst.,
with nearly 1,200, having been absent just twenty-four days,
during which time I travelled over a thousand miles, captured
seventeen towns, destroyed all the Government supplies and
arms in them, dispersed about 1,500 Home-guards, and pa-
rolled nearly 1,200 regular troops. I lost in killed, wounded,
and missing, of the number that I carried into Kentucky,
about ninety."

From his encampment, near Sparta, Morgan seems to have
gone, personally, to Knoxville—perhaps to consult with Kirby
Smith—for, on the 4th of August, 1862, he issued this stirring
order to his men from that place:

"SOLDIERS—Your country makes a fresh appeal to your
patriotism and courage!

"It has been decided that Kentucky must be freed from the
detested Northern yoke, and who are so fit to carry out this
order as yourselves?

"The road is well known to you. You have already taught
the tyrants at Tompkinsville, Lebanon, and Cynthians, that
where Southern hearts nerve Southern arms, our soldiers are
invincible.

"To an enemy be as tigers—to our Southern brethren be as lambs! Protect their homes, respect their homes! Is it not of your fathers, mothers, sisters, and friends?

"Soldiers! I feel assured that you will return with fresh laurels to enjoy in peace the fruits of your glorious victories. In the mean time, let your avenging battle-cry be 'Butler!' but shout 'Kentucky' to your kindred and friends.

JOHN H. MORGAN,
Colonel of Cavalry, C. S. A.

A week afterwards, he was again off, and on the 12th of August, at night, he forded the Cumberland river with one thousand men and four pieces of artillery. He then surprised and captured the whole of Colonel Boone's command at Gallatin, without firing a shot; pushed on for the railroad in the rear of Nashville, so as to destroy the track and cut off Buell's supplies; and, reaching the tunnel near that place, succeeded in causing a portion of the roof to fall, and thus effectually block the way. This done, and hearing that a force from Nashville was after him, he retreated across the Cumberland, but eventually gave the Federal cavalry battle in the neighborhood of Gallatin. The result was a disastrous and humiliating flight on the part of his pursuers, and a complete, triumphant victory to Morgan and his command.

About this time, Bragg in one part of Kentucky, and Kirby Smith more to the eastward, were advancing towards the northern part of the State, and on the 29th of August, Morgan moved his gallant legion to unite with his department-commander. The union was effected near Lexington, and the triumphant reception Morgan there met, from the inhabitants of his native city, we have already described, as also the subsequent retreat of the army, in which Morgan had to join his cavalry, covering the rear. On recrossing the Cumberland mountains, he was detached to follow his old occupation of harassing the enemy, after his own peculiar fashion. He rested a short time, and then renewed operations in the neighborhood of Nashville, materially obstructing the enemy's supplies, and doing other serious injury. One anecdote concerning his movements at this period is thus related:

"About the middle of November, he came across a small mail-stage, travelling the route between Bowling Green and Nashville. Of course, he quietly captured the affair, and be came the possessor of a large quantity of Uncle Sam's postal matter. The most interesting correspondence was the letters of the various reporters for the Yankee press—the New York *Tribune*, *Times*, etc.

"One letter was from J. L. Able, proprietor of the stage line, to his agent at Bowling Green, imploring him for God's sake to send more stages through, as that '—— rascal, John Morgan, was travelling around, and would be sure to catch them.' Thus advised, the —— rascal aforesaid waited for the next stage, and captured that also. We do not know whether Mr. Able will continue his line."

After this, for about a month, Morgan seemed to be very quiet, and the Federals began to think themselves rid of their troublesome customer. But, "Lo! and behold! one fine night, during September's new moon, the great raider dashed into Huntsville with fifteen hundred men, killed and wounded two hundred, and captured two thousand, destroyed all of the camp equipage, and crossed the river with his captives, and what spoils he could carry. This was the cleverest of all Morgan's successes, and both sides admitted that he was the best man in such business on the 'job.' I will add, here, that this capture was a disgraceful Federal defeat, and so called by Rosecrans." *

Whatever may have been the delights of this wild adventurous life to our hero, it appears that he still had thought for other interests more common to the heart of man. We find that at Murfreesboro, on Sunday, December 4th, 1862, after being promoted to the rank of major-general, this gallant cavalry chief was in the evening married to Miss Ready, daughter of the Hon. Charles Ready, and sister of Mrs. Cheatham, of Nashville.

This pleasant and peaceful episode, however, was soon left far in the distance, for the warrior-groom is found the day following dashing away into Kentucky, ardently as ever, bent on new conquest and achievement, deferring the quiet enjoy-

---

* This statement, from the pen of a Northern writer, is confirmed by all other accounts.

ment of the wedding trip till the events of the next twenty days should be accomplished.

The account of his operations at this time we will briefly give in the words of another : "General Morgan's command returned to Tennessee Saturday last. In their campaign in Kentucky, the Bacon Creek, Nolin, Elizabethtown, Shepherd - ville (eighteen miles from Louisville), and other bridges, were totally destroyed for the distance of eighty miles. The trestle work of the two first was at Muldrough's Hill, twelve hundred feet long and ninety feet high. The number of prisoners captured at these various places amounted to two thousand. The destruction of the railroad is complete from Green river to Shepherdsville, a distance of seventy-five miles. At Springfield, General Morgan was surrounded by twenty-six thousand of the enemy, and, for awhile, it seemed his situation was desperate, but he escaped with his entire command."

While this expedition was in progress, the battle of Murfreesboro was fought, ending on the day before Morgan's return. Afterwards, as already mentioned, the army rested for some time, and probably that portion under Morgan did the same, he being then absent for about a month with his bride. In February, he rejoined his command at Sparta, Tennessee, and during that month, March, and April, had frequent engagements with parties of the enemy sent against him, meeting with repulse more frequently than before. On the 21st of April he was at McMinnville—his headquarters—with his wife, when General Reynolds, sent by Rosecrans, unexpectedly came upon him with a large force. Morgan barely escaped with his life, but the lady was captured, though not, however, long detained.

For awhile, now, there was no opportunity for the exercise of Morgan's peculiar tactics, but in June, having planned another raid, the boldest and most important he had yet undertaken, he left Sparta, on the 27th, for a dash through Kentucky into Ohio and Illinois. Of this daring affair, who has not heard? A brief account of it, however, we cannot omit, often told as has been the tale.

On the 2d of July, Morgan, with a force of 2,028 effective men and four pieces of artillery, crossed the Cumberland river at Barkesville during the night, using canoes and dug-outs,

improvised for the occasion; drove back Hobson's force of Federal cavalry--marched on to Columbia, and defeated Wolford's Kentucky command—dashed forward to Stockdale on the Green river, and there fought a heavy battle with the enemy on the 4th of July.   In this encounter, he was repulsed with severe loss; but, quickly reorganizing his shattered forces, on he went again to Lebanon—had a hard fight of five hours, captured the place, with a vast amount of stores, over four hundred prisoners, and many fine horses, but with the loss of Morgan's gallant young brother Tom, a lieutenant in his command.   On the 7th, Bragdensburg was reached—two fine steamboats captured—the Federal gunboats, and three hundred Home-guards fought, and then the bold raiders crossed the Ohio river to the Indiana shore, next day.   The following day they arrived at Corydon—engaged over four thousand State militia—dispersed them—moved on, without halting, through Salisbury and Palmyra to Salem—played some tricks with the telegraph wires, and obtained important information—then forward again towards Lexington, after destroying bridges, depots, and doing other considerable damage.

From Lexington, Illinois, and following the course of the Ohio, the command passed on to near Vernon, where General Manson, with a heavy force, awaited them.   Two hours skirmishing, as a feint, then enabled the main body to move on Dupont, while squads cut the railroad in several important places.   It was night-time, and Morgan's bonfires aroused the good people everywhere, who, however, deemed the illuminations to be part of a celebration gotten up for the Federal victories at Vicksburg and Gettysburg, little dreaming of the daring band in their vicinity.   But daylight dissolved the charm, and a stampede everywhere ensued.

Versailles was the next place reached ; and here a company of militia was adroitly, and to themselves unwillingly, brought into Morgan's power, who, however, kindly released and sent them home again.   Thence to Harrison, and at dusk on to the suburbs of Cincinnati, skirting it closely on the night of the 13th.   At daylight, they were eighteen miles east of the great city, having traversed over fifty miles since the sunset previous. Men rode their horses fast asleep, and were only aroused by Morgan himself, chatting, laughing, joking, or giving orders to

one and all.   Camp Dennison was passed without any attack
from the enemy, and Camp Shady reached—seventy-five army-
wagons and much forage destroyed ; and then Morgan moved
between Chillicothe and Hillsboro, on one side, and Gallipolis
on the other.   On the morning of the 19th, after thus passing
through the States of Indiana and Ohio, and turning once
more to the South, they again reached the river at a ford above
Pomeroy.   Here a Federal gunboat and a large body of troops
suddenly attacked them, inflicting some loss, and compelling
Morgan to go further up the Ohio.   Fourteen miles beyond,
they then attempt the passage again—fording, or rather swimming across.   Some now reached the opposite shore, when, a
second time, the gunboats were upon them.   Forward, therefore, they must go.   A few miles further, and they try it
again—into the stream they dash—the gunboats come in
sight—are close upon them—many of the command get
across—Morgan's noble mare swims bravely—falters—strikes
out again—then boldly makes the shore.   The command is
now hastily gathered together—a heavy force, at Buffington,
under General Judah, is attacked and scattered—fresh Federal
reinforcements arrive—on all sides the hunted raiders are surrounded—12,000 United States troops are in Morgan's rear—
8,000 more in front and on his flank, and about 10,000* militia
hunting on his track in all directions.   His men, at length
compelled to give way, fly wherever there is a chance of escape.   One portion of a few hundred take the Gauley road, in
West Virginia, and safely arrive at Lewisburg, near White
Sulphur Springs ; another party strikes for Kentucky, and
many others are captured, amongst them Colonels R. Morgan,
Basil Duke, and Smith.   John Morgan, however, succeeds in
escaping, hardly pressed on all sides, and chased like a hunted
bear.   Up the Ohio he bends his way : is faced there : turns
back again,—then crosses into the State of Ohio once more—
next proceeds towards McArthur, Athens, Zanesville, and
northward, to the neighborhood of Wheeling.   Thereabouts he
moves in various directions, until, at length, on Sunday, July
26th, he was fairly hemmed in, four miles south of Lisbon, and
captured by Major Rae, of General Shackleford's command.

---

* The account says 80,000 !   *Vide* " Times' " report.

This officer, with an excellent guide, had followed a cross-road, and managed to get in the rear of his chase. Morgan saw himself hopelessly entrapped, and sent forward a flag of truce, informally surrendering. General Shackleford then arrived, with his cavalry, and the formal surrender was completed about 2 P. M., in the shade of an apple-tree, on a farm.

Morgan affected indifference, and talked lightly of his misfortune. His well-known blooded mare he made over to Major Rae, and his pair of silver-mounted, ivory-handled revolvers to Colonel Wolford. An eye-witness of his capture describes his appearance as follows :

" His looks, at least, are not those of an ordinary man. He is fully six feet high, broad-shouldered, and compactly built ; has soft auburn hair, gray eyes, reddish whiskers, florid complexion ; a pleasant smile, when talking ; a musical voice, and shows to advantage a splendid set of teeth. He wore a gray roundabout and pantaloons, with a wide-brimmed, black felt hat, and morocco boots, with his pantaloons inside."

Morgan was taken to the Ohio Penitentiary, and there incarcerated—not as a captured military officer or a soldier—but as a common felon. He and his comrades, Colonel Duke, and others—had their persons searched—hair and beards shaved, were bathed, and clad in prison suits, in accordance with the ordinary jail discipline. The cruelties which followed were unprecedented in prison discipline, and disgraceful to the age in which such atrocious inhumanity was tolerated. The incarceration occurred on the 30th of July, 1863, and now, at last, said those who had so long felt his daring exploits, he was secure—hard and fast within stone walls, and strongly guarded. Four months afterwards, almost to a day, the bold chief, with two or three companions, electrified the country by making his escape ! This bold enterprise was accomplished by digging through the floor of their cell, to a sewer leading to the river ; but how it was so adroitly done, undiscovered, is to this day a marvel.

Of course, every effort to catch him again was employed ; but John Morgan evaded all the plans laid down for his entrapment, and succeeded in crossing the Tennessee river into the Confederate States, about the middle of December. Very few, if any, occurrences in this remarkable war have been

more marked with romantic and extraordinary incidents, than those belonging to John Morgan's escape and flight from the Ohio Penitentiary. He arrived at Danville on the 25th of December, and was welcomed in the most enthusiastic manner. A short time afterwards, with his wife, he visited Richmond, where his reception was equally flattering to him. By March he had a strong force under him again. On the 8th of April, 1864, he left Richmond, once more to take the field.

During the following summer, with varied experience of success and reverse, he pursued the gay tenor of his way, with unabated zeal, while his enemies vainly pursued him, their resolution strengthening with every new disappointment.

On the 3d of September he advanced upon the town of Greenville, East Tennessee, situated on the great line of railroad from Virginia to Georgia, *via* Knoxville. There he halted for the night, in the house of a Mrs. C. D. Williams— his staff being with him. Before retiring to rest the pickets were carefully attended to; but as the enemy, under General Gillem, were at Bull's Gap, sixteen miles distant, every thing was deemed secure. His betrayal, however, was at hand, and a woman—least suspected—was about to disclose his hiding-place to his foe. Young Mrs. Williams, daughter-in-law of the landlady—when the favored moment appeared—mounted a horse, and, unnoticed, rode to the Federal commander, who immediately sent a force to surround the house at daybreak. Morgan and his staff, hastily aroused from their slumbers, vainly tried to effect their escape. Bravely the chief resisted, endeavoring to fight his way through them, when a soldier— private Andrew Campbell, company G, Thirteenth Tennessee Cavalry—dashed forward, as he passed through the doorway into the street, and shot him dead.

Thus, on Sunday morning, September 4th, 1864—a day in the week always singularly eventful to him—the career of this justly celebrated and extraordinary man was suddenly and unexpectedly brought to a close.

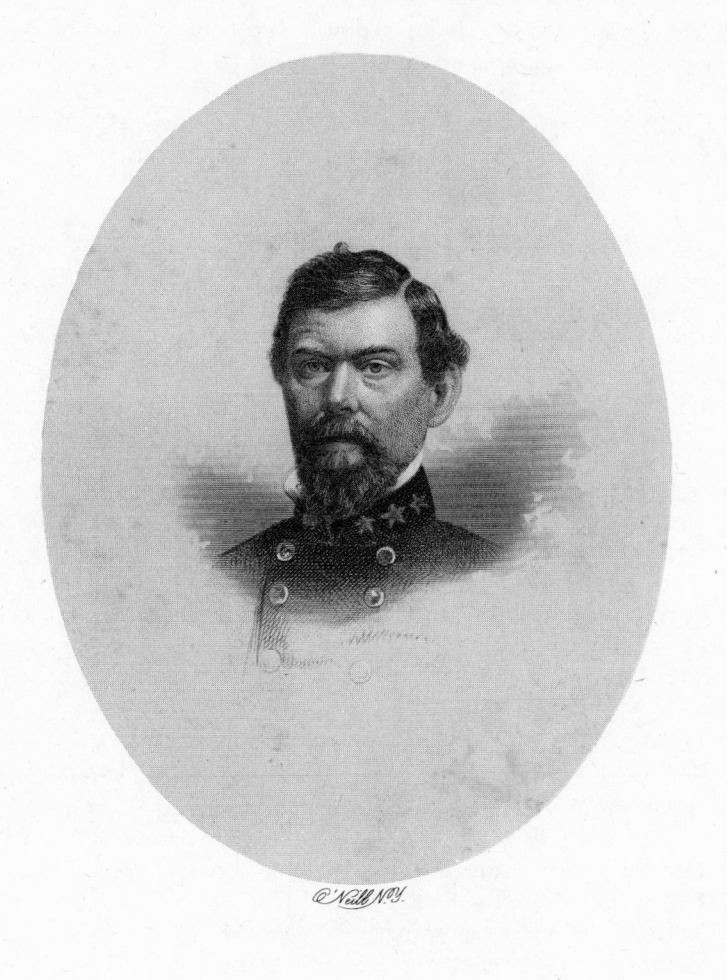

LT. GEN. HARDEE.

LIEUTENANT-GENERAL WILLIAM J. HARDEE.

AMONGST those of the army who have embraced the Southern cause, it would be difficult to find one more generally known in military circles, and, to some extent, in the literary world, than the subject of this sketch. Born about the year 1817, at Savannah, in the State of Georgia, it was to have been expected that he would unite with her fortunes, whatever they might be; nevertheless, so distinguished had he become under the flag of the old government, that it would seem, at the time, almost impossible for him to sever his connection with it. That innate love for the place of one's birth, however, which, more or less, all true men possess—even though circumstances, or the occupations of life, may take them from it—no doubt greatly influenced Colonel Hardee in his course. He was, and still is, one of those brave spirits and gifted minds, whom the world has long known and learned to respect. His native State had just reason to be proud of him, for he was not only the second officer of highest rank, from Georgia, in the old army, but was the author of one of the best works on military tactics that had been published.

In 1834, Hardee entered West Point as a cadet, and graduated with honor four years afterwards. He was then gazetted as second-lieutenant, in the Second United States dragoons, and was sent to Florida, where he served for two years. On the 3d of December, 1839, he was promoted to a first-lieutenancy, and was sent by the Secretary of War to the celebrated military school of St. Maur, about eighty leagues from Paris. There, he was regularly attached to the cavalry department of the French army, and, after completing his studies, —making himself a thoroughly good officer, with a perfect knowledge of that branch of the service—he returned to the United States, bringing a flattering letter of recommendation

from Marshall Oudinot to the Secretary of War at Washington.

Lieutenant Hardee's regiment was now stationed on the Western frontier, and quickly rejoining it, he soon became actively employed in defending the advanced settlements from Indian depredations. On the 18th of September, 1844, he was promoted to be a captain of dragoons, and then accompanied General Taylor across the Rio Grande to the Mexican campaign. There, his company was the first to engage the enemy, at a place called *Curricitos*, where, after vainly endeavoring with his gallant little band to cut his way through the Mexican ranks, he was overwhelmed by superior numbers, and taken prisoner. He had to remain a captive for several months, and then was exchanged in time to take part in the siege of Monterey. For this and other engagements he was promoted major of cavalry on the 25th of March, having then joined the forces under General Scott, at Vera Cruz, and displaying great gallantry in an affair at Medelin, near that place. The subsequent battles in Mexico are well known. Major Hardee greatly distinguished himself in all of these, to the gates of Mexico; and, for such meritorious conduct, he was made a brevet lieutenant-colonel. Afterwards he was promoted, in the regular army, to the rank of major in the famous Second cavalry regiment, where the colonel and lieutenant-colonel were A. S. Johnston, and R. E. Lee. It was at this time, Colonel Jefferson Davis, then Secretary of War, detailed him to prepare a system of tactics better adapted for the use of the infantry than those adopted, and this was compiled and published, as "Hardee's Tactics; or, the United States Rifle and Infantry Tactics," 2 vols. On the completion of the work, in July, 1856, he was ordered to West Point as commandant of cadets, with the local rank of lieutenant-colonel, and was employed there—with the exception of one year's leave of absence in Europe—until he was promoted full lieutenant-colonel of cavalry, which position, however, he resigned on the 31st of January, 1861.

In the month of October, 1860, events forshadowed that mighty convulsion which has since taken place in the nation. Virginia was even then preparing to "resist all attempts at coercion," and "an encampment of nearly two regiments of

cavalry were to be formed at the Fair ground, near Richmond, on the 7th of November." At that time Colonel Hardee was staying in New York awhile, but it seems from a letter, written at Richmond, dated October 31st, 1860, that he
was then, by permission of his commander-in-chief, to go down
to Richmond, and "instruct these regiments in military tactics." At all events, we find him at Montgomery about the
end of February, 1861; he then offered his sword and services
to the Confederate government. They were gladly accepted,
and he was at once confirmed as colonel of the First regiment
of infantry. He was then assigned to duty at Fort Morgan,
Mobile, and directed to take Grant's Pass, and all their approaches to Mobile, under his charge. In the month of June,
Hardee was appointed a brigadier-general, and sent to Arkansas, with his command, embracing that portion of the State
south and west of the White river—General Polk being the
department commander of the Mississippi and adjoining region.

General Hardee's services in the West were of great importance to the cause he had joined. Before his arrival, Arkansas
had appointed a military board to arrange about transferring
the entire force of the State to the Confederate government,
provided, however, that their arms were to be used simply in
self-defence. A deputation went to Richmond, but no promise
could be given as to their future disposition. But, on the 4th
of July, 1861, an agreement was made with General Hardee,
and, with a single exception, the several regiments were transferred to his command, the whole force numbering about 6,000
men.

At this time, McCullouch was in charge of the Indian territory, on the Arkansas frontier, and General Price was operating with Governor Jackson, in Missouri. General Hardee,
however, soon prosecuted the war with vigor, in the department of which he had control. In the early part of August
he went to Greenville, Mobile, taking with him artillery and
small-arms, in consequence of having received promises of reinforcements. But he was much disappointed. The men we
afraid of being called away from their own State, and, there
fore, would not join. His hopes thus proving abortive, he
turned his attention to Pilot Knob, and the Iron Mountain

railway; but, ultimately, he abandoned his designs in that part, and returned to his headquarters at Pocohontas.

Shortly afterwards he was transferred to Kentucky, and in September his movements led General Shoepff, the Federal commander, who was advancing against General Zollicoffer, to suppose he intended flanking him from Bowling Green, and this helped to produce the Federal retreat from Wild-cat. At the end of October, General Hardee was dispatched with a force of about 3,000 men to Green river, Ky., to attack the Federals at Camp Andy Johnson, under General Ward, but a sudden rise in the river enabled the latter to retreat, and Johnston recalled Hardee to the more important position at Bowling Green. He was appointed a major-general, and, on the 17th of December, 1861, the battle of Mumfordsville, Ky., was fought by a portion of the troops under his command—Brigadier-general Hindman leading the advance. Hardee's report of this is as follows:

HEADQUARTERS, CENTRAL ARMY OF KENTUCKY, }
BOWLING GREEN, December 21, 1861. }

SPECIAL ORDER No. 64.

On the 17th instant, our forces, under Brigadier-general Hindman, partially engaged a superior force of the enemy near Woodsonville. In the action we sustained a loss of four killed and nine wounded. The enemy was driven back, and left about fifty killed, and seven prisoners. The conduct of our troops was marked by impetuous valor. On charging the enemy, Colonel Terry, of the Texas Rangers, was killed in the moment of victory. His regiment deplores the loss of a brave and beloved commander—the army one of its ablest officers.

The general commanding returns his thanks to Brigadier-general Hindman and his command for their conduct in the initiative of the campaign in Kentucky, and he hails the brilliant courage shown in the affair as a bright augury of their valor when the actual hour comes for striking a decisive blow.

By order of Major-general HARDEE.

D. H. WHITE, Act. Assis't Adjutant-general.

At Bowling Green he was located all the winter, as second in command of the army at that post, and, it is reported that,

so rigorous was he in guarding the rights and property of noncombatants, that he arrested a general for burning the houses at Cave City and other places on the Louisville and Nashville railroad.

Prior to, or at the commencement of April, 1862, Hardee was appointed a major-general; and, in the arrangement for the battle of Shiloh, his corps—the third—was directed to move in advance, and he was to make all " proper disposition of the artillery along the line of battle." His zeal, ability, and skill in this battle, were afterwards very highly spoken of by Beauregard in his official report.

From this time General Hardee's corps was attached to Bragg's army, and accompanied it in all its movements, to the battle of Perryville. There he commanded the left wing of the army, and very successfully conducted the operations committed to his direction. His conduct on this occasion and throughout the campaign, procured for him the appointment of lieutenant-general, ranking in the Confederate army after Longstreet.

At the battle of Murfreesboro, during the last days of December, 1862, Lieutenant-general Hardee took a conspicuous part. His corps, consisting of Breckinridge's and Cleburne's divisions, were formed on the west bank of the Stone river, until ordered to advance. Then, it is related, the sight was a most magnificent one. Two columns deep, with a front of nearly three-fourths of a mile, the line well preserved and moving forward with great rapidity, on went the men, their bayonets glistening in a bright sun which had broken through the fog.

In the month of May, 1863, General Hardee was visited by the British officer we have before quoted from, and he says " I found that he was in company with General Polk, and Bishop Elliot, of Georgia, and also with Mr. Vallandigham. The latter (called the Apostle of Liberty) is a good-looking man, apparently not much over forty, and had been turned out of the North three days before. Rosecrans had wished to and him over to Bragg by flag of truce; but, as the latter declined to receive him in that manner, he was, as General Hardee expressed it, 'dumped down' in the neutral ground between the lines, and left there. He then received hospitality

from the Confederates in the capacity of a destitute stranger.
. . . When I presented my letters of introduction, General
Hardee received me with the unvarying kindness and hospitality which I had experienced from all other Confederate
officers. He is a fine, soldierlike man, broad-shouldered and
tall. He looks rather like a French officer, and bears the
reputation of being a thoroughly good soldier. He is a
widower, and has the character of being a great admirer of
the fair sex. During the Kentucky campaign last year, he
was in the habit of availing himself of the privilege of his
rank and years," by mixing freely and socially with the
families of the farmers; and several good jokes arose from it.
One may be mentioned. " An old lady told him he ought
really ' to leave off fighting at his age.' ' Indeed, madam,'
replied he; ' and how old do you take me for ?' ' Why, about
the same age as myself—seventy-five,' she answered. The
chagrin of the stalwart and gallant general, at having twenty
years added to his age, may be imagined."

In July, 1863, General Hardee* was assigned to duty in
command of the department formerly held by General Pemberton; but when Rosecrans marched on Chattanooga he was
recalled to Bragg's army, and the second corps placed under

---

* The following anecdote is related of him during this period :

While on a forced march in some of the army movements in Mississippi last
summer, General Hardee came up with a straggler who had fallen some distance in the rear of his command. The general ordered him forward, when
the soldier replied that he was weak and broken down, not having had even
half rations for several days.

"That's hard," replied the general, "but you must push forward, my good
fellow, and join your command, or the provost guard will take you in hand."

The soldier halted, and looking up at the general asked—

" An't you General Hardee ?"

" Yes," replied the general.

" Didn't you write Hardee's Tactics ?"

" Yes."

" Well, general, I've studied them tactics, and know 'em by heart. You've
got a order thar to double column at half distance, an't you ?"

" Well," asked the general, " what has that order to do with your case ?"

" I'm a good soldier, general, and obey all that is possible to be obeyed, but
if your orders can show me a order in your tactics, or anybody else's tactics,
to double distance on half rations, then I'll give in."

The general, with a hearty laugh, admitted that there were no tactics to
meet the case, and putting spurs to his horse, rode forward.

him. The battles of Chickamauga, Lookout mountain, and Missionary ridge, followed, as previously related, and, finally, General Hardee was appointed to temporarily succeed Bragg in the general command.

On assuming command, Lieutenant-general Hardee issued the following general order to the soldiers of the army of Tennessee:

DALTON, GA., December 2, 1863.

General Bragg having been relieved from duty with this army, the command has devolved upon me. The steady purpose, the unflinching courage and unsullied patriotism of the distinguished leader who has shared your fortunes more than two years, will long be remembered by the army and the country he served so well.

I desire to say, on assuming command, that there is no cause for discouragement. The overwhelming numbers of the enemy forced us back from Missionary ridge, but the army is still intact and in good heart; our losses were small and were rapidly replaced. The country is looking to you with painful interest. I feel I can rely upon you. The weak need to be cheered by the constant successes of the victors of Shiloh, Perryville, Murfreesboro, and Chickamauga, and require such stimulant to sustain their courage and resolution. Let the past take care of itself. We care most to secure the future.

W. J. HARDEE, Lieutenant-general.

With reference to this appointment, it was said that " the command had devolved upon Lieutenant-general Hardee, an excellent corps commander, who has borne himself well in many of the hardest-fought battles of the war, and who, at Missionary ridge, most gallantly maintained his position until the rest of Bragg's army gave way. Hardee was one of the very few—probably the only prominent officer—who avowed his readiness to serve under Bragg when the President visited the army to ascertain its wants. Modesty is so rare now-a-days that all were surprised to hear that Hardee declined the command on the ground that he was not qualified for it; and, it was only as a temporary arrangement that he agreed to accept this important trust."

Shortly afterwards, a very important address from the generals in command of the army of Tennessee, was sent to the Confederate Congress. This address referred to measures best calculated, in the judgment of the signers (General Hardee's name being at the head of the list), to maintain the efficiency and vigor of the army, and was read in the House on December 29th, 1862.

In the month of January, 1863, General Hardee obtained leave of absence for a short time, and, on the 13th, was married to Miss Mary T. Lewis, of Greensboro, Alabama.

In May, General Johnston having assumed full command of the army, Hardee's movements were again merged in those of the commander-in-chief, and the Confederate forces. The battles that followed have been narrated in previous sketches. Hood succeeded Johnston. Atlanta was evacuated; and Hardee, when President Davis visited the camp, in September, was relieved at his own request, and appointed to the command of the department of South Carolina, with his headquarters at Charleston. The subsequent events are well known. Sherman marched upon Savannah, and Hardee went there beforehand to make arrangements for its defence. It was, however, found vain to attempt resistance, and, on the 21st of December, 1864, this important city was evacuated by the Confederates, and the victorious Federal forces entered in triumph. Since then, General Hardee, in conjunction with

General Hardee then retreated to Charleston, which he was compelled to evacuate on the 14th of February, and move towards Columbia, where a council of war was held between Beauregard, Hampton, himself, and a General Butler of the Southern Confederacy. At this council it was determined to abandon Columbia, and Johnston shortly afterwards assuming chief command of the forces, Hardee's corps became one of the three into which the Southern army was now divided. Previous to the general surrender, Hardee remarked that it would be next to murder to continue fighting, now Lee had yielded.

After obtaining his parole, General Hardee repaired to Alabama, where the last accounts, in October, settle him down to the cultivation of a plantation derived through his wife.

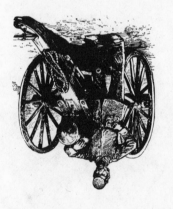

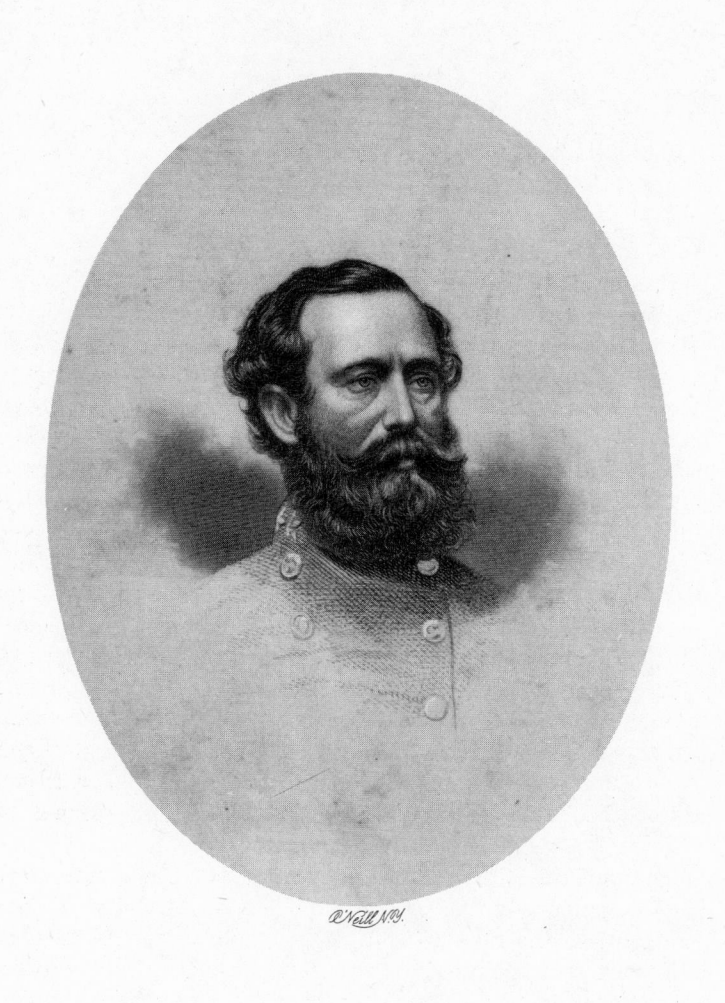

GEN. WADE HAMPTON.

LIEUTENANT-GENERAL WADE HAMPTON.

———

THE gallant officer whose career we now notice, was born in the city of Charleston, South Carolina, in the year 1818. His father was Colonel Wade Hampton, who greatly distinguished himself in the war of 1812, and was an aid-de-camp to General Jackson, at the battle of New Orleans. He was an eminent and esteemed citizen of South Carolina, distinguished as an enlightened and liberal agriculturist, and greatly respected for his elevated and pure character as a man. Colonel Hampton's father was also an eminent military officer—General Wade Hampton—of the revolution, and a prominent citizen of South Carolina. Thus, the present General Hampton is descended from men who have well and bravely fought in their country's cause. His early education was received at South Carolina College, where he graduated with much distinction; and then, while quite a young man, married the youngest daughter of General Francis Preston, of Virginia, by whom he had three children, two of them becoming officers in the Confederate army. After the death of this lady, he married the daughter of Governor McDuffie, of South Carolina.

The pursuits of Hampton, previous to the present war, were almost exclusively those of a planter, though he served in both branches of the South Carolina Legislature with distinction. His argument against the opening of the African slave trade, was spoken of as a master-piece of elegant and statesmanlike logic, dictated by the noblest sentiments of the Christian and the patriot.

At the commencement of 1861, he was considered one of the richest planters of the South, and owned the greatest number of slaves. When hostilities commenced, he immediately raised a splendid legion of six companies of infantry—himself their

leader, and though the cost must have been very great, he contributed largely towards the equipment.

At the latter end of May he had all nearly ready, but some delay occurred before they could be marched to the seat of war in Virginia, yet he had the good fortune to arrive in time for the battle of Manassas, July 21, 1861. Here he was immediately ordered forward to a position near the Lewis House, as a support for any troops engaged in that quarter. When the Confederates, during a part of the day, were falling back near the Robinson House, Hampton, with his legion, greatly aided Generals Bee, Bartow, and Evans, in recovering the lost ground. Beauregard says, "about noon the commands of Bee, Bartow, and Evans, had taken shelter in a wooded ravine behind the Robinson House, and this was stoutly held at the time by Hampton, with his legion, which had made a stand there, after having, previously, been as far forward as the turnpike, where Lieutenant-colonel Johnston, an officer of brilliant promise, was killed, and other severe losses were sustained. . . . . I then placed Hampton's legion, which had suffered greatly, as a reserve to protect the right flank against any advance of the enemy from Stone bridge," and, when a charge was made, in conjunction with the 18th regiment (Withers', of Coke's brigade), he captured several rifle pieces, which were immediately turned upon the foe. Finally, he greatly aided in "restoring the fortunes of the day at a time when the enemy, by a last desperate onset, with heavy odds, had driven the Confederates from the fiercely contested ground about the Henry House." His "soldierly ability" was especially noted by the commander-in-chief, who said that "veterans could not have behaved better than his well-led regiment."

In the last charge, however, Colonel Hampton was not personally present, having previously been wounded in the head; but so highly did Beauregard appreciate the legion, that he gave himself, for the time, to the vacant post of their retired commander.

We must not, however, omit mentioning that, during a part of the fight, when Colonel Hampton's horse was shot under him, he seized a rifle, and said to his men, "Watch me, boys; do as I do." He then shot down, successively, several of the

Federal officers who were leading their forces against him. General Beauregard then came up, and said, "Take that battery." Just at that moment the flag of the legion was shot down. Beauregard said, "Hand it to me; let me bear the Palmetto flag." He did bear it in the fury of the fight. Colonel Johnston, of the legion, was slain in the charge.

The Hampton legion promised to defend the flag presented to them by the ladies of the Palmetto State, while one of them remained to step the field of conflict. That this promise was sacredly redeemed, no one can doubt, when he comes to learn that of the eight hundred who went into the field on that Sunday, one hundred and ten sealed their fidelity with their blood, such being the number of their killed and wounded, according to the reports.

In the subsequent battles on the Peninsula, from the beginning of operations at Yorktown, the Hampton legion was ever conspicuous, and at the battle of Seven Pines was especially noticed. It is said that the loss amongst them, in killed and wounded, was a fraction over one-half their number. "The charge of this body of men was gallant and daring beyond all description; and Colonel Wade Hampton was wounded in the foot." During the battle of Gaines's Mill, June 29th, the Hampton legion again displayed great valor, and, indeed, throughout the whole seven days' contest.

Hampton was now promoted to the position of Brigadier-general of cavalry, under Major-general Stuart, and zealously seconded that gallant officer in all his daring exploits. We may, however, give one or two illustrations of General Hampton's own personal doings in these expeditions. In the retreat from Antietam, when the enemy's cavalry, under Pleasanton, attacked Lee's pickets in front of Sheperdstown, Hampton's brigade had retired through Martinsburg, but, on being recalled, speedily returned, and aided Colonel W. F. H. Lee in repulsing the foe.

A few days afterwards, he accompanied Stuart on his successful expedition into Maryland, as already mentioned in previous sketches. When they arrived near Chambersburg, the following incidents occurred, as related by the Federal colonel, A. K. McClure. He says:

" After travelling a mile westward, we were brought to a

halt by a squad of mounted men, and informed that General Hampton was one of the party, to whom we should address ourselves. It was so dark that I could not distinguish him from any of his men. Upon being informed that we were a committee of citizens, and that there was no organized force in town, and no military commander at the post, he stated, in a respectful and soldierlike manner, that he commanded the advance of the Confederate troops; that he knew resistance would be vain, and he wished the citizens to be fully advised of his purpose, so as to avoid needless loss of life and wanton destruction of property. He said he had been fired upon at Mercersburg and Campbellstown, and had great difficulty in restraining his troops. He assured us that he would scrupulously protect citizens; would allow no soldiers to enter public or private houses, unless under command of an officer upon legitimate business; that he would take such private property as he needed for his government or troops, but that he would do so by men under officers who would allow no wanton destruction, and who would give receipts for the same if desired, so that claim might be made therefor against the United States government. All property belonging to or used by the United States, he stated, he would use or destroy at his pleasure, and the wounded in hospitals would be paroled. Being an United States officer myself, I naturally felt some anxiety to know what my fate would be if he should discover me, and I modestly suggested that there might be some United States officers in the town in charge of wounded, stores, or of recruiting offices, and asked what disposition would be made of them. He answered that he would parole them, unless he should have special reasons for not doing so, and he instructed us that none such should be notified by us to leave town. Here I was in an interesting situation. If I remained there it might, in General Hampton's opinion, be special reasons for not paroling me, and the fact that he had several citizens of Mercersburg with him as prisoners did not diminish my apprehensions. If I should leave, as I had ample opportunity afterwards to do, I might be held as violating my own agreement, and to what extent my family and property might suffer in consequence, conjecture had a very wide range. With sixty acres of corn in shock, and three barns full of grain, excellent

farm and saddle horses, and a number of best blooded cattle, the question of property was worthy of a thought. I resolved to stay, as I felt so bound by the terms of surrender, and take my chance of discovery and parole."

During the time Chambersburg was occupied, General Hampton was appointed military governor; and, in reference to his whole proceedings, Stuart, in his report, observes: " Brigadier-general Hampton . . . is entitled to my lasting gratitude for his coolness in danger, and obedience to orders."

General Hampton, in the beginning of December, 1862, entered Dumfries one morning about three o'clock, and captured several Federal soldiers, besides doing much damage to government stores. A few days afterwards he made a rich haul on a government train in the neighborhood of Occoquan. There were twenty-seven cars laden with the choicest articles for the gay Christmas season. Many of the articles captured were labelled " Christmas presents for General Burnside," and consisted of fine brandies, segars and wines. Besides these there was a good supply of sutlers' stores, embracing boots and shoes, gauntlets, and nearly every other article necessary for the comfort of man during the cold season. In addition, 170 soldiers who were guarding the train were made prisoners.

A little later, in the beginning of January, 1863, he crossed the Rappahannock, with one hundred and twenty cavalry, and fell in with ninety-two men, including five officers, of the Pennsylvania cavalry, capturing them without a shot being fired, and obtaining a great prize of valuable carbines, one hundred horses and their equipments, not to mention the warm overcoats of the men, which are no slight item in the month of January.

At the battle of Gettysburg, General Hampton was wounded thrice—once in the hip, from a shrapnel, and two severe sabrecuts in the head. This compelled him to retire awhile from his command; but his active spirit would not brook a longer absence than was imperative. Therefore we find him again zealously engaged with Stuart, the two Lees, and his gallant men, in many other raids and adventures. These, however, have already been alluded to, and we must pass on to the time

when, having been made a major-general, he had command of
the cavalry, after the death of Stuart.

During the latter part of May and beginning of June, 1864,
he was constantly engaged pressing the enemy's cavalry, and
obtained several advantages over them.   On the 12th, Hampton and Fitz Hugh Lee encountered Sheridan, Custer, Torbert,
and Gregg at Trevilan station ; and on the 20th successfully
attacked the Federals stationed at the White-house.   Five days
afterwards, the enemy's cavalry advanced to a place called
Nance's shop, and intrenched themselves.   Hampton quickly
followed, and drove them away, pursuing them till 9 P. M.,
to within two miles of Charles City Court-house.   "Great
credit," says Lee, in his report, "is due to General Hampton
and his command, for their handsome success."

On the 26th of August he attacked a body of the enemy's
cavalry, about four miles beyond Reams' station, and routed
them.   It was about this time he was made commander-in-
chief of all the cavalry in the army of North Virginia, and
was thenceforth considered as General Lee's Master of Horse—
a position of no slight dignity in such times.   But the most
exciting affair, and especially one peculiarly serviceable, was
his foray upon the commissariat of General Grant.

In the middle of September, there arrived in the Federal
camp 2,486 head of cattle, in splendid order.   These were put
to graze in the neighborhood of Sycamore Church, not far
from the James river, east of City Point, and had been collected by the Federal commissariat with great care.   Hearing
of this, Hampton, with W. F. H. Lee's division, Rosser's and
Dearing's brigades, and Graham's and McGregor's batteries,
started early one morning to capture them.   Taking a wide
circuit round the Federal army, the Confederates suddenly
came upon the surprised forces, stationed on their right,
on Thursday night.   A fight ensued : the enemy's position
was carried ; and the cattle not only captured, but safely
driven back to the Confederate lines, after another sharp engagement with some cavalry under General Gregg.   What the
great prize really was, may be judged from the following remarks in a Richmond paper: "The Federal commissaries buy
beeves of the largest size for the use of their armies in Virginia.   The expense and trouble of transportation, which are

in proportion to numbers, make this very expedient. The beeves taken in Hampton's late expedition are judged, by a Loudon grazier, to weigh 800 pounds net. Twenty-four hundred and eighty-six beeves at 800 pounds, would make an aggregate of 1,988,800 pounds, or within a fraction of *two millions of pounds*. This, distributed in daily rations of a pound each, would feed 1,000 men for nearly 2,000 days, 10,000 men for 200 days, or 50,000 for 40 days, and so forth. It is a very nice addition to our commissariat, for which we are very much obliged to Mr. Grant, and particularly to General Hampton and his braves."

A short time after this, he again " routed the enemy, capturing two stands of colors, and about five hundred prisoners, including five colonels, and thirteen other officers."

On the 27th of October he attacked the enemy in the rear, while General Mahone struck them in the flank, on the Boydton plank-road. It is said, that on this occasion "General Hampton and his cavalry rendered a service which the country cannot too highly appreciate."

Hampton was now made a lieutenant-general, and on the march of Sherman's army through South Carolina, was detached from Lee's immediate command to join the forces then under Beauregard. As his family residence was at Columbia, very naturally he was adverse to any measures that would abandon the place; and it is stated that during the two days' council of war held there, he would only attend once. When the city was fired, and a ruinous destruction followed, he was accused of having done the deed, though he immediately decried it. Some sharp correspondence also took place between him and the Federal officers on the subject of prisoners, and on the night of the 19th of March he succeeded in surprising Kilpatrick's command, and, for a time, putting it to flight. Kilpatrick, however, soon rallied, and by a great effort of personal daring, retook the camp, and kept Hampton from any further success.

During the remainder of the campaign, General Hampton was conspicuous for his dauntless efforts to resist the Union advance, and when the final surrender came, reluctantly yielded to the sad necessity which ended the war. He retired to his home, such as it now was, and then advised " all true patriots

to devote themselves, with zeal and honesty of purpose, to the restoration of law and the blessings of peace." In October, 1865, Hampton was nominated at Charleston for governor of South Carolina, though not a candidate, nor desirous of being one—nor was he elected; and, in thanking his fellow-citizens, he advises " a concurrence with all measures now adopted by the President, whose course towards the people of the South he believes to be wise and generous."

D1017108